FOXYMORON

Unholy Triptych: Rupert Murdoch, News Corp, FNC

MICHAEL STRADA

ISBN: 146991560X
ISBN 13: 9781469915609

PRECIS

FOXYMORON

An unholy triptych morphs seamlessly into Foxymoron 1.) Rupert Murdoch; 2.) News Corp; 3.) Fox News Channel (FNC). With America so politically bifurcated, pundits and politicians spew out mean-spirited hyperbole. Can academics help defang the venom?

If so, inter-disciplinary scholarship helps: 1.) Authoritarian Personality (Social Psychology); 2.) Paralinguistics (Communications); 3.) Suspension of Disbelief (Humanities); 4.) Ethnocentrism (Anthropology); 5.) Critical-Thinking-Skills (CTS) (Philosophy/Psychology); 6.) Best-Practices Bench-Marking (Business).

A consensus has emerged in academe: Undergrads should be taught CTS for lifelong learning in an age of flux. Case studies suggest that teaching students CTS costs little money, is grounded in stellar research, small is beautiful institutionally, and much depends on leadership.

What impedes progress? 1.) Professors fall in love with their voices; 2.) Straight lecture=zero risk (unlike best-practices); 3.) Administrators defer too readily to academic freedom (a cultural norm without legal clout); 4.) Half of undergrads attend Division I mega-universities prioritizing research over teaching, huge classes led by Teaching Assistants, and reputations earned via marketing sports. Unmitigated lecture is derided by some critics as "worst-practices bench-marking."

My title oozes paradox, as does Professor Mardy Grothe's *Oxymoronica: Paradoxical Wit and Wisdom from History's Greatest Wordsmiths* (Harper Collins, 2010). Grothe says "Most people associate oxymoron with a contradiction in terms, such as military intelligence, pretty ugly, or acting naturally. However, a deeper meaning triggered by paradox usually makes perfect sense." (p. 76)

Her book explains all of these words' etiologies. A few that I like:

"I am deeply superficial;" "Even their ignorance is encyclopedic;" "I love my country too much to be a nationalist;" "Melancholy represents the pleasure of being sad;" "Less is more;" "Free love is much too expensive;" "Nations are peaceful only when at war;" "If you really want to live, attend your own funeral;" "Wisdom comprehends one's own ignorance;" "A verbal contract isn't worth the paper it's printed on."

Paradox first appeared in English dictionaries during 1540, a century before oxymoron's debut; and for centuries, both were derided in both Great Britain and America. Only in the last century have they risen greatly in public esteem. (p. 118)

I was mulling over several fat titles when this leaner one came from ex-student, Nancy Kadar, who watches FNC often. For a true-believer liberal like me, how better to illustrate "a contradiction in terms" than FNC?

It contains this Précis, 10 dense Chapters (>350 citations), six Appendices, and a Coda.

DEDICATION

*Chicken-Hawk Ditto-Heads
whose religion dictates that the Rush-
Meister epitomizes fair and balanced*

FOXYMORON

UNHOLY TRIPTYCH: RUPERT MURDOCH, NEWS CORP, FOX NEWS CHANNEL (FNC)*

*Ten trips to Russia familiarize me with Orthodoxy's fixation on sacred triptyches: Ornate tri-panel paintings containing inspiring imagery; irony permeates my analysis of Foxymoron's Unholy Triptych

CHAPTER ONE:

"Common Sense=Necessary-but-Insufficient Condition for Rational Public Policy"

BACKGROUNDER:

Question: On which topic does the American public afford politicians unfettered "suspension of disbelief"? [i] A.) Patriotism; B.) Religiosity; C.) Individualism; D.) Common Sense. I think the sexier areas of patriotism, religiosity, and individualism generate enough heated discourse for critics to expose serial excesses. However, common sense draws scant attention: An apt metaphor might be that the last thing fish would ever notice is water. So too with those considering common-sense an unimpeachable public good, greasing a cognitive race to the bottom.

Wiktionary defines common sense as "Ordinary sensible understanding; one's basic intelligence which allows for plain understanding and without which good decisions or judgments cannot be made."[ii] I consider the smartest way to approach the nexus between politics and common sense as this: a necessary-but-insufficient condition for rational public policy. Furthermore, modern science so routinely exposes common-sensical errors as to render citing them moot.[iii]

FNC's common-sensical culture relies on braggadocchio paralinguistics to convey authoritarian[iv] subtext messages to its niche demographic, enabling a self-fulfilling *"suspension of disbelief."* Several feminist writers led me to explore FNC's snug fit with alpha male values; and, following his 2011 interview with Barack Obama, Bill O'Reilly coaxed a willing "guest expert" to interpret the sharp exchange between them as typical of "alpha males," in which the Big O visibly luxuriated.

INTRODUCTION:

This chapter challenges common sense's unassailability, providing its researched-laden best-practices antidote: Critical-Thinking-Skills (CTS.) Consensuses occur rarely in U.S. higher education, yet a preponderance of college-level institutions and professional organizations have coalesced around an overarching goal for undergraduate education: *teaching students CTS for life-long learning in an age of flux.*

My last decade teaching sought enhanced course syllabi catalyzing soft-data portfolios for the daunting task of evaluating teaching CTS to students. This germinated during my 16-year half-time assignment at FACDIS,[v] an award-winning interdisciplinary consortium at WVU, later applied at my home institution (West Liberty University); culminating in two articles on the Assessment movement in academia, two more on the latent potential of enhanced syllabi,[vi] and *Benefits of Model Syllabi* (University Press of America, 2007), 246 pp.

A subset of academic CTS, philosopher Don Lindsey's ARCHIVE OF FALLACIOUS ARGUMENTS provides a treasure trove exceeding 20 pages available online at: http://www.don-lindsey-archive.org/skeptic/ arguments.html. He identifies, defines, and illustrates more than 70 well-documented common rhetorical fallacies.

The role of CTS to investigate media bias will be addressed in subsequent chapters. Wiktionary strikes me as essentially centrist when defining emotive political terms, thus I rely on it here. Concerning media bias, it contends: "Media Bias: (USA) A political bias in journalistic reporting, in programming selection, or otherwise in mass communications media. Fox News (FNC) is often cited as an example of *conservative media bias*, yet its viewers claim that CNN is guiltier of *liberal media bias.*"6

Joined at the hip with Kindle, Amazon Books CEO Geoff Bezos stays ahead of competitors by focusing on very serious readers, not casual ones seeking glitz. Kindle provides instantaneous access to a treasure trove of information sans computer. I accessed 400 books for this research.

STANDING ROOM ONLY (SRO): BOOKS BONKERS OVER COMMON SENSE

Common sense is fine—it's merely **insufficient** for the complex world we inhabit wherein change remains the only constant, and employable skills keep morphing. I was amazed by the ubiquity of books treating common sense as an undeniable public good, thus I opened this chapter with that trick question about the relationship between patriotism, religiosity, individualism, and common sense (as related to suspension of disbelief.)

Elsewhere I've written "Science proves that things are not always what they appear to be, rendering commonsensical understanding inadequate. Common sense alone suggests the Earth is flat, our sun revolves around the Earth, and that heavy bodies fall faster than lighter ones. Yet we have long known all of these expectations as false. Common sense encourages inaccurate observations, over-generalizing about the significance of anecdotal experiences, and making judgments based on what we expect or desire to see." 7

Let's examine *Do the Right Thing: Inside the Movement That's Bringing Common Sense Back to America* , by ex-Arkansas Governor and paid FNC pundit, Mike Huckabee (Kindle, 2008). He refers to his victory over Mitt Romney and John McCain in the 2008 Iowa Republican primary as symbolizing a desire for Republicans to return to common sense fiscal conservatism after Bush II's profligacy, and how his humble roots as a second native of Hope, Arkansas to aspire to the American presidency. Like the Big O (Bill O'Reilly) in his memoir, *A Bold Fresh Piece of Humanity*, Huckabee wallows in the *ipso facto* false assumption that humble origins guarantee sound judgment.

In one place Huckabee says "I decided to run for president because I had beliefs and the record to unite our party. I had the proven ability to attract the independent and the undecided Democrat votes we would need to win general elections. People saw me for who I am, a firefighter's son, a Main Street guy, free from the corruption of K Street or the greed of Wall Street. Plus, I had the proven executive and emergency leadership experience to be president." (p. 192) But fortunately scholars possess ways to spot specious reasoning, including philosopher Don Lindsay's ARCHIVE OF FALLACIES.[vii]

Huckabee warns why election of a Democrat in 2008 would defang the War On Terror (WOT) irreparably: "Then there's the WOT. A Democratic President won't fight the WOT with the intensity and single-mindedness that it demands. As unbelievable as it sounds, Democrats still don't understand how viscerally, obsessively, and fanatically the Islam-fascists hate us and how determined they are kill us destroy our Judeo-Christian culture and civilization. We can put it very simply: the Islamo-fascists want to destroy our way of life and kill us. Period. The conflict in Iraq is just one battle in this generational, ideological WOT, as Korea and Vietnam were battles during the Col War. The Democrats are quick to criticize the war in Iraq, but they're criticizing tactics in this one battle without offering any overall strategy for winning the broader war. They seem to have almost no plan." (p. 239)

The unintended consequences of the WOT, however, are explored thoroughly in a PBS television program aired on 16 January 2011 by one of the most respected newsmagazines: *Frontline*. The cumulative effects of secretive WOT overachieving since 9/11 are revealed in frightening detail begun by *Washington Post* investigative journalist Dana Priest, then pursued by the ACLU and other mass media. A myriad of ex-insiders, led by former Presidential adviser on anti-terrorism, Richard Clarke, describe details about how new military intelligence technologies developed in Iraq and Afghanistan now precariously reduce privacy in America.

Like the Big O, Huckabee seems to have majored in redundancy, name-calling, reductionism, Straw Man Fallacies, and Fallacy by Emotive Language in college. Don Lindsay's Straw Man Fallacy refers to "Attacking an exaggerated or caricatured version of your opponent's argument;" and, the *Fallacy by Emotive Language* means "Using emotionally loaded words to sway the audience's sentiments instead of their minds. Manipulation of emotions such anger, spite, envy, and condescension can be rhetorically useful." B.S. (Bad Science)

Exposing Huckabee's sophistry is too easy, so I'll settle for just one more: Second Amendment rights. "When I was governor, I signed a law *protecting* gun manufacturers from exposure in the courts. I also signed laws permitting former law-enforcement officials to carry concealed handguns and removing restrictions on concealed-handgun permit holders. I was the first governor in the country to have a concealed-handgun license, and of course, I'm a lifetime NRA member." (p. 318)

He explains how his love of hunting enabled his upset victory over Bob Dole in 2008: "Iowans love their Second Amendment rights with the same zeal as Arkansans, and one of the ways they love them best is in pheasant season. It's a tradition that brings generations of families and friends together to enjoy the great outdoors and to share the thrill of the chase. Pheasant hunting in Iowa is viewed with the same fervor as duck hunting in Arkansas. I've often said that in Arkansas, duck hunting is not a sport; it's a religious experience." (p. 323)

Without catching his breath, "Because of the campaign I was pretty much going to miss all of duck season in Arkansas. . . . As a concession to my giving up my duck season, my advisers and I decided that whatever we were doing on opening day of Iowa pheasant season, I'd be in the field with a shotgun and orange vest. The hunt turned out to be one of those rare and wonderful moments when something I truly enjoy also happened to be fantastic PR. No matter how far behind we were in the polls, on that day we could own the media." (p. 328)

Don Lindsay's ARCHIVE OF FALLACIES would identify this one as *Argument by Scenario* ("A story linking unrelated items as proof of their relatedness.") Also pertinent here is the *Appeal to False Authority* ("The speaker claims unique expertise of dubious validity.")

Dennis Boyles' hometown retrospective appeared in 2007: *Superior, Nebraska: The Common Sense Values of America's Heartland*, is more than a tad corny, but surely earnest. Boyles emulates Huckabee with mega-paragraphs:

"To most people on the East and West coasts, Superior, Nebraska is just another dot on the mysterious map of the Midwest, a place out there, somewhere off the right side of the aircraft. For decades—and especially during the last two presidential terms—people in small towns like Superior have been ignored, or worse, insulted by people from the big cities who don't know much about the middle of America except how it votes, which is sometimes but not always Republican. Blue-state pundits have reviled people like the ones you see walking up Central Avenue as Babbetts and bigots, hicks and Jesus freaks. It's not just a lazy way of thinking, it's a political weapon based on a century-old stereotype, and its use has been spreading since Reagan was President. Even the Midwest's liberals, eager to mimic elitists on the coasts, now think of their neighbors this way. They probably have to, since the only alterative these days is to grant them a little good faith, something partisans right and left find impossible." (p. 58) B.S. (Bad Science)

The author also succumbs to circuitous logic, "But the Midwest's most valuable commodity of all is the common sense of its durable inhabitants. Too bad it doesn't come in barrels, because there's a huge reservoir of the stuff out there, and part of the goal of this little book with its innocuous subtitle is to help export some of it to places where it's desperately needed." (p. 63)

Conservative talk radio in America's heartland reigns supreme, therefore, the counter-intuitive story of *Ed Schultz's* political epiphany intrigues, as does his shift from talk radio to MSNBC more recently The son of educator Mary and father George, Ed's intellectual journey from right to left occurred relatively slowly over the decade dominated by Bush II's common-sensical rule, coming through in his, *Straight Talk From the Heartland: Tough Talk, Common Sense and Hope from a Former Conservative* (Kindle, 2007).

"How did a prairie-dwelling, red-meat eating, gun-toting former conservative become the hope of liberal radio? It all started with this annoying habit I have of speaking my mind. Sometimes when I open my mouth all hell breaks loose. Other times I feel like a voice in the wilderness and I wonder 'Does anybody get this?' This time the right man was listening. Big Eddie was coming through loud and clear. When (wife) Wendy and I attended the State of the Union Address in January 2003, we had no idea how profoundly it would change our lives and begin to re-script the landscape of American talk radio. I came to Washington unsettled by the changes occurring in America. The economy was floundering. We were on the eve of war and the mainstream press had largely been cowed by the administration and a climate of fear had allowed the Patriot Act to pass almost unchallenged and unread in Congress. The neo-cons had hijacked the Republican Party, and it seemed, America itself. The Democrats looked weak and ineffective. Right-wing talk radio was spewing its propaganda relentlessly, decrying liberals as unpatriotic, angry, hateful, and just plain loony. And it was working. Democrats were going frustrated with the constant hammering they were taking: Three hours of Rush Limbaugh; three hours of Sean Hannity; three hours of Michael Savage; three hours of Michael Reagan. The list goes on and on. I believe that if Rush Limbaugh had been a liberal in 2000, Al Gore would have won that election. That's the difference talk radio can make." (pgs. 71-72)

He credits his second-wife, Wendy, with much more than just progressive politics. They met while he was a conservative talk show host in Fargo, North Dakota. She was director of a homeless shelter in the same city where Big Eddie had been excoriating homeless as lazy and the unemployed as freeloaders. While he was aware of the Big Eddie adulation from simple folks as getting a little old, it was a chance encounter with the gentle little lady that brought a lot of things together for him. His switch from con/pol to lib/pol brought cries of disingenuousness, but Schultz chalks it up to conscience.

Ed Shultz identifies in one five-letter word the cause of America's current malaise: greed. "I worry about the very soul of this nation. This is the greediest generation America has ever seen. Man, I look around and wonder when we're going to think about the next generation. What kind of a world are we leaving them? The wealthiest need a tax cut? Sure, break out the credit card and give our children the bill. Where's the morality that conservatives talk about? Lost in the relentless rush for profit at any cost, that's where. And the middle class is getting trampled. Unchecked greed creates inequality. The hard slant of politics to the right in this country is hurtling us toward oblivion in ways most Americans have yet to grasp." (pp. 186-87)

A postscript to Shultz's consists of his finding a new home with MSNBC, which I love for taking on FNC assertively without replicating their violence-prone aggression. I don't find his analysis as penetrating as colleagues like Rachel Maddow, Lawrence O'Donnell, Dylan Ratigan, Martin Bashir, or Andrea Mitchell. (Bravisimo)

The next common sense sufficiency book does not make us wait for any subtitle to get the deeper message inside. Cline Calhoun's 2010 entry, *The Common Sense of Christianity,* begins by admitting that he possesses no B.A., M.A., Ph. D., or even garden variety divinity degrees. Not broached apologetically, in fact, Calhoun claims down-home credentials owing to his *tabula rasa* purity. His only feign toward scholarship consists of this caveat: "Unless otherwise noted, in this work I will quote from the New King James version bible which many scholars agree is the most reliable translation available of God's word." (p. 82) And his Preface ends with this moniker:

CLINE CALHOUN, CHRISTIAN.

His first chapter, *"Progressive Christianity,"* begins thus: "I recently bought and read a book by Glenn Beck entitled *Common Sense*. I cannot recommend strongly enough the need for every American to read his words of wisdom. Not necessarily wisdom from formal education and degrees, but the natural wisdom that comes with man's God-given common sense, at least for those who choose to use it." (p. 98)

The author obviously believes in the existence of human free will by virtue of his tacking on at the end here: "at least for those who choose to use it." Yet, he refers in later contexts to an antithetical Islamic-like belief in fateful pre-destination. Methinks intoning Christianity enables many people to switch on their suspension of disbelief with alacrity; however, anyone familiar with CTS understands this circle can't be squared.

A few pages later, "We are told in God's word that the writers of the scriptures were inspired by the Holy Spirit, the most powerful force in the universe. As Christians we must have faith that this same Holy Spirit has provided us with the complete word of God as we have in our possession today, the Bible. To think otherwise is to tell God 'I think you left something out, your word is not perfect or complete.' And that, my friend, is treading on thin ice!" (p. 143-44) B.S. (Bad Science)

For CTS practitioners, this is known as the Fallacy of the Slippery Slope ("The assumption that something is wrong because it could slide towards something much worse.") Don Lindsay's ARCHIVE OF FALLACIES.

Later the author mimics Glenn Beck's clarion call for a resurgent two-pronged fundamentalism: literal interpretation of the American constitution matching extant religious fundamentalism (literal interpretation of the Bible). Earlier in life I found fascinating all of the books written by ex-British Nun, Karen Armstrong, but recommend in this context her middle one warning of the dangers inherent in fundamentalism globally.

Author Cline Calhoun provides fodder in ways I couldn't even begin to imagine with these words about a twofer: "As America should return to the Constitution of the United States, we, as Christians, need to take a leap-frog back in time to the days of early Christianity, abandon the doctrines and principles of man, and take a close look at the common sense of Christianity." (p. 334)

Dennis Murray's 2009 book is called *Taming Hate through Common Sense,* and it expresses an antithetical logic to that advanced above by Cline Calhoun (who insists on collapsing common sense and Christianity seamlessly). Murray, however, claims that "Common sense and religious beliefs have connected until recent centuries. We need to separate them clearly now, in order to have a worldwide common sense. We can do this by looking closely at religion and common sense and by finding new common sense that works for all of us." (p. 30) Why don't these volunteer experts on common sense ever define what they mean by it?

After imploring us to separate common sense and religion, Murray conflates them bizarrely in chapter three, entitled "Adam and Eve": "Adam and Eve is a bible story, but it is also part of common sense. In fact, it is part of the foundation of common sense. The story of Adam and Eve is about the three things in the world around us that threaten hope: that we have to die; that we are capable of hate; and, that we have to work hard to sustain life. Death, hate, and work—the big three—they give us different fears." (p. 48) Then, on the very next page, we get this: "Adam and Eve offered a wonderful explanation of these three fears. It said the world is good at its core because there is a loving powerful divine creator." (p. 49)

In the next 2007 book by Juli Idelman, I did intuit her book's theme from the title: *Common Sense from the Purple State,* i.e. the real America unimpressed by the ideological rigidities of hostile Democrats (Blues) and Republicans (Reds): the pragmatic, common-sensical, silent majority, no-nonsense independents driving the Tea Party movement. And if you remember your ROYGBIV spectrum, blending blue and red yields purple (not one of the seven primary colors). Maybe Idelman's musings warranted a brief article, but a book?

As if it wasn't obvious where she was going with this Purple State thing warranting capitalization, she zaps us in the Preface: "The Purple State is a theoretical place where the millions of Americans discouraged by the current condition of our political process are said to reside. While there are no doubt degrees of purple within our group—some more blue, some more red, some such a complete blend of either—the common ground we share is the growing exasperation with the bickering of the Democratic and Republican parties and the impasses these verbal jousting matches forge." (p. 24) Who can possibly argue with the American bifurcation thesis today? However, a cute title does not a paradigm shift make.

Lindsay's ARCHIVE OF FALLACIES offers two equally applicable ripostes to Juli Idelman's statement above: 1.) *Fallacy of the Excluded Middle* ("Assuming only two alternatives exist.") This mental laziness also goes by synonyms such as false dichotomy, faulty dilemma, or bifurcation). 2.) The *Reductive Fallacy* ("Oversimplifying, as Einstein said, everything should be made as simple as possible, but no simpler.")

Of course, it's veritable food fight in the political trenches now but I think that academics can help infuse some civility to the discourse. Dehumanizing adversaries into enemies represents a dysfunctional zero-sum-game mentality. We all understand that intuitively; however, appropriate responses require CTS sophisticated enough to deal with an ineffably complex world.

From Juli Idelman's cute musings about the color purple, we now turn to Jacob Larson's recent prosaic overkill in *Common Sense From a Common Man: One Man's Opinion on Life's Common Conflicts* (Kindle, 2006) Book titles can only be expected to carry so much water on their shoulders, and Larson's sneers at economy.

His Preface sounds reminiscent of familiar themes, such as "This book is not written for the 'intellectual.' It is written for the person with a degree in interpersonal relationships, people like me, who go to work each day, surrounded by the drama of life, looking for the truth in the reality we live in, yet bound by the time it takes to research the subjects we struggle through daily." (p. 25) I know that globalization's down-sizing has forced publishers to cut corners, but so many of these statements beg for an editor.

He devotes a chapter to the male/female dynamic and begins it with "In case you haven't noticed, men and women are different. I know, a shocking revelation, but it's true. Men and women are obviously, noticeably different." (p. 34) A Big Duh to that erudition! Several pages later, "Now both sexes are trapped in a world where two incomes are *required* in order to make rent. Our children are being fed *home-cooked* meals from strangers. And the differences that brought the two sexes together have now become a source of conflict. *Progressive?* Is that the kind of progress we are looking for? In our cry for equality, we have forgotten who we are. We have given our sons an excuse to be lazy, bound our daughters to a life of financial dependence on a job, and justified with the lie of being *fair* "(pgs. 58-59)

Let me mull over this illogic: bad things happening in America result from pursuing the lie of trying to be *fair?* How can efforts to behave fairly self-evidently constitute a lie? This is what Don Lindsay refers to as the *Fallacy of the Single Cause* ("Using only one causal explanation when several exist.")

Speaking of verbose titles, get David Burnett's 2008 book (even though his name is not actually Joe): *A Regular Joe's Take: A Common Sense Approach to Understanding the Political Issues that Determine Who We Should Vote for in the 2008 Presidential Election.* "I am just a regular Joe living in suburban USA. I just felt the need to make sense of the issues using good old fashioned Common Sense instead of relying on all the misinformation that is fed to us through the media and the campaigns themselves." (p. 19) Again, fundamentalists use admittedly bifurcated America as a blank check.

Shortly thereafter, "Let's face it, the media is Liberal and they vote Democrat. That is ok as they have that right. But regretfully because of their agenda you can't trust the information they provide. Even as a Democrat, you can't trust what you have been told what is true or accurate and it may be misleading. Do you knowingly want to make a decision about the future of our country based on knowingly biased information? I don't." (p. 38) This statement by David Burnett fits what Don Lindsay calls the *Fallacy of Argument by Selective Observation* ("Counting the hits but forgetting the misses on any subject"), a.k.a. cherry-picking.

Even more FNC, Burnett reveals his beliefs about the media, "Whether it is the mainstream media, Republican talk radio, or even such new sources of information like Fox News who claim to be fair and balanced. I agree to a certain extent that they may be balanced, but I don't believe it to be 100 percent accurate. They do have a tendency to create a Republican angle on things. That's okay. They have that right just like all the network news programs have the right top angle towards Democrat interpretation." (p. 47) Segments of the foregoing fail to constitute valid sentences and are blatantly ungrammatical. For example, on page 57 Burnett gets away with an absurd word usage when he writes "My goal for the book is to share my thoughts in this *manor*," duh, he must mean in this "manner." My freshman students soon learned to avoid such chicanery.

In *Statistics with Common Sense* (2003) Australian math Professor David Kault shows how both common sense left alone and statistics left alone can lead to bogus conclusions regarding public policy or new medical treatments. However, in tandem these phenomena synergize one another.

He says "Statistics is primarily a way of making decisions in the face of variability and uncertainty. Often some new treatment is first tried on a few individuals and there seems to be some improvement. We want to decide whether we should believe the improvement is 'for real' or just the result of 'chance variation'. . . . In many professional areas people want to answer the same basic question: 'Does this make a real difference?' In the modern world this question is answered by statistics." (p. 16)

Then on the next page he posits its inherent duality, "Statistics has conquered the world of modern decision making; statistics can of course be used wisely, but this depends on the user properly understanding the meaning of the answers from the formula or the computer and understanding how to combine these answers with common sense." (p. 17) Don Lindsay's *Innumeracy Fallacy* works here ("Misunderstanding the nature of statistics; for example, statistics can show that of those people who adopt the habit of eating, very few survive.")

In another familiar-sounding title, Richard Matthews' *Resurrecting Common Sense in America* (Kindle 2009), who authored a series of essays entitled "Resurrecting Common Sense in America" covering varied topics. The hook for Matthews' efforts consisted of a banner headline on the cover of *Time Magazine,* "The Decade from Hell," chronicling the panoply of bad news stories for the previous decade since the millennium. The "Decade from Hell" "was an assessment one that many persons in America have come to share. But it is not one I happen to agree with." (p.24) Then, he leads into "You see my friends, many if not all the problems facing America today remain the same as what our fathers, or father's fathers or even our original founding fathers faced." (p. 25)

He closes his simplistic syllogism with this: "We the People of these great United States of America can change the future of this country. All we need to do is Resurrect Common Sense in America." (p.36) Enjoy the read, Richard A Matthews. He reiterates the standard fundie argument: we should deal with the world's unprecedented complexities by reverting back to a more idyllic past.

In the first chapter, "The Dream" Matthews uses bogus words supposedly attributable to historical figures disputing the artificial Straw Man Fallacy of the "Decade From Hell," in order of appearance: Walter Cronkite, Thomas Paine, Adam Smith, Pope John Paul II, Benjamin Franklin, Thomas Jefferson, John Kenneth Galbraith, Ronald Reagan, William Randolph Hearst, Dwight and Milton Friedman. Matthews presenting his musings as a dream enables him to blend fact and fiction into faction.

Author Dan Bael similarly beats the political fundie drum to death. His version of the over-wrought title is: *Common Sense from the Common Man: A Common Man's Survival Guide for Common Men* (Kindle, 2010); it's hard to find a more redundant title among this prosaic genre. How do these simplistic scribes interpret the complexity of the human experience on Earth as justification for rejecting the bounty of CTS sketched here? What accounts for such eagerness to crawl up into an intellectual fetal ball?

Bael begins his paen to ignorance thus: "Why Should I listen to this guy will probably be the first question that comes to your mind. Well, for starters, the book is entitled *Common Sense from the Common Man* and that's exactly who I am: a common man. The next thing I'm sure you're asking yourself is: so if this guy is so common, why should I listen to him? The answer to that is simple: I've got knowledge and I'm willing to share it with you. If you want to take said knowledge, act on it, and maybe even better yourself in the process, then good for you. If you choose to do nothing with the knowledge that I'm offering—well, you already bought the book, so no skin off my back." (pgs. 85-86) B.S. (Bad Science)

Author Bael totally confuses belief with knowledge supposedly based on his Common Man Curriculum Vitae. (C.V.) Self-fulfilling prophesies, redundancy, and circularity also flow from his words. Then the disingenuous conclusion: if you disagree with me, who cares, because "you already bought the book." Philosopher Don Lindsay discusses the *Non Sequitur Fallacy* ("Something does not follow. For example, arguing that your religion helps you, therefore it is undoubtedly true").

The author describes himself as a "giving kind of guy," therefore offers as knowledge #1 "The Bael Formula:" SUCCESS = MOTIVATION X KNOWLEDGE + SKILL. Believing that merely placing his beliefs here in caps provides sufficient *gravitas* for a common-sensical diatribe. Another gem Bael altruistically shares with us: "I've found that we as humans need to exercise our figurative 'common-sense muscle' so that it doesn't atrophy from lack of use. I think the best way to do this is by reincorporating common-sense into our daily lives as much as possible." (p. 158) *The Reification Fallacy* ("An abstraction discussed as if it were actually concrete. For example, nature abhors a vacuum") works well here.

David Abel also covers familiar turf in this specious genre of common-sensical sufficiency in his *Common Sense Apologetics: One God, One Book, One Way* (Kindle, 2010). And, of course, it's his way or the highway. He similarly cuts to the quick in his Introduction:

"There's really no point for Christians to tiptoe around these basic facts: God Exists, the Bible is His unique and only written word to mankind, and eternal life in Heaven comes through Jesus Christ alone. I know full well that these statements give offense. They sound arrogant, narrow-minded, and exclusive. However, what I intend to argue is that these statements needn't be taken with offense; they needn't be inflammatory, or arrogant, or narrow-minded. On the contrary, my argument will be that these statements carry the greatest measure of love, logic, inclusion, and moral certainty." (p. 79)

First, facts and religious beliefs are mutually exclusive concepts and surely not coterminous as portrayed here; also, if critics take his words as "arrogant, narrow-minded, and exclusive," maybe they have a valid point; and, as for "love": this represents another Reification Fallacy; as for "logic": the applicable fallacies here reach double-digit intellectual sins; and David Abel's Catholic "inclusion" rings fatuous in a world where his religion constitute less than one-fifth of humanity.

A few pages later, Abel proves disabled when he confuses two words with wholly different meanings (intimated vs. intimidated): "Unfortunately, many have been *intimated* into automatically assuming a weak position when attempting to discuss their faith with non-believers. Christians tend to freeze up when confronted with the question: 'Why should Jesus be the only way to heaven?' Too often, the Christian will cede the intellectual high ground with the mythical belief that the skeptic/atheist is operating from a standpoint of scientific and historical superiority." (p. 89) Well, with many hundreds of religions to choose from, maybe that's why Christians freeze up?

Later, he falsely labels all critics of Christian fundies as "atheists;" and, provides a pep talk for defending Christianity's values against cheaters relying on logic: "Throughout the book we will see that though the atheist tries to use intellect as a club—in the end—it turns out to be more like a crutch. Further, believers in Christ should be confident that when all the evidence is assessed, it points to the truth of Christianity, not away from it. Let none of you who are believers in Jesus Christ be intimidated by anyone who purports that your faith must swim against the tide of intellectual pursuits. As I will argue, just the opposite is true." (p. 99)

Next, Fergus O'Connell chimes into the chorus with *The Competitive Advantage of Common Sense: Using the Power You Already Have* (2003), taken from a Prentice-Hall Financial Times Series on business-related issues. If you are beginning to think that infatuation with common sense is monopolized by political/religious fundies, the acceptance of O'Connell's book into a serious Prentice-Hall effort described thus by P-H: "In an increasingly competitive world, it is quality of thinking that gives an edge—an idea that opens up new doors, a technique that solves a problem, or an insight that simply helps make sense of it all. "

Furthermore from the P-H editors, "We work with leading authors in the various arenas of business and finance to bring cutting-edge thinking and best learning practice to a global market. It is our goal to create world-class print publications and electronic products that give readers knowledge and understanding about which can then be applied , whether studying or at work." (p. 34)

One unusual title links common sense's popular status of unconditional positive regard with sophisticated science, by Frances Beinecke, president of the Natural Resources Defense Counsel: *Clean Energy Common Sense* (Kindle, 2008). The Foreword by environmental activist Robert Redford refers to Beinecke's as in the mold of Thomas Paine's 47-page pamphlet *Common Sense* sold 150,000 copies and was extrapolated in the *Declaration of Independence.* Redford suggests that Beinecke's *Clean Energy Common Sense* (Kindle, 2010) "a modern version of Paine's revolutionary classic, calling on us, as a nation, to rise to the challenge of global climate change, an environmental ill of astounding proportions, while there's still time to act." (p. 44) Oiy vey!

But while common sense is a necessary but-insufficient condition for rationality generally, common sense's popularity must be combined with serious science to avert devastating consequences of climate change. Two centuries ago Paine said "I offer nothing more than simple facts, plain arguments, and common sense;" similarly, Redford describes "Beinecke's book as providing those same qualities in this concise but powerful format." (p. 71)

Like Robert Redford (above) and Glenn Beck (below) the author of *Common Sense for the 21st Century* (Kindle, 2010) pays homage to Thomas Paine's classic. Author Beverly Eakman writes that "Paine's own thoughts had evolved by the time he wrote a subsequent tome, *The Rights of Man*, which established him as one of the foremost thinkers of his era. One can agree or disagree with his logic; that is not the issue. The point is that in a free society a person should have the luxury of changing opinions; the individual ought not to be chained to a former, and perhaps less mature, viewpoint. That is the essence of 'free conscience' without which liberty cannot exist. For this reason, Thomas Paine remains a 'great' among American thinkers." (p. 178)

Glenn Beck's Common Sense: The Case against an Out-of-Control Government Inspired by Thomas Paine, which was published with the Tea Party Movement peaking and co-authored this with Joseph Kerry. Beck does not limit his mendacity-laden fantasies to his 5 PM slot on FNC, generously placing them in print as well, documented by several systematic critics. Many of his fundamentalist principles have been cited above, but he possesses a bully pulpit infinitely larger than those cited above.

The New York Review of Books is about as good as that art gets on this planet. Mark Lilla's 16-page comprehensive review of books by and about Glenn Beck called "The Beck of Revelation" characterizes the essence of Beck's standard pitch as this: "Around the beginning of the 20th century, power-hungry elites convinced 'ordinary' Americans to abandon the Founders' principles in the name of progressivism, eroding our rights in a steady process that has culminated in Barack Obama's socialism."[viii]

Viewers of Beck's now-defunct prime-time FNC gig know the drill. What he adds here in *Common Sense* is abandoning the creed since Reagan about American entitlement to Affluenza. Beck scolds Americans for forgetting that "capitalism isn't about money, it's about freedom." (p. 6) He claims that only by returning to the virtues of the Founding Fathers can we be saved: "Americans have changed. Our parents and grandparents relied on debt only to buy a home or a car or put someone through college, but we rely on it to live the lives we *think* we have earned; suddenly our summer vacations, flat-screen televisions, boats, clothes, and dinners out at fancy restaurants were all 'purchased' with debt. If we didn't have the money we acted like we did. We felt we deserved to have it all—big homes, big cars, big TVs." (p. 13)

Beck has referred to himself as an "ex-circus clown" and many of his critics concur. However, Mark Lilla has plowed through most of Beck's writing and says Beck is best understood as a "demagogue," and it's fruitless to search for the underlying essence of demagogues, they simply reflect populist passions rather than create them. Therefore, Beck is always a work in progress.

Wyatt Webb's *What To Do When You Don't Know What To Do: Common Horse Sense* (Kindle, 2006) is quite misleading. Why? Because his story of long-term drug abuse, alcohol, and cigarettes jumped up and bit him in his fifties when he suffered a heart attack. His near-death experience was extremely painful and he was lucky to wind up in the care of a capable and personable cardiologist in Tucson, AZ named Dr. Gregory Koshkarian, a rare 24/7 kind of healer understanding the mind/body/spirit dynamic.

Webb also benefited from previous addictions counseling that taught him how to cope with fear/anxiety by systematically responding to it in five stages: 1.) Acknowledge the fear; 2.) Quantify the fear; 3.) Imagine worst-case scenario; 4.) Gather information and support; 5.) Move on. (p. 154) (Webb's bio shares much with Glenn Beck's)

Webb writes that "In truth, the laws of cause and effect hadn't let me get away with those years of abuse. They took their toll on my physical body, but the lessons I learned were invaluable. I'm really glad to be alive writing this book from a place of awareness that I wouldn't have had I gotten away with something. It's just a further affirmation that accountability is necessary for us to grow, and to remember who we are." (p. 171) Finally, a reasonable observation.

Another title portending more common sense as a sufficient-condition for rationality, Webb benefits here from going beyond the standard common-sensical mantra by embracing CTS, cause-and-effect insights, and the immutability of the scientific method. A nice segue to the rest of this introductory chapter, which builds upon common sense's insufficiency for rational politics and CTS coming to the rescue. It seems to me that a good way to separate valid common sense gems from facile reversion to conventional wisdoms is the CTS mission. Why? Humorist Will Rogers said it most tersely, "Common sense ain't so common."

Veteran journalist Charles Pierce holds his profession responsible for lowering the American discourse in a highly satirical, acerbic new treatise, Pierce harkens back to James Madison's warning that the Enlightenment's intellectual bounty in America could be subverted by the emergence of nihilist "cranks" in America. His title kind of says it all: *Idiot America: How Stupidity Became a Virtue in the Land of the Free* (Kindle, 2009). Its blurb comes along with a series of questions with Pierce, especially this one most pertinent to my subject here.

"**Question:** Is there a specific turning point where, as a country, we moved away from trusting the gut rather than intellect? **Answer:** I don't know if there's one point you can identify as its specific beginning. The conflict between intellectual expertise and reflexive emotion—often characterized as 'good old common sense,' when it's neither common nor sense—has been endemic to American culture and politics from the beginning. I think that my profession (journalism) went off the tracks when it accepted as axiomatic the notion that 'perception is reality.' No. Perception is perception and reality is reality, and if the former does not conform to the latter, then it's the journalist's job to hammer and hammer the reality until the perception conforms to it. That's how 'intelligent design' gets treated as 'science' simply because a lot of people believe in it." (p.121)

Finally, a common sense blog blurts out the return to American classics mantra in one paragraph of its homepage: "We are currently are led by cadres of highly educated 'experts' who have guided our activities for the past fifty years. It is time to reestablish trust in ourselves and take back the governance of our own lives. This site is dedicated to the proposition that ultimate responsibility and authority rest with the people. For too long we have deferred these powers to our business leaders, professors, media, and members of government at all levels. Allowing them to make decisions on our behalf without paying sufficient attention to their actions has proven to be neither wise, nor to our benefit." See: http://www.commonsense-blog.com/

COUNTERVAILING LITERATURE ON CTS:

Common sense's insufficiency bleeds through a recent tale by journalist Joe Queenan in which his scientist daughter came to the aid of his son. Author Queenan confesses to a long-held belief that "People who left their beds unmade would never be successful in life—that an unmade bed signified sloth, indifference, and lack of moral character," and his long-standing battle with his son on this score. He jests that the information age is the bane of all conscientious parents, why?

Because his scientist daughter recently emailed an article to both Dad and little bro "Discussing why sleeping in an unmade bed is healthier than sleeping in a made one. According to a study at Kingston University in London, Ontario that a disheveled bed enables pockets of moisture in a mattress to dry out faster—thereby dehydrating and killing dust mites and other annoying creatures."[ix]

Consensuses in American higher education are rare, but the evidence suggests that a preponderance of institutions and professional organizations now accept the same daunting goal for undergraduate education: *Teaching CTS to students for lifelong learning in an age of constant flux.* I spent the last decade of my teaching career tweaking ways to use model syllabi as conduits for teaching CTS.

In addition to philosopher Don Lindsay's ARCHIVE OF FALLACIES I also recommend two books by Robert Gula: *Nonsense: Red Herrings, Straw Men and Sacred Cows: How We Abuse Logic in Our Everyday Language* (Kindle, 2007) ; and, *Nonsense: A Handbook of Logical Fallacies* (Kindle, 2002); The latter includes double the number found in Lindsay's ARCHIVE.

To me, the essence of CTS consists of *skepticism* that refuses to take things at face value and asks tough questions probing unexamined assumptions. CTS was first introduced into academic policy dialogues by philosophers and psychologist, whose disciplines evolved from very different traditions.[x] One psychologist considers the hallmark of CTS to consist of "an enquiring mind to ask good questions," another focuses on "willingness to engage in active reflection," and a third refers to making "judgments about truthfulness."

Two oft-quoted philosophers, Richard Paul and Linda Elder, describe the crux of CTS as "asking tough questions that *probe*: unexamined assumptions, evidence, alternative views, as well as the consequences of our opinions and behavior, by taking charge of the structures inherent in thinking and imposing intellectual standards on them." [xi] They also believe that several personal traits characterize CTS aficionados: some are passive (like humility, empathy, and civility) others more active (such as courage, integrity, and curiosity).

Another pair of philosophers teaching at Bowling Green State University provide a textbook that I have used: M. Neill Browne and Stewart Keeley present precise guidelines for teaching CTS and pitch the importance of CTS because modernity is replete with dueling experts having a vested interest in most controversial questions; therefore, we need to think rigorously for ourselves, including awareness of interrelated key questions asked at the right times.

Ten Critical Thinking Questions:

1. What issue is involved and what conclusions reached?
2. What reasons are given for this viewpoint?
3. What words or phrases are ambiguous?
4. What value conflicts underlie this controversy?
5. What hidden assumptions are made here?
6. Does the reasoning contain fallacies?
7. How good is the evidence?
8. Are there multiple sources of causation at work here?
9. Are statistics used deceptively?
10. Is significant information omitted?[xii]

Since abstract concepts like CTS confuse students, I used a concept's antithesis. With CTS, nothing epitomizes its negation better than *group-think,* a theory developed by Illinois University social psychologist Irving L. Janis. Groupthink fosters conformity and self-censorship in all decision-making bodies such as corporate boards, faculty senates, and foreign-policy venues. I used a film based on Janis' book identifying case studies in which groupthink did in fact occur (Pear Harbor; Bay of Pigs Invasion; Gulf of Tonkin Incident, and Bush II's Iraq War); as well as others (such as Cuban Missile Crisis) where it did not occur, and why.

Since CTS emanate from two distinct disciplines: philosophy (humanities) and psychology (social sciences) the title of every relevant book does not contain CTS. For example, a recent one by D. Q. McInerny called *Being Logical: a Guide to Good Thinking* fits into this category. Its author writes that "Logic, taken as a whole, is a wide, deep, and wonderfully varied field, and I would be pleased if my readers were to become more familiar with it. . . . My governing purpose was to write a practical guide-book, presenting the basic principles of logic in a way accessible to novices." (pgs. 155-56) His book evolves through five stages:

1) Proper frame of mind for logical thinking;
2) Foundational truths under-girding logic;

3) Argumentation (logical public expression;
4) Attitudes that foster illogic;
5) Fallacies (particularities of illogic.)

McInerny also cites a classic I still like: William Strunk and E.B. White, *The Elements of Style* as motivating him to replicate their treatise on thoughtful writing with one on thoughtful thinking. This linkage of sound writing and sound thinking is expressed by McInerny thus: "Being logical presupposes sensitivity to language and a knack for its effective use, since language and logic remain inseparable. It also has healthy respect for the firm factual nature of the world we live in, for logic is about reality." (p. 174)

I appreciate fully the author's next words: "Critical thinking is neither the easiest subject to teach not the easiest to learn. It incorporates so many different skills that even defining it proves much more difficult than other subjects. But, in the long run, these skills are all aimed at making wise decisions about what to believe and how to act. Furthermore, we believe it is best taught by integrating logic (formal and informal) with a variety of other skills helping us make sound decisions about claims, actions, policies, and practices." (p. 103) Cal State University professors Brooke Moore and Richard Parker's 2009 book is simply called *Critical Thinking*.

Scottish professors Gary Kemp and Tracy Bowell's 2009 book was intended as a college textbook, and reads easily: *Critical Thinking: A Concise Guide*. They observe that "We are frequently confronted with *arguments*: these are attempts to *persuade* us—to influence our beliefs and actions—by giving us reasons to believe this or that, or to act this way or that. This book will equip you with concepts and techniques used in the identification, analysis and assessment of arguments. The aim is to improve your ability to tell *whether* the argument is and whether you ought to be persuaded by it." (p. 225) They don't get into the proper function of commons sense per se, but they do go after its specious cousin: "pseudo-reasoning."

Kemp and Bowell cite the importance of "why" questions challenging conventional wisdoms. However, CTS goes further by demanding good reasons, not settling for perfunctory answers. By presenting good answers we make legitimate *arguments*. I like their use of italics and bolding as something akin to to the *paralinguistics* (tone of voice, facial expressions, body language) I keep referring to regarding FNC. They contend that in courts of law critical thinking possesses life and death consequences; and, they concede that developing CTS entails hard work, but pays huge benefits. Following an "ignorance is bliss" mantra will suffice for many humans, but proves inadequate in modern civil societies.

In *Critical Reasoning: A Practical Introduction* by Anne Thompson (Kindle, 2009, 3E), she attacks the common misperception that when we engage in critical reasoning that means we are incessantly attacking the ideas of others to excess. Fair-minded CTS also showers praise on sound, evidence-based logical arguments. Also intended as a higher education textbook, Thompson defines terms carefully and illustrates concepts with useful examples. A literature professor, she pays tribute to American CTS pioneers such as John Dewey, Edward Glaser, Steven Norris, Robert Ennis, Richard Paul and Michael Scriven. She credits Alec Fisher as the catalyst for transferring this endeavor across the Atlantic.

Another Brit, Timothy Crews-Anderson, authored *Critical Thinking and Informal Logic* (Kindle, 2007) and touches upon the ironic ubiquity of loose thought amid a paucity of reason among us. "Try to imagine for a moment a field of human endeavor that does not require reasoning. This is likely impossible as there is little our species does not involving our ability to think. Philosophers have postulated that if there is anything essential to the human being, it is the capacity for reason. Indeed, thought is so fundamental that only rarely is one without it. The operations of the mind come so easily that we scarcely realize they are ongoing. It is perhaps for this reason that the notion of thinking *skillfully* may seem strange." An apt analogy here might be the idea that the last thing a fish would ever notice is water. (p. 13)

Crews-Anderson observes that incisive critical thinkers take the process seriously by consciously asking the right kinds of probing questions. And, as with most human activities, skill development does not occur without much practice. "It is probably unreasonable to expect them to come easily, but it's almost certain that time and effort will pay a heavy dividend." (p. 34) I know this certainly rings true in my experience.

Hy Ruchlis' *Clear Thinking: a Practical Introduction* (Kindle, 2008) includes a lengthy Foreword from Isaac Asimov. Asimov points out that there are about two million species alive today and maybe 20 times that ever on Earth, "practicing complex, and even abstract reasoned thought. Almost all of us can do it. Indeed, it is our only true badge of humanity." (p. 7) Also, taking a jab at common sense, Asimov contends "Because fakers and charlatans offer people the lure of easy thinking, they are followed avidly by much of the public. Millions listen gullibly to the astrologers, the spoon-benders, the mind-readers, spiritualists, cultists and other shoddy retailers of nonsense. And it is the habit of easy, emotional pseudo-thought that makes it so hard to wean people from this kind of folly." (p. 37)

Author Ruchlis provides chapters covering:

1) Importance of Clear Thinking;
2) Nature of Facts;
3) Superstition and Science;
4) The Reasoning Process;
5) Language and Reasoning;
6) Common Errors in Reasoning;
7) Astrology: A Case Study in Defective Reasoning;
8) Conflicting Opinions;
9) Stereotypes and Discrimination;
10) How Opinions are Influenced;
11) Reasoning Errors in Advertising;
12) The Big Picture.

American academic Julian Meltzoff wrote a book based on 17 years teaching graduate students how to design and evaluate research, resulting in *Critical Thinking about Research: Psychology and Related Fields* (Kindle, 2010). What was his complaint? Plenty of books about research design teach students how to create their own research, but few teach them how to assess those of their peers. The years 1990-2010 featured what was known as the "assessment movement" in American academe and he brings that vague concept to life here.

Author Meltzoff opens his Introduction deftly with these words:

"How should scientific evidence be evaluated? After reading a research article, one person may be fully convinced by the evidence offered; a second person may think the same evidence may be true but regards it, on balance to be equivocal and feels obliged to suspend judgment; and a third may disdainfully dismiss it with scatological words of unmistakable meaning. Their differing judgments are informed by different views concerning what constitutes proof, are influenced by their different beliefs about the evidence needed to establish proof, and are limited by the amount of knowledge they possess about the methods used to gather evidence in the search for truth. They are also affected by variation in ability to think critically as a positive quality, not as a pejorative reference to mean-spirited fault-finding." (P. 97)

Another entry in the CTS genre appears in Professor John Papazafiroulos' *Dare to Think for Yourself: How to See through the Deceptive Falsehoods which are Thrown Your Way* (Kindle, 2008) who he wrote this brief book because so many students suggested it. Preparing students for lifelong learning represents a stellar theme in today's progressive literature. To wit: "It is important that we continue to learn throughout our lives, and that we question those who give direction to what we should or should not do. The ability to think critically will become, in my opinion, a matter of survival. Knowledge is the only true power. Wealth, positions, relationships, beliefs, and health can all be taken from you. What you know, however, can never be taken away." (p.12)

Reflective judgment and critical thinking are viewed as equally valid public goods in the CTS literature. This becomes readily apparent in Patricia King and Karen Kitchener's *Developing Reflective Judgment* (Kindle, 2006) where the author claims two unique corners in this market: 1.) Describing the series of stages that lay the foundation for and lead to reflective thinking; 2.) Covering the extensive research literature on which this "developmental model" is firmly grounded. (p. 77)

Regarding the nice fit between reflective judgment and CTS, the authors note "We are aware that what we call reflective judgment is related to what other researchers are studying as critical thinking. While certain aspects of the definitions overlap, other aspects remain quite distinct." (p. 55) These University of Minnesota professors' text contains much data (hard and soft), diagrams, charts, and ambitious scope. The professional shorthand for their theory is referred to as the Reflective Judgment Model (based on Reflective Judgment Interviews); they claim this book represents the only comprehensive examination of this model.

Much of the CTS literature deals with teaching it to captive students, however, the next book's focus is on adult learners. Jack Mezirow, ed. offers *Fostering Critical Reflection in Adulthood: a Guide to Transformative and Emancipatory Learning* (Kindle, 2005). I like the notion that change remains the only constant in our universe. Mezirow's Introduction says "The pervasiveness and significance of change in modern society have become axiomatic. Freed from the inevitable dependency imposed by the socialization process, adult learners can make dramatic gains in self-direction. Understandably, one may find transformative learning threatening, exhilarating, and empowering." (p. 29)

Several pages later, he claims that his multi-authored chapters "Suggest methods and program approaches for precipitating and fostering transformative learning in the context of the classroom, special workshops, informal groups, counseling sessions, and the workplace. Each contributing author has identified and analyzed a useful method of analysis or approach to program development to help adults learn." (p. 49)

Philosopher George Santayana's century-old classic, *The Life of Reason,* is now available again. Greek rationalism, resurrected by the Renaissance and Enlightenment (ironically via Middle Eastern Islamic scholars during the Middle Ages) receives its proper kudos in Santayana's classic. "As it is improbable that there will soon be another people so free from preoccupations, so gifted, and so fortunate as the Greeks, or capable in consequences of so well exemplifying humanity, so also it is improbable that a philosopher will soon arise with Aristotle's scope, judgment or authority, one knowing so well how to be both reasonable and exalted." (p. 337)

By juxtaposing the concepts of religiosity and ethics, Santayana points to a fundamental Greek irony: "If the happy freedom of the Greeks from religious dogma made them the first natural philosophers, their happy political freedom made them the first moralists. It was no accident that Socrates walked the Athenian agora; it was no petty patriotism that made him shrink from any other scene." (p. 304)

An older book by PARADE magazine contributor, Marilyn vos Savant, is *The Power of Logical Thinking: Easy Lessons in the Art of Reasoning and Hard Facts About Its Absence in Our Lives* (St. Martin's Griffin, 1997), 228 pp. Purportedly the individual with the highest recorded I.Q. she took a lot of flak from mathematicians and statisticians over a debacle in print known as the "Monty Hall Dilemma."

Her book seems aimed primarily at what might called "math anxiety" found in the general population. A review in BOOKLIST opines that "vos Savant shows us how even the most well educated can be semiliterate in the arts of reasoning and problem solving. She illustrates how easily we are duped by 'counter-intuitive' problems that run against the grain of instinct." (common-sensical insufficiency)

Anthony Weston's succinct *A Rulebook for Arguments* (Kindle, 2009) skips much of the theory and analysis about CTS and specializes in lists of dos and don'ts. He calls it less a textbook than a rulebook. He offers "simple rules for putting good arguments together. We do not want our students to come out of critical thinking courses knowing only how to shoot down (or just at) selected fallacies. Critical thinking can be practiced in a far more constructive spirit." (p. 110)

Weston asks: "What's the point of arguing? Many people think that arguing is simply stating their prejudices in a new form. This is why many also consider arguments pointlessly unpleasant." One dictionary defines "argument as "disputation," implying something akin to a verbal fistfight. While that can happen, their key main purpose is to offer reasonable evidence supporting a conclusion. They represent efforts to support certain views with reasons; as such arguments are anything but pointless, they are essential." (p.132)

The author also admits that while CTS are labor-intensive, they slowly grow on their practitioners. "The practice of argument has some inherent attractions of its own. Our minds become more flexible, open-ended, and alert; we come to appreciate how much difference our own critical thinking really makes." (p. 159)

Academician H. William Dettmer's *The Logical Thinking Process: A Systems Approach to Complex Problem Solving* (Kindle, 2007) includes scores of heuristic figures and illustrations. Dettmer is currently Senior Partner at Goal Systems International, a consortium of management professionals, and has 23 years prior experience in applying the logical thinking process to businesses, governments, and Non-Governmental-Organizations (NGOs) around the world. The book specializes in the use of "logic trees" in real-world applications, and is replete with diagrams of all sorts.

A more standard treatise on logic consists of Nicholas Capaldi's *The Art of Deception: an Introduction to Logic* (Kindle, 2008) based on the viewpoint I expressed earlier that in educational settings it helps students if instructors not only define their terms, but also define their antitheses. Concerning arguments, Capaldi asserts that one kind of argument intuitively unacceptable is one arriving at a false conclusion from true premises. For example:

"Premise 1: Terrorists call for the immediate withdrawal of US troops from Iraq.

Premise 2: US liberals call for the immediate withdrawal of US troops from Iraq.

Conclusion: Liberals are terrorists." (p. 115)

The deep divide I'm drawing here between common-sensical thought and CTS has much in common with Chet Raymond's *Skeptics and True Believers* (Kindle, 2006). It seems to me that in each case we are referring to a fundamental divide at the level of human nature, not merely America or Western Civilization.

Raymond notes "Skeptics are children of the Scientific Revolution and the Enlightenment. They are always a little lost in the vastness of the cosmos, but they trust the ability of the human mind to make sense of the world. They accept the evolving nature of truth and are willing to live with a measure of uncertainty. Their world is colored in shades of gray." (p. 112).

"True Believers are less confident that humans can sort things out for themselves. They look for help from outside from God, spirits, or extraterrestrials. Their world is black and white. They seek simple and certain truths provided by a source that is more reliable than the human mind. True Believers prefer a universe proportional to the human scale. They are repulsed by diversity, elitism, and intellectuals." (p. 114) I also admit to a strong affinity for the Skeptics over True Believers among us.

SKEPTICS SOCIETY:

I first encountered this concept via Eric Hoffer's classic book, *True Believers,* which *Skeptic* magazine recommends because it gives a skeptical view of the oft-quoted notion a of safety-in-numbers (e.g., "Ten million Elvis fans can't be wrong!") According to its editor, "Hoffer's book confronts the idea that ALL mass movements are born out of unhealthy constructs, they appeal to emotion over logic, and swell their ranks with the weakest, not the strongest members of society." I like rank-orderings forcing us to prioritize.

My favorite CTS magazine is *Skeptic,* available both in hard copy and online. It has been published by the Skeptics Society since 1992. For general inquiries contact them at skepticssociety@skeptic.com; and to subscribe: subscriptions@skeptic.com. The Skeptics Society provides a marvelous Austhink compendium labeled: "Critical Thinking on the Web: A Directory of Quality Online Resources": http://austhink. com/critical/pages/skepticbooks.html Their top ten skeptics CTS books based on a e-Skeptic hotline request selected by subscribers consisted of:

1) Carl Sagan, *The Demon Haunted World: Science as a Candle in the Dark;*
2) Michael Shermer, *Why People Believe Weird Things;*
3) James Randi, *Flim Flam!: Psychics, ESP, Unicorns and Other Delusions;*
4) Martin Gardner, *Fads and Fallacies in the Name of Science;*
5) Theodore Schick and Lewis Vaughn, *How to Think About Weird Things;*
6) James Randi, *The Faith Healers;*
7) Michael Shermer, *How We Believe;*
8) Martin Gardner, *The New Age: Notes of a Fringe Watcher;*
9) Stephen Jay Gould, *The Mismeasure of Man;*
10) Robert Park, *Voodoo Science: The Road from Foolishness to Fraud.*

The Skeptics society Website also contains many excellent links, including ones on Group Thinking (groupthink), Fallacies, Great Critical Thinker, Magazines & Journals, Terrorism, Course Syllabi, and Web Page Evaluation. Also, "The Skeptic's Guide to the Universe" is a weekly Podcast talk show produced by the New England Skeptics Society (NESS) in association with the James Randi Educational Foundation (JREF). It features latest news and topics from the world of the paranormal and fringe science.

Austhink also provides a top ten CTS for quality online resources:

1) *Argument Mapping Tutorials* (six online tutorials in argument mapping, a core requirement for critical thinking);
2) *The Skeptic's Dictionary* (more than 400 definitions and essays);
3) Gary Curtis, *The Fallacy Files* (excellent website on fallacies);
4) *Butterflies and Wheels* (News and Articles);
5) Peter Facione, *Critical Thinking: What It Is and Why It Counts*;
6) John Stuart Mill, *On the Liberty of Thought and Discussion;*
7) *Chance* (best website for helping students thinking critically about statistics);
8) Richard Heuer, *Psychology of Intelligence and Analysis* (cognitive psychology's contributions to critical thinking);
9) Ian Johnston, *Writing Argumentative and Interpretive Essays* (handbook);
10) Michael Shermer, *Baloney Detection: Parts I and II.*

Their website also cites Francis Bacon's famous 1605 take on CTS: "For myself, I found that I was fitted for noting so well as the study of Truth; as having a mind nimble and versatile enough to catch the resemblances of things ...and at the same time steady enough to fix and distinguish their subtler

differences; as being gifted by nature with desire to seek, patience to doubt, fondness to meditate, slowness to assert, readiness to consider,

carefulness to dispose and set in order; and as being a man that neither affects what is new or admires what is old, that hates every kind of
imposter."

Taking one volume of *The Skeptic* volume 10, number 3, includes such
topics as "Special Evolution Issue: Intelligent Design and Creationism."
Authors and title of the five main articles: Brandon Muller, "Blame it on
the Jews: Anti-Semitism and the History of Jewish Conspiracy Theories;"
Simon Morris, "Toward a Theology of Evolution? Humans were inevitable
on Earth, but are we alone in the Cosmos?"; review by Donald Prothero of
Simon Morris' *Life Solutions: Inevitable Humans in a Lonely Universe;* Peter
Corning review of David Wilson's *Darwin's Cathedral: Evolution, Religion,
and the Nature of Society;* and, "Is God in the Equations?" a review by Joe
Cuchiara of Harold Morowitz, *The Emergence of Everything.*

Another thoughtful piece in volume 10, number 3 is David Eller's
"Macroevolution and Microcreationism: Another Flaw in Intelligent
Design Creationism," which begins thus: "A standard tactic used by
creationists to attack evolution is to contrast microevolution (intra-
species evolution), which they accept, and macro-evolution (inter-
species evolution)., which they adamantly reject. They assert that
while microevolution may be true, it is trivial, and the major claim of
evolution—the evolution and emergence of species—is either unsub-
stantiated or false."

Furthermore, "This failure to account for macro-phenomena, such as
human life, the Earth, or the universe, suggests creationism as the only
plausible alternative for life's origins. This conclusion suffers from
the Fallacy of the Excluded Middle or false dilemma. But ironically,
the 'success' of the 'scientific' creationist enterprise, particularly in its
most recent and serious incarnation (i.e., Intelligent Design, ID), has
itself up to this point rested on claims regarding a few minor fragmen-
tary subspecies processes rather than the macro-processes that that it

so keenly denies to evolution." In a 12-page treatise Eller debunks this mega-mythology.

CTS RESOURCES ONLINE:

An online resource I wish I knew about earlier is called INTERNET DETECTIVE:

"A free, online tutorial designed to help students develop the critical thinking skills required for their Internet research. Originally designed in 1998 by the European Union and later translated into many languages, INTERNET DETECTIVE has tutorials offering practical advice on evaluating the quality of websites; and, highlights care in selecting online information sources for university or college work."

The tutorials runs for one hour and rely on a light-hearted film noir detective motif to teach critical thinking skills, comprised of these segments: 1.) What's the story?; 2.) The good, the bad, and the ugly; 3.) Detective work; 4.) Get on the case; 5.) Keeping on the right side of the law. The service is currently based at two British universities: Bristol and Manchester Metropolitan.

Co-editor Emma Place (Bristol U.) emphasizes "Students are increasingly turning to the Internet to find information for their coursework assignments, but they can be naïve in the sources they choose. Concern exists among lecturers (professors) and librarians that students degrade their work by either referencing inappropriate information sources, or by failing to use the best scholarly materials available to them."

I told my students that when I was in their position, knowledge was conceived largely as quantifiable content (stuff), including much trivia. In modernity's age of information overload, raw information inundates us from all directions. The key skill now? CTS to separate the gold from the gunk; sound qualitative judgments enabling us to rank-order the significance of competing hard-and-soft data.

See: http://www.vts.intute.ac.uk/detective/

A more diverse, multi-faceted website also focused on education is called THE CRITICAL THINKING COMMUNITY based at The Foundation and Center for Critical Thinking, which "Aims to improve education from primary schools to higher education by presenting workshops, conferences, publications, and professional development programs emphasizing instructional strategies. Socratic questioning, critical reading and writing, higher order thinking, assessment, research, quality enhancement, and competency standards."

See CRITICAL THINKING COMMUNITY:

http://www.criticalthinking.org/store-page.cfm?P=products&itemID=1 67&cateID=132&...

I like most of their publications, but none fits my purposes here better than a book by two authors encountered above: Richard Paul and Linda Elder, who have the importance of ethnocentrism down pat concerning media bias globally: *How to Detect Media Bias & Propaganda in National and World News* (Foundation for Critical Thinking, 2008).

In their Introduction, "The underlying logic beneath bias and propaganda in news media worldwide is simple and discernible. Each culture's unique world view colors what it sees and how it sees it, translated into the news media's coverage of events and their respective meanings. However, the truth about news events gets much more complicated when these national prisms conflict. Critical readers of the news media in each nation must come to grips with this reality and read/act accordingly. Critical thinking is a complex set of skills that reverses what is natural and instinctive in human thought." (p. 3)

In other words, ethnocentrism constitutes the fallback position for humans and must be both recognized and resisted.

Furthermore, tunnel vision should be challenged if we seek greater objectivity: "Achieved insights from various sources include weaknesses and partiality that can be integrated more comprehensively upon reflection." (p. 6) In my view, Fox epitomizes the ethnocentrism and tunnel vision decried by authors Paul and Elder. Hopefully, my ten chapters will convince you as well.

Based in Vancouver, BC, another online CTS resource is called TC2 (The Critical Thinking Consortium) addressing all levels of education. Since 1993, TC2 has been embedding CTS into curricula worldwide, and what they call their COURSEPACKS strike me as unique: "Comprehensive digital resource containing detailed lesson plans, ready-to-use student booklets and interactive visual displays for use with Smart-board technology." See: http://www.tc2.ca/wp/

Finally, a new resource developed by Robert Ennis, Emeritus Director of the Illinois Critical Thinking Project. His definition: "Critical thinking is reflective cognition helpful in deciding what to believe or do, therefore it involves creative activities such as formulating hypotheses, plans, and counterexamples; planning experiments, and seeing alternatives. "

See: http://www.criticalthinking.net/

CONCLUSION:

This chapter began linking the filmic humanities concept of "suspension of disbelief" to SOP at FNC, where punditry conflates common-sensical thinking as both a necessary-and-sufficient condition for political discourse. The subtext of Fox's culture relies heavily on paralinguistics (a.k.a. paralanguage) to convey authoritarian values to its niche alpha male demographic.

Getting beneath their mere words, FNC personalities such as The big O, Sean Hannity, and Glenn Beck all ooze on-air braggadocchio, somewhat less offensive (though no less specious) in their writings. Please find me another FNC critic asserting a strong correlation between paralingusitc manipulation by these three pundits.

1   Film critics refer to the concept of "suspension of disbelief" signifying success by the director in convincing the viewer to eschew skepticism and embrace credulity, similar to what novelists perform with the printed word. One definition of this term consists of "People's acceptance, for the sake of appreciation of art (including literature) of what they know to be a nonfactual premise of the work of art":

"Suspension of disbelief," WIKTIONARY: http://en.wiktionary.org/wiki/suspension_of_disbelief.
Suspension of disbelief strikes me as equally germane to the role of Fox news in American politics, where Conservative "true believers" see Fox as the talisman affirming a parochial world view bereft of evidence illustrating author Eric Hofer's introduction of that term to our public lexicon several decades ago.

2   "Common Sense," WIKTIONARY: http://en.wiktionary.org/wiki/common_sense.

3   "Alpha Male," WIKTIONARY: "The term alpha male is sometimes applied to humans referring to a man who is powerful through his courage and a competitive goal-driven, take-charge attitude. With their bold approach and confidence alpha males are often described as charismatic. While they are often over-achievers recognized for their leadership qualities, their aggressive tactics and competitiveness can also lead to resentment by others." (http://en.wikipedia.org/wiki/Alpha_male)

4   The West Virginia Consortium for Faculty and Course Development in International Studies (FACDIS) has received about $1.5 million in federal funding and we have always relied upon course syllabus enhancement as the royal road to verifying the pedagogical fruits of our efforts, leading me to publish two articles and then a book on this unexamined subject. Based at West Virginia University with outreach programs to over 375 interdisciplinary faculty members in all of our 15 higher education institutions FACDIS celebrated our 30th year of service at our annual workshops in November 2010.

5   Assessment Movement: "The Value-Added Assessment Initiative (VAAI) and Higher Education Quality Control," *Peer Review;* by invitation (Association of American Colleges and Universities), Spring 2002; and, "Assessing the

Assessment Decade," *Liberal Education* (Association of American Colleges and Universities), vol. 87, no. 4 (fall 2001), pp. 41-49.

Syllabi on Steroids: "Neglect Not the Syllabus: The Humble Syllabus as Creative Catalyst," THRIVING IN ACADEME SECTION (by invitation) *NEA Higher Education Advocate* (circ=90,000) vol. 18, no. 2 (June 2001), pp. 5-8; "The Case for Sophisticated Course Syllabi," *To Improve the Academy, 2000 Edition* (Anker Publishing, 2000), pp. 162-76.

6   Don Lindsay, ARCHIVE OF FALLACIOUS ARGUMENTS:

    http://www.don-lindsay-archive.org/skeptic/arguments.html

7   Mark Lilla, "The Beck of Revelation," THE NEW YORK REVIEW OF BOOKS (9 December 2010):

    http://www.nybooks.com/articles/archives/2010/dec09/beck-revelation/

8   Joe Queenan, "Kids Have Discovered a Diabolical New Use for Science: Rebutting Their Parents," SMITHSONIAN MAGAZINE (December 2010), p. 108.

9   Michael J. Strada, *Benefits of Model Syllabi* (University Press of America, 2006), p. 3.

10   Richard Paul and Linda Elder, *Critical Thinking: Tools for Taking Charge of Your Professional and Personal Life* (Kindle 2008), p. 32.

11   M. Neil Browne and Stewart Keeley, *Asking the Right Questions: A Guide to Critical Thinking* (Prentice Hall, 2009), pp. 12-14.

CHAPTER TWO:

"American Politics/My Politics"

POLITICAL SCIENCE AND THE SOCIAL SCIENCES:

Social sciences consist of: anthropology, economics, geography, political science, psychology, and sociology. Given human behavior's complexity, specialization has evolved since the Enlightenment (1700-1800). Getting behind the eyeballs of each discipline to glean what matters most to its practitioners; in political science, the answer remains clear: Power (the ability of Actor A to get Actor B to behave in a manner in which B would not otherwise do).

Political actors consist of individuals, unions, NGOs (non-governmental-organizations), and larger entities such as countries because the competitive process remains similar at the micro, macro, and mega-levels of analysis. The philosophical guru who molded modernity's fixation on power as the currency of politics was Italian Renaissance thinker Niccolo Machiavelli.

Politics relies on ideologies (ideas in action) coalescing around core values (such as equality or competitiveness), in groups prioritizing them. Ideologies simplify a complex world, making sense in ways congenial to our beliefs. Certain ideologies defend the status quo, while others hope to tear down business-as-usual. Modern ideologies comfortable defending the status quo (conservatism) stand in stark contrast to those seeking progressive policies (liberalism).[xiii]

The political spectrum sorts out individuals and groups espousing contrasting policies. It is typically divided in three: the political center (home turf for moderates); the political left (home turf for liberals); and, the political right (home turf for conservatives). Moving from the center toward both extremes, we encounter radicals acting out to promote change or toil against it. Berkeley political scientist Austin Ranney describes what he refers to as "universal features of politics at all levels": 1.) Conflict; 2.) Group behavior; 3.) Employment of tactics."[xiv]

CLASSIFYING GOVERNMENTS:

The key to categorizing 190-some governments consists of how power is distributed: in a concentrated manner or diffusely? Democracies distribute power diffusely, and have spread like wildfire across the globe for two centuries, especially in recent decades. The good news globally is that most powerful/affluent countries today qualify as democracies, according to the human rights NGO called Freedom House.[xv]

However, no pure democracies exist wherein all citizens participate freely in public affairs. But on a decidedly imperfect planet Earth, indirect democracy is valued for providing someone or something to represent the interests of a majority of us. Democracies try to protect both their denizens' civil liberties (freedoms) and civil rights (equality).

Political scientists list four attributes essential to democracy: 1.) Popular sovereignty; 2.) Political equality; 3.) Popular consultation; and 4.)

Majority rule/minority rights.[xvi] Two world-class democratic models are the parliamentary form (epitomized by the United Kingdom's fusing governmental powers in its cabinet); and, the presidential from (represented by the USA) where powers get divided between three branches: legislative (rule-making), executive (rule-administering), and judicial (rule-adjudicating).

Countries like France and Germany merge parliamentary and presidential types quite well. Most scholars believe that democracy has at least won the intellectual argument in all world regions (even Africa, Latin America, and Eastern Europe) except the Middle East, where popular uprisings have torn apart countries like Iran, Syria, Tunisia, and Egypt. This remains the only region in which the intellectual fight between modernity (i.e., democracy) and traditionalism (i.e., dictatorship) appears uncertain.

The ugly word scholars reserve for those rigid, hierarchical leftovers from the Middle Ages? Dictatorships: As humans evolve cognitively, archaic dictatorships have failed in the quality-of-life issues social scientists emphasize, epitomized by the United Nations' annual Human Development Index (HDI) measuring not only gross economic productivity, but subtler quality of life matters.

The two most virulent forms of dictatorship came and went during the twentieth century, Fascism in Germany and Japan; as well as Communism, which lasted longer than Fascism spreading from the Soviet Union to 12 other countries. Only four of those still remain: China, North Korea, Cuba, and Vietnam. Dictatorships distribute power in a concentrated manner and are broken down into two variants by extent of control over denizens:

1.) *Authoritarian regimes*: Status-quo oriented and desirous of maintaining the privileged status of a wealthy ruling class, with no agenda for radically restructuring society through mass mobilization.

2.) *Totalitarian regimes*: Occurring in the 20th century as a virulent strain of dictatorship known by this moniker; i.e., both Communism and Fascism fit here. They are led by an elite party using terror and mass media to further a discrete ideology.

The historical record demonstrates that totalitarian regimes are much more dangerous to their neighbors' health and security than are authoritarian regimes. In some ancient dictatorships, one convenient method of monopolizing power consisted of governments ruled by royals (kings and queens) as legitimization for exercising power.

And all matters political must factor in British historian Lord Acton's famous 1877 lecture at Cambridge University. However, his dictum typically gets misquoted. The misleading imposter runs "power corrupts, and absolute power corrupts absolutely," containing considerable determinism absent in the subtly-nuanced original: *"Power tends to corrupt, but absolute power corrupts absolutely,"* wherein the word "tends" makes all the difference.

Thus, the correct quote is more relativistic. Insights tapped into by Acton, I believe, operate at the level of *humanity*, not merely national or individual levels of analysis.

Consequently, while power-holders don't always act corruptly, it happens often enough for sentient beings to apply CTS to words tumbling from politicians' mouths. History reveals that things like term limits help to establish accountability. [xvii]

ALTERNATING LIBERAL/CONSERVATIVE BOOKS ON AMERICAN POLITICS:

Punch "American politics" into Kindle and hundreds of books appear. As stated below, if the choice comes down to liberalism versus conservatism, I'll almost always pick the liberal option, thus I refer to myself as very liberal ideologically. In the interest of fairness, I will alternate reporting on liberal and conservative tomes in this backgrounder chapter. All of these books appear high on this e-reader's rank-ordered sales compendium.

Predictably, I really like Cheyney Ryan's *The Chicken-hawk Syndrome: War, Sacrifice, and Personal Responsibility.* (Kindle, 2009) My contemporary, Ryan first began to doubt the validity of America's massive war machine in trying to outsmart the Selective Service System's grossly unfair methods during Vietnam. While Ryan's current book deals specifically with the serial absurdities of Bush II's 2003 Iraq War, the author claims naivete about America's bloated Pentagon budget (exceeding those of all other countries combined) until recently.

Ryan's snappy title reflects a key question familiar to most news junkies: How is it that so many of the gung-ho warmongers demanding to take out Saddam Hussein in 2003 based on illusory reasons were so conspicuously absent when the chips were really down for America from 1965-1975 in Vietnam's rice paddies?

Ryan plumbs the depths of this collective shroud of sorrow, providing well-documented evidence for the "chicken-hawk" behavior of Bush II, Dick Cheney, Paul Wolfowitz, Donald Rumsfeld, Scooter Libby, Dan Quayle, Bill O'Reilly, and many others. In chapter four I review Bill O'Reilly's latest book, *A Bold Fresh Piece of Humanity,* and his rationalizations for dodging the draft during Vietnam. Ryan defines a chicken-hawk as "Someone who vigorously endorses a war and its sacrifices while diligently *avoiding* such sacrifices himself." (p. 18)

The author says "The chicken-hawk issue is a real one; not an incoherent slur, toothless epithet, or rhetorical ploy. Nor is it a purely partisan, involving few politicians. The chicken-hawk syndrome raises important ethical questions of war and personal responsibility. It raises basic political questions about the citizenry's connection—or lack thereof—to the wars that are fought in its name." (p. 83) Ryan's Quaker father volunteered for WW II and served heroically, in that most justifiable of all 20th century wars.

Sara Palin's *America By Heart* (Kindle, 2009) starts with her speech Tax Day in Boston, MA, which she concludes thus "What I've learned from all this traveling and meeting and talking and reading is this: the spark of patriotic indignation that inspired the Americans who fought for our freedom and independence has been ignited once again! Americans are reawakening to the ideas, the principles, the habits of the heart, and discipline of the mind that made America great." (p. 1)

Furthermore, "This isn't a political awakening. It's an *American* awakening coming from real people—not politicos or inside-the-Beltway types. These Americans grow our food, teach our children, run our small businesses, help out those less fortunate, and fight our wars. They've seen what is happening in America, so they've decided to get involved. They feel like they are losing something fundamentally good about their country, which they've decided to take back, because they love this country and are proud to be Americans." (pp. 102-03)

And just who is preventing regular Americans from taking back their country? Barack Obama and like-minded lefties trying to impose unwanted policies on our political heartland: "President Obama and the current Washington crowd have promised us a 'fundamental transformation of America.' The left seems to think that there's something wrong with America—not something wrong with our policies or our government, but something wrong with our country and what we value." (p. 115)

"Hell-bent on changing it fundamentally, they don't share the timeless values that so many of us hold dear: our belief in our God-given freedom, our faith in free markets, and our certainty that the truths of our American founding are the way to a more perfect union." (p. 123) Her placing quotation marks around the words "fundamental transformation of America" imply that she is actually quoting from some official document or official spokesperson, but she is not.

The Alaska Governor who quit, and ran for V-P raises one of her favorite Hollywood movies, *Mr. Smith Goes to Washington,* starring Jimmy Stewart. "The wonderful thing about this movie is that it doesn't just cheerlead for America, or engage in a theoretical discussion of our founding documents (the Declaration of Independence and the Constitution) but rather puts these documents and their ideas into a human context. It shows us the love, charity, and humanity that they embody when they are honored and adhered to." (p. 243)

The other side of the ideological coin bleeds through the pages of Barack Obama's *The Audacity of Hope: Thoughts on Reclaiming the American Dream* (Kindle, 2007). His tome contains chapters on: Republicans and Democrats; Values; Our Constitution; Politics; Opportunity; Faith; Race; The World; and Family.

Sarah Palin's contention that Obama remains clueless about the value of the U.S. Constitution is belied by his devoting a full chapter to it here. Written during his first term as Illinois Senator after a career teaching constitutional law and doing community organizing, Obama addresses some of the same themes his stellar words at the 2004 Democratic Convention.

Obama recounts his first run for office when citizens consistently asked him two questions:

"1.) Where'd you get that funny name?; and 2.) You seem like a nice enough guy, so why do you want to go into something nasty like partisan politics?" (p. 35) To which he smiled and nodded saying: "I understood the skepticism, but there was—and had always been—another tradition to politics, a tradition stemming from the country's founding to the glory of the civil rights movement, a tradition based on the simple idea that we have a stake in one another, and that what binds us together is greater than what drives us apart, and that if enough people believe in the truth of that proposition and act on it, then we might not solve every problem, but we can get something meaningful done." (p. 40)

He concludes that Americans' basic hopes and expectations are really quite modest and consistent regardless of race, region, religion, and class: "Most of them thought that anybody willing to work should be able to find a job that paid a living wage. They figured that people shouldn't have to file for bankruptcy because they got sick. They believed that every child should have genuinely good education—that it shouldn't just be a bunch of talk—and that those same children should be able to go to college even if their parents were not rich. They wanted to be safe from criminals and from terrorists; they wanted clean air, clean water, and time with their kids. And when they got old, they wanted to be able to retire with some dignity and respect." (p. 121)

After easily winning the primary and general elections for the Senate held previously by Democrat Carol Moseley Braun, he says "There was just one problem. My campaign had gone so well that it looked like a fluke. Political observers would note that in a field of seven Democratic primary candidates, not one of us ran a negative TV ad. The wealthiest candidate of all—a former trader worth $300 million—spent $28 million on a barrage of positive ads, only to flame out in the final weeks due to an unflattering divorce file that the press had got unsealed." (p. 136)

And, "My Republican opponent, a handsome and wealthy former Goldman Sachs partner turned inner-city teacher, started attacking my record before his campaign was similarly felled by a divorce scandal of his own. For the better part of a month, I traveled Illinois without drawing fire.... And finally, the Illinois Republican Party inexplicably chose as my opponent former presidential candidate Alan Keyes, who had never lived in Illinois and who proved so fierce an unyielding in his positions that even conservative Republicans were scared of him." (p. 272)

Flipping ideological prisms once again, let's look at former-Bush II advisor Karl Rove's *Courage and Consequence* (Kindle, 2010). His initial words epitomize the essence of his message, "On 11 September 2001 I was the first person to tell President George W. Bush that a plane slammed into an office tower in New York City and was aboard Air Force One. I was caught in the sweep of history much larger than someone from my origins could anticipate. It was a turning point for a presidency and the country. The courage and conviction I saw among those aboard Air Force One and in the White House in the years ahead gave me the confidence of having been on the right side of the fight." (p. 282) Just where would his party have been without 9/11's cataclysm?

However, absent from Rove's recollections are these facts: 1.) Republican Neocon white papers (**Project for a New American Century**) excoriated Clinton for squandering America's unipolar moment in the 1990s; 2.) Those same white papers lamented the need for an unlikely "New Pearl Harbor" for Republicans to expand the Post-Cold War Pentagon budgets; 3.) Multiple warnings about 9/11 which Bush II ignored vacationing in Texas; 4.) Only one 9/11 in our history, why then?

Rove accounts for his politics stemming from the rugged individualism many Republicans profess to adore, which he claims in reductionist fashion amounted to geopolitics: "Republicanism fit with my childhood of growing up in the Rocky Mountain West, a place of big horizons, long vistas, and most important of all, a palpable sense of freedom. There is something about the West that encourages individualism and personal responsibility, values I thought best reflected by Republicans." (p. 199)

He recalls at age 9 placing a Nixon bumper sticker on his bike's basket, drawing the attention of a much larger 13-year-old girl ebullient over John Kennedy. "She had a few years and about 30 pounds on me, pulled me from my bike and beat the heck out of me, leaving me with a bloody nose and tattered ego. I've never liked losing a political fight since." (p. 204) Pick any leading contemporary psychological theory and apply its relevance here to Rove and the disputed Bush v. Gore election of 2000 in which Republicans wallowed in dishonor, but eventually prevailed.

During high school, Rove waxes eloquently about his role on the school debate team: "I had no particular skill at sports or with girls. But I did have one useful ability: I could talk and argue. I was fortunate that at Olympus High, and the state of Utah generally, high school debate was a big deal, an activity where a bookish boy could find affirmation. I joined the debate team, found my tribe, and was off." (p. 240) His sounds a lot here like Newt Gingrich's autobiography before running for President in 2012.

Rove excoriates ethically-challenged journalists who he says practice psychobabble to attack political adversaries. In particular, he discusses a campaign directed against him in 2004 when he was developing strategy for Bush II's re-election featuring the traditional marriage theme in the culture wars. Reports had surfaced about Rove's retired-father, a geologist by profession, who reputedly had turned gay in his senior years. Rove and Dick Cheney strike me as similar in many respects, including this familiar dilemma.

He claims that John Kerry blundered in 2004 when by accusing both Dick Cheney and Karl Rove of "chicken-hawk" status. Why blunderous? Because "Kerry sounded as if he were attacking us as unpatriotic among the 15.97 million men who received student deferments during the Vietnam War. And he was making two terrible mistakes for a candidate: he let anger drive his decision, and he concentrated his fire on an aide rather than the other candidate. Any day Kerry spent attacking me was a day he wasted." (p. 617)

I assume readers are supposed to be impressed by both the precision and magnitude of deferments (15.97 million.) However, compared to all these other Republican memoirs, Rove's is notably more serious and reflective, and I commend him for that. But a chicken-hawk is a chicken-hawk is a chicken-hawk!

In his last of four similar books, journalist William Hartung's *Prophets of War: Lockheed-Martin and the Making of the Military-Industrial Complex* (Kindle, 2010) thematic predictability fails to detract from its gravity.

When full-page color ads began appearing in the *Washington Post,* scribes there commenced joking that "At a time when many companies had been cutting back on advertising budgets, Lockheed-Martin's barrage of huge ads for keeping the F-22 Raptor alive in February and March 2009 was the main thing keeping this venerable old paper afloat." (p. 20) Exactly 187 raptors have been produced as of this writing.

The Raptor costs $350 million per plane (most expensive combat aircraft ever) with the ignominious tagline that it's never been used in combat and its one trial ended unimpressively. And, even Secretary of Defense Robert Gates wanted to scrap it during simultaneous wars. Nevertheless, Lockheed-Martin lobbies for its continuation with claims like it has the "radar signature of a bumble bee;" and, the "only 24/7/365 All-Weather Stealth Fighter;" plus, "providing first-look, first-shot, first kill air dominance capability;" not to mention, "when we meet the enemy we want to win 100-0, not 51-49." (Clever PR, but wholly devious).

Author Hartung writes that "At the heart of the lobbying campaign in Congress was the mantra of 'jobs, jobs, jobs in 44 states.' (p. 50). Again cutting to the quick, Hartung identifies one problem with this impressive flurry of job claims: "They were grossly exaggerated. Utilizing standard techniques that estimate numbers of jobs generated by different economic activities, the $4 billion being spent on the F-22 would create less than half as many jobs as the manufacturer was claiming." (p. 54)

When a *USA Today* reporter asked for details about location of the jobs, the company figuratively pleaded the fifth: "Lockheed-Martin claimed that such information was proprietary and refused to provide it. Never mind that the manufacturer gets almost all its revenues and profits from the federal government—when it's time to come clean about how it is using our tax money, it's none of our business." (p. 64)

The author argues "The irony is that almost any other form of spending, from education to health care to mass transit to weatherizing buildings (even a tax cut) creates more jobs than military spending," However, "their advocates lack the well-oiled lobbying machine that a firm like Lockheed-Martin can bring to bear." (p. 71)

Army War College professor Williamson Murray has stated on the record: "The F-22 is the best fighter in the world, no doubt about it. But there isn't any opposition out there, like having a boxing tournament for high school and bringing Mike Tyson in." (p. 97) Influential bipartisan Congressmen Jack Murtha (D-PA) and Jerry Lewis (R-CA) attempted to pull the plug of the F-22 using the profligacy argument often, but failed.

Another reason for the Raptor's longevity: the ease with which Pentagon requests were not only met but exceeded after 9/11. "The increase in military spending from 2001-2003 was more than the *entire military budget* of most countries, including the UK and China. In this climate, no major weapon system was likely to be cut, no matter how irrelevant to fighting Al Qaeda." (p. 126) He credits then-Defense Secretary Robert Gates with confounding the conventional wisdom in April 2009 not only declaring the Raptor DOA, expanding other more vital expenditures(e.g., higher pay; child care; housing; and education for the troops).

Leaning rightward, whereas Bill O'Reilly's authoritarian braggadocchio gets muted in print, his paralinguistics (TV body language, tone of voice, and facial expressions) infuriate liberals like me more on the FACTOR. This FNC kingpin's hubristic autobiography I assess in chapter four, however, now I report on his shrill paean arguing that Barack Obama seeks a new American Revolution inconsistent with our revered traditions.

In *Pinheads and Patriots: Where You Stand in the Age of Obama,* (Kindle, 2011) his Introduction states "In fact, much of it will be devoted to discussing the present occupant of the Oval Office. President Barack Obama is, perhaps, the most polarizing chief executive since Abraham Lincoln. Yes, opinions about Bill Clinton and Bush the Younger divided the country, but not in the way views about Mr. Obama have. Some Americans sincerely believe he is trying to change the fundamental core of the United States. You hear this refrain all the time: 'When do I get my country back'." (p. 143) O'Reilly fans love it so much that he has added the pinhead/patriot motif as his FNC closer.

Why the weasel word, "perhaps," in this context? Is Obama the most polarizing figure since Lincoln, or not? If so, on what does he base this startling conclusion? Was he asleep at the journalistic switch while LBJ tore us asunder during Vietnam? Or, when Nixon went bonkers with his enemies list and resigned ignominiously? Or, when Bush II lied about almost everything relating to his Iraqi War of choice?

Like me, O'Reilly wasn't alive during FDR's massive transformation of America, but even he reads history occasionally (Although inaccuracies in his recent book on the Civil War suggests otherwise). And exactly where does he hear this refrain all the time: "I want my country back;" No one has ever said that to me about Obama. And, if someone other than he really "considers Obama the most divisive president since Lincoln," please name them so we can assess their credentials. The exact number of endnotes in each of his books is identical (0), constituting intellectual fraud.

O'Reilly thanks his readers and viewers for making him "rich and famous," not mature, intelligent, empathic, or heaven forbid, truthful. What clearly matters most to him is the "rich and famous" thing; the rest mere gamesmanship. He has the brass balls to say self-serving things like: "I have a responsibility to provide you, the reader, with an honest appraisal of your situation in this age of Obama. I can't embrace ideology, myth, or propaganda. I've got to cut through the fog and define whether socialism, corruption, incompetence, and yes, even evil are in the air." (p. 164) Evil again?

O'Reilly's delusional "no spin zone" best analogizes Rod Steiger's "Twilight Zone" in the 1950s. How dare he self-identify a unique imprimatur of political independence when his predictability belies it daily! "Why? He says it best, "It's very simple, you guys have made me rich and famous." (p. 111) It's sick to believe that you can get away with saying anything aggressively.

When I was interviewing Vietnam War resisters in the late-1990s who remained in Canada, one who impressed me greatly was Michael Klein, Professor of Family Medicine at the University of British Columbia. Later on I discovered that his daughter, Naomi Klein was doing some courageous investigative reporting for the *Toronto Globe & Mail.* Her most recent book, *The Shock Doctrine*, (Kindle, 2007) examines the long reach of Milton Friedman's Chicago School of Supply-Side Economics.

"Friedman articulated contemporary capitalism's core tactical nostrum, what I have come to understand as the 'Shock Doctrine.' He observed that 'only a crisis—actual or perceived—produces real change.' When that crisis occurs, the actions taken depend on the ideas then lying around. That, I believe, is our basic function: to develop alternatives to existing policy, to keep them alive and available until the politically impossible becomes the politically inevitable.' Friedmanites stockpile free market ideas." (p. 173).

Friedman honed his *Shock Doctrine* advising Augusto Pinochet, Chilean dictator, in the mid-1970s. Two shocks were extant in Chile: 1.) From Pinochet's violent coup; and 2.) From severe hyperinflation. Friedman's unambiguous advice? "Impose a rapid-fire transformation of the economy—tax cuts, free trade, cuts to social spending, and deregulation. It was the most extreme capitalist makeover ever attempted anywhere, and became known as the "Chicago School Revolution...." (182) "In the decades since, whenever governments have imposed sweeping free-market programs, the all-at-once shock treatment has been the method of choice." (pp. 183-84) And, Pinochet's pervasive pattern of well-documented "torture cells" often accompanied Dr. Friedman's remedy.

After citing other examples, she describes New Orleans' Katrina disaster as a new capitalist leitmotiv: "By the time hurricane Katrina hit New Orleans, and the nexus of Republican politicians, think tanks and land developers started talking about 'clean sheets' and exciting opportunities, it was clear this was now the preferred way of advancing corporate goals: using moments of collective trauma to engage in radical social and economic engineering." (p. 208)

Naomi Klein closes her rhetorical circle with these words: "Seen through the lens of this doctrine, the past 35 years look very different. Some of the most infamous human rights violations of this era (which have often been seen merely as sadistic acts carried out by anti-democratic regimes) were in fact either committed with the deliberate intent of terrorizing the public or were actively harnessed to prep for radical 'free-market' reforms." (p. 236)

Returning to right-wing politicos, let's examine Bush II's missive which he has been all over the airways promoting in 2011, *Decision Points* (Kindle, 2010). "My goals in writing this book are twofold. First, I hope to paint a picture of what it was like to serve as president for eight consequential years. I believe it will be impossible to reach definitive conclusions about my presidency—or any recent president, for that matter—for several decades. The passage of time allows passions to cool, results to clarify, and scholars to compare different approaches. My hope is that this book will serve as a resource for anyone studying this period in American history." (p. 27)

"Second, I write to give readers a perspective on decision-making in a complex environment. Many of the decisions that reach the president's desk are tough calls, with strong arguments on both sides. Throughout the book, I describe the options I weighed and the principles I followed. I hope this will give you a better sense of why I made the decisions I did. Perhaps it will even prove useful as you make choices in your own life." (p. 33) His title seems apt enough, since he often reminded us that "I am the decider," missing the more nuanced reality that he's not the ONLY decider in a system of checks and balances.

The first chapter is called "Quitting," and finally we get some real-life discourse regarding intervention with alcoholics (and other addictions). His epiphany at age 40 was triggered by wife Laura's simple question asked calmly: "Can you remember the last day you didn't have a drink?" Well and good, W, welcome to the human race, the American public understands and even empathizes. Why the two-decade ruse of floor-to-ceiling denial of the obvious?

Also, "For months I had been praying that God would show me how to better reflect His will. My scripture readings had clarified the nature of temptation and the reality that love of earthly pleasures could replace love of God. My problem was not only drinking, it was also selfishness. The booze was leading me to put myself ahead of others, especially my family. I loved Laura and the girls too much to let that happen. Faith showed me a way out. I knew I could count on the grace of God to help me change." (p. 71)

He writes of the difficulties inherent in implementing the decision to cease drinking. "As my memory of the last hangover faded, the temptation to drink became intense. My body craved alcohol. I prayed for the strength to fight off my desires. I ran harder and longer as a way to discipline myself. I ate a lot of chocolate because my body was screaming for sugar. Chocolate was an easy way to feed it. This also gave me another motivation for running: to keep the pounds off." (p. 76)

As for his family's rather schizoid Connecticut/Texas identity he says "While I was growing up in Texas, the rest of the Bush family was part of a very different world. When I was about six years old we visited Dad's parents in Greenwich, CT. I was invited to eat dinner with the grownups, I had to wear a coat and tie, something I rarely did in Midland outside of Sunday school. The table was elegantly set. I had never seen so many spoons, forks, and knives, all neatly lined up. A woman dressed in black with a white apron served me a weird-looking red soup with a white blob in the middle, I took a taste, and it was terrible. Soon everyone was looking at me, waiting for me to finish this delicacy." (p. 203)

Whereas Bush I had been a World War II hero, the son was saddled with the "chicken-hawk" label associated with the Texas Air National Guard during Vietnam. "Serving as a guard pilot appealed to me. I would learn a new skill. If called, I would fly into combat. If not, I would have the flexibility to do other things. At that point in my life, I was not looking for a career. I viewed my first decade after college as a time to explore. I didn't want anchors to hold me down. If something caught me attention, I would try it. If not, I would move on." (p. 357)

The absurd, "if called" scenario, was about as likely as humidity-free summers in his beloved Houston. And, of course, his pilot training proved a godsend when he flew onto an aircraft carrier sporting the huge Iraqi war banner in 2004: "Mission Accomplished" blaring the vilest of untruths.

He concludes the National Guard gloss with these words: "I will always be proud of my time in the Guard. I learned a lot, made lifelong friends, and was honored to wear our country's uniform. I admire and respect those who deployed to Vietnam. Nearly 60,000 of then never came home. My service was nothing compared to theirs." (p. 402)

Bush II has been known to over-achieve the art of understatement, and this line may live on as his signature example for the historians whom he feels confident will judge him favorably. With all of the unbelievable mistakes he made while in office, he says his main regret consisted of losing sleep over a Black rapper accusing of him of racism after Katrina (Let's file this one under inscrutability squared.)

When he invaded my space in Wheeling, WV, pitching his War On Terror (WOT) in 2005, I had a large sign made. One side read "Mendacity Kills," while the other side tweaked the same theme with "Truth's Nadir."

I hope Bush II lives to hear some favorable assessments from historians, because he has no dearth of bright critics now. Among them, Eric Alterman and Mark Green, *The Book on Bush: How George W Misleads America* (Kindle, 2004), appearing during that year's re-election campaign. They note that the 2000 campaign Bush bore almost no resemblance to the subsequent policy Bush: "It was not easy, at least at first, to discern just how differently from his campaign rhetoric Bush intended to govern. There were few precedents for Bush's transformation, either in America's political past or in his own personal history." (p. 86)

While they acknowledge that some adversaries underestimated Bush II's political acumen, they focus more on "his self-defined limits of intellectual inquiry." They quote him saying in 1986 that "I was never a great intellectual," and "We Bushes are not serious, studious readers. We read for fun." In 1999, Bush explained to conservative commentator Tucker Carlson that he disliked reading long books, especially about policy, and in 2003 he admitted to FNC that he rarely read beyond newspaper headlines." (p. 97) (Perfect for FNC's authoritarian demographic)

Alterman and Green describe Bush's low knowledge base and lack of intellectual curiosity as less worrisome when found among less ambitious politicians. "However, the advent of the second Bush administration witnessed a fully united Republican Party driven by the engines of the religious right, big business, and the neoconservative worldview—and piloted by a famously stubborn Texan." (p. 119)

About the prophetic neocon scenario fantasized about in 1994's PROJECT FOR A NEW AMERICAN CENTURY, the events of 9/11 operationalize the "Pearl Harbor imperative," Alterman and Green seize upon its serendipity: "Following 11 September 2001, President Bush fell under the sway of a group of *neoconservative ideologues* placed in his administration by Dick Cheney and focused primarily in the Pentagon and Vice President's office. These ideologues viewed the attacks less as a national tragedy than a strategic opportunity to implement a program of unilateral global empire for the United States, beginning with a 'preventive' war against Iraq." (p. 123)

Because Bush II was willing to deceive Congress and the public about both the level of threat Iraq presented, as well as its nonexistent connections to Al Qaeda, he perpetuated a war decried by populations from virtually every nation on earth. Meanwhile, candidate Bush's promise of a foreign policy "humble in how we treat nations that are figuring out how to chart their own course was consigned to the dustbin of history." (p. 158)

The authors use case studies to pinpoint the crux of his M.O.: "In each of these cases, the Bush modus operandi has been to say one thing while doing another, whether promising tax saving for everyone but giving the lion's share to the wealthy few or vowing to protect America from threats while inflating nonexistent ones and ignoring those against which we can be defended. How does he do it? A variety of techniques add up to what playwright Arthur Miller refers to as Bush's 'power of audacity'." (p. 186)

Alterman and Green quote *Slate* journalist Michael Kinsley: "What's going on here is akin to lying-by-reflex. If someone accuses you of saying the world is round, you lunge for the microphone declaring your passionate belief that it is flat. The ferocity is often accompanied by insouciance...." And, furthermore "The characteristic Bush II form of dishonesty is to construct an alternative reality on some topic and to regard anyone who objects to it as a sniveling dweeb obsessed with nuance, while the

President has more consequential things to worry about." (p. 251) (My initial exposure to the Imperial-laden connotations of Bush I and Bush II.)

Conservatism receives a nice boost in the next book, Ronald Reagan's son, Michael is joined by Jim Denney with the release of *The New Reagan Revolution: How Ronald Reagan's Principles Can Restore America's Greatness* (Kindle, 2008.) Based solely on one 5-minute speech by Ronald Reagan, they try to jazz it with ancillaries.

A lengthy Foreword by 2012 presidential candidate-to-be Newt Gingrich's inspirational words about Saint Reagan, called "Like Father, Like Son." Gingrich gives Reagan credit for everything good that occurred under the sun in that glorious decade (1980s): "I became House minority whip in March 1989, shortly after Ronald Reagan left office. The American economy was booming, the Soviet Union on the brink of collapse, and the Berlin Wall would topple before the year's end. President Reagan had accomplished his mission." (p. 44)

Gingrich overachieves in his Foreword: "My good friend Michael Reagan has written a compelling book about what you and I must do to defend freedom in our generation. *The New Reagan Revolution* is honest, insightful, and thought-provoking. In these pages, Michael Reagan reveals insights about his father, that have never been shared before." (p. 56) And one more quote from Gingrich: "There are disturbing parallels between America in the 1970s and America today. Then, as now, our nation seemed to be in decline, our national security in doubt, our economy unraveling. The principles of Ronald Reagan turned America around before, and they can do so again." (p.73)

Michael shares his reaction to his father's devastating defeat by Gerald Ford in the 1976 presidential primary: "I remember what I was thinking, the same thing we were all thinking: This is it; Dad's too old to run for president again. He was sixty-five and would be approaching seventy in

1980. All of us, including Nancy thought this was the end of the road." (p. 231)

Playing the divine-intervention-card, Michael Reagan and Jim Denney state: "God chooses the time for all the great events of history. He chose the right time for Ronald Reagan's election. On 30 March 1981 God arranged events to the split second to prevent my father from being killed by an assassin's bullet. And He chose the right time for the Iron Curtain to fall. I believe God places the actors on the grand stage of history, and as they play their parts, the drama of history unfolds." (p. 394)

A liberal book counters virtually all facile claims made by Bush II in his retrospective: *Decision Points? The Truths Behind George W. Bush's Autobiography in His Own Words (Declassified Documents of Bush II)* (Kindle, 2011). Declassified documents are provided here under six different headings: 1.) Before the Presidency; 2.) Iraq, WMD and Torture: Justifying War and Torture; 3.) Pleading Ignorance; 4.) Dissenting Views from Public Officials; 5.) Background Documents; 6.) State of the Union Addresses.

David Horowitz and Richard Poe's 2006 diatribe accuses the Democrats of everything-but-treason, *The Shadow Party Seized Control of the Democratic Party* (Kindle, 2006). Their Introduction wastes no time: "The War in Iraq marks a new era in America's political life. Never previously has one of America's two major parties attacked a sitting president and wartime commander-in-chief with the ferocity manifested by leaders of the Democratic Party today. Never before has the country been so divided in the early stages of war on foreign soil." (p.36) Never, ever?

Horowitz and Poe write "Bipartisanship in wartime has been a hallmark of American foreign policy since the Second World War. Republicans displayed it when President Clinton went to war in Bosnia and Kosovo— wars conducted without congressional authorization or UN approval, but which Republican leaders nonetheless supported. Such bipartisanship is strikingly absent in America's war in Iraq. It has been undone by a Democratic leadership committed to more radical goals." (pp. 48-49)

If so, maybe it's because Republicans have forever been in bed with the MIC (military-industrial-complex) promoting serial wars contrary to broader national interests! Also, Bush II's Iraqi lies led to record-breaking popular demonstrations among both adversaries and allies. Maybe Democratic criticisms represent a more intelligent role for America in the world than bad cop. See Don Lindsay's ARCHIVE OF FALLACIES for Argument from Spurious Similarity ("Claiming that two situations are highly similar, when the aren't")[xviii]

Paranoia requires a sinister bogey-man, and FNC is addicted to lies about the same individual demonized by Horowitz and Poe here as "Lenin" both willing and able to overthrow America's political system. "The 'Lenin' behind our revolution, however, is billionaire finance wizard George Soros, allegedly directing a 'Shadow Party' network of holding companies coordinating the revolution. Once attained, that power will be used to effect a global transformation—economic, social and political—a post-Berlin Wall reincarnation of the old radical dream." (p. 74) They don't define a shadow party, or explain what makes it so bad.

Republicans know how to play the "fear card" justifying obscene Pentagon budgets precluding funds for education, scientific research, or reducing the national debt. And, unfortunately Democrats in 2011 were apparently afraid of attacking the sacrosanct Pentagon budget for fear of being called weak on defense. Democrats represent part of the problem with current American politics by their unwillingness to play the "peace card" lying at their feet.

Barry Goldwater will never rise to Ronald Reagan's level of adulation in the Republican pantheon because he never came close to winning the presidency, but his classic *The Conscience of a Conservative* (Kindle, 1960) still ranks pretty high in Kindle sales (a useful barometer of political popularity). First printing March 1960 (10,000 copies); second printing April 1960 (10,000 copies); third printing May 1960 (50,000 copies). A few quotations from its dust jacket prove instructive.

On the Cold War: "A tolerable peace must follow victory over Communism.... We should withdraw diplomatic relations from all Communist governments including the Soviet Union. It would give heart to the enslaved peoples and help them overthrow their captors."

On States Rights: "The cornerstone of our Republic, our chief bulwark against the encroachment of individual freedom by Big Government, is fast disappearing under the piling sands of absolutism. No powers regarding education were ever given to the federal government. Despite the recent holding of the Supreme Court, I am firmly convinced that the Constitution does not permit any interference whatsoever by the federal government in the field of education."

On the Supreme Court: "I have great respect for the Supreme Court as an institution but I cannot believe that I display that respect by submitting abjectly to the abuses of power by the Court and by condoning its unconstitutional trespass into the legislative sphere of government."

On Foreign Aid: "It is not only ill-administered but ill-conceived. It has not made the free world stronger, it has made America weaker."

On Labor: Right to Work laws derive from the Natural Law. They are simply an attempt to give freedom of association the added protection of law.... Let us henceforth make war on all the monopolies whether corporate or union....The champions of freedom will fight against the concentration of power wherever they find it."

Robert McChesney's Foreword to another recent book is called "The Golden Age of Irony," and states "The heavyweight champion of irony at FNC is Bill O'Reilly, whose **FACTOR** remains its most successful program. Every session begins with his pronouncement that his show constitutes a 'no-spin zone' where all the B.S. and hot air that politicians and hustlers try to spew before the American people to mask their naked self-interest will be exposed for the tripe it is. He claims to slice through the crap and reveal the truth to the masses."

McChesney calls O'Reilly the consummate spin-meister. McChesney likewise claims that Peter Hart's book exposes the bullying tactics of O'Reilly. Hart's book was one of the first to expose O'Reilly's systematic sophistry, yet his observations remain valid in 2011.

O'Reilly's favorite tactic? "Faced with a factual statement he's unable to rebut, he accuses his guest of stating an opinion. For example, when a journalist mentioned Israel's 'illegal settlers' (7/18/00) he replies 'All right, that's your opinion.' When a drug-policy advocate said 'marijuana impairs driving less than alcohol' (1/3/00) the predictable answer was 'well, that's your opinion;' and, when NGO Greenpeace's John Passacatando asserted that drilling in the Arctic National Wildlife refuge would only yield six to nine months of oil (5/10/01); 'that's your opinion'." (p.22)

Don't journalists invite guests on because they possess some meaningful opinion or information? The Big O, however, he loudly asserts his opinion as incontrovertible fact. Nice gig if you have both the big mouth and the bully pulpit to ridicule your guests. But Hart opines that part of the hidden agenda at FNC is to browbeat public acceptance of its uniqueness for possessing no political agenda.

Glenn Beck and Kevin Balfe deserve praise for an economical title (5 letters) in their *Broke* (Kindle, 2010), an anomaly for this windbag, Their Acknowledgments, however, go on forever, naming more than 100 persons as absolutely vital to the finished product. Like Beck's others, the subtext reads like a primer for blending political and religious fundamentalism as a savior for what ails America's psyche. He warns us that he has no economic expertise, but when did that ever stop him? Here, Broke refers to profligacy concerning not only the national debt, but all areas of life.

"This book is about understanding that our system of government is broken because we ourselves are broken in spirit, broken in trust, and broken in our faith. It's about understanding that debts and deficits aren't the disease; no, they're just symptoms of the suspects targeted by Roger Ailes' oft-leaked memos to his staff: for example, Obama's very existence; Democratic egalitarian philosophy; Ethical Humanists; Intellectuals; and, of course Internationalists.

However, for the first time in this book, Beck jettisons The Reagan Mantra (we can have it all without sacrificing any of our biggest toys) and sides with a more Tea Party-oriented call for the kind of hair-shirt sacrifices that Christians learned to live with in the Middle Ages. It's clear that Beck considers Christian fundies the chosen from whom much should be expected. "Live large and put it on the charge," Beck calls this current American syndrome. I predict his relationship with that the reigning Republican orthodoxy epitomized by the Bush clan will increasingly distance themselves from Beck.

Beck even has the testosterone here to use the E-word (Empire) traditionally dissonant to Republican ears. Maybe he's beginning to hear the critics calling him a court jester, clown, idiot, ignoramus, or mental midget. Anyway, I was surprised to see him quote highly-respected financial historian Niall Ferguson: "If you really want to see when an empire is getting vulnerable, the big giveaway is when costs of serving the debt exceed the cost of the defense budget." (p. 141)

And, "Despite the eye-rolling that normally ensues when anyone tries to mention the fall of the Roman Empire, David Walker's 2005 warning to the National Press Club was not hyperbole; he was dead on. In fact, the parallels between America and the latter stages of the Roman Empire unfortunately go much, much further than most people are comfortable admitting." (p. 169) Once you perceive America as the most dominant Empire since Rome, you are poised to shed tons of conservative orthodoxy.

Ex-Treasury Secretary in the Clinton administration, Robert Reich, attended the September 2009 G-20 Summit in Pittsburgh, PA, and agreed with the policies advocated by the current Head of Treasury, Timothy Geithner, that the emergency measures taken in response to the Great Recession (2008-10) were working and should be continued. However, in *Aftershock:The Next Economy and America's Future* (Kindle, 2010). Reich takes the analysis deeper concerning cause and effect for the worst Recession since the 1930s.

He challenges the press' conventional wisdom that the Great Recession consisted merely of Americans borrowing too much in the past and necessity of tightening belts and increasing savings. According to Reich, "The problem was not that Americans spent beyond their means but that their means had not kept up with what the larger economy could have been able to provide them. The American economy had been growing briskly, and our middle class naturally expected to share in that growth. But it didn't. A larger and larger portion of the economy's winnings had gone to the people at the top." (p. 72)

Equally prescriptive, Reich explains some arcane economics elegantly: "The central challenge is not to rebalance the global economy so that Americans save more and borrow less from the rest of the world. It is to rebalance the American economy so that its benefits are shared more widely in America, as they were decades ago. Until this transformation is made, our economy will continue to experience phantom recoveries and speculative bubbles, each more distressing than the one before." (p. 78)

Much about economics seems counter-intuitive, so I stick closely to Reich's careful prose on this subject. "In the late 1970s, the richest one percent of the country took in less than nine percent of the nation's total income. After that, income concentrated in fewer and fewer hands. By 2007, the richest one percent took in 23.5 percent of total national income. It is no mere coincidence that the last time income was this concentrated was in 1928." (pre-1929 crash) (p. 123)

Conservative Black newspaper columnist Thomas Sowell's *Dismantling America: And Other Controversial Essays* (Kindle, 2010) uses the motif of a "perfect storm" as a hook for linking scores of his old columns into the same kind of simplistic caveats about America in decline espoused by Bill O'Reilly, Glenn Beck, David Horowitz, and Alan Poe.

His paranoid refrain pulls no punches regarding Barack Obama "While the Obama administration in Washington is not the root cause of the ominous dangers that face this country, at home and abroad, it is the embodiment, the personification and the culmination of dangerous trends that began decades ago. Moreover, it has escalated those dangers to what may be a point of no return. The specifics of the missteps and misdeeds of this administration are among the things chronicled, here and there, in the essays that follow." (p. 23)

Sowell seems truly perplexed as to "how such an administration could be elected in the first place, headed by a man whose only qualifications to be President of the United States at a dangerous time in the history of our world were rhetoric, style and symbolism—and whose animus against the values and institutions of America had been demonstrated repeatedly over a period of decades beforehand—speaks volumes about the inadequacies of our educational system and the degeneration of our culture." (p.92) What a prescient fellow, this Sowell, after a mere two years of Obama rule he has all the answers. Serial fallacies roll off of Sowell's tongue like candy and I'll resist piling on.

Next let's peek at a snappy title by Crooks & Liars investigative journalists John Amato and David Neiwert, *Over the Cliff: How Obama's Election Drove the American Right Insane* (Kindle, 2010). The Foreword by Dexter

Digby states "When the liberal blogosphere formed in the early Bush administration, it comprised a small community of dedicated political observers, reaching out to one another trying desperately to make sense of how the right-wing media had developed the capacity to shape the political discourse." (p. 18)

David Neiwert's blog, *Orcinus,* quickly rose to the top; and his series "Rush, Newspeak, and Fascism" expressed seminal insights on how right-wing extreme ideas have come to permeate our political culture. "A couple of years later, John Amato changed the way blogs themselves were constructed by offering commentary and videos online (well before YouTube) on his blog *Crooks and Liars,* exposing media absorption of the right-wing agenda. It was only natural that they would team up to write this book." (p.38)

Losing a presidential election results in bitter disappoint, however, Amato and Neiwert write that "Among a certain subset of Americans, it went well beyond the usual despair. For them, 5 November 2008 was the end of the world. Or, at least, the end of America as they prefer it, resulting in the venomous violence peculiar to the American right. (p. 75) This is harkens back to the "authoritarian personality" studies by Teodor Adorno decades ago.

The authors also describe the paper trail documenting cases of noose-stringing, mega-bonfires, anti-nigger chants, and spray-paintings of "hang Obama by a noose" across a wide swath of mostly Southern conservative college campuses. But similar acts of unseemly hooliganism occurred in other parts of America as well.

Amato and Neiwert describe a bizarre scene the day after the election in Midland, MI, where "a discarded Ron Paul activist named Randy Gray (dismissed from the Paul campaign when his white-supremacist activism was revealed), dressed in full Ku Klux Klan regalia, stalked the sidewalk in the middle of a busy intersection waving the American flag. Gray was toting a pistol but police let him go when he told them his behavior was unrelated to Barack Obama's election." (p. 99)

Numerous arsons also occurred in much of the country. A school bus in Rexburg, ID, taunted the tiny minority of Obama supporters by chanting, 'assassinate Obama.' "An Obama supporter in Forsyth County, GA, who had attended Obama's historic inauguration ceremony discovered later that her house was burned to the ground, her fence painted "Your black boy will die." (p. 122)

The Atlanta-based Southern Poverty Law Center (SPLC) counted more than 200 "hate-related" incidents in the week after Obama's election. The white-supremacist neo-Nazi Web site called Storm-front added more than 2,000 new members the day after the election. Storm-front's founder, Don Black, spoke about his group's promising future: "I get nonstop e-mails and private messages from new people who are mad as hell about the possibility of Obama becoming president. . . . This is scaring a lot of people who maybe never considered themselves racists, and it's bringing them over to our side." (p.155)

The authors argue, convincingly, that for conservative die-hards, the election was, and will always remain about race: "To a significant segment of the American Right, 2008 indeed marked the end of the world as they knew it; small wonder, then, that the most extreme among them erupted in violence." (p.330)

The wave of rumors fabricated by the right about Obama found their way into the campaign, but the one striking me as not only the most absurd, but most provable questioned the candidate's U.S. citizenship. His campaign requested the prestigious FactCheck.org to examine his birth certificate. This, and all other veracity police, found these charges baseless.

For example, "Our staff has now seen, touched, examined, and photographed the original birth certificate. We conclude that it meets all requirements from the State Department to prove U.S. citizenship. Claims that the document lacks a raised seal or a signature are false. We have posted high-resolution photographs of the document as supporting documents to this article. Our conclusion: *Obama was born in the USA just as he has always said.*" (p. 395)

Decidedly different sets of assumptions and relevant facts ooze from Conservative Dinesh D'Souza's *The Roots of Obama's Sudden Rage* (Kindle, 2010), a subject he knows well, since this makes D'Souza's third book on Obama, and a person of color himself. Here he observes "Barack Obama is an enigmatic figure, a puzzle both to his adversaries and to his supporters. Somehow the Obama of the election campaign seems to have metamorphosed into a very different President Obama." (p. 17)

He and others complain that the old reassuring Obama is gone and has been replace by a new more detached, unreadable and, to some, even menacing Obama. "It's hard for Americans to respond to Obama because we aren't sure where he is coming from, what motivates him." (p. 32) Again, the Conservatorium spewing paranoia about liberals somehow magically changing stripes completely once in power. All presidents change somewhat, but I think the kind of "gotcha" evidence for this scenario best fits Bush II.

I was pleased to see a conservative writer willing to use a few sophisticated concepts and avoid bashing intellectuals as irrelevant. However, concerning the flip-flop theme, where was D'Souza when Bush II's campaign wooed us with "I'm a uniter, not a divider;" "nation-building endeavors end badly;" or, promising a "modest foreign policy footprint?"

In an earlier book, D'Souza argued that "racism in America is no longer systemic, but merely episodic. It existed, but no longer controls the lives of blacks and other minorities. Dinesh opines that racism no longer explains why some people in America succeeded and others didn't." (p. 63) The author uses Obama's election as affirmation that what he suggested in 1995 certainly reflects a "post-racist" America in 2008.

By 2010, D'Souza was convinced that black activists and scholars had become extremely disappointed with the man they helped elect. "Obama's indifference to black issues was the central theme of a 2010 summit organized PBS host Tavis Smiley, echoed the thoughts of other panelists when he said the time has come for the president to be more aggressive about the African-America agenda." (p.47)

Black academic Michael Eric Dyson expressed this viewpoint more bluntly on MSNBC: 'This president runs from race like a black man runs from a cop." (p. 106) Like most commentators, however, D'Souza misses the obvious point that calling Obama Black is inaccurate. Confucius said that meaningful dialogue between humans begins with calling things by their proper names.

Obama's ancestry is most accurately described as 50/50 racially, since he had a black father and white mother. He lived in both cultures, unlike someone like Jesse Jackson or Al Sharpton, who did not. The concept of culture is more pertinent here than that of race; and, the American Anthropological Association (AAA) went on record in 1998 that "Race as a biological fact does not exist."

Culture, however, can't be dismissed by any discipline. Other social sciences such as sociology, economics, political science, and psychology believe that if people "perceive" race as meaningful, then a self-fulfilling prophecy ensues.

D'Souza has devoured all of Obama's writings and describes his story as "both enthralling and incredibly revealing of his current motivation and outlook; and that Obama's books tap three dreams: 1.) The American Dream; 2.) Martin Luther King's Dream; and 3.) The Obama Dream." (p. 189).

According to the author, while the origins of the first two are obvious, the third is not—because it derives from his father as revealed in Obama's

Dreams from My Father. D'Souza belabors the obvious writing that our president's pivotal dream is "markedly different from the one espoused by George Washington, Benjamin Franklin, and Abraham Lincoln." (p. 194) Duh. The key figure here for D'Souza is Frantz Fanon.

Expanding the fallacious guilt-by-association process inter-generationally, DeSouza posits a magical transition of revolutionary fervor on behalf of the poor from Fanon to Obama senior to Obama junior, at least he's willing to try using psychological insights typically pooh-poohed by conservatives as intellectual psychobabble, (e.g., both Bushes).

The author's problems, however, stem not from considering psychological variables relevant to public policy analysis, but from his weak logic positing the thesis that Frantz Fanon's books influenced the Senior Obama, Obama admired his Dad, and that the key to explaining the enigmatic President lies in the multi-generational transfer of revolutionary fervor on behalf of the oppressed in this world.

That Obama read some works admired by his father in his youth written by Frantz Fanon, a Martinique psychiatrist who joined the Algerian National Liberation movement, means nothing. Educated people read thousands of books, many of which inspire us to adopt various attitudes and beliefs. However, we mature via reading other perspectives that better contextualize information and attitudes.

Ascribing near-magical properties to Frantz Fanon's words, where does D'Souza derive the testosterone to offer such a grand hypothesis? Maybe here: 1.) D'Souza is a conservative intellectual working hard to pinpoint Obama's essence (expertise); 2.) The author believes that he alone has discovered an intellectual sin committed by our president, entitling him to cash in on the symbolic reward (spoils to the victor).

Specifically, D'Souza accuses Obama of plagiarizing a story from Fanon's book *Black Skin, White Masks* in order to score polemical points via a fictive event supposedly from Obama's own youth, but really deriving from Fanon's. Let's give D'Souza the benefit of the doubt here and accept his story. Where would that rank on a moral equivalency scale with lying blatantly to sell a disastrous war effort?

Professor Andrew Bacevich has traversed an arduous career as an Army officer in Vietnam, post-war critic of Vietnam policy within the Army, Professor at Brandeis University, author of many thoughtful books, and father of a son who died serving America in Iraq. Fortunately, he has three surviving daughters. His new book, *Washington Rules: America's Path to Permanent War* (Kindle, 2010) lives up to his high standards of integrity and scholarship. The term epiphany isn't used here by Bacevich, but it should be.

The author had spent many years in Europe soldiering, but had never visited the Cold War's core symbol (Berlin's Brandenburg Gate) until the Wall came down on 11/9/89. In a chaotic later scene involving hawkers of cheap Russian military watches, bayonets, medallions and bits of Red Army uniforms he writes:

"These were loose ends of a story that was supposed to have ended neatly when the Berlin Wall came down. As we hurried in search of warmth and a meal, I began slowly to entertain this possibility: the truths I had accumulated over the previous two decades as a professional soldier— especially truths about the Cold War and U.S. foreign policy—might not be entirely true. . . . I started, however hesitantly to suspect that the orthodoxy might be a sham. I began to appreciate that authentic truth is never simple, especially when handed down from on high (whether by presidents, prime ministers, or archbishops) is inherently suspect." (p. 105)

His embarrassment at achieving such insights so late in life ties into his regretting "too often confusing education with accumulating and cata-loguing facts," but years later he better appreciates that genuine wisdom often occurs through painful self-discovery involving lots of cognitive dissonance. In an age of information overkill, the requisite skill involves making qualitative judgments about paradoxical matters. He doesn't use the word CTS but that's what he means.

Bacevich's duties increasingly took him behind what our military called "the trace" (Iron Curtain), which he refers to traveling there as "akin to entering a time warp." For example, "The villages through which we passed were forlorn and the small farms down at the heels. For lunch, we stopped at a roadside stand. The proprietor happily took our Deutsche-marks, offering us inedible sausages in exchange. Although the signs reminded us that we were still in a land of German speakers, it was a country still recovering from World War II." (p. 138)

Unlike Bacevich, I had traveled to Berlin twice during the Cold War and twice after 11/9/89. Also, ten trips to Russia between 1985-1995 ena-bled me to witness the profound changes underway, alternately thrilling and depressing. Bacevich's story helps me to better comprehend how an intelligent, sophisticated, and reflective fellow like he could have swal-lowed American Cold War propaganda whole.

While he was serving in Vietnam, I was dodging the draft to avoid ending up there. Very many little things helped me to anticipate the Cold War's demise. Bacevich deserves credit for discussing many painful examples of his gradual education, including his son's death fighting in Iraq.

Later, "George W. Bush's decision to launch Operation Iraqi Freedom in 2003 pushed me fully into opposition. Claims that once seemed ele-mentary—above all claims relating to the essentially benign purposes of American power—now appeared preposterous. The contradictions that found an ostensibly peace-loving nation committed to a doctrine of preventive war became too great to ignore. The folly and hubris of the policy makers who heedlessly thrust the nation into an ill-defined and open-ended 'global war on terror' without the foggiest notion of what victory would look like, how it would be won, and what it might cost approached standards hitherto achieved only by slightly mad German warlords." (p. 213)

Allow me to deviate from my left/right juxtapositions here with another epiphany-laden memoir of another ex-Army careerist turned academic, Stephen Melton, *The Clausewitz Delusion: How the American Army Screwed Up the Wars in Afghanistan and Iraq* (Zenith Press, 2007). He uses Clausewitz's famous quotation about "war constituting politics by another means" as the hook for explaining what went wrong in America under Bush II. Yes, and he trumps Bacevich by having two of his sons serve between 2001-2007.

Countless observers have chronicled how-and-why Bush II's neocons led us astray, but only ex-veteran Melton takes back further than Leo Strauss and Anthony Lewis to Carl von Clausewitz tied into distinguishing the traditional nature of "defensive wars" from the modern paradigm of "offensive wars" as fundamentally different.

"In the late-1970s, Clausewitz's recondite *On War* became the Army's new intellectual touchstone, viewed as revealed wisdom from a more sophisticated European military tradition. Having lost faith in ourselves after Vietnam, the Army replaced William Tecumseh Sherman with Carl von Clausewitz as it philosophical foundation. In the blink of an eye, center of gravity analysis and decisive battle replaced attrition as the Army's war paradigm." (p. 126)

He makes it clear that solving our post-Vietnam funk by reinventing ourselves as 19th century Prussians led us to overlook more relevant lessons gleaned from our own history.

The Prussian theoretician was too grounded in "intangibles such as genius leaders" rather than empirical science and history's bounty of case studies. This distortion led to a "commander-centric emphasis."(p. 142)

Editor Julian Zelizer's 2010 tribute to Bush II, *The Presidency of George W. Bush: A First Historical Assessment* contains chapters by many contributors from academe whose opinions naturally vary quite significantly. In his Introduction, editor Zelizer cites four major objectives established by the new Bush Administration:

1.) To craft federal policies facilitating economic and demographic shifts underway since the 1970s;

2.) To accelerate the progress on twin policy goals: Deregulation and tax reductions thereby weakening government and unleashing market forces;

3.) To aggressively pursue Executive-centric national security championed by Neoconservatives since the Vietnam War; and;

4.) To construct a governing Republican coalition comparable to what Democrats established after 1932. "A potential Republican coalition, according to Bush's political guru (Karl Rove) would be rooted in non-coastal states while securing the Republican base to include voting blocs traditionally thought Democratic, from working-class whites from the industrial Midwest (already tempted by Reagan's GOP in the 1980s) to new immigrants in the Southwest (Hispanics)." (p. 203)

Princeton University Professor of History Zelizer writes that "In pursuing all four objectives, the exercise of presidential power became one of the defining characteristics of the Bush administration, as Mary Dudziak and I show in our respective chapters. The expanding authority of the executive branch was a primary objective of President Bush and Vice President Cheney since the day they took office in January 2001." (p. 208)

Also, "Conservatives came to see presidential power, grounded in a distinct interpretation of the law, as the best available tool for combating the liberals who dominated Congress and federal agencies." (p. 213) This book consists of 12 substantial chapter by 11 different authors, and it's scholarship excels.

Bush II certainly got off to a very rocky start. Zelizer writes "Further complicating Bush's presidency was the fact that he had been elected in an extraordinarily close and contested election. Problems with the ballots in Florida had resulted in a recount, court battles, and a controversial Supreme Court decision in December via *Bush v. Gore* needed to cement his victory. As a result, some Americans did not accept his presidency as legitimate, feeling the election had been literally stolen from Gore." (p. 134)

And concerning 9/11, he pens this: "Though all of these matters were on their agenda upon winning office, the attacks of 11 September 2001, dramatically intensified their drive to see these policies enacted into law and caused the president to expand his reach into areas such as nation-building in Iraq. They undertook a radical expansion of interrogation techniques, including the use of torture breaking with national precedent and circumvented international accords on the treatment of detainees." (p. 176)

John Dean's newest book takes the gloves off regarding Bush II in his *Worse than Watergate: the Secret Presidency of George W. Bush* (Kindle, 2010). As former presidential counsel to Richard Nixon who testified at the Watergate hearings, Dean knows from whence he speaks.

His Preface begins: "George W. Bush and Richard Cheney have created the most secretive presidency of my lifetime. Their secrecy is far worse than during Watergate, and it bodes even more serious consequences. Their secrecy is extreme—not merely unjustified and excessive but obsessive. It has created a White House that hides its president's weaknesses as well as its vice President's strengths. It has given us a presidency that operates on hidden agendas. To protect their secrets, Bush and Cheney dissemble as a matter of policy. In fact, the Bush-Cheney is strikingly

Nixonian, only with regard to secrecy far worse (and no one will ever successfully accuse me of being a Nixon apologist). Dick Cheney, who runs his own secret governmental operations, openly declares wanting to turn the clock to pre-Watergate years—a time of an unaccountable and extra-constitutional imperial presidency. To say that their secret presidency is undemocratic is an understatement." (p. 38)

Proceeding along a similar trajectory, Dean later notes that "This book began as an admonition, an approach both 'beware of Bush' and 'Bush beware.' Only ignorance or bliss, I figured at the time, could lead another President and White House to make the same kind of mistakes we made during Nixon's presidency. As I proceeded, however, it was evident that the post 9/11 activities and operations were carefully calculated policies and plans." (p. 60)

During the 2000 presidential campaign, Dean says he read W's campaign autobiography, *A Charge to Keep*, ghost-written by his aide Karen Hughes to get a better feel for this incurious presidential aspirant, "A work described by the *Texas Observer* as a political memoir so bad that reviewers have been calling around looking ghost readers to read it. Indeed, his selective biography was useless." (p. 196)

Bush II has never left much of a paper trail, so Dean began interviewing family friends about "Junior," and was surprised to discover "concern bordering on fear" of speaking openly about the Bush clan. "Repeatedly, I was told that Bush is known for taking revenge against those who fail to keep the family's confidences." (p. 198)

Our next author has very similar of opinions about Barack Obama, in *Trickle up Poverty: Stopping Obama's Attack on Our Borders, Economy, and Security* (Kindle, 2010) by Michael Savage. The author lives up to his last name in this shallow diatribe. His recurring metaphor entails a destructive child who enters one room of a house dismantling priceless watches into unfixable wrecks, and then doing a reprise in second, third, and fourth rooms.

Clueless, the child continues wreaking havoc without adult supervision. No one seems to care. "I've been watching in stunned amazement as Obama the Destroyer systematically takes apart America, piece by piece, while the complicit fifth-column government media complex and the lapdog political leaders remain silent. Barack Hussein Obama is tearing down everything that was built before this man was even born." (p. 33) Unlike most other conservatives, Savage keeps repeating the failed campaign strategy of fixating on Obama's middle name (Hussein).

Savage warns "Mark my words: History will show that Obama the Destroyer is impoverishing the middle-class with taxation, regulation, and a desecration of our cherished freedoms. Moreover, as I will demonstrate in this book, Barack Obama is a naked Marxist-Leninist whose sole ambition in life is to transform America into the USSA: United Socialist States of America." (p. 62)

While the Great Recession was profoundly troubling, and Obama's stimulus package essentially an extension of Bush II's initial response, Savage will brook none of the nonsense about Obama doing his best with inherited serial disasters: "I'd like to chalk up this disturbing trend as nothing more than ineptness on his part. It's not. Let's be clear: *the trickle up poverty and economic meltdown* is quite by design. The sooner you accept that fact, the greater the chance we have of saving this county." (p. 82)

Ex-speech writer for Rudy Giuliani, John Avlon, describes himself as a "fiscal conservative but social progressive" in his new *Wingnuts: How the Lunatic Fringe is Hijacking America* (Kindle, 2010). The Foreword to Avlon's book comes from editor-in-chief of *The Daily Beast,* Tina Brown, one of many British journalists who trekked across the Atlantic because freedom of the press has such a rich history in America.

She writes "Our political commentator John Avlon was a clear choice to kick off our BEAST BOOKS series. His assiduous reporting and his smart, passionate commentary have impressed colleagues and readers alike. All along, he has been keeping detailed track of America's descent into bitter partisanship despite the advent of a president who fervently hoped for a politics that would be the very opposite." (p. 46)

Brown also contends that "To discount the Wingnuts as entirely delusional is too easy. And it's a mistake: When we are so repelled by the language that we deny a genuine point, we merely aggravate the paranoia that agitates many of the Wingnuts. Many of the miseries that have beset Americans in recent years have been too complex to explain easily." (p. 66) Brown traces similar arcs for Father Coughlin, Huey Long, and Joseph McCarthy in our history, but concludes more pessimistically: "What is new is the multiplying reach and volume of the Internet, concentrating the toxicity of destructive emotions circulating in the political bloodstream with unparalleled velocity." (p. 92)

Early in his book, author Avlon states "Wingnuts see politics as ideological blood sport, an all-or-nothing struggle for the nation's soul. They find purpose by dividing America into 'us against them.' And for those with a vested interest in stirring the crazy pot, all this is good for business. Hate is a cheap and easy recruiting tool, but it can be murder on a democracy." (p. 180)

As to his own politics, Avlon avers "I am not a Democrat. I am not a Republican. I'm an American. I find the far left and far right equally insane. But in the opening years of the Obama administration, the Wingnuts on the right have been screaming the loudest." (p.190) Furthermore, "As I've traveled across the country interviewing the luminaries and lowlights among the Wingnuts, I've heard a consistent refrain: Armageddon days are here again." (p. 200)

Finally, "Popular broadcasters amp up the outrage to increase ratings. FNC host Glenn Beck announces that America is on the road to socialism, fascism and communism—take your pick—with the kicker 'The country may not survive Barack Obama.'" (p. 230)

All this anger incites violence. For example, Marine Lance Corporal Kody Brittingham wrote a letter about why he intended to assassinate Barack Obama: "My vow was to protect against all enemies, both foreign and domestic. I have found, through much research, evidence to support my current state of mind. Having found said domestic enemy, it is my duty and honor to carry out by all means necessary to protect my nation and her people from this threat." (p. 236)

Amy Chua's provocative title portends what follows: *World on Fire: How Exporting Free Markets and Democratization Kill Minorities* (Kindle, 2010), a tome well-researched by this product of the wealthy Chinese ethnic minority in the Philippines (1% controls 60% of its economy).

Her economic/financial pedigree plays into the storyline. "This book is about a phenomenon—pervasive outside the West yet rarely acknowledged, indeed often even viewed as taboo—that turns free market democracy into an engine of ethnic conflagration. The phenomenon I refer to is that of *market-dominant minorities:* Ethnic minorities who for widely variant reasons, tend under market conditions to dominate economically, often to a startling extent, the indigenous majorities around them." (p. 168) Her personal history of privilege has alerted her to a phenomenon she describes as "found in every corner of the world."

Chua even suggests that "Market-dominant ethnic minorities are the Achilles hell of free-market democracy. In societies with a market-dominant ethnic minority, markets and democracy favor not just different people, or different classes, but different ethnic groups. Markets concentrate wealth, often spectacularly, in the hands of the market-dominant minority, while democracy increases the political power of the impoverished majority. In these circumstances the pursuit of free market democracy becomes an engine of potentially catastrophic ethno-nationalism, pitting a frustrated indigenous majority, easily aroused by opportunistic politicians, against a resented, wealthy economic minority. This scenario is playing out in country after country today, from Indonesia to Sierra Leone, from Zimbabwe to Venezuela, from Russia to the Middle East." (p. 176)

Fine, but how does Chua fit into American politics? "Global anti-Americanism has many causes. One of them, ironically, is the global spread of free markets and democracy. Throughout the world, global markets are bitterly perceived as reinforcing American wealth and dominance. At the same time, global populist and democratic movements give strength, legitimacy, and voice to the impoverished, frustrated, excluded masses of the world—precisely the people, in other words, most susceptible to anti-American demagoguery. . . . For the past twenty years Americans have been grandly promoting both marketization and democratization throughout the world. In the process we have directed at ourselves the anger of the damned." (p. 185) I had not been exposed to this theory before, and think Chua presents it capably.

Rebounding back across the political spectrum, let's peek inside *Glenn Beck: The Redemptive Story of America's Favorite Political Commentator* (Kindle, 2009) by Xander Cricket, who points out that Beck has morphed from dominance of talk radio to dominance of talk TV via Rupert Murdoch's FNC cable network.

Early on, Cricket observes: "Glenn defies political categorization. He shuns both Republicans and Democrats, generally drifting somewhere between libertarian and conservative. He is a person who genuinely searches for the truth, wherever that might lead him, and is open to new arguments on any topic. He makes clear to the audience he is a work in progress; He spent many years as a self-absorbed, pony-tail wearing, anything-goes drug addict. In the span of only a few years, he was transformed into a charitable, clean-cut, pro-life family man who investigated just about every belief system before settling on

Mormonism. He remains willing to listen, evidenced by the fact he has changed his mind on several occasions through conversations with callers on the show." (p. 83) Try to find a more naïve characterization of Glenn Beck in print!

Then, more FNC-specific, she says: "The Glenn Beck Program is as much about entertainment as it is about his opinions. He keeps the studio frigid so he won't sweat too much, and though he's been diagnosed with ADD, he opts not to take the medicine so as to remain his usual, animated self. Some days, his performance consists more of theater than substance. A segment on the corrupt characters responsible for the housing crisis might devolve into a half-hour impersonation of Barney Frank, followed by a series of sarcastic diatribes leaving some degree of doubt as to which points Glenn is espousing and which he is mocking. He is an expert in the art of satire, and so conveys his message in extremely memorable ways. If someone does not get the point, he or she has at least last a lot of fun listening." (p. 97) Beck makes tens of millions each year, so maybe he has bought off his chirping Cricket?

Cricket then proceeds to this observation. "The reason he is reviled by the Whoopi Goldberg/Barbara Walters circle (hosts of the View where sparks flew during an interview) is because he refuses to play the game. He is irreverent toward the political establishment. He calls out hypocrisy. He scorns political correctness. He demands honesty from himself and those around him. He forces people to recognize their inconsistencies. For three million viewers of his show, it all makes for great entertainment. For those in the 'mainstream' of society, he's intolerable—a truly sick twisted freak." (p. 113) Serial choppy sentences of the "See Jane run" variety bespeak simpletonia.

We lean sharply leftward with Deborah Jaramillo's trenchant, *Ugly War, Pretty Package: How CNN and Fox News Made the Invasion of Iraq High Concept* (Kindle, 2009), recent recipient of a Ph. D. degree. She claims rather boldly that "To divorce televised war coverage from the entertainment industry is to de-contextualize it in the most fundamental way." (p. 120)

In addition to "This book explores how CNN and FNC positioned and packaged the American military's invasion of Iraq in 2003 for a domestic audience. I place those two networks and the 2003 invasion of Iraq in the context of postclassical Hollywood filmmaking, one offshoot of which is high concept—a filmmaking practice inextricably linked to media conglomeration, new technologies, and an incessant self-preserving drive to market." (p. 50)

I'm glad to see her including CNN among the usual suspects enabling Bush II's absurd war of convenience. For example, "If on the first day of the ground war in 2003 we see CNN's Walter Rodgers barreling through the dessert in real time, we are transfixed by the image of sand and dust pouring out from the Humvee in front of him as well as his pseudo-poetic phrases that fetishized the U.S. military's 'wave of steel'." (p. 119) [xix] Right, but where was she while all this unfolded? Independent journalists like Dany Schechter were constantly speaking out loudly.

In January 2011, I was reading Gideon Rachman's *Zero-Sum Future: American Power in an Age of Anxiety* (Kindle, 2011) which chronicled his coverage of the Davos, Switzerland, 2009 Economic Summit two years prior, arguing that the Great Recession had in fact dislodged the fundamental logic of international relations. "It is no longer obvious that globalization benefits all the world's major powers, and it's no longer clear that the United States faces no serious international rivals. And it is increasingly apparent that the world is facing an array of truly global problems—such as climate change and nuclear proliferation—that are causing rivalry and division between traditional allies." (p.7)

Then, "After a long period of international cooperation, competition and rivalry are returning to the international system, a win-win world is once again giving way to a zero-sum world," believes Rachman. (p. 109), Even more ominously for America he suggests: "The emergence of a zero-sum world undermines the key assumptions of U.S. foreign policy since the end of the Cold War." (p.113)

And, "Both Bill Clinton and Bush II believed that it was in America's best interests to encourage the rise of major new powers, such as China and India, because globalization was bending history in America's direction." (p. 134) Referring to the 2007 Davos summit, this publisher and former US-presidential candidate gushed: "This is the richest year in human history. The best way to create wealth is to have free markets and free people, and more and more of the world is realizing it." (p. 161)

Three years later, however, Obama's chief economic adviser, Larry Summers was saying to the assembled plutocrats at Davos that "One in five American male workers between ages 25-50 was now unemployed. In the 1960s, 95 percent of the same group had been working. Summers strongly implied that Chinese trade policies were largely to blame." (p. 171)

As to dynamics inhering in the oddest couple's trade relationship, Rachman notes: "Rising economic tensions between America and China may well lead to a serious increases in American trade protectionism. That in turn would feed Beijing's paranoid fear that America is ultimately intent on blocking China's rise—poisoning political relations between the world's two most important powers, and so destabilizing the global system." (p. 176)

The author similarly plumbs future problems with the third economic giant: a single-currency expanded EU with serious fiscal dilemmas. And, in the aftermath of the Great Recession, "Much talk at Davos suggested 'the need for a 'new Bretton Woods,' the 1944 conference laying the foundations for the economic architecture of the postwar era." (p. 202)

Finally, "This dark new international mood contrasts sharply with the liberal dream of the past 30 years for a more prosperous and peaceful world, pulled together by the ineluctable forces of globalization and regulated by markets and American power." (p. 217) In American academe, a whole sub-genre of research had blossomed under the rubric of the theory of the democratic peace." (p. 243)

A book by Stanley Kurtz fixates on Barack Obama's work experiences as a "community organizer" is called *Radical-In Chief: Barack Obama and the Untold Story of American Socialism* (Kindle, 2010). As usual, the political right has simple answers to complex problems, a la Kurtz: "Ever since Barack Obama's meteoric rise to the presidency began, Americans have been asking themselves this question: 'what on earth in a community organizer?" (p.3) The answer, it turns out, solves the riddle of Obama's political convictions. Community organizing is really a socialist profession, impugns Kurtz.

Ergo, "Particularly at the highest levels, America's community organizers have adopted a deliberately stealthy posture—hiding their socialism behind a 'populist front.' These organizers strive to push America toward socialism in unobtrusive, incremental steps

calling themselves 'pragmatic problem-solvers' all the while. Barack Obama's colleagues and mentors were some of the smartest and most influential stealth-socialist community organizers in the country." (p. 24) But if they're so smart, why are they dedicated to such an implausible revolutionary outcome?

How does this cabal of closet socialists manage to be both "stealthy" and "influential" simultaneously? That must require some fancy footwork, but the author opines they comprise "some of the smartest people in the country. "(p. 47). Again, fundies' anti-intellectualism bleeds through.

Ex-Los Angeles Prosecutor Vincent Bugliosi has written another book, the latest called *The Prosecution of George W. Bush for War Crimes* stemming from "war damages, uncorking literally hundreds upon hundreds of thousands of people will involuntarily re-create in their mind's eye, over and over again, what happened to their loved ones." (p. 107) . Bugliosi examines carefully each of the various reasons provided by Bush II for war in Iraq, and concludes they can each be easily disproven under legal rules of evidence.

Bugliosi also discusses alternative explanations, considering them weak. "In fact, because it (WMD) was virtually the sole reason given by Bush in his march to war, the only reason given by Congress in its 11 October 2002 joint resolution authorizing war was national security, nothing else. (p. 142)

The resolution reads: 'The president is authorized to use the armed forces of the United States as he determines to be necessary and appropriate in order to defend the national security of the United States against the continuing threat provided by Iraq'. . . And in Bush's report to Congress on 19 March 2003, the day the war began, he spoke of nothing else but Hussein's WMD and our national security. There wasn't even a hint or mention of any other motive for war." (p. 321)

Only after WMDs went MIA in Iraq did Republicans begin chirping that the real reason was "the fanciful notion of changing the political culture of the Arab world to our liking, if Bush's REAL purpose was to ignite a restructuring of the Middle East by giving birth to democracy in Iraq, he had no right to keep this motivation secret from the American people." (p. 335) Bugliosi concedes that during wartime, of course legitimate reasons exist to "protect the truth with a bodyguard of lies," but residents of any democracy have a right to know the reasons for that war." (p. 341) A similar book is called *Scourge: The Demise of Critical Thinking in the Age of "the Secret,"* by Newton Fortuin (Kindle, 2007).

I think that the best recent book to close this tit-for-tat lefty/righty dialogue is called *Bipolar Nation: Will the Real Majority please stand up?*

(Kindle, 2010) by Austin Pearl. Reducing anything undesirable to syndrome status is supposed to awaken a desire to find an antidote.

With Pearl, knee-jerk hyper-partisanship is belittled as dysfunctional not only for civil society, but rational policy: "In order to raise awareness of the aforementioned condition and hopefully begin to roll back its effects, we're going to document it for the first time. I hereby declare the existence of *the partisan sickness,* defined as a condition in which the patient has a prepackaged negative judgment of any and all actions of the opposing political party; often resulting in unpleasant dinner conversations, emotional arguments, and a higher than normal usage rate of the terms 'fascist' or 'communist'." (p. 110)

It's impossible to dismiss Pearl's central point: the noise level politically has become deafeningly shrill, civility has lost its appeal, and obnoxious behavior seems to raise TV ratings not just marginally but significantly. He also blames over-reactions to 9/11 as highly contributory to hyper-partisanship. Author Pearl's solutions walk and talk very much like he understands CTS.

Incivility is, however, only one-half of the partisanship walnut. Pearl traces ways in which America's unique culture *as contrasted with Europe wherein political consensuses are more prevalent than our split right down the middle.* The cover photo symbolizes the titular *Bipolar Nation* well because it depicts a split facial image with each of our two most recent presidents each given exactly 180 degrees of the photo.

Polls consistently reveal America to consist of fairly equal triads: liberals, moderates, conservatives. Ergo, whoever wins over the independents these days takes home the big prize. Also, the structures of our presidential election system marginalize Third Parties in our duopoly, never a problem in parliamentary systems. In 2011, Tea Party enthusiasts believe they will prove the exception to the rule, but American electoral history suggests otherwise.

MY PERSONAL POLITICS:

My ideological proclivities on the traditional prism (liberal/moderate/conservative) seem transparent. They also bleed through my main thesis: FNC's common-sensical culture fails to employ CTS, relying heavily upon paralinguistics to convey stereotypical alpha-male authoritarian messages enabling its niche demographic to engage in a self-fulfilling suspension of disbelief. Too simplistic for 21st Century denizens.

If the choice consists of this continuum, I'll almost always pick progressivism, as well as proclivities for the Democratic Party, except when co-opted by the Military-Industrial-Complex to approve obscene Pentagon budgets fueling our deficit. However, the most apt descriptor of my core values would be the label humanistic internationalist. Thus I comment below concerning four other relevant prisms for contemporary Americans.

The prisms consist of: 1.) Liberal/conservative; 2.) Realist/idealist; 3.) Ethnocentric/cultural relativist; 4.) National/global; 5.) Common-sensical/CTS. These ideologies orient our policy preferences on controversial economic, political, social, cultural, and ethical issues. The campaign portfolio of an American presidential candidate typically addresses more than 100 issues.

And what's my take on the hottest new voice in 2011, the Tea Party movement?

All sentient souls know that deficit spending represents a classic slippery slope. Many scholars predict that the extant mightiest Empire since Rome will implode via Imperial Overstretch. First: America's archipelago of military bases in 120+ countries worldwide is unprecedented. And second: Military spending in excess of all 190+ countries on the planet when we have no rivals. The Great Recession and U.S. indebtedness may represent what some call a "natural governor" forcing us to forsake Imperial Overstretch or go broke.

A life-long Democrat, I hurt when our side acts badly, for example: FDR placing 330,000 Japanese-American citizens in camps; Harry Truman's deaf ear to Japanese feelers for conditions of peace; his failure to consider the scientists calling for an A-bomb demo; and starting Cold War hyperbole with the specious Domino theory. Similarly, JFK's failure to apply CTS instead accepting CIA plans for Bay of Pigs invasion; Likewise, LBJ's bevy of lies about Vietnam; Ditto for Jimmy Carter's vacillation over the Iranian hostage rescue; More recently, Bill Clinton on the Rwandan genocide, his signing the repeal of Glass-Steagill legislation; and Bosnian rescue delays.

Similarly, I have to admire Nixon's brilliant installation of floating exchange rates in 1971, founding the EPA, and China gamble. Elsewhere I have contrasted Bush I's rational decision-making concerning Iraq and Bush II's irrational mendacity. Bush I oversaw the Cold War's end with adroit humility. Finally, Ronald Reagan deserves credit for coming to his senses by replacing his first-term "evil empire" rhetoric with a second-term rapprochement with the Soviets, who turned out to be human beings after all.

The issue on which conservatives believe they own the moral high ground is the one they keep raising in the House as a rider to everything from budgets to bridges: abortion. I minored in philosophy in college under a CTS-minded professor, Marvin Kohl. I wrote a term paper on abortion arguing exactly my current position (pre-Roe v. Wade): the only thing worse than legal abortion is illegal abortion; therefore, for health reasons it should be legalized in three circumstances: rape; incest; mother's life is endangered.

Of course, it's awful and I decry wanton overuse in 2011, but even that is better than illegality. If conservatives were truly pro-life quality, they would favor beneficent euthanasia, and outlaw capitol punishment. The frequency of wrongful deaths proved via DNA testing can't be ignored forever. And, of course, Bush II and Rick Perry built Texas governorships as guilt-free mass executioners in a state to the right of Attila the Hun.

Sexism also enters into these issues, for example, how many female Catholic Bishops exist in America? And how is it that pedophile priests kept getting transferred rather than fired by their male bosses? The science overwhelmingly reveals that women contribute only slightly to pedophilia, it's a male's ball game. In 2012, the House GOP chaired a panel on women's issues with zero distaff invitees.

Regarding the 2011 insurgent Tea Party, our system creates huge infra-structural advantages for bipartisan serial role reversal, whereby neither opposition party is willing to hold the ruling party truly accountable in ways other than marginal. Our history is replete with examples of single-issue populist young children rising to challenge the adult parents before wilting. After forcing the adults to either adopt or reject the kids' policy alternatives, the kids disappear from the headlines they need like oxygen.

Deficit spending was aberrant until Lyndon Johnson funded his Vietnam War off the books to avoid raising taxes, with predictable stagflation ensuing in the 1970s. Since then, the norm for both Republicans and Democrats (for reasons politically explicable but economically indefensible) habituated floor-to-ceiling deficits. Simple solutions to complex problems prove illusory, and the Tea Party activists reek of reductionism regarding both the causes and cures for federal deficits.

Furthermore, where was the Tea Party during Bush II's wholesale profligacy? When his Vice President testified before Congress, Cheney predicted that Iraqi oil revenues would cover the expenses of Operation Iraqi Freedom, leaving little for America to contribute, that prediction proved not only false but utterly laughable. The meter is still running for that war, but final figures will total more than $1 trillion. Since Bush II bullied and bribed reluctant allies to join a "coalition of the willing" for a war their populations begged them to decry.

I consider Bush I to have laid painstaking plans for his 1990 Iraq War, executed it crisply, and dealt with its unpredictable consequences reasonably. His military sang from the same sheet of music and intelligence was integral to the entire operation. Equally important, it was a genuinely UN-sanctioned endeavor and he secured up-front commitments from Saudi Arabia, Germany, Japan, and others ultimately contributing 80 percent of the expenses.

In striking contrast, Bush II's feisty Under-Secretary of State (Richard Armitage) answered a Senator's question as to whether America could handle two simultaneous wars he responded with the hubris endemic to Bush's team: "I think we can walk and chew gum simultaneously."

And 10 months prior to a next election cycle, what are we to make of Barack Obama's first term which began with enthusiastic promises of a new paradigm consisting of pragmatic bipartisanship? *Atlantic* scribe, James Fallows, provides considerable perspective in "Obama Explained" (March 2012). Conducting copious research involving all the usual suspects, his core question: "Chess master from his election campaign, or pawn pushed around by political opponents and overwhelmed by macro-economics?"

Despite the pitfalls of assessing presidents in "real time," Fallows digs beneath stereotypes to subtext analysis. He draws upon his experiences positing that several factors contribute to failed presidencies: first, the analytical inability to deal with complex short-term and distal decisions flying at them nonstop; second, lacking eloquent rhetorical clarity to communicate effectively; third, empathic emotional intelligence enabling a feeling for where others are coming from; fourth, personal adaptability; fifth, comfortable enough in own skin to see through hubristic temptations. (pp. 58-59)

He sees whether or not they achieve reelection as the crucial variable profoundly influencing how we judge presidents them in perpetuity, which

Fallows characterizes as largely beyond their control; that is, they remain largely at the mercy of unforeseeable events such as recessions, wars, and subterfuge. Second terms enable presidents to apply lessons won the hard way during earlier experiments. "If Barack Obama loses this fall, he will forever seem a disappointment: a symbolically important accidental figure raising hopes he could not fulfill and meeting insurmountable difficulties." (p. 70) The author contends that Obama inherited such a noxious legacy from Bush II that only a second term can salvage his historical legacy.

He sketches Obama's first-term failures: 1.) Underestimating the severity of the economic crisis; 2.) Insufficient responses to the Great Recession; 3.) Coddling financiers; 4.) Honeymoon capital squandered excessively on health care reform; 5.) Naivete over GOP bipartisanship; 6.) Accepting GOP premise that federal deficits represent our top priority. (p. 73)

Successes are afforded equal time and include: 1.) Averting an economic meltdown; 2.) Rejoining the community of good global citizenship; 3.) Health care reform vexing presidents for a century; 4.) Demonstrated the crucial quality of "adaptability" to circumstances in flux; 5.) Unexpected achievements the weakest part of his portfolio: foreign affairs leadership. (p. 80)

Unclear is whether Obama will convince a majority of the public that his persona consists of the coolly rational adult in the room, or coldness absent the empathy exuding from the ultimate "comeback kid," Bill Clinton. "The payoff for Mr. Obama's strategy of remaining Mr. Reasonable consists of this prospect: occupying the acceptable center, as the Tea Party steers Republicans hard right." (p. 83)

A second useful prism dichotomizes realism versus idealism. I define realism as placing a premium on competitive national interest defined as power and suspicious of cooperative endeavors among states. Its antithesis I define as believing that human reason can find ways to avert war and promote cooperation via common elements uniting all peoples. I find affinity with what the nobler (albeit problematic) alternative in each case. Here realism holds a natural pole position since it generally conforms to our obvious material best interests. Realism and idealism can be contrasted on these dimensions:

Realism:	*Idealism:*
Pessimistic human nature	Optimistic human nature
Pragmatic emphasis	Ethical emphasis
Action is potent	Ideas are potent
Human rights tangential	Human rights vital National
National interest=seeking power	National interest=doing good
Peace through strength	Peace through cooperation

A third ideological prism compares ethnocentrism with cultural relativism. So accustomed are humans to our own circumstances that we take them for granted. Therefore, the easy fallback prism consists of ethnocentrism: Judging the customs of other cultures by one's own culture and assuming them inferior. Ethnocentrism taps into our comfort level with the familiar. Its antithesis, however, cultural relativism defined as a fair-minded egalitarian attitude that cultures are not better or worse, merely different. Again I feel an affinity with cultural relativism as the nobler alternative.

A fourth useful prism contrasts nationalism and globalism. Nationalism maintains the traditional personal identity with the sovereign nation-state as humans did for three centuries. Globalism consists of a post-national paradigm whereby you consider yourself as a global citizen identifying more with the human family than the national tribe. Here I gravitate strongly towards globalism.

A fifth useful prism is common-sense versus CTS, (see chapter one). Common-sensical thinking comes easily to us, but the intellectual bounty of adopting the CTS prism has been proven among humans since the Scientific Revolution. In sum, I strive for what seem the nobler-but-tougher choices of liberalism, idealism, cultural relativism, globalism, and CTS.

Relying solely on the first of these analytical tools (liberal/conservative) helps to understand where others are coming from, therefore it proves a necessary-but-insufficient political lexicon. All five of these prisms inter-act freely with one another and if we want to understand humans as quin-tessentially social beings, they assist our quest.

13   Michael J. Strada, *Through the Global Lens: An Introduction to the Social Sciences* (Prentice Hall, 2009), paraphrasing pp. 312-315.

14   Austin V. Ranney, *Governing: An Introduction to Political Science* (Prentice Hall, 2007), pp. 4-5.

15   "Political Freedom in Global Perspective," Source: Freedom House Inc., 2007.

16   Strada, pp. 316-18.

17   "Lord Acton's Lecture" http://www. Libertystore.net/LSTHINKACTON.html

18   Don Lindsay, ARCHIVE OF FALLACIES, Argument from Spurious Similarity: http://www.don-lindsay-archive.org/skeptic/arguments.html

19   Danny Schecter, EMBEDDED; WEAPONS OF MASS DECEPTION; HOW THE MEDIA FAILED TO COVEER THE WAR ON IRAQ (Prometheus Books, 2003).

CHAPTER THREE:

"Foxymoron's Mercurial History"

BACKGROUNDER:

Rupert Murdoch (RKM), News Corp, and FNC blend smoothly in global consciousness and in reality. The last two decades witnessed FNC's voracious soap opera. Yet, I think the Foxymoron trifecta has peaked and headed for an ignoble nadir. The London phone-hacking 2011 scandal is utterly compatible with the triptych's history.

All RKM biographies are examined below. However, a sneak preview of reviews for two of the authors (Michael Wolfe and Wendy Rohm) is provided here. BBC producer/reporter Eve Conway writes that "Rohm's book provides insights into the driving force behind Murdoch's global media ambitions for the new millennium and looks at his high-stakes strategies in several world markets."

McKinsey consulting firm's Director, Michael Wolfe, says that "Rohm's book examines how Rupert Murdoch's News Corp is fighting the battle for access to the world's audiences/advertisers." Similarly, Eric Nee, senior writer at *Fortune Magazine,* opines that Rohm "sheds light on one of the world's most powerful yet enigmatic figures who single-handedly created one of the largest media companies on earth."

BSMG Media's Tim Grace claims "RKM's vision transcends media (and the technology required for its dissemination) to impact the creation of ideas in ways that even the Internet does not yet manage. . ., armed with the expertise acquired in previous high-stakes ventures." Lastly, the *London Daily Mail's* Daniel Jeffreys argues that Rohm "explains how Murdoch continues to forge unorthodox paths in new media that no other media barons have yet had the stamina to explore, never mind weather the risks involved."[xx]

NEWS CORPORATION:

This publicly-traded conglomerate was founded in Adelaide, Australia, by RKM in 1979 as a holding company for News Limited, assets inherited from his father (Sir Keith Murdoch), along with the Australian tabloid newspaper *The News* in 1952. News Corporation currently resides in New York City (alongside Fox News). Current leaders of News Corp include Rupert Murdoch (Chairman and CEO), Chase Carey (COO), David Devoe (CFO), Lawrence Jacobs (Vice President), and James Murdoch (CEO: Europe/Asia).

It produces films, television, cable programming, satellite television, magazines, newspapers, books, sports, and websites. It's symbol on NASDAQ? NWS. Often abbreviated as News Corp, the statistical profile in 2009 included these impressive numbers in US dollars: Revenue (30.5 billion); Operating Income (5.7 billion); Net Income (3.4 billion); Total Assets (53.2 billion); Total Equity (23.2 billion).[xxi] It employs 64,000 persons and ranks third among media conglomerates (behind Disney Company and Time Warner Company). Its website? Newscorp. com (http://www.newscorp.com/)

RKM achieved his crucial breakthrough in America by purchasing the *San Antonio Express News* in 1973, followed in quick succession by the supermarket tabloid the *National Star* and the *New York Post*. Then, in 1981, News Corp announced purchasing the Metro-media group of stations, greasing the skids eventually for a fourth broadcast network in America (FNC).

On 4 September 1985 Murdoch became a naturalized U.S. citizen, a enabling ownership of a television station here. With the Metro-media deal closed, Murdoch soon launched the Fox News Channel (FNC) in 1986, whose growth occurred dizzingly fast and by 2010 the upstart was being viewed in 96 percent of U.S. households. Murdoch envisioned FNC as a direct competitor to Ted Turner's ground-breaking CNN 24-hour news channel. FNC caters to a loyal niche market of "authoritarian personalities" identified in American politics by Thedor Adorno decades ago.

Then in 1986-87, News Corp challenged the influence of unions working in its British newspapers, and Murdoch imported several senior Australian media moguls, including John Dux, managing director of the *South China Morning Post* with violent confrontations between the unions and Murdoch's tough guys. He also moved his London News Corp operation to Wapping in the East End, where nightly battles occurred. Also, "Delivery vans and depots were frequently and violently attacked, and ultimately the unions capitulated."[xxii]

By 1992, RKM's risk-taking led to huge debts, and News Corp sold off many American magazines acquired in the mid-1980s, as well as spinning off long-held Australian magazine interests as Pacific magazines. "Much of this debt came from its stake in the Sky Television satellite network in the U.K., which incurred massive losses in its early years, subsidized with profits from its other holdings until forcing rival satellite operator BSB into merging in 1990: (BSkyB) has dominated the British pay-TV market since."[xxiii]

In 1993, News Corp acquired a 64 percent stake of Hong Kong's STAR TV satellite network for more than $500 million, completing its total purchase in 1995. At that time, Murdoch sung the populist praises of satellite networks thus: "Telecommunications have proved an unambiguous threat to totalitarian regimes everywhere. Satellite broadcasts make it possible for information-hungry residents of closed societies to bypass state-controlled television channels."[xxiv]

The validity of RKM's U.S. citizenship was criticized since News Corp's home base (Australia) trumped his convenient new de facto citizenship. By 1995, the American FCC had begun investigating charges that Murdoch's ownership was illegal; however, the FCC (under President Clinton's watch) surprised pundits by ruling in Murdoch's favor stating that his ownership of FNC was in the public's best interests. Almost simultaneously, News Corp revealed a deal with MCI Communications creating a major conservative news website called *The Weekly Standard.*

Critical-Thinking-Skills (CTS) routinely assess the source's reputation on controversial issues. The highly-regarded U.K. journal, *The Economist,* jumped all over News Corp in 1999 with investigative reporting that "the corporation's complex structure, international scope, and use of off-shore tax havens enabled it to pay minimal taxes compared to its competitors."[xxv] Also, the BBC (another stellar source) reported that News Corp had made $20 billion in profits over 11 years while completely avoiding paying net corporation taxes, which amounted to roughly $350 million in taxes.[xxvi]

Frenetic growth continued after the new millennium. In 2003, Murdoch acquired a 34 percent stake in DirecTV Group (formerly Hughes Electronics and once the biggest U.S. satellite TV system) from General Motors for $6 billion; and, in 2008, DirecTV Group was sold to Liberty Media's John Malone in exchange for shares in News Corp. A year earlier, a higher-profile News Corp acquisition discussed elsewhere here occurred when Murdoch purchased Dow Jones, publisher of the *Wall Street Journal,* for $5.6 billion.

Derided for his tabloid-laden portfolio, Murdoch was apparently willing to pay top dollar to land what experts consider one of the top troika of American dailies. Also in 2007, "the corporation spun off a business news channel from Fox News – Fox Business Network."[xxvii] On 8 February 2007, Murdoch assured guests at the McGraw-Hill Media Summit that "A Fox Channel would be more business-friendly than CNBC, since that channel leaps on every scandal, or whatever they perceive as one."[xxviii] In 2009, News Corp established an entity called NewsCore (global wire service to provide news content to News Corp's outlets.)

Shareholder ownership resonates profoundly in large conglomerates and several recent developments on this front have been widely reported. In 2005, the Murdoch family possessed only 29 percent of News Corp, but most of these consisted of voting shares, facilitating effective control in RKM's hands. However, John Malone of Liberty Media owned a large stake, half of which were voting shares.

Therefore, in November 2006, New Corp transferred 38.8 percent managing interest in DirecTV Group to John Malone's Liberty Media, which bought back Liberty's 16.3 percent shares in News Corp, leaving Murdoch with tighter reins on the latter firm. And Murdoch sold 17.5 million "class A" shares in December 2007.[xxix]

A juicy Saudi subtext also exists here: Prince Alwaleed bin Talal al-Saud's Kingdom Holding Company possesses 7 percent of News Corp shares, and second largest shareholder of News Corp. Prince Alwaleed is the same person contributing most heavily to construction of the controversial Islamic Center planned near ground zero in New York City in 2011.[xxx]

News Corp's Management Conferences feature secretive record-keeping, with uninvited journalists denied access. Invited celebrities, politicians, journalists, and News Corp executives discuss timely topics. The 2006 Conference, held in Pebble Beach, CA, led by RKM, notable for a source leaking the agenda to the *Los Angeles Times*. Issues covered dealt with geopolitics, terrorism, new media, Europe, and Islam and the West (with Israel's President Shimon Peres participating in the latter). Among the invited speakers: Rupert Murdoch, Newt Gingrich, Arnold Schwarzenegger, Bono, John McCain, Nicole Kidman, and Al Gore.

Critics have jumped all over News Corp for conflicts of interest and huge political donations. Most recently, two cases flared up in 2010:

1.) Republican Governors Association (RGA): News Corp donated $1 million prior to the 2010 elections. The Democratic Governors Association (DGA) demanded transparency criticizing FNC for bias. DGA head Nathan Daschle wrote to the chairman of News Corp and to FNC head Roger Ailes: "In the interest of some fairness and balance, I request that you issue a formal disclaimer to your coverage when your programs cover governors or gubernatorial races between now and election day." A Fox spokesperson responded thus: "There is a strict line between business and editorial at Fox News."[xxxi] Yeah, right.

2.) In the summer of 2010, News Corp likewise donated $1 million to the U.S. Chamber of Commerce, and the Chamber aggressively supported Republican efforts to retake Congress in 2010. Many critics complained that these two behaviors by a large media company clearly violated ethical norms, though probably not legal ones.

FOX NEWS CHANNEL (FNC):

As a direct offshoot of Rupert Murdoch's News Corp, FNC has already been sketched briefly. However, other significant controversies include: Fox began broadcasting on 7 October 1996 under the direction of Murdoch's founding CEO, Roger Ailes, ex-CNBC executive and long-time Republican consultant. The name Fox actually derives from the

Australian-American mogul's May 1985 purchase of 20th Century Fox Film Corporation.

Within a year, Fox Film had increased its profits tenfold. That purchase was assisted by American industrialist Marvin Davis with the shared intention of competing with both CNN and the three mainstream networks (CBS, NBC, and ABC). By 2009, FNC captured the number two position among primetime viewers (behind USA Network).

It's website? Foxnews.com.[xxxii]

Even fools can't deny the rapid ascension of FNC, however, its growth is mitigated by several ancillary considerations. Firstly, much research reveals that Americans are exceedingly bifurcated ideologically today: truly a schizoid 50/50 nation unmatched in any other OECD top-29 world economies. Consensus-builders among politicians and journalists describe efforts in futility. I'm hoping academicians like me can do better.

Secondly, FNC's quantitative gains parallel those of News Corp generally. However, this fact is countervailed by the burden of negative qualitative assessment among experts. High ratings do not impress sophisticated analysts; in essence, FNC epitomizes worst-practices bench-marking among the literati. Fortunately, the only time thus far that the networks and CNN were stupid enough to "out-fox Fox" was in the 2003 Iraq War.

Thirdly, liberal Ted Turner's CNN dominated cable news for two decades. Many wealthy conservatives (like Joseph Coors and the Koch brothers) were chomping at the bit for exactly what they got in spades with FNC's transparently Republican apologias.

The American pendulum has swung for too long toward common-sensical thinking, and I believe now finally swings back toward CTS. Quarter-truths and half-truths appeal to niche authoritarians, but they possess a short half-life, eventually coming back to haunt truth butchers. CNN and the networks need not feel tempted to out-fox Fox, a role better suited to MSNBC.

Fourthly, RKM has relied on unethical practices pandering to the lowest common- denominator. His cheating continues being exposed by investigative reporters around the globe. For example, the shocking phone-hacking scandal based at his London paper, *World News Today,* continues to reveal myriad ethical voids cohabiting Murdoch enterprises.

Finally, Fox's clever-but-specious exploitation of subtext paralinguistics to trigger authoritarian alpha-male stereotypes will lose its infotainment shock value. Encyclopedia Dramatica's Jimmy Wales refers to it as "Faux News" (a comedy network for gullible Republicans).[xxxiii]

On 7 October 1996, FNC reached only 10 million households, none in either New York City or Los Angeles. Reviewers watched the first day's effort the only place available: Fox's studios. The initial newscast was called *The Schneider Report*, presented by host Mike Schneider. From the outset, Fox's evenings were filled with opinion shows led by Bill O'Reilly, Catherine Crier, and the Sean Hannity/Alan Colmes testosterone-mis-match. Fox emphasized colorful graphics and bullets spoon-feeding the audience.

From these inauspicious beginnings, RKM found clever ways to accelerate adoption by cable companies. For example, "Fox News paid systems up to $11 per subscriber to distribute the channel. This contrasted with the normal practice, in which cable operators paid stations carriage fees for the programming of channels."[xxxiv]

When Time Warner bought out Ted Turner's Broadcasting Empire (including CNN) a federal antitrust consent decree demanded that Time Warner carry a second all-news channel and Time Warner chose MSNBC. Fox claimed this violated an unwritten agreement to cover Fox News as the secondary channel; News Corp pressured NYC Republican

Mayor Rudy Giuliani to lean on Time Warner to go with Fox rather than MSNBC, and it worked.[xxxv]

Time Warner filed a lawsuit against New York City, alleging interference with educational channels for commercial programming. News Corp followed with an antitrust suit against Time Warner for unfairly protecting CNN and an acrimonious public battle ensued between Turner and Murdoch. Complicating matters even further, Giuliani's wife was employed as a producer on Murdoch's WNYW-TV and ultimately Time Warner and News Corp signed a settlement agreement permitting Fox to be carried by NYC cable systems, as well as by Time Warner.

In May 2008, FNC launched "high definition channel simulcasts of its programming in selected regions of the United States. Time Warner is carrying this channel in New York City, Kansas City, and San Antonio." And in October 2008, Direct TV added the HD channel, as did Cox Communication shortly thereafter.[xxxvi] Fox keeps a program archive and also handles the Fox Movie-tone newsreels, and ITN. FNC presents live programming up to 15 hours daily. With its rapid growth, Murdoch's conglomerate has also begun Fox News Radio and a Fox News website, as well as Fox Business News.

However, TV popularity did not translate online (low-Neteracy Fox fans). In August 2010 viewers per month were: CNN=48 million; MSNBC=47 million; FNC=24 million.[xxxvii] Live Internet streaming arrived at Fox in September 2008 on its website called "The Strategy Room," designed for seniors. Informality dominates its airtime and leading programs include: "God Talk Hours," "News with a View," and "Business Hour." A year later Murdoch's network added a website, "The Fox Nation," encouraging readers to post comments.[xxxviii]

FNC experienced a 300 percent increase in viewership during the early stages of the 2003 Iraq War, averaging 3.3 million viewers daily.[xxxix] Also, Bush II's address to the RNC in 2004 notched 7.3 million viewers as compared to 5.9 for NBC, 5.0 for CBS, and 5.1 for ABC. However, in 2005 the network experienced a brief decline in ratings for every single prime time program, only to rebound during the North Korean Missile Crisis and the Lebanon War in 2006.

FNC is the only network to internalize Bush II's specious global War On Terror (WOT). The term war used to have precise meaning in international law; Bush II's WOT has bastardized the term Why does Jingoism constantly over-achieve solely on Fox? It features an interlocking directorate benefiting enormously from America's obscene military budget. The boring nature of international peace represents Fox's worst nightmare.

In September 2009, the Pew Research Center released a study of public opinion towards Fox News. It revealed that "72 % of Republican viewers rated the channel favorably, while 43 % of Democrats and 55 % of all viewers shared this opinion. However, FNC also had the highest negative ratings of all outlets studied at 25 %." Pew also concluded that partisan divergence concerning Fox news increased substantially after 2007. [xl] Again, given America's political bifurcation, is severely bifurcated ideologically, how can such figures surprise anyone?

I see FNC's deceptiveness as multifaceted; therefore, its irony-laden marketing slogans matter. Its slogan of "fair and balanced" decried by critics was actually first prefaced by the words "real journalism." Since fair and balanced should be the ubiquitous default position, why does only FNC bait its critics with such superfluous bromides?

Al Franken's book, *Lies and the Lying Liars Who Tell Them: A Fair and Balanced Look at the Right* (Plume Books, 2003), now-Senator Franken cites examples of FNC' bias, relying on solid research. Bill O'Reilly insisted on Fox suing Franken in August 2003, but dropped the lawsuit three days later when Judge Denny Chin refused their request for an injunction. Chin wrote in *Fox v. Franken* that the case was "wholly without merit, both factually and legally; and also that Fox's trademark on the phrase 'fair and balanced' could be invalid."[xli]

Liberal online advocacy organization, AlterNet, filed a "cancellation petition" with the U.S. Patent and Trademark Office (USPTO) to have Fox's "fair and balanced" slogan rescinded as nondescript. In court, AlterNet introduced Robert Greenwald's trenchant documentary film "Outfoxed: Rupert Murdoch's War on Journalism," as evidence because it chronicles cases of conservative bias stemming from leaked internal memos sent to staff (some by Editorial V-P John Moody), stipulating policy positions.[xlii]

After losing several early motions in the lawsuit, AlterNet withdrew its case.[xliii] Other slogans have failed to generate as much heat as the "fair and balanced" one, but include: "we report, you decide" and "You Decide 2008" for that election.

Another FNC case study strikes me as particularly telling: Fox V-P William Sammons, at the peak of the health care debate said: "Use the term 'government-run health insurance,' or when brevity is a concern, 'government option' because if you call it a 'public option' Americans are split, but if you call it the 'government option,' they are overwhelmingly against it."[xliv]

Chroniclers of online political untruths continue popping up, and I like PolitFact (Pulitzer Prize Winner), MediaMatters, and AlterNet, as well as the prestigious online Ariana Huffington Post researchers. Appendix D here addresses "veracity police."

Media Matters for America annually releases "Ten most egregious examples of distortion by FNC." Featured in 2010 are several examples of cropping quotes from President Obama, V-P Joe Biden, and ex-VP V-P Al Gore out of context, using image manipulation software editing the appearance of reporters from the *New York Times,* and bogus footage from other events suggesting a larger-than-life number of participants at a 5

November Tea Party rally in the nation's Capitol. Media Matters also jumped all over a 4 December 2009 "questionable graphic" in which Republican pollsters (Rasmussen Reports) featured data in a climate change poll amounting to 120 percent.[xlv]

In 2009, FNC disrespected Obama's White House, which returned the favor. On 20 September 2009 when Obama spoke on all other outlets except for Fox. Sending an unambiguous message concerning dismissive remarks about the president's health care proposals made by Sean Hannity and Glenn Beck, as well as Fox's clearly biased coverage of that topic. Similarly, on Fox News Sunday, host Chris Wallace referred to White House officials as "crybabies."[xlvi]

Obama's Senior Advisor (David Axelrod) met with FNC's News Director (Roger Ailes) in a futile effort to defuse this PR bomb. Two weeks later, WH communications director Anita Dunn stated boldly that "Fox is not a news channel; it operates as either the research arm or the communications arm of the Republican Party." President Obama chimed in with "If media are operating basically as a talk radio format, then that's one thing; however a news outlet represents something quite different."

Then-Chief of Staff Rahm Emmanuel responded "It's important to not have the CNN's and others of this world basically be led by Fox."[xlvii] More than a year later, however, Obama himself appeared on the O'Reilly Factor for an interview that the Big O later said involved two alpha males duking-it-out; consistent with my assertion that Fox triggers alpha-male (authoritarian) responses via inflammatory subtext paralinguistics.

Fox hacks often ridicule our good neighbors to the north. FNC is offered in Canada by eight cable companies, but not by the country's third largest carrier (Videotron), which has refused to follow suit. FNC's jingoism has rubbed Canadians the wrong way several times.

In 2005, a late-night Fox comedy shtick called "Red Eye with Greg Gutfeld" made disparaging remarks about the Canadian military, including "inappropriate and disrespectful comments on the Fox channel regarding the Canadian military efforts in Afghanistan." Well-documented outrage emerged from many Canadian journalists and politicians. One Canadian media carrier (Shaw Communications) provided its customers stuck with FNC another option.[xliii]

A multi-award-winning Canadian investigative documentary program is known as "The Fifth Estate" and it has also crossed polemical swords with Fox News. For three decades this best-practices CBC institution has aired more than 1,600 stories and over 600 shows. A remarkable variety of Canadian, American, and international awards been won by this program. Exactly 243 honors, including several Oscars and Emmys. "Its mission? Incisive original investigative journalism challenging hidden assumptions, questioning conventional wisdoms, and giving voice to victims of injustice."[xlix]

One that interested me was called "Sticks and Stones" in which reporter Bob McKeown examines FNC and can be viewed entirely (42 min.), as well as briefer video interviews with both Bill O'Reilly and Ann Coulter. Ancillary information on both O'Reilly and Coulter is provided, as well as letters from viewers, and American responses. Their website includes numerous key links and bibliographic references.[l]

Let's take a look at Fox's daily programming schedule in 2011, and it becomes clear how editorial-laden its offerings are in Table 3.1.*

Table 3.1:
Fox's Daily Offerings:

Time:	Format:	Program:	Host:
6-9	Opinion	"Fox & Friends"	Gretchen Carlson
9-11	News	"America's Newsroom"	Bill Hemmer
11-1	News	"Happening Now"	Jon Scott
1-3	Opinion	"America Live"	Megyn Kelly
3-4	News	"Studio B"	Shepard Smith
4-5	Opinion	"Your World"	Neal Cavuto
5-6	Opinion	"Glenn Beck Show"	Glenn Beck
6-7	News/Opinion	"Special Report"	Bret Baier
7-8	News	"Fox Report"	Shepard Smith
8-9	Opinion	"The Factor"	Bill O'Reilly
9-10	Opinion	"Hannity"	Sean Hannity
10-11	Opinion	"On the Record"	G. Van Susteren
3-4 am	Opinion	"Red Eye"	Greg Gutfeld

* times not listed (repeat programming) [li]

MURDOCH'S STATESIDE ALTER EGO: ROGER AILES

Probably no other American has advanced the FNC agenda as profoundly as Roger Ailes, who grew up in an eastern Ohio factory town (Warren). From his youth, Ailes suffered from hemophilia and became accustomed to hospitalization. He was inducted into both Warren High and Ohio University Halls of Fame.

His early TV career began in nearby Cleveland and later moved to Philadelphia as property assistant, producer, and executive producer for then-locally-produced variety talk program "The Mike Douglas Show," ultimately syndicated nationally. Ailes' work was nominated for a Daytime Emmy Award but failed to garner this honor in 1968.

Producing "The Mike Douglas Show" enabled him to meet Richard Nixon, who had "considered TV as a mere gimmick." Subsequently, Nixon hired Ailes as a consultant in a 1968 effort "to make the stiff Nixon more likeable and accessible to voters," as chronicled in journalist Joe McGinniss' best-selling critique *The Selling of the President* (1968). Nixon represented Ailes' first political consultancy after he founded Ailes Communications in 1969.[lii]

Then, in 1984, he entered Ronald Reagan's campaign late and is widely credited with coaching Reagan to victory in the second presidential debate with Walter Mondale, after two other aides had botched prepara-tion for Reagan's first debate. Reagan's jest about not holding Mondale's youthful lack of experience against him defused public concerns about Reagan's advanced age.

Followed in 1987-88 by Bush I's come-from-behind victory against Michael Dukakis in which he scripted and produced the now-infamous "Revolving Door" ads. A full expose of Ailes' role in Bush I's 1988 cam-paign is skewered in the award-winning documentary film, *Boogie Man: The Lee Atwater Story.*

Ailes has denied producing the Willie Horton ad, which featured this convicted rapist furloughed by Governor Dukakis. Democrats complained that the group responsible, National Security Political Action Committee (NSPAC) was merely a front for the Republican National Committee (RNC). A Federal Election Committee (FEC) investigated but remained deadlocked (3-3 vote), letting Ailes off the hook.[liii] The accusation of "dirty tricks" has shadowed Ailes' resume, as revealed in Kerwin Swint's biography.

However, the dark maestro's final campaign effort failed in November 1991, when Richard Thornburgh failed to win a Senate seat in Pennsylvania. One year later, Ailes retired from consulting gigs; however, his fingerprints are all over a memo cited by Bob Woodward in his book, *Bush at War*, in which Ailes counsels Bush II "the American public would be patient as long as they were convinced the President was taking the harshest measures possible."

About Woodward's book, Ailes said: "Woodward got it all screwed up, as usual; the reason he's not as rich as Tom Clancy (novelist) is that while they both make stuff up, Clancy at least does his research first."[liv] Ailes has consistently refused to release a copy of the memo he sent to Bush II. Ailes has written only one book, with long-time aide John Kraushar: *You Are the Message: Secrets of Master Communicators* (Crown Business, 1989).

Its cover states "You are the message; what does that mean, exactly? It means when you communicate with someone, it's not just the words you choose to send to the other person that make up the message. You're also sending signals about what kind of person you are—by your eyes, your facial expression, your body movement, your vocal pitch, tone, volume, and intensity, your commitment to your message, your sense of humor, and many other factors. The receiving person is bombarded with symbols and signals from d you. Everything you do in relation to other people causes them to make judgments about what you stand for and what your message is, 'you are the message' comes down to the fact that unless you identify yourself as a walking, talking message, you miss the critical point. The words themselves are meaningless unless the rest of you is synchronized. The total you affects how others think of and respond to you."[lv]

Ailes' own words articulate my harping on FNC's exploitation of braggadocchio paralinguistics unleashing the suspension of disbelief with its alpha-male authoritarian demographic.

He stresses the "seven-second imperative," which he calls the time-frame available for presenters to win over others to their core message. Another bromide: "Be natural, don't force an emotion;" also, "Perceptions count more than content," plus, "Be prepared;" and, "Record yourself on audio and video;" "The magic bullet: being likeable;" "Be interesting, use analogies from other fields and pungent metaphors." Endless lists dot the landscape this handbook.

In 2011, only one book has been written about Roger Ailes: Kerwin Swint, *Dark Genius: the Influential Career of Legendary Political Operative and Fox News Founder Roger Ailes* (Union Square Press, 2008). Some Republican will eventually come out with a book defending Ailes' career, but not just yet. Incidentally, Ailes' 2009 FNC base salary ($5 million, with bonuses $23 million).

Thoughtful *Atlantic* journalist James Fallows recently assessed journalism's condition and argues that Roger Ailes must be contextualized as "doing something new" in ways similar to Henry Luce's mastery of photography in "Life" magazine, or Ted Koppel's use of satellite technology to introduce live interviews with prominent guests around the world.

Fallows writes: "The core of Ailes' success has not simply been that Fox was more entertaining to watch than pallid CNN. It has been, in the words of Richard Wald (ex-NBC News head) 'you can't beat Roger fighting on territory he's already left behind.' That is, Fox is doing something different from the other networks. If you say Glenn Beck got a fact wrong, or how many of Fox's female on-air broadcasters are babes in very short skirts, Ailes' answer will be: So?"[lvi]

In my view, Fallows' assertion that FNC not merely a quantitative change, but rather a paradigm shift, is only partly valid, since I predict it's heading for a nadir-ville damned soon. Roger Ailes refused Fallows' requests for an interview prior to his April 2011 article.

In 2008, Ailes purchased two local newspapers in Cold Spring, NY, where he owns a summer mansion, called the *Putnam County News and Reporter* (4,000 circ.) and the *Putnam County Courier.* And according to reputable online journal called *Politico,* friends and colleagues have been recommending his candidacy for President in 2012.[lvii]

Two other case studies involving criticisms of Fox/Ailes occurred in early 2011. First, an open letter from 400 rabbis from all Jewish denominations issued on UN-designated Holocaust Remembrance Day called on News Corp's Rupert Murdoch to censure Roger Ailes/Fox commentator Glenn Beck for shameless exploitation of Holocaust imagery to discredit their political opponents.

Ailes retorted by calling executives of the NPR Network that ran the story "Nazis," eventually apologizing to a Jewish religious group but not to NPR radio. Another Fox executive rejected the protest letter branding it "the work of a George Soros-backed leftwing political organization."[lviii]

Second, the *New York Times* reported that legal documents show that Ailes beseeched former-employee (and current publisher), Judith Regan, to lie to federal investigators about an affair she had with New York City Police Commissioner Bernard Kerik (nominated for Homeland Security Secretary).

Why lie? To protect a presidential bid by Rudolph Giuliani. According to court documents, Judith Regan audio-taped an incriminating conversation between her and Ailes. Two days later, political commentator Barry Ritholtz revealed Ailes had cancelled a New York City benefit the following month because of a possible indictment. [lix]

Roger Ailes' first wife graduated from Ohio University with him, but he left her to work on the 1968 Nixon Presidential campaign. His second wife, Norma A. Ailes, had a previous son (Shawn Ailes Visco Ferrer) whom the couple raised together. They divorced and Ailes remarried again in 1997, this time to the former Elizabeth Tilson. Republicans seem so in love with "family values" that keep creating new ones.

DARK GENIUS:

That Roger Ailes has severely impacted the news business no one doubts. However, whether that represents a very good thing or a very bad thing remains open. As noted by several authors, rarely has America been so bifurcated politically as in 2011, and just as the public is vehemently divided over FNC, so must it be about Roger Ailes.

Kennesaw State political scientist Kerwin Swint's 264-page biography thoroughly explores his complex subject. Its title suggests paradoxical implications: *Dark Genius* (Union Square Press, 2008), and in 2011 I can find no extant review of it. The product description refers to Ailes as "this Oz-like figure."

In the early-1990's, Ailes was hired to run the first TV financial network, CNBC, where he experimented with the first talk-show sensibility to the boob tube. A policy dispute with CNBC's Board, however, led to his premature departure, after which Ailes was gobbled up by Rupert Murdoch as FNC' one and only Director to date. This was also soon after Murdoch had purchased the *Wall Street Journal* from the dysfunctional Bancroft family. Then, in 2007 Ailes/Murdoch launched the Fox News Business Channel.

Kerwin Swint's cover states "Over the span of several decades, Ailes has played a key role in the growing reach of conservatism, first in politics, then in mass media. Part history, part media criticism, part current events, *Dark Genius* tracks the rise, dominance, and relevance of political television, and how it has been used and abused by its master." After reading it, I think the author definitely considers FNC highly biased, yet his work represents exemplary scholarship (>300 endnotes), zero hyperbole, which I suggest that academicians provide best.

I will focus on seven of Swint's 17 chapters. First, chapter three ("Fairness Is For Sissies"), which is all about Ailes' mastery of exploiting "wedge issues" in political communications. Wedge issues refer to Ailes' penchant for "identifying openings, areas of concern or fragmentation in the American political and moral landscape amenable to exploitation—then going hard after them. When the name of the game is winning, and little else, this leads to some pretty crass and shallow activities on the part of campaigns, consultants, and sometimes political party officials."[lx]

Regarding wedge issues, Swint goes back to Nixon's use of it as the cornerstone of the Republicans' 1968 "Southern Strategy;" and, Bush I's similar imagery conjured up by Republicans again with the notorious 1988 "Willie Horton ads," depicting paroled murderer Horton's mug shot.

Swint writes, "For the past 40 years, conservative Republicans just haven't known what to do with black people." (p. 32) Their policy response consist mainly of "law and order campaigns." Another alter ego consists of the "Sissy Factor," attributable to "law and order's liberal critics." Swint blames Roger Ailes for contributing mightily to this sordid phenomenon.

Also, about the Willie Horton ads "One could make the argument that the Willie Horton issue helped drive Ailes out of politics in the early 1990s,. Considerable evidence also suggests that much of Ailes' career since then has been based at least partly on the desire to exorcise the

Willie Horton demon from his past." (p. 37) Alluding to the well-known guilt-ridden complex known as the "Alfred Nobel Syndrome," Swint suggests that Fox News represented Ailes corollary to the dynamite king's founding his Nobel Prizes.

Chapter four is also titled coyly, "Machiavelli's Love Child," and opens with this quote from Ailes: "You don't have to be a patsy by sitting there allowing people to kick you and then edit your remarks to make you look like an idiot." (p.45) Niccolo Machiavelli, the legendary 16th century politician and author of the world's best-known handbook for political cunning and treachery, *The Prince,* might have produced a character such as our hero, Roger Ailes, methinks.

After all, Machiavelli advised that there was a difference between public ethics and private ethics, and that political goals and ethical considerations are not related. He described the importance of establishing a reputation of strength, and stressed the importance of subterfuge and deception." (p. 46)

"To help Bush I to shed the wimpy image dogging him through the Reagan years, and in early-1988, several sources suggest that Ailes' master stroke consisted of preparing Bush to pick an on-air fight with CBS anchorman Dan Rather, and, then to coach him gently through that hostile (and now historic) confrontation. The timing was crucial for Bush: two weeks before the Iowa caucus, neck-and-neck with his main opponent (Sen. Bob Dole of Kansas)." (p.47)

Swint elaborates further, "During the actual interview, Bush had plenty of help. According to numerous sources, including CBS Producer Howard Rosenberg, Ailes was standing nearby holding up cue cards prompting the Vice President to use certain phrases. It might have seemed like an old Mike Douglas Show flashback—Ailes stage-managing Bush's performance on live TV. In response to Dan Rather's questions, Ailes would furiously scribble down pithy comebacks and hold up the card for Bush to see. As Rather pressed, it turned into more of an argument than an interview." (p.48)

Chapter five's title proved somewhat more enigmatic, but Swint carefully teases it out for us: "Coors to You." It should be subtitled: Fox's Harbinger. Colorado beer-magnate Joseph Coors has long expressed the public view that America's news media shifted decidedly leftward in the 1960s with disastrous consequences for the country.

Swint puts it this way, "Coors was the crucial player in the emergence of the New Right during the 1970s and 1980s. In essence Coors supplied the money. During the 1960s, the Coors family became one of the most prolific and generous underwriters to right-wing causes. Included were dozens of the best-known political organizations in America. For example, the Christian Broadcast Network, Heritage Foundation, Hoover Institution, Manhattan Institute, Ethics and Public Policy Center, and the Free Congress Foundation; as well as less savory players like the John Birch Society and Neo-Nazis." (p. 60)

Lesser- known is the saga of Television News, Inc. (TVN) in 1975 with Coors money because of his "strong belief that the network news is slanted to the liberal left side of the spectrum and does not give an objective point of view to the American public." (p. 60) Furthermore, "The idea for a conservative television news service like TVN originated with Robert Pauley, a Boston investment banker sharing Coors' disdain for news media bias." (p.61) Jack Wilson was Coors' Vice President in the TVN newsroom. This debacle lasted only a few years, but went through four news directors owing to internal squabbles. Yup, one was named Roger Ailes.

Therefore, 20 years before Rupert Murdoch and Ailes successfully launched FNC, Joseph Coors, Jack Wilson, and Roger Ailes failed badly with TVN. Why? Swint cites several factors: 1.) Murdoch's deeper pockets and willingness to absorb losses; 2.) Murdoch's penchant for risk-taking;

3.) Murdoch's global distribution network; 4.) Murdoch's considerable pull with the Federal Communications Commission (FCC).

How the 1988 ad continued plaguing Roger Ailes is deconstructed by Swint in Chapter seven's "Hatching Willie Horton." Swint's chapters are all introduced with pithy quotes, this one by Lawrence Noble, General Counsel, Federal Election Commission (1987-2000), concerning claims that the FCC failed to investigate charges of illegal coordination between Roger Ailes, the Bush campaign, and creators of the Willie Horton ad: "The Commissioners wouldn't authorize a full investigation. I always thought there was more there than meets the naked eye, but we just weren't allowed to proceed." (p. 86)

Bush I staffer Jim Pinkerton came across video from the 1988 Democratic primaries in which Al Gore criticized fellow candidate Mike Dukakis as "too liberal to be elected president" because of a week-end furlough program in Massachusetts, arguably the most liberal of all states. (On the other side of the coin, I'm currently watching the Democrats drool over the unusually-ugly Republican primaries in 2012).

Swint states "Roger Ailes and Lee Atwater, Bush's campaign director, knew a golden opportunity when they saw it, and one had just fallen into their laps." (p. 87) The only question was how to exploit this gem; and the answer came in what author Swint refers to as the "two-track strategy:" 1.) Bush I's official entourage would criticize Dukakis' weak "law-and-order" credentials as governor; 2.) An extant campaign finance legal loophole allowed outside groups such Republican-backed NSPAC "to spend unlimited amounts of money on a candidate's ads." (p. 88)

About race as a "brass-knuckle wedge-issue" sans ethics, Swint details how Ailes organized focus groups in Paramus, New Jersey, involving moderate Democrats considered possible swing voters (a la Ronald Reagan). Hundreds of week-end furloughs passed without incident, but Willie Horton's surely did not. This black male brutally raped a white woman named Angie Barnes and terrorized her husband, Clifford. Swint quotes Ailes as saying to staffers beforehand, "The only question is whether we show Willie with a knife in his hand or without one." (p. 90)

Chapter eleven changes gears by contextualizing Ailes' role more widely within talk radio's brief history: "Talk Is Cheap. . . Talk Radio Is Priceless!" The unambiguous quote de jour comes from one of the genre's pioneers, Joe Pyne: "Get Off the Line You Creep!" Regarding Pyne, Swint sees a harbinger of modern in-your-face, obnoxious pseudo-TV news. Pyne's career peaked when he moved to California and became syndicated on more than 200 radio stations. A subtitle for this chapter should read: FNC: Talk Radio's natural and logical consequence.

Swint writes that "Roger Ailes' programming experiments at CNBC and America's Talking (AT) represented the first attempt to transfer what had worked on in talk radio to television. Then, when he went to work for Rupert Murdoch he essentially replicated much of this formula in developing FNC, building much of its viewership on the fan base of talk radio. Let's not forget that Ailes' first job was at a radio station where he learned what grabs a listening audience's attention." (p. 129)

I have not yet discussed Rush Limbaugh's significance described in Swint's endnote-laden tome. Self-educated, Limbaugh dropped out of Southwestern Missouri State University where his mother stated "Rush flunked everything." He hails from a small-town family rife with lawyers, which Swint interprets as stylistically revelatory of disputation.

A huge sports fan, his conservatism derives partly from a WW II-pilot father loathing Communism. Swint concludes that Rush surely has no self-esteem problems, since he often refers to himself as "Talent on loan from God." Talk radio requires long soliloquies, and some of his most tasteless ones land him in hot water. For example, when he said "Donovan McNabb was getting built up by the media because he was black;" or, "accusing Parkinson's Disease-sufferer Michael J. Fox with exaggerating the effects of the disease." (p. 132)

However, Swint turns the calendar further back to 1945 and disc jockey Barry Gray who became bored with spinning platters, and "Put a telephone to the microphone so that his audience could listen to his conversation with popular bandleader Woody Herman. It was spontaneously brilliant, and a huge hit with the listening audience." (p.. 135) His station manager concurred and they integrated the motif into their repertoire.

Liberal political scientist Kerwin Swint sketches the yawning left/right gap in American talk radio today. A June 2007 study by The Center for American Progress notes "Out of 257 news/talk radio stations nationally, 91% were conservative, and only 9% progressive." (p. 136) He cites a similar study describing roughly 100 talk radio stations in America are liberal, whereas the Rush Limbaugh program alone exceeds 600 stations. Critics either call for reinstating the now defunct Fairness Doctrine, or amending local licensing requirements to seek more diverse political opinion over the airwaves. (p. 138)

Chapter thirteen: "Fox News: A Current Affair Meets CNN" and its hook quotation cites Rupert Murdoch's retort to Roger Ailes' observation that "You know they're laughing at us" upon Fox's launch. Murdoch's unimpressed rejoinder: "They always laugh at first. That never bothers me." Swint observes that Ailes once compared watching CNN news to visiting a funeral parlor, for its "mundane, vanilla, and passionless style." (p. 155)

CNBC's prototypical program called "America Talking" was developed by Roger Ailes, and Swint notes "That programming at CNBC became, in essence, the prototype for Fox News. Ailes himself has admitted this in several interviews, and the man who hired him at CNBC to run 'America Talking' (Bob Wright) believes that it's essentially an offspring of CNBC's "America Talking." (p. 156)

Because of Murdoch's deep pockets, Fox represented the perfect storm for Ailes to replicate "America Talking" writ large. He faced none of the shortcomings saddling Joseph Coors and Jack Wilson 20 years earlier. A corrective for the news media's perceived by Coors and others as too liberal now existed.

Author Swint examines Fox personnel from top to bottom, concluding that conservatism is the glue binding them together and making "fair and balanced" represent thumbing their noses at everyone else. Ken Auletta quotes from his interview with Bill O'Reilly: "These people, not only in the print press but other network people, and some powerful people in boardrooms, are basically frightened of the Fox News Channel. They understand that the power has shifted into an organization right of center." (p. 158)

Counter-intuitively, when Auletta inquired as to whether a more accurate tagline for Fox News might be: "We report, We decide," the Big O concurred "Well, you're probably right." (p. 159) Endless examples can be cited of O'Reilly pontificating wholly incompatible policies.

Author Swint says that only Greta Susteren among Fox hosts is not overtly conservative, and I concur. Ditto for his description of Brit Hume: "Hume is the cream of the crop at Fox News—a solid journalist with a nose for the news and a sophisticated understanding of American politics." (p. 160) True for Hume earlier in his career, but sounding a tad slow these days.

Swint also discusses what I refer to as a "bevy-bleached-blonde-babes" oozing sexuality, which he also indirectly links to Fox's dominant demographic of alpha male viewers.

His last chapter fittingly deals with humor/comedy, the subject of my chapter nine. Labeled 'The Fox Follies," he opens with an old show-biz saw that "dying is easy, but comedy is hard." And you don't need to share his or my liberal palate to understand that, to date, we lefties have won this competition going away.

First, there's Comedy Central, a whole network devoted to tickling our collective funny bones. Jon Stewart's "The Daily Show" and Stephen Colbert's "Colbert Report" have been trend-setting, award-winning hits for many years. The late Mort Sahl, George Carlin, and Carl Reiner were decidedly liberal, as is Jay Leno. According to Swint, performing artists generally, and stand-up comedians in particular see the world through progressive lenses. Dennis Miller is tapped-out as FNC's go-to-guy.

Fox's trial balloon? It was sold to a skeptical Roger Ailes by executive producer Joel Surnow, called "The Half-Hour News Hour." Surnow describes himself as a "right-wing nut job" and all those alpha males at Fox must have cringed at the very notion of trying to emulate wimpy Comedy Central. "Surnow first pitched the Half-Hour comedy program to executives at Fox, who said "no." Joel trumped them by convincing Ailes to take a gamble." (p. 204) It was intended to tap into Rush Limbaugh's ditto-head army, who did one cameo appearance. It flopped quickly.

However, Joel Surnow still refuses to accept The Half-Hour's cancelation as evidence that FNC can't do humor well. He advocates a future successor, but none has appeared. In Swint's words: "All those Comedy Central shows are really funny. The Half-Hour News Hour wasn't; at least not often enough to build interest for the show." (p. 207) It mimicked a proven winner, Saturday Night Live's "Week-End Update" segment, enabling libs to own the Monday morning water-cooler forever.

RUPERT MURDOCH BIOGRAPHIES:

Kindle yields a plethora of Murdoch biographies, and I'll begin with my favorite title: Paul La Monica's, *Inside Rupert's Brain* (2009), including 8 Chapters: 1.) "Start Spreading the News;" 2.) "Crazy Like a Fox;" 3.) "Hooked on Cable;" 4.) "The Sky's the Limit;" 5.) "Wheeling and

Dealing;" 6.) "Rupert 2.0;" 7.) "The Battle for Dow Jones;" 8.) All in the Family."

I find La Monica comparing favorably to Kerwin Swint's serious scholarship. The author expresses "A desire to take a more sober and less emotional look at the controversial Murdoch's successes and failures. For better or for worse, Murdoch has transformed the news industry, Hollywood, and the rest of the media world. Often critics eventually imitate him, a fact that thrills Murdoch (the original maverick)." (p. 236)

The Dow Jones takeover, including the prestigious *Wall Street Journal,* solicits plenty of ink as the author hones his "maverick" theme. On 8 February 2007 the enigmatic Murdoch told a gathering of media executives, "We're cooling on the idea of buying Dow Jones. The *Wall Street Journal* is obviously a wonderful brand, but I don't think we'd ever get it or that they would sell it." (They=Bancroft family.) (p. 237) But his overwrought bid for Dow Jones ($5 billion) resulted in a sale quickly. Critics pondered why Murdoch would pay so much for an icon of the Old Media when his larger strategy was supposedly going digital?

Ironies pervade Murdoch's career, and La Monica luxuriate in them. Among them the apparent contradiction between Murdoch's frenetic "quest for journalistic respectability," while saddled with a stable of low-rent tabloids. Concerning the Dow Jones gambit: "Often Murdoch has quickly fallen out of love with acquired assets if they fail to grow." (p. 239) For example, News Corp purchased the Los Angeles Dodgers in 1998, ditching it six years later. Similarly gobbling up the American satellite business (DirecTV) in 2003, then selling to rival tycoon John Malone in 2006.

La Monica describes Murdoch as enamored with his image as a world-class risk-taker, which no observer can dispute. To wit, he notes that investors have almost always disagreed with the majority of Murdoch's acquisitions. And Murdoch never seems to tire of making them "eat crow." The prime example was the universal disrespect of network media experts when FNC challenged the Big Three American networks (ABC, CBS, NBC) and CNN.

Likewise, skepticism greeting his decision to take on liberal media icon Ted Turner's CNN in 1996. How could sufficient audience be generated for a second 24-hour all-news network? I remember that it struck me as a long-shot in 1996, without having any understanding then of Fox's value-added in tapping the alpha-male authoritarian demographic. Ditto for News Corp's purchase of social-networking neophyte, MySpace, which grew significantly under Murdoch (he boasts that by 2008 its profitability had grown 20-fold).

More recently, October 2007's launch of Fox Business opposite CNBC, which Murdoch criticized for "focusing on day traders and high-level financial news catering to Wall Street junkies. Fox Business, on the other hand would have more of a Main Street appeal." (p. 163)

The Nielsen Ratings refused to publish Fox Business' early statistics because they were so dismal. My view of Fox Business in 2011? The Foxymoron political agenda drives Fox Business so blatantly that it will soon fade from the scene. Its top attack dog: O'Reilly's clone: Neal Cavuto.

More publicized and more recent is veteran American journalist Michael Wolff's *The Man Who Owns the News: inside the Secret World of Rupert Murdoch* (Kindle, 2010), including a whopping 18 chapters. Wolff thanks native Aussie research assistant, Leela de Kretzer, who had worked for two Murdoch papers, for assisting in more than 120 interviews together, sat with Murdoch for 50 hours, and crossed the island nation repeatedly. Likewise with British journalist Christopher Silvester for convincing numerous people in the know to make Murdoch available. Wolff also expresses appreciation for the extensive print literature on Murdoch (KRM).

His obsession with all things KRM began with a 2007 article for *Vanity Fair* on the Dow Jones takeover. The entire KRM project required 12 months to complete. And somewhat surprisingly, he acknowledges that "None of this would have been possible without the singular cooperation of this book's subject, who not only was (mostly) a patient and convivial interviewee but also opened every door I asked him to open. He has been as helpful in facilitating this book as I can imagine any CEO ever being with a writer who owes him nothing." (p. 54)

Wolff's words about KRM's pivotal Dow Jones takeover fascinate me: "He'd started to think that his triumph in the quest for Dow Jones was an opportunity to rebrand—the kind of marketing frippery he usually disdained. He was even toying with the idea of changing the name of News Corp, that oddly boring, generic-sounding throwback to the company's earliest days—his first paper in Adelaide, Australia, was the news—to something more indicative of his and News Corp's philosophical reason for being." (p. 131)

His younger son, James, fought diligently for such a rebranding. He had pioneered News Corp's new-media initiatives during the 1990s, then taken over British Sky Broadcasting (BSkyB) operating the dynasty's holdings in the UK. Wolff observes that by the 1990s, RKM was favoring James as heir apparent. Prior to then time, he had showered praise first upon elder son, Lachlan; then on daughter Elisabeth. Also, a second marriage had produced two cute young daughters (Chloe and Grace) via his then-39 year old wife, Wendi. This was Murdoch's third trip to the altar.

Murdoch's immediate slicing-and-dicing at the *Wall Street Journal* helped exacerbate a chasm between the journalistic establishment, epitomized by the *New York Times,* and the journalistic upstarts symbolized by RKM's News Corp. During his first address to the assembled *Journal* staff, which Wolff characterizes thus: "Murdoch's intention, which he began to announce with something like a sadistic glint, was to use his new acquisition to go to war against the venerable gray lady cohabiting New York City, not the least of which was ground zero for the journalists who held him in contempt." (p. 218)

Wolff assesses Murdoch's willingness to put up with the inconvenience of extended interviews, and providing the author with endless contacts in these words: "I assume this book is part of his branding and legacy strategy—but if so, it has lacked most typical marketing or PR controls. There was no approval of the manuscript or agreement to provide News Corp with a prior look. Nor were there any restrictions on what I might ask about." (p.295)

Furthermore, RKM represents "A game but difficult interview subject. He trails off before finishing sentences; he speaks in what is frequently merely a low mumble; his Australian accent remains thick and his Aussieisms often opaque; he sometimes dips into an alarming reverie where he either naps or carefully weighs his words." (p. 304)

Wolff tries to capture Murdoch's humanity, getting beyond temptingly facile stereotypes, calling RKM both "a good gossiper," and "very shy," and a "better listener than talker." However, the author also juxtaposes these observations: "He's often disconcertingly direct or abrupt—cutting to the chase, breaking the social flow. It's a tic. It's unsocialized. Lacking any depth of self-awareness (and being impatient with what that implies), he's not all that interesting when it comes to talking about himself; he can't tell you why he does things, and has never been all that interested in that question. But he can be trenchant about other people—he possesses a snap sense of their weaknesses." (p. 355)

Again the maverick theme, "The reputation that will form around Murdoch derives not least from the impression that there is something uninvited about him—and his failure to recognize that he's welcomed, or, conversely, his enjoyment of that fact." (p. 370)

Kindle also yields Aussie journalist Neal Chenoweth's *Rupert Murdoch: The Untold Story of the World's Greatest Media Wizard* (2007), featuring even more chapters than Wolff's: 1.) "A Business of Ferrets;" 2.) "A Muddle of Moguls;" 3.) "Voltaire's Undergraduate;" 4.) "The Drunken Sailor;" 5.) "The Party Line;" 6.) "The Fugitive;" 7.) "The Pretenders;" 8.) "Lost In Space;" 9.) "Herb Allen's Porch;" 10.) "The Apple Fumble;" 11.) "Wired;" 12.) "The Poker Player;" 13.) "Divided Royalties;" 14.) "The Testing of Pat;" 15.) "Man for All Seasons; "16.) "The Mouse Wars;" 17.) "The Trouble With Tony;" 18.) "Rupert's Rocket;" 19.) "The Manhattan Window." The Introduction also includes a very detailed timeline for relevant players.

Chenoweth muses often about Murdoch's legacy in a country one-tenth the American population where the man owns 70 percent of all newspapers. "I became a Murdoch watcher because Rupert was always the best story in any Aussie town." (p. 275)

While praising HKM's back-handedly being a decent listener maybe due to his rudimentary speaking skills. "He's walking down the corridor flanked by his senior executives, and he's the one who stops to ask the guy mopping the floor about his exertions. And he's fidgeting. He's listening to you, but you know he's having at least a dozen other mental conversations of his own. You're talking to a butterfly mind that still manages a bewildering command of detail. The humor, which shows when he's sneaking up on you, is deadpan and terrifyingly funny. The man is interested in everything and nothing." (p. 327) Talk about paradox!

Like Deep Throat's Watergate admonition to "follow the money," Chenoweth opines "Murdoch hasn't achieved such immense power by accident. While he is a great media man, he remains above all a great businessman. In Murdoch's world, the money does the talking. It is impossible to understand what he has achieved and how he has gained his power without following the torturous deals that have produced them. Murdoch is a product of his finances: a creature of the cash trails that wind through the tax havens of the world before returning to the US, Europe, and Australia." (p. 383)

Next, let's check in on American journalist Sarah Ellison's *War at the Wall Street Journal: inside the Struggle to Control an American Business Empire* (Kindle, 2010), with 23 chapter, Prologue, Epilogue, and Cast of Characters.

The chapters: 1.) "The Fix;" 2.) "Cousins;" 3.) "The Unraveling;" 4.) "The Newsroom;" 5.) "Billy;" 6.) "The Chase;" 7.) "The Letter;" 8.) "The Wait;" 9.) "Personal and Confidential;" 10.) "Not No;" 11.) "Exploring Alternatives;" 12.) "Family Meeting;" 13.) "Editorial Independence;" 14.) "Decisions;" 15.) "First Day;" 16.) "Meet Mr. Murdoch;" 17.) "Interregnum;" 18.) "Chiefs;" 19.) "Taking Bullets;" 20.) "Resigned;" 21.) "Thompson's Journal;" 22.) "One of Us;" 23.) "Urgent." Based on her writing for the *Wall Street Journal*, the book draws on extensive sources.

Ellison describes deftly a monumental soiree aboard Barry Dillard's yacht in August 2007, where Dillard hosted the oddest of couples: Arthur Sulzberger, Jr.'s and wife, Gail Gregg, juxtaposed with Rupert Murdoch, and his new wife, Wendy Deng. Deng began as a 31-year old Chinese employee at Star TV in the 1990s when he was also falling in love with doing business in China.

As background, Dillard and Murdoch shared a history together since the former helped the latter start FNC in America, abandoning him when Murdoch refused to share Fox ownership with Dillard. Author Ellison waxes smoothly about that evening on Dillard's yacht:

"The guests aboard Dilllard's beautiful 118-foot cruiser knew that reality was the creation of the highest bidder. Their media empires didn't report the news; rather, they chose and shaped it. Yet tonight's stated purpose was not strictly business: At the top of the agenda was viewing Diller's new IAC (Inter-Active-Corp) headquarters from the water, with a tour to follow. Diller, a comfortable host and bit of a showman, had arranged things a week earlier. The evening light would perfectly showcase the rather controversial building, designed by architect Frank Geary to evoke eight wind-whipped sails gliding onto the river. But the strangely graceful edifice was no one's notion of the big news story that evening." (p. 114)

Diller had formerly run Paramount Pictures, and another guest was New York City Mayor Michael Bloomberg, also an ex-CEO and current owner of Bloomberg TV.

Sharing the stage that night was a $5 billion offer to buy Dow Jones, Inc., owner of the prestigious Wall Street Journal, winner of 33 Pulitzer Prizes during its 105-year existence. One of the last multi-generational newspaper families, the Bancrofts were deeply divided concerning their response.

In Ellison's words: "The purchase had ensured that the later generations of the Bancrofts were banded together, however reluctantly or tentatively." Providing context, she also points out that in 2007, Murdoch's worth was valued at $9 billion, ranking 31st on *Forbes'* list of wealthiest Americans.

As for Ellison's assessment of the Sulzbergers' suzerainty over the King Kong of serious journalism? "The year had been terrible for the Times with an ever diminishing paying readership and plummeting ad revenues; the company would end up mortgaging its headquarters to slimy Mexican billionaire Carlos Slim Helu at usurious rates of interest." (p. 149) While several of the Bancrofts came to see the purchaser as a "savior," the author refers to Gail Greg as continuing to call Murdoch "dreadful." She and husband, Arthur, met as aspiring journalists amid optimism unleashed by Woodward and Bernstein.

Wendy Goldman Rohm's 2002 book is somewhat older but useful nevertheless. *The Murdoch Mission: The Digital Transformation Of a Media Empire* includes 12 chapters: 1.) "The Dream Beam;" 2.) "Walled Garden;" 3.) "Big Guns;" 4.) "The Patent Lord;" 5.) "Rupert, James, and the Dragon;" 6.) "Patriarchs in Decline;" 7.) "Footholds ;" 8.) "On the Peak;" 9.) "Rupert and Rupees;" 10.) "In the Land of the Giants;" 11.) "Bubble;" 12.) "The Code." An apt subtext for this book might read something like "going global digitally."

She writes "Mythology about Murdoch, the man and his practices, runs rampant, but up close he is a surprising and complex individual who often defies being pigeon-holed. More than anything, he is independent; ironically, an iconoclast who traffics in icons." (p.55) I began my current chapter with little empathy for Roger Ailes or Rupert Murdoch; however, these biographies give me greater appreciation for their complexity.

Rohm traces assiduously the importance of Sky Global (his new holding company) in the Murdoch weltanschauung. He was hoping that Sky Global would represent his "integrated platform for interactive multimedia content distribution." In 2001, Murdoch attempted to acquire pay-television giant, Direct TV, owned by General Motors' Hughes Electronics, and run by Mike Smith. Murdoch's merger attempt was backed by a $70 billion offer. By this time, such behavior defined Murdoch's rapacious M.O.

Rohm labels his inner sanctum of key advisors The Big Six: COO son Lachlan; CFO David Devoe; President Peter Chernin; Chief Counsel Arthur Siskind; and Sky Global CEO Chase Cary. The author believes News Corp then was motivated by these recent mega-merger competitors: AOL Time Warner; and, Vivendi Universal. Murdoch believed his competitive advantage consisted of having adopted a truly global paradigm in 2001.

The author describes her work: "This is a story of Murdoch's difficulties, successes, and single-mindedness in the course of shaping his corporation for the new millennium—both through technology and global platforms—and tutoring his sons Lachlan and James to become leaders in the process." (p. 38) The strategy for the previous decade concentrated on Asia generally, and China specifically. But now add South Asia's India to that burgeoning list. In short order, Murdoch had captured leadership in Indian TV programming. Further, "In India, he went from being vilified as a supposed pornographer and culture destroyer to being regarded as royalty: the number one Hindi TV broadcaster." (p. 52)

Aussie journalist Denis Cryle's book, *Murdoch's Flagship,* contains six chapters: 1.) "A Wild Ride;" 2.) "Plaudits and Patrons;" 3.) "Labor's Bane;" 4.) "Liberal to Neo-Conservative;" 5.) "Turning a Profit;" 6.) "Kingmaker." It amounts to a 25-year examination of newspapers in Australia, especially what he refers to as "Murdoch's Flagship, i.e., *The Australian.*" This rear-view mirror approach explains huge changes in Rupert Murdoch, and his domestic newspaper experiences, wherein he worked out a distinctive style long before the rest of the world caught on.

Cryle describes 1975 as pivotal for nation, newspaper, and owner alike; all were influenced significantly by the disastrous American withdrawal from Vietnam. Following the government of Sir Robert Menzies, who had kow-towed to the American line, creating a "new social awareness; described by the author as entailing both internationalism over nationalism, and, diplomacy over militancy." (p. 26)

Murdoch's newspaper experienced "A dramatic reinvention from the outspoken liberal paper under Adrian Deemer to the crusading right-wing paper edited under Leslie Hollings. Yet, the rapidity and extent of this transformation, attributed to Murdoch's own disillusionment with 'bleeding heart liberal causes,' requires scrutiny." (p. 93)

"By 1989, after 25 years of daily publication, it was time for the *Australian* newspaper to celebrate. Rupert Murdoch's national newspaper had struggled financially for almost two decades before turning the corner in the mid-1980s. The toughest years had been the earliest in Canberra, where both the paper and its mission began. There was an epic quality to this compelling story, and a potent oral mythology had arisen around its young proprietor, which pervaded the 1989 event." (p. 155)

The author of *Big Shots, Business the Rupert Murdoch Way: Ten Secrets of the World's Greatest Dealmaker* (Kindle, 2002) covers some familiar turf, yet provides new insights as well. Australian journalist Stuart Crainer's book contains ten chapters: 1.) "Go With the Flow;" 2.) "Goodbye Mister Nice Guy;" 3.) "Place Your Bets;" 4.) "Lead From the Front;" 5.) "King of the Nitty Gritty;" 6.) "DNA Marketing;" 7.) "Speed Freaks;" 8.) "Think Tomorrow Today;" 9.) "Ambition Never Dies;" 10.) "Drive the Company."

Crainer writes that "Some thought that Rupert Murdoch might be consigned to corporate history's dustpan. During the dot-com bubble of the late-1990s, he appeared briefly out of step with the times. He looked older physically, and attracted less media attention, as the main action seemed to have moved elsewhere, even a peripheral figure. News Corp looked like yesterday's role model: a sprawling colossus in an age of nimble-footed start-ups." (p.23)

Crainer's opinions seem as pertinent in 2011 as when made seven years earlier concerning succession to the throne: "The media may conjecture but it is doubtful that anyone other than RKM really knows who will take over News Corp and maybe he does not know. In the meantime, Murdoch watchers can only observe the careers of the respective candidates and speculate." (p. 71)

The FNC versus CNN battle provides value-added by quoting Ted Turner's court depositions; namely "a slimy character" and "a dangerous person," after Murdoch's *New York Post* blasted Turner's wife (Jane Fonda). Turner challenged Murdoch to a public boxing match, but Murdoch used the seniority system to decline. Add humorist-turned-politician Sen. Al Franken's (D/ WI) similarly unrequited invitation to a conservative journalist and the "nerdy" stereotype attributed to liberals dissolves in its own acid.

The *News International* phone hacking scandal broke in 2011, exposing sleazy tactics by RKM's people in London, and I wasn't surprised when Charlie Rose devoted a full segment to it; or, that C-SPANN carried live coverage of Murdoch and son James testifying before Parliament for three hours of wall-to-ceiling denials. I consider FNC to have lost its ephemeral zenith, losing credibility with all but its niche authoritarian demographic.

What did surprise me on that July 2011 day, however, was the appearance of a Kindle book on the scandal by Kevin Prahl (2011), *Rupert Murdoch and the News International Phone Hacking Scandal: How it All Went Down* impresses not merely for its timeliness, but also its detail. A fine TIMELINE of the key events run from February 2010 to 19 July 2011, precisely three days before I read this excerpt.

The Introduction is entitled, "How It All Started," and begins thus: "In January 2003, Andy Coulson took over as editor of THE NEWS OF THE WORLD following the move of editor Rebekah Brooks (then Rebekah Wade) to sister paper THE SUN. Brooks had been NEWS OF THE WORLD editor since May 2000, when allegations surfaced that the tabloid had accessed the voicemail of murdered school girl Milly Dowler. In 2003, Brooks and Coulson appeared before a parliamentary committee, where Brooks admitted to paying police for information." (p. 7)

On 22 July 2011, I picked up USA TODAY (middling ideologically), whose topic was the News Corp scandal. Its own editorial was titled, "After Decades of Buccaneering, Murdoch Runs Up Against Limits," and it opened with these words: "Even the seamiest of Rupert Murdoch's tabloids couldn't make up a story juicier than the phone-hacking scandal now roiling British politics—not that they wouldn't try." (p. 3A)

It ends comparably, "As in the Watergate scandal of the 1970s, the question is: What did they and their associates know, and when did they know it? When the answers are in, the Murdochs may learn the same painful lesson that Richard Nixon ultimately did: It's the cover-up that gets you." (p. 8A)

USA TODAY also quoted from *The Wall Street Journal:* "When News Corp and CEO Rupert Murdoch secured enough shares four years ago to buy Dow Jones, Inc., this column welcomed our new owner and promised to stand by the same standards and principles we always had. That promise is worth repeating now that politicians and our competitors are using phone-hacking years at a British corner of News Corp to assault *The Journal.*" (p. 8A)

I saw biographer Michael Wolfe on TV thrice: "The hacking scandal is the perfect denouement to Murdoch's career. Hacking is not at all an aberration, or an error of judgment or strategy; rather, an expression of the company's fundamental identity." (p. 6A). Similarly Alan Rusbridger, editor of the London Guardian, in *Newsweek* "For a generation or more, British public life has molded itself to accommodate the Murdochs. As the company grew dramatically (e.g., double BBC income) and became more aggressive—a small team of criminal investigators were employed to work over anyone in public life." (p. 8A)

CONCLUSION:

I'm glad that CNN, ABC, CBS, and NBC News did not fall prey to out-foxing Fox, leaving that to MSNBC. Quoting from at least two sides of any issue, applying CTS, and selecting guests from across the political spectrum are objectives worth preserving. Best-practices bench-marking occurred during CBS' Golden Age in the 1950s, and should be emulated.

Conversely, I'm thrilled by MSNBC evolving into the left's confidently assertive tit-for-tat answer to FNC. The key word here is assertive, distinguishing MSNBC from FNC's aggressive rhetoric. Otherwise, we indeed sink to their level.

Finally, an interview by MSNBC correspondent Alex Witt with her network's President, Phil Griffin, epitomizes what I am saying. Assertive is the only word adequately describing Griffin's comments on 7 January 2012: "We don't follow, we lead;" and, "in this business you either adapt or you die;" plus, "Before 9/11, cable was largely about covering legal forums of contention as most scintillating. However, after 9/11, issue-areas became more highly politicized; and, that's when we really took off." Bravisimo.

xx. Wendy Rohm, *The Murdoch Mission* (http://www.amazon.com/Murdoch-Mission-Digital-Transformation-Empire/dp/04713836...)

xxi. WIKIPEDIA: "News Corporation Facts and Figures" (http://en.wikipedia.org/wiki/News_Corporation)

xxii. TIME MAGAZINE: (1993-08-23): "Revolution on Fleet Street" (http://www.time.com/time/magazine/article/0,9171,960821-2,00.html)

xxiii. Philip Shenon (1993-08-23) New York Times: "The Media Business: Star TV Extends Murdoch's Reach" (http://query.nytimes.com/gst/fullpage.html?)

xxiv. GUARDIAN: Guardian.co.uk (http://www.guardian.co.uk/commentsfree/2008/apr/22/chinathemedia.rupertmurdoch)

xxv. ECONOMIST: Anthony Patterson "Rupert Murdoch Laid Bare" (http://www.vision.net.au/~apaterson/politics/economist_murdoch.htm)

xxvi. BBC News: (25 March 1999), "Tax Free: Branches of Rupert Murdoch's Zero Status" (http://news.bbc.co.uk/1/hi/special_report/1999/02//99/e-cyclopedia/302366.stm)

xxvii. HOLLYWOOD REPORTER: (16 October 2007): "Fox Business Makes TV Debut" (http://www.hollywoodreporter.com/hr/content_display/news/e3i118a16d2ff59590bd77181d8da9c9fb9)

xxviii. BUSINESS WEEK: (February 2007): "Rupert Murdoch Speaks His Mind" (http://www.businessweek.com/bwdaily/dnflash/content/fcb2007/db20070208_987706htm?chan=search)

xxix. USA TODAY: (22 December 2006): "News Corp and Liberty Media" (http://www.usatoday.com/ money/media/2006-12-22-newscorp-liberty_x.htm?POE=NEWISVA);

THE AGE: 16 November 2007, "News Corp. Murdoch Trust Sells Shares" (http://www. theage.com.au/news/BUSINESS/News-Corp-Murdoch-trust-sells-shares/2007/11/16,1194 766914058.html)

xxx. FINANCIAL TIMES: (22 January 2010), Kenneth Li: "Alwaleed Backs James Murdoch" (http://www.ft.com/cms/s/0/7b0b1924-06f5-11df-b058-00144fea-bdc0.html?nclick_check=1)

xxxi. POLITICO: 30 September 2010, Ben Smith: "News Corp Gave $1 Million to Pro-GOP Group" (http://www.politico.com/news/stories/0910/42989.html)

xxxii. WIKIPEDIA: "Fox News Channel" (http://en.wikipedia.org/wiki/Fox_News_Channel)

xxxiii. ENCYCLOPEDIA DRAMATICA: Jimmy Wales, "Faux News" (http://encyclopediadramatica.com/Faux_News)

xxxiv. MULTICHANNEL NEWS: Richard Katz (1996-05), "Bold Grab for Subscriptions: Murdoch Offers $11 to Carry Fox News" (http://www.webcitation.org/5uRUOfPQa)

xxxv. NEW YORK TIMES: Mark Landler (4 October 1996), "Giuliani Pressures Time Warner to Transmit a Fox Channel" (http://query.nytimes.com/gst/fullpage.html?res=9504E3DA123FF937A35753C1A960958260)

xxxvi. ENDGADGET: Darren Murph (17 October 2008), "Fox News Turns HD on DirecTV"(http://hd.endgadget.com/2008/10/17/fox-news-turns-hd-on-directv/)

xxxvii.EBIZMBA: (1 September 2010), "15 Most Popular News Websites" (http://www.ebizmba.com/articles/news-websites)

xxxviii. NEW YORK TIMES: (15 February 2009), "For Talking Heads, A Spot to Relax and Sip Coffee on Webcam" (http://www.nytimes.com/2009/02/16/business/media/16fox.html)

xxxix. BBC: (13 August 2003), "War Coverage Lifts News Corp" (http:news.bbc.co.uk/2/hi/business/3148015.stm)

xl. PEW RESEARCH CENTER: (10 November 2010), "Press Accuracy Rating Hits 20-Year Low" (http://pewresearch.org/pubs/1341/press-accuracy-rating-hits-two-decades-low)

xli. CNN NEWS: (22 August 2003), Phil Hirschkorn, "Fox News Loses Attempt to Block Satirist's Book" (http:www.cnn.com/2003/LAW/08/22/fox/Franken/)

xlii. USPTO BOARD: (2 June 2004), "Official Documentation of Petitioned Cancellation of 'Fair and Balanced' Trademark Phrase" (http://ttabvue.uspto.gov/ttabvue/v?pno=92042790&pty=CAN&eno=1)

xliii. ASSOCIATED PRESS: (19 July 2004), Jake Coyle, "Advocacy Group Challenges Fox News Slogan"

xliv. BUSINESS INSIDER: (9 December 2010), "Leaked Fox Memo Reveals News Division Told to Echo GOP Talking Points" (http://www.businessinsider.com/leaked-fox-news-memo-reveals-news-division-told-to-echo -gop-talking-point-2010-12)

xlv. MEDIA MATTERS FOR AMERICA: (11 November 2009), "Hannity Video Switch-Up Just the Tip of Fox News' Video Doctoring Iceberg," (http://www.webcitation.org/5uRUNmQyk); MEDIA MATTERS FOR AMERICA (8 December 2010), Simon Maloy, "Fox News Fiddles With Climate Change Polling" (http://www.webcitation.org/blog/2009/2000911119/ts_ynews/ynews_ts988)

xlvi. NEW YORK TIMES: (12 October 2009), Brian Stelter, "Fox Volleys With Obama Intensifying" (http://www.nytimes.com/2009/10/12/business/media/12fox.html); and, US NEWS & WORLD REPORT (23 October 2009), "White House: Fox Pushed Team Obama Over the Brink" (http:"www.webcitation.org/5uRUSCZig).

xlvii. NEW YORK TIMES: (23 October 2009) Jim Rutenberg, "Behind the War Between White House and Fox" (http:///www.nytimes.com/2009/10/23/us/politics/23fox.html?_r=1); and CBS NEWS (23 October 2009), "President Obama's Feud With Fox News-CBS Evening News" (http://www.webcitation.org/5uRUTlhWd)

xlviii. CBC NEWS: (23 September 2009), "Fox Host Apologizes for Mocking of Canadian forces" (http://www.cbc.ca/arts/tv/story/2009/03/23/redeye-soldiers-mocking.html); and, EDMONTON SUN (14 May 2009), "Shaw Customers Allowed to Give Fox the Heave-Ho" (http://www.edmontonsun.com/news/canada/2009/05/14/9462046-cp.html)

xlix. CBC NEWS: "About the Fifth Estate" (http://www.cbc.ca/fifth/history/index.html)

l. CBC NEWS: "Sticks and Stones" (http://www.cbc.ca/fifth/sticksandstones.html)

li.   WIKIPEDIA: "Fox News Channel Programming" (http://en.wikipedia.org/wiki/Fox_Channel)

lii. WIKIPEDIA: "Roger Ailes' Career" (http://en.wikipedia.org/wiki/Roger_Ailes_Career)

liii. NEW YORK TIMES: (30 June 1988) "New Polls Show Bush Shaves Dukakis Lead" (http://www.nytimes.com/gst/fullpage/.html?res=940DE6DE1031F93 3A05755C0A96E948260); SALON MAGAZINE: Floyd Brown, "Operative Behind Willie Horton Ad," (http://www.salon.com/news/opinion/joe_conason/2008/04/25/floyd_brown); INDIANA UNIVERSITY LAW SCHOOL: (1997-03-17), "The Death of an Honorable Profession" (http://www.law.indiana.edu/ilj/volumes/v72/no2/bogus.html#N_1_).

liv. WASHINGTON POST: (19 November 2002), Lloyd Grove, "Roger Ailes-Bob Woodward Smackdown?" (http://www.washingtonpost.com/ac2wp-dyn ?pagename=article&node+contentId=A7351-2002Nov18&notFound=true); CNN ALL POLITICS: (19 November 2002), "Fox Chief tooCozy With White House?" (http://www.archives.cnn.com/2002/ALL POLITICS/11/19/ cf.opinion.fox.debate); NY DAILY NEWS: Paul Colford, "Fox News Boss Disputes Woodward's book," (http://www.nydailynews.com/archives/ news/2002/11/19/2002-11-19_didn_t_help_w_ailes_sez__fo.html).

lv.   CROWN BUSINESS: "Product Description for book by Roger Ailes and John Kraushar" (http://www.amazon.com/s/ ref=nb_sb_noss?url=node%3D154606011&field-keywords=Ro...)

lvi. James Fallows, "Learning to Love the Shallow, Divisive, and Unreliable New Media, *The Atlantic* (April 2011) p. 44.

lvii. POLITICO: (23 October 2009), Mike Allen, "Friends Pushing Ailes for President" (http://www.politico.com/click/stories/0910/fox_head_could_make_ run.html)

lviii. GUARDIAN: (27 January 2011), "Rabbis Call for Murdoch to Censure Roger Ailes and Glenn Beck for Offensive Holocaust Remarks" (http://www.guardian. co.uk/media/2011/jan/27/rabbis-murdoch-fox-glenn-beck-holocaust).

lix. NEW YORK TIMES: (25 February 2011), Russ Buettner, "Fox News Chief, Roger Ailes, Urged Employee to Lie, Records Show" (http://www.nytimes.com/2011/02/25/nyregion/25/roger-ailes.html); SALON: (27 February 2011), Justin Elliot, "The Story Behind the Roger Ailes Indictment Story" (http://www.salon.com/news/fox_news/?story=/politics/war_room/2011/02/27/ailes_indictment_story).

lx. Kerwin S. Swint, *Dark Genius* (Sterling Publishing, 2008), p. 31.

CHAPTER FOUR:

"Self-Described 'Bloviator': a.k.a. The Big O"[lxi]

BACKGROUNDER:

If you've seen any episodes of Bill O'Reilly's pseudo-news shtick (the FACTOR) you don't need to read his earlier books: *The O'Reilly Factor; The O'Reilly Factor for Kids; The No Spin Zone; Who's Looking Out for You?; Culture Wars.* However, I recommend his latest memoir, *A Bold Fresh Piece of Humanity* (Broadway Books, 2008), 256 pp., which he says "Is all about defining the experiences that have shaped my thinking, propelling me into becoming one of the most controversial human beings in the world." (p.1): As if that represents an unimpeachable public good!

As always, he exudes egocentrism here. Yet I find his braggadochio les obnoxious than on the boob tube, because of what communications scholars call paralinguistics: "The non-verbal elements of communication used to modify meaning and convey emotion, such as pitch, volume, intonation, and body language."[lxii] It requires all my scholarly discipline with the FACTOR not to: 1.) Scream at his lazy illogic; 2.)

Flash my longest finger at his image; or 3.) Email nasty words to his website.

My chapter ten features a plethora of smart O'Reilly/FNC critics. But let me know if you find another critic addressing paralinguistics enabling the suspension of disbelief prevalent among Fox's "authoritarian personality" niche. Only another interdisciplinary academician would discover the diverse relevant literatures from business, sociology, anthropology, political science, psychology, philosophy, and the humanities, getting behind Foxymoron's eye-balls.

I admire incisive book reviews written by journalist Christopher Hitchens, likewise for his recent retrospective, *Hitch 22*. Having now read O'Reilly's disingenuous navel-gazing, I muse as to whether these two contemporaries reared on different continents actually hail from separate planets. This chapter is dedicated to Hitchens' acumen for analytical rigor.

All readers really need to memorize is the first paragraph of O'Reilly's cover to swallow the hook for his narcissism: "One day in 1957, in the third-grade classroom of St. Brigid's parochial school, an exasperated Sister Mary Lurana bent over a restless young William O'Reilly and said, *'William, you are a bold fresh piece of humanity.'* Little did she know that she was, early in his career as a troublemaker, defining the essence of Bill O'Reilly and providing him with the title of his brashly entertaining issues-based memoir." His fans score a perfect 100 on the Gullibility Scale!

The "bold fresh piece of humanity" mantra is milked shamelessly by the Big O. Given his well-documented proclivity for quarter-truths aimed at half-wits,[lxiii] my first reaction is to question the quotation's veracity, since no sagacious nuns populated my Catholic schools. A natural southpaw, my lasting badge of Catholicism consists of lousy hand-writing. One of my master's degrees is in Counseling Psychology, and I officially diagnose him with Attention Deficit Disorder (ADD).

INTRODUCTION:

Even more germane to his abrasive incivility, however, is the literature emerging from the late social-psychologist Theodor Adorno's penetrating research.[lxiv] First published in 1951, then in 1993, Adorno sought answers to the perplexing appeal of Nazi anti-Semitism, pioneering interdisciplinary sharing both methods and insights from sociology and psychology. This broader literature focused on the complex interplay between anti-Semitism, prejudice, and ethnocentrism.

However, his examination of a mindset congenial to an American political niche referred to as *"the authoritarian personality,"* aptly describes FNC niche demographic. Adorno claimed that America nurtures a persistent authoritarian personality in about one-fifth of its citizens. Meshing seamlessly with Adorno's literature is contemporary feminist research on "alpha male" stereotypes among primitive thinkers. After his 2011 interview with President Barack Obama, O'Reilly coaxed a guest "expert" into referring to them both gleefully as "decidedly alpha male."

The Big O's Introduction is *modestly* entitled, "Reading This Book Will Dramatically Improve Your Life." Master of reductionism, O'Reilly blurts out the obvious early and then hammers it home: "There is little doubt that the way I think today has its roots in my traditional childhood home and in the strict Catholic schools that I attended. Therefore, we'll take an incisive look at those influences as well as other significant events in the life of O'Reilly, all with an eye toward convincing you that the point of view I bring to the world is worthy, and might even help you in your life" (p.5) Always the selfless altruist in his delusional mind!

Oiy vey! Committing the intellectual sin of *Single Causation,* only Catholic schools are credited with producing this "bold fresh piece of humanity." It may have beaten down others like me, but somehow empowered this energizer bunny on steroids. He and I grew up in suburban New York State neighborhoods clearly middle-class in composition; both of our fathers possessed college degrees, yet he repeatedly refers to his milieu as "decidedly working class." (i.e., zero privilege)

It strikes me that what got him out of Levittown, NY, consisted of several factors, but uppermost his *education* generally, not specifically Catholic. His 15 chapters deal with all manner of trivia, but none devoted to education. Also, each chapter begins with a brief quote (zero from scholars past or present). Any mention of *academics* in his book discounts the pertinence of anything they might say.

His serendipitous two-year stint teaching in a poor Miami high school did for him exactly what teaching in West Virginia did for me: kept us the hell away from Vietnam's killing fields. The Selective Service System possessed no conscience, and educated young men found ways to finesse it. O'Reilly and I were contemporaneous draft dodgers, yet he remains in full-bodied denial. Six of my best friends went to Canada and I would have joined them if drafted.

Whole books have been written on the *"chicken-hawk phenomenon"* citing a strong statistical correlation between Neo-con cheerleaders for the 2003 war in Iraq seemingly allergic to service from 1965-75, when desperately needed by their country. In the social sciences, correlation does not guarantee causation; however, by the smell test, the chicken-hawk phenomenon reeks.

THE BIG O: CHAPTER-BY-FLABBY CHAPTER

I examine key chapters in *A Bold Fresh Piece of Humanity*. This book of 247 pgs. contains zero endnotes and no index, requiring a failing grade in even my most basic college course; plus, it oozes anti-intellectualism. [lxv] Ditto for lazy thinking, the twin sister of common-sensical thinking With his deep research pockets, couldn't he come up with one lousy endnote to bolster any of his untethered bloviations? That's blatant intellectual fraud.

I refer call him as the Big O because he's only an inch shorter than the original Big O (world-class hoopster Oscar Robertson), which he exploits to lean threateningly over his pseudo-debaters wherein FACTOR participants have little time to respond to his loaded questions and ad hominem attacks. This is known as the Fallacy of Argument by Vehemence.

Secondly, I call him the Big O because he considers himself a world-class "bloviator" and Oscar Robertson was undoubtedly a world-class basketball phenom. Philosopher Don Lindsay's online ARCHIVE OF FALLACIOUS ARGUMENTS not only lists well over 50 notorious ones, but provides definitions and trenchant examples. Please see: ARCHIVE OF FALLACIOUS ARGUMENTS: http://www.don-lindsay-archive.org/skeptic/arguments.html.

When I ditched Catholicism in college I decided to minor in philosophy under a humanistic mentor, Professor Marvin Kohl, providing me with a more sane ethical system for this recovering Catholic, on the advice of my roommate, Tom Harvey, fellow recovering Catholic and southpaw. Harv was more rebellious than I, and when the good nuns tried to make him write righty, he refused and his Dad backed him up.

Coincidentally, Harv grew up in East Meadow, Long Island, contiguous to the Big O's tough "working-class Levittown" and laughs at calling Levittown anything but middle class. I also followed Harv's recommendation to minor in philosophy under, Dr. Kohl, exposing me to CTS, ditching two law school acceptances in favor of a Ph.D. to emulate my model educator.[lxvi] The last decade of my career featured using model course syllabi catalyzing CTS, which I also trace back to Dr. Kohl.

Politics:

Often the Big O explains that the "bold fresh guy" exists and thrives because he remains immutably **unaligned** regarding not only Democratic/Republican parties but liberal/conservative ideologies as well. In chapter one he writes, "Only independent thinkers can deliver unbiased appraisals of complicated problems;" (p.7) If not considered independent, the Big O's entire *raison d'etre* disappears, much like Bush II's entire foreign policy sans 9/11.

In chapter one, the Big O describes his "bold fresh guy" reaction to the ignominy of being turned down by a panel of Marist College professors because, in his words, "I was a Philistine who could not be trusted to represent the college in a sophisticated foreign country—or any other destination, for that matter." (p.16) He proudly recounts that "I'm not the kind of guy that readily accept the word no;" then, as a scribe on the school newspaper, he threatened to accuse them of "anti-Irish bias, or Levittown bias, or whatever bias I could conjure up." (p.17)

He says that they folded and he won; a disingenuously pyrrhic victory, since he didn't really want to go, later rejecting outright all criticisms of the Vietnam War's critics who assailed him in England: "I was no fan of the Vietnam War, but even at 19 years of age, I loved my country and understood its essential nobility," (p.18) and furthermore, "To this day, I believe much of the anti-Americanism in Europe was driven by simple jealousy. America is a big, loud dog that generally struts its stuff." (p. 19) I wonder if that ethnocentric sagacity also derives from a grade school nun?

For 16 years I held leadership positions in a two-time national award winning statewide interdisciplinary consortium (FACDIS),[lxvii] involving decisions concerning students applying to study abroad. Like his faculty detractors at Marist, his "Philistine problem" he raises surely would have affected me, but not as much as his ethnocentrism problem.

The fall-back position for our species has always been the easy one: go along with jingoistic de-humanization of other peoples enabling us to kill them in good conscience. The more noble posture, cultural relativism, requires more integrity and serious reflection. No book and documentary film better explain this war-enabling dehumanization process better than psychologist Sam Keen's *Faces of the Enemy* (1998).

I'm four years older than the Big O, so the Vietnam War was the signature ethical dilemma upon his return from England, yet he says "Basically I stayed out of the fray. I was back on the football team, writing for the paper, and counting the days until graduation." (p. 22) His point here is that he bought into neither the conservative flag-wavers, nor the radical SDS chorus, remaining a uniquely independent thinker. Lots of other options existed in-between the false dichotomy he poses here, known as the Fallacy of the Excluded Middle among philosophers (Assuming there are only two alternatives when in fact more exist).

For example, assuming Atheism is the only alternative to Fundamentalism; or, being a traitor the only alternative to a loud patriot."[lxiii] Actually, a worst-practices CTS textbook could be written on the fallacious arguments presented here by O'Reilly. All of the shortcomings of common sense described in chapter one as a necessary-but-insufficient condition for rationality apply here in spades. My textbook, *Through the Global Lens: an Introduction to the Social Sciences* (Prentice Hall, 2009, 3E), 464 pgs. contains about 75 illustrative case studies, including one on the "Moral Dilemma Facing Vietnam War Draftees."

SELF-RELIANCE:

Establishing his independence credentials, the Big O opens chapter two with an inane quote from rock and roller Eric Clapton: "You've been told, so may be it's time that you learned." The chapter is replete with his personal life lessons erroneously assuming they remain relevant in a very different America milieu today. He and I both came of age amongst prosperity, zero national debt, miniscule unemployment, and a robust middle class.

Today we continue reeling from the Great Recession (2008-10), near-double digit unemployment, with the rich getting richer while the poor get much poorer. Why? Massively unsustainable Republican tax breaks for the wealthiest 1% of Americans begun by Ronald Reagan and pushed over the cliff by Bush II. When the Big O came of age, journalism was expanding rapidly with commensurate job opportunities. Today even top students (which he wasn't) can't tap into a journalistic career track.

When I was hired in 1969 an equally fertile academic landscape existed. Today state budget crunches dictate anemic fringe benefits, heavier course loads, larger classes, fewer tenured positions, and reliance on adjunct professors. I don't envy my successors. Then add the baby-boom demographic, social security/Medicare expenses, and affluenza becomes an endangered species in our heartland.

One liability of common-sensical thinking derives from simple solutions for complex problems typically proving illusory. The Big O commits the Fallacy of Reductionism here habitually. In chapter two on self-reliance, he writes: "It's simple. I believe almost every American can prosper if he or she does what is absolutely necessary. That is: learn a skill and work hard. If that mantra were drilled into America's children, this country would be a far better place." (p. 39) Simplistic drivel.

Please notice the moniker of success he uses here; not good character, citizenship, ethics, or intelligence. But rather PROSPER, i.e. *mucho dinero*. Get real, Billy boy, for a staunch proponent of realpolitik that's a patently surreal conclusion. It is also fallacious reasoning to contend that just because something applied to him in the pre-globalization era applies to contemporary youngsters in what master metaphorician Thomas Friedman calls the newly "flat world."

Globalization represents another vital force about which the Big O seems utterly clueless. As I write elsewhere, "Considerable complex meaning comes wrapped up in this single word. It enrages some people while elating others. No one, however, escapes globalization's reach in the contemporary era. But that does not mean that individual and groups must remain victims of globalization, because instantaneous communication empowers us in ways impossible before."[lxix]

In my social science textbook, I cover five categories of globalization: economic, environmental, communications, military, and cultural. In addition, "common metaphors employed to pump life into this somewhat abstract concept include the global village, spaceship earth, our shrinking world, web of interdependence, world without walls, world community, vanishing boundaries, human family, global commons, and borderless athletes." (p.7)

FEAR:

Once again he wallows in worn-out clichés as if experiencing epiphanies; his prosaic opening quotation on a subject about which everyone has an opinion: *"Fear is your friend if you can control it."* CUS D'AMATO, FAMED BOXING TRAINER. Give me a friggin' break, man! 400 years of human progress since the Renaissance and Cus D'Amato represents the epitome of civilization's wisdom concerning fear?

His prosaic prose and illogic appear juvenile for a man now in his sixties. "Why am I telling you all of this? Because I believe that overcoming fear is an essential key to living a useful and honorable life. Taming fear also trains a person to stand up against injustice. This is very important." (p.51) Then, on the next page writing: "But make no mistake; to attempt righting wrongs means conflict, and you will suffer. Most people are afraid of that suffering, so most people sit it out. My father was a role model in this regard, a good man afraid to stand up."

On the following page, his specious logic warrants his labeling himself as evil:

Major premise: "Refusing to choose puts one in the evil category by default, because bad things then go unchallenged." (p.2)

Minor premise: "Some will call me delusional, but I truly believe that I was put on this earth for a reason and confronting evil is that purpose." (p.53)

Logical conclusion: O'Reilly epitomizes evil because about the ethical dilemma for our generation (the Vietnam War) he "chose to sit that one out because it was chaos;" and proved his independence by not buying into the only two ideological extremes available (warmongers vs. SDS). When in reality many other sane choices existed for those with the intelligence to choose. His own words render him evil by exposing his "refusal to choose" during a profound national crisis. (p. 60)

EVIL:

This chapter is where his narrowly self-righteous Pre-Vatican Catholicism overachieves most carelessly. For a guy who prides himself on direct expression, why use the word "truly" on page 53 regarding evil? Because it conveys his true-believer religious imprimatur concerning the sanctity of his behavior; it shows he doesn't merely believe it, but *truly* believes it, sending an important esoteric message to the authoritarian personalities who revere FNC.

His disdain for sound logic entails a Fallacy known as Pious Fraud ("a fraud done to accomplish some good end, on the theory that the end justifies the means.") He also admits here that he tones down his religiosity on the FACTOR because his job with FNC is a secular one. Apparently considering himself impervious to embarrassment after a self-evidently successful career, he comes out of the closet in this book.

When his prosaic opening quotation brings the devil into it, you know sound judgment has just left the building. He says repeatedly here that Catholic schools had the greatest impact on his successful life. So why not quote some sage Catholic theologian about the devil/evil nexus? Instead, he uses the Eagles rock group's song "Somebody": "No one knows about the times you've had, you've been so evil, you've been so bad, There's the devil to pay for what you've put them through, and you've got a feeling someone's following you." (p. 61)

The Big O quotes from his earlier book, *Culture Warrior*, which he wrote in response to critics ridiculing his "War on Christmas" campaigns. But concerning evil in his retrospective, he lays out a classic Straw Man Fallacy "Some people do not acknowledge evil at all. For them, it doesn't exist." (p. 64) Oh, really? If so, tell us which people? The term "some people" seems gutlessly vague to me. If he is correct, his deep Fox pockets should be able to cite one example! I know that I certainly don't believe what he suggests. Without this deeply flawed assumption about "some people," his whole chapter about evil collapses into self-fulfilling prophecies.

In a rare reflective moment, he observes that "My definition of evil, like just about everything about me, is simple and straight-forward" (p. 59), which likely works well with simple-minded FACTOR viewers, but clashes with the hard reality that we live in a universe both ineffably complex and sublimely aesthetic (both of which the Big ignores). An hour surfing the Internet's Hubbell space photos would neatly snuff the simple-minded, commonsensical viewpoint about the cosmos. No gray areas, nuance, or ambiguity exist in the Big O's *weltanschaung*.

He ends the chapter thus: *"You either fight active evil or you accept it. Doing nothing is acceptance. There is no in between."* (p.67) So, according to the Big O, you either is, or you ain't. No gradations along a spectrum of good/evil? Franklin Roosevelt, Lyndon Johnson, Richard Nixon, Bush I, and Bush II all lied to us about their reasons for war. However, I would rank-order FDR's as least egregious; then Bush I; then Nixon; then Bush II; then Johnson as most egregious. CTS require that we make thoughtful qualitative judgments in all areas of life. Common-sense forever remains a necessary-but- insufficient condition for rationality.

RELIGION:

The Big O insults other educated readers in this chapter by incorrectly assuming that his little slice of conservative Catholicism is all one needs to know. This intellectual sloppiness is compounded by his complete ignorance about the vital distinctions between religiosity, spirituality, and ethics. This kind of tautological argument commits the intellectual sin of Begging the Question ("Reasoning in a circle").

I experienced a balanced public/private education, better contextualizing the pre-Vatican II Catholicism that the Big O clings to so tenaciously. He has the balls here to criticize "lapsed Catholics" who bolted during the endless sexual abuse cases in recent decades. He rationalizes conveniently distinguishing between the nobility of the Church and some evil persons deserving punishment. Presenting one side of any issue is known as the Fallacy of Argument by Dismissal ("An idea is rejected without saying why"), and he basks in it here.

A more sophisticated explanation for *priestly abuse* than the specious "few bad apples argument," is two-fold: 1.) The centrality of the confession ritual exonerating sinners with a few hail Maries rather than medical rehabilitation; and 2.) The celibacy rule (adopted in the twelfth century for strictly economic reasons). Could it be any more obvious that the rarity of abuse by married Anglican priests or Jewish rabbis or Muslim imams screams out at us?

Concerning my balanced schooling, I did K and first-grade in an "old school" Catholic setting in Buffalo, NY. Too young to object, I obeyed the nuns' Draconian orders, including chucking my left-handedness to write "properly." My subsequent lousy writing I can live with and forgive.

However, I spent grades 2-8 in a sophisticated campus school attached to the college my Dad had attended. My experiences there were uniformly healthy and our Church-going experiences benign enough that I wasn't prepared for my Catholic High School where I ended up in Father Edward

Coyne's (*a sadistic alcoholic*) freshman religion class for the entire year. Early on, I remember a classmate named Dennis Wilson being forced to kneel in front of the class for an entire period. His sin? He said, "Yes, sir" to the priest not "yes, father." Whose bleary-eyed response was: "Who do you think you're addressing? A Protestant Minister?"

Coyne belted out the "hellfire" theme, my first exposure, and it really scared me. Hell had been strictly an abstract concept to me earlier, but not during my year with this sadist. My interaction with girls up until then was normal and wholly without guilt. Coyne changed that sufficiently for a few classmates to label me "The Puritan." Like the Big O, I played four sports, was class president, and not homely. I won a combined award for citizenship/scholarship, but the more apt award would have been for fewest kisses experienced.

These words from Big O require no riposte: "Somehow I recognized that Catholicism was basically a good thing, even though some of the people associated with it were loons. Unlike many, I never equated crazy priests and mean nuns with the core tenets of the faith. I just thought they were bad employees. I never took their nuttiness and applied it to Jesus or even to the Pope. To my limited mind, Jesus came off as a pretty good guy. He ran around healing people, was nice to his mom, and even forgave the savages who nailed him to the cross. As the song says: Jesus is all right with me." (p. 71)

Our utterly rebellious "bold fresh piece of humanity," however, folded when his mother insisted that he become an altar boy (the most frequent abuse-recipients.) "To be an altar boy, she *really* wanted that. And even though memorizing a bunch of Latin prayers and getting up at six in the morning to kneel on a cold marble altar was not my idea of a great time, I did what my mother wanted with a minimum amount of whining." (p. 70)

He concludes this bizarre chapter with: "The end-game, of course, is to earn God's reward in the afterlife by rejecting evil. And in Catholicism and other Christian religions, the actions of Jesus demonstrate how to do that." (p. 88) His use of the words "of course," here qualify for the parochial Fallacy called Not Invented Here ("Ideas from elsewhere are made unwelcome").

The Big O hints at divine inspiration in his Catholic fundamentalism the same way Bush II waxed about his Protestant fundamentalism more than once. Okay, apparently being born-again saved Bush II's marriage and spurred a personal rebirth after 40 years spent unimpressively. When asked if he ever consulted Bush I about politics, Bush II's straight-faced response was: "I consult with a higher power."

RELIGION PROPERLY CONTEXTUALIZED:

My social science textbook includes an eight-page discussion of religion as a social institution based on more than 30 endnotes, and I paraphrase snippets from it here. Religion comprises one of the five pivotal social institutions (along with the family, education, economics, and politics).

Diverse answers to the question of *why* religion exists as a cultural universal are provided by three sociologists: 1.) Emile Durkheim believes that religion performs an integrative function binding believers into a coherent social whole; 2.) Edward Tylor expresses a more direct answer explaining humanity's need to explain a bewildering world; 3.) Bronislav Malinowsky emphasizes religion's ability to allay our death anxieties as the only one of 1.8 million species on Earth who ponder our mortality.

While specific religions vary tremendously, they all entail belief in some form of metaphysical power, most often involving an image of a higher spiritual entity, opinions about an afterlife, ethical codes of conduct, and a sacred place of worship. Therefore, religions usually share beliefs (faith) that certain things or (ideas) are sacred; practices (rituals) based on sacred beliefs, and a moral community (church) stemming from that group's beliefs and practices.

Rituals bring believers into closer contact with the sacred. When Muslims face Mecca to pray, or Catholics go to confession, or Jews participate in a bar mitzvah, or Hindus bathe in the Ganges River, an internal logic renders these activities spiritually meaningful for participants, but opaque to outsiders. Increasingly, rituals from disparate religions find themselves lumped together. For example, the Chamulas of Mesoamerica borrow the worship of celestial objects from the ancient Mayans merging it with worshipping Jesus Christ from the conquistadores. This is especially pronounced wherever *colonialism* has imposed new religions forcefully.

Recorded human history dates back to the Agricultural Revolution, ten millennia ago. Anthropologists trace physical evidence of religious rituals back at least 40,000 years. Early hunting/gathering societies practiced *Animism* (the belief that natural objects make up part of a spiritual world, of which the sun, moon and stars represent reverential objects). Attempts to communicate with ancestral spirits also permeate animist rituals.

Following on the heels of the Agricultural Revolution were ancient civilizations in places like Egypt, Persia, Greece, and Rome. These societies shifted dramatically away from nature to a more abstract pantheon of gods, called *Polytheism* (Recognition of numerous gods without considering any of them as supremely ordained). Some gods, such as Vishnu, the creator god in Hinduism, are impersonal. Others take on a more anthropomorphic (humanlike) countenance. Anthropomorphism reaches its zenith during the past 2,500 years with the flourishing of *monotheistic* religions (Judaism, Christianity, Islam).

Counted globally, the number of religions runs into the thousands. United Nations data suggest that about 80 percent of world population profess some kind of religious beliefs, two-thirds of whom report practicing their faith actively. Table 7.1 identifies world religions on a percentile basis. Clearly, the Big O's Catholics comprise less than one-fifth of believers worldwide.

TABLE 7.1: WORLD RELIGIONS

Roman Catholics	18.7%
Muslims	18.3%
Nonreligious	16.3%
Hindus	13.5%
Other Christians	8%
Protestants	6.9%
Buddhists	6.0%
Other religionists	4.7%
Atheists	4.2%
Chinese fold religionists	2.6%
Sikhs	0.4%
Jews	0.2%
Confucians	0.1%
Shintoists	0.1%

Social institutions evolve, with an overall decline in religious author-ity, has led to *secularization* in pluralistic societies (accompanied by declining church attendance.) Less able to justify beliefs and practices as traditional religion's sphere of influence shrinks, CTS helps in sort-ing through seclarization's challenges. This doesn't diminish the human need for spirituality, it's just that traditional fit between religiosity and spirituality has loosened enormously. Sociologist Robert Bellah describes America's separation of church and state producing what he calls *"a civil religion"* based on nationalism, American exceptionalism, and emotive symbols like the American flag.

The global trend towards secularization has produced its own back-lash—namely, the revival of fundamentalism. Ronald Reagan success-fully tapped into this sentiment during the 1980's. That era also saw a new "electronic church" linking mass television and radio audiences in ways profitable to a new class of evangelists. The electronic churches faltered, however, when Jim Bakker paid blackmail to a woman he had a sexual liaison with and was imprisoned in 1989 for defrauding his con-tributors.[lxx]

A profound dilemma consists of religion constituting a cultural universal, therefore not dismissible; however, humanity's first try (Animism) strikes me as more credible and functional than its successor (Polytheism), or the current paradigm (Monotheism). Animism springs directly from human experience via sheer physicality; whereas its successors emanate from wild human imaginings: Polytheism seems too confusing; Monotheism too fantastical to me.

Significantly, humans have historically worshipped two completely dif-ferent types of divinities: the Transcendent God versus the Personalized God. For me, the personalized God makes sense only to explain its thor-ough anthropomorphism. How convenient that He/ She/It as the spitting image of us!

As inhospitable conditions around the universe are revealed by scien-tists, the sublime beauty of our sacred turf not only to be nurtured, but worshipped. Animist religions boldly trump both of their successors in this respect. And, of course, Monotheism's Big Three have proven awful stewards of planet Earth. Our species' greatest achievement (CTS/science) suggests that dichotomizing science and religion remains naive at best, and utterly false at worst.

Why? Because scholars like Garrett Leacy hypothesize that science will ultimately solve the remaining mysteries; in other words, through "Divine Geometry" God will show up in the equations, producing the elusive "Theory of Everything" sought by Einstein. Laurentian University neurologist professor William Lattimer conducts experiments with a "God Helmet," targeting the brain's right-temporal lobe with electrical stimulation accompanied by a "God Experience," in more than 80% of his subjects.

Doesn't CTS/Science represent the only paradigm worthy of 21st Century humanity, rendering Bill O'Reilly's pre-Vatican Catholicism ineffably primitive?

SAVING THE WORLD:

Back to the life of O'Reilly, the Big O entitles this chapter to mock idealists like me naïve enough to devote entire careers to educating young people. He spent only two years teaching in a tough Miami neighborhood that made Levittown look like East Hampton. As usual, he resorts to the Fallacy of Single Cause and the Fallacy of Reductio Ad Absurdum by crediting Divine Intervention with landing him a two-year stint at Monsignor Edward Pace High School: "God does have a sense of humor, no question. After watching me terrorize teachers for years, the Almighty dropped a teaching job right into my lap. And you say you don't believe? The year was 1971." (p. 89)

That year fell mid-way in America's longest war (ten years) until recently surpassed by Afghanistan. Rather than the Deity, I think the Big O should be thanking his local draft board in Levittown, NY. His teaching stint bought him time until the lottery system was instituted. And a mere two years at Monsignor Edward Pace sufficed for the Big O to develop firm convictions about high school teachers' delusions about "saving the world." He describes himself as the exception to the norm of permissive instructors incapable of disciplining their unruly classrooms (ad nauseam: the bold fresh guy).

Photos in this chapter all include him wearing *stylishly-long hair*, but shouldn't Mr. Independent sport a traditional short brush-cut, since he's immune to fads? A picture on page 91 is captioned: "I brooked no nonsense. If a kid clowned around, he or she was sharply warned. Second time, an appropriate sanction was swiftly delivered to the miscreant."

And later, "many of the other teachers at Pace presided over undisciplined classroom environments that wasted time and accomplished little." Surprise, surprise, the Big O then goes ego tripping, "I realize that might sound self-righteous, but that's how I saw it. I was getting paid to do a job, and no defiant kid was going to stop me. Period." (p. 94) I love the definitive one-word closer: "Period."

Then he uses the title to chide deluded losers mired in public education. "During my two years teaching high school, I learned an enormous amount about life, liberty, and the pursuit of happiness. But one lesson stands all the others: you can't save everyone." (p.98) It was fortuitous that his *draft-dodger teaching stint* produced such erudition, Why? Because lessons learned in Vietnam would be hellishly more brutal—kill or be killed!

CONSERVATIVES VERSES LIBERALS:

As if he hadn't already beaten the God card into the ground, his quotation for this chapter reads, "One nation under God, indivisible." THE PLEDGE OF ALLEGIANCE

The text begins: "Not too many liberals lived in my Levittown neighborhood; this was not a place for progressives. Many of the denizens were

former military, and almost all had attended the school of hard knocks."
(Except for the Big O, who dodged the draft and enjoyed a private school
education). In seventeen years there he recalls only two liberals. (p.129)

Later he observes dryly that "Levittown, by design was all white. The real
estate agents simply would not sell to blacks." (p. 133) Again belaboring
the obvious, he intones that "Levittown is working-class territory. Few
there are exploring a move to San Francisco."(p.134)

In this chapter he repeats the absurdity that he's uniquely qualified as
courageous enough to stand up against evil; yet he remained unaligned
throughout the 1960's cultural revolutions (consisting of more than just
the Vietnam War), and in his own words "I sat that one out." He recently
wrote a book called *Culture Warrior,* yet at the time when his core values
were being severely challenged in America, he remained somehow nobly
above the fray.

"So, as the late 1960s roared on, both sides held little attraction for me.
The conservative side was angry and sometimes bigoted, and the liberal
side equally angry and often hateful toward their own country. With neither choice appealing, I remained on the sidelines, swimming, running,
huffing, and puffing. Looking back, I'm glad I stayed unaligned." (p.134)
Each side was angry, therefore his response was opt out? What characterizes the Big O schtick on the FACTOR as poignantly as red, raw anger?
Yet during this crisis, he cowers from a bifurcated America? With forty
years' hindsight he's still glad he blinked. Also, I should be constantly
referencing his serial Fallacies of the Excluded Middle.

His token stab at introspection occurs on page 135, where he chucks the
ludicrous moniker of non-aligned journalist motivated solely by bringing evildoers to justice *"As for me, the bold fresh guy, I now am branded a
conservative by some in the crazed, dishonest, ultraliberal media, and do you know
what? That's fine with me. As stated, I hold many traditional, conservative
views and am proud of them."* (p.135)

While vociferously denying ideological identity in countless contexts, by conflating "traditional" and "conservative" as synonyms here (which they surely are not) he tries to finesse the logical inconsistencies leaking from both his book and his well-documented track records on the issues. Note the sleazy name-calling: "crazed, dishonest, ultraliberal media" with zero grounding in specifics. Also, the Fallacy of Begging the Question runs rampant.

He engages in the Fallacy of Argument by Dismissal ("Crazed, dishonest, ultraliberal media"); The Fallacy of Victimhood ("Innately unfair attacks on him"); Ad Hominem personal attacks on his critics not their actual words)–mighty difficult with zero endnotes? Plus, rampant name-calling (appealing to the simple-minded); also, the Fallacy of Hypothesis without Evidence (by calling the general news media self-evidently ultraliberal); Fallacy of Victimhood (poor O'Reilly besieged by ignoble critics). Leading these ignoble forces, confidently claims the Big O, is the faceless scourge of ultra-liberalism.

Concerning global warming: "My take again is simple: only the Deity knows if the current warming trend on earth is man-made or part of a long-term natural cycle. To debate the cause of global warming is a complete waste of time." (p.141)

This passage reveals several fallacies: Having Your Cake ("Almost claiming something, but backing out"); Fallacy of Factual Error ("The presence of one error of fact often means others will be uncovered"); Fallacy of Inflation of Conflict ("If scholars debate a point, they must know nothing"); Stacking the Deck ("Using the arguments that support your position, but ignoring or somehow disallowing the arguments against"); Arguing to the Future ("Arguing that evidence will someday be discovered which will someday be discovered supporting your viewpoint"; Poisoning the Well ("Discrediting sources used by your opponent"); Argument By Dismissal ("An idea rejected without saying why"); Poisoning the Wells ("Discrediting the sources used by your opponent.") See ARCHIVE OF FALLACIES.

The Big O's "only God knows" may have sufficed as humanity's best guess during the bleak Middle Ages, when Catholicism monopolized the intellectual roost. But more than a few things have happened during modernity: for example, unearthing of Greek Rationalism by Muslim Scholars; The Renaissance; Enlightenment; Scientific Revolution; Industrial Revolution; Critical-Thinking-Skills (CTS) leading to impressive research at thousands of universities worldwide.

HEROES AND ZEROES:

He justifies the unethical *"ambush"* endemic to the FACTOR: "If you watch the FACTOR these days, you know that we often 'ambush' bad guys: that is we arrive with cameras rolling and confront them with tough questions." And, "To some a TV ambush is a controversial technique, but I believe it is absolutely necessary. We live in a time when powerful people can hide behind hired spinners and concrete walls, evading scrutiny for evil deeds. Villains can easily say 'no comment' and avoid explaining their destructive actions. This is not okay." (P. 148)

The emotionally-loaded term "bad guys" is a cop-out demonizing supposed miscreants without explaining why. Militaries lead the league globally turning adversaries into enemies in order to kill them (otherwise a cultural taboo for humans). Also, he didn't like it at all when paparazzi hounded him relentlessly over his sexual harassment lawsuit. And who gets the right to identify reputed "bad guys?" The Big O oozes hypocrisy in justifying FNC "ambushes."

Washington Post journalist, Howard Kurtz, covers all of the sordid details in a comprehensive article entitled, "Bill O'Reilly, Producer Settle Harassment Suit: Fox Host Agrees to Drop Extortion Claim."[lxxi] Kurtz writes that "Concerning the lurid details of what *Andrea Mackris* alleges were phone-sex conversations between them. On the FACTOR, O'Reilly asked fans not to believe everything you hear and read."

He thanked FNC and FACTOR fans for not abandoning him: "You guys looked out for me and I will never forget it. This brutal ordeal is now officially over and I will never speak of it again." However, while he asked that we not believe everything we hear, he may have a harder time requesting suspension of disbelief for what fans might *see* online these days. The Big O didn't know at that time that lurid tapes and transcripts would later materialize online. Google "Sexual Harrassment and Bill O'Reilly" and you'll plenty to see and hear. Finally, he invokes in this passage the Fallacy of Victimhood ("Subject deserves sympathy because he has been treated unjustly by someone else.")

His riposte of FNC's most assertive competitor, MSNBC (Microsoft being the MS part merged with NBC News, owned by General Electric) wallows in hyperbole. "A few years ago, some commentators on the MSNBC cable network launched personal attacks on Fox News personnel, the Bush Administration, and other Americans they considered on the conservative side. The attacks were vicious and unprecedented. Never before had a network used such slander and defamation on a regular basis. The reason for this foray into the gutter was business, pure and simple. MSNBC was losing big time in the ratings to Fox and CNN. Simply put, the network's performance was embarrassing to NBC and big daddy General Electric didn't like it. . . . That's when MSNBC decided to go into the hate business. You've heard a million times that 'sex sells,' well so does rank hatred to a given demographic." (p.150)

The Big O's assertion about MSNBC's attacks as "vicious and unprecedented" are rendered absurd by O'Reilly's SOP: alpha-male bullying to peddle hatred. As for corporate sponsors influencing the contemporary news business, pristine days of real separation between news and entertainment have been replaced by what scholars call "infotainment:" epitomized by FNC's "gazundheits" to Rupert Murdoch's every sneeze. Fact and fiction meld seamlessly into faction at Fox, enabling *suspension of disbelief.*

As a liberal, I'm thrilled that MSNBC has assumed a confidently assertive (not aggressive) role counter-vailing FNC. By 2011, MSNBC had found its groove. Not bound by three networks or CNN's objectivity, analysts like Rachel Maddow, Darren Ratigan, Rev. Al Sharpton, Ed Shultz, Martin Bashir, and Lawrence O'Donnell can opine effusively. And, while corporate investors worry about ratings, I don't. Most entertaining for me is little-known Rachel Maddow because of her ballsy humor, intelligence, articulate prose, poised delivery, and integrity.

I watch the News Emmys on CSPAN every September, and in 2011, Rachel won in her category. I believe in the significance of best-practices bench-marking by professional peers: whether it's the Oscars, Emmys, or Statewide/National Exemplary Professor awards. Likewise for academia's guarantor of excellence for everything from publications, educational grants, Fulbright Awards, and tenure: blind peer review.

Back to the Big O, he closes this chapter claiming a bogus *"fail-safe"* against that most human of all traits (believing one's own bullshit): "I fully understand the danger of losing perspective, of seeing evildoers hiding in my closet. Luckily, I believe that I've developed a fail-safe way of keeping a realistic outlook and not becoming a dragon-slaying loon. My magic potion: old friends." (p.154)

That's cute, but inconsequential since camaraderie-based groupthink constitutes another cultural universal well documented by scholars, rendering his "fail-safe" ruse laughable. Hopefully, the FACTOR'S deep research pockets will expose him to the leadership of social psychologist Irving Janis on groupthink.[lxxii] Evidently, none of his "fail-safe buddies" minored in philosophy like me. The fail-safe concept was developed around the profoundly vital issue of nuclear security and I resent his pinching it here for such pedantry.

Three vastly superior reality checks occur in academia: 1.) the CTS superior to common sense; 2.) Fallacy Archives and books; [lxxiii] 3.) Blind Peer

Review (inter-subjectivity) whereby one's assertions are assessed by multiple anonymous experts. The regular working-class guy from Levittown has three higher education degrees from Marist, Boston University, and Harvard (the latter he has criticized as a "haven of pin-headed elitism"). My question to him: "Why does he remain so willfully ignorant of the intelligentsia's bounty?"

POWER:

The Big O fails to recognize the subtle continuum between power and influence, buying into dichotomous either-or thinking. In his words: "Let's begin the power presentation with the president I know best. Three times I have interviewed George W. Bush, and here is my assessment: I believe he is an honest man. I believe his presidency was challenged by extraordinarily difficult circumstances that only a few other chief executives have ever faced. The terror attack on September 11 instantly changed the world, introducing a complex set of unique circumstances to Americans. Understanding that, I do cut President Bush some slack, unlike many in the media." (p. 193)

Wow! The bold fresh guy never shilling for the powerful could have taken his profound analysis directly from White House press releases since this is precisely the party line spewed out by Bush II *ad infinitum*. Couldn't an experienced journalist at least have added a few original words and arguments of his own? Does he believe the rest of us were asleep for eight years? More extraordinarily difficult circumstances that George Washington, Thomas Jefferson, Abraham Lincoln, Ulysses S. Grant, FDR, or Lyndon Johnson?

Senator Chuck Schumer (D-NY) presciently said that "Coupling 9/11 with any verb is all the Republicans believe they need to justify their policies." Richard Clark ,longest-serving National Anti-Terrorism Adviser in U.S. history, does more than hint that Bush II was the sloppiest of all his presidents and clearly inattentive for several months before 9/11, in his memoir. .

Groovy man! 9/11's unique disaster occurs early in Bush II's watch; neo-conservative hawks who subsequently became policy-makers write policy papers excoriating Clinton for squandering what Charles Krauthammer boldly labels "America's uni-polar moment" post-Soviet Union; and their hawks accused Clinton of *self-inflicted weakness.*

It's the role of the loyal opposition to offer policy options, but it amazes me how blatantly the Republicans called for bellicosity as the answer to all of their problems. Yet, the mainstream media not only passed on reporting this prophetic paper trail then, but continue doing so in 2011. Why are these undeniable facts ignored and Bush II given a free-pass on the trivial matter of 9/11?

I think it's because we have a "duopoly" in America, whereby each party takes its turn feeding at the public trough unaccountably. The only system worse than a "duopoly" is a "monopoly," but that sets the best-practices bar pitifully low. In absolutely no three-party, or multi-party system, do we find comparable looking the other way. Clinton was impeached for a B.J., and Obama won't even consider impeaching Bush. It's not that Obama is immune to piling on, it's that he merely exudes the patience of a "duopoly."

National Geographic Channel did a 2009 documentary on the "9/11 Truthers" clinging to disproven, bogus theories about 9/11. They conclude that these few observers who have remained steadfastly implacable about clinging to false hopes is best explained as case studies in aberrant psychology, and I think that analysis holds up very well. But since Bush II stonewalled completely about 9/11, no wonder scores of wild conspiracy theories flourished!

CTS helps to discern the gold from the gunk, and those labeled "Truthers" by National Geographic's documentary got mired in gunk. Not that some gold doesn't exist in the same neighborhood. Bush II"s neo-cons possessed both motive and opportunity to realize the Holy Grail of global military hegemony (i.e., Empire).

The Big O summarizes the Iraq War thus "In fact, the mantra that Bush 'lied' about Iraq is itself a lie and completely absurd on its face'. . . . Of course, the WMD intelligence turned out to be wrong, but there's a big difference between a mistake and a lie.... It is important to remember what happened there (Iraq): America did nothing immoral by removing a murderous dictator who had violated the First Gulf War cease-fire 17 times, and who was hell-bent on causing trouble for America. No, the USA did not fail morally; we just weren't very smart in anticipating the complexity of the Iraqi battlefield." (pp. 194-95.)

Yikes! Lies and mistakes do not vary ethically in gravity? Scholars had cited Saddam Hussein among the 50 most-egregious dictators in world, but never among the top ten. What expertise enables the Big O to consider Saddam among the very worst? If so, PARADE magazine's annual list would have at least included him in their top ten. And what does "hell-bent on causing trouble for America" mean exactly? So should we also take out Hugo Chavez, Fidel Castro, and Robert Mugabe? Actually, Bush II's neocons figured out the battle-field quite well, it was Iraqi politics about which they proved will-fully ignorant.

Concerning WMD and Iraq, veteran journalist Danny Schechter's trench-ant book and documentary film are brilliant: *Embedded: Weapons of Mass Deception: How the Media Failed to Cover the Iraq War* (Prometheus Books, 2003), 286 pp. To wit: "there were really two simultaneous wars involv-ing WMD, one fought by armies of soldiers using bombs; the other a shadow war employing cameras, satellites, and armies of journalists spewing Pentagonese."[lxxiv] Schechter also heads Globalvision.org, an international media company producing newsmagazines, documentaries, and TV specials.

BBC journalist and author of *The Best Democracy Money Can Buy*, Greg Palast, reviewed *WMD*: "Once again, Danny Schechter has the goods on the Powers That Be. This time he's caught America's press puppies in *flagrante delicto* embed with the Pentagon. Schechter tells the tawdry tale of the affair between officialdom and the news boys—who, instead of covering the war, covered it up. How was it that we saw the liberatees only from the gun hole of an Abrams tank? Schechter explains this lubricious twist as the creation of a frightening new Military-Entertainment-Complex (MEC)."

Finally, regarding an off-the-record interview the Big O had with Bush II, he opines: "In the dining room adjacent to the Oval Office, we talked for about 30 minutes. I was impressed by the President's knowledge and analysis of history. He clearly believed his tough strategy against Islamic extremists had prevented further attacks on U.S. soil and that history would vindicate the Iraq campaign. You can decide about the President's belief. But I can tell you that personally, he seems to be a very good guy." (p. 196) How pertinent is whether a President "seems to be a nice guy" in a private interview with a biased journalist? Wow, this fallacy is called the Argument by Personal Charm ("getting the audience to cut you slack unjustifiably, a variant of schmoozing").

Finally, a website dedicated to mocking FNC's constantly-growing-news-nose also solicits funds for boycotting FNC can be found at: http://www.foxnewsboycott.com/featured/donations/ and sells other good-ies like FAUX NEWS t-shirts, TV-GONE pocket-sized zappers, and results from online surveys. The last one asked respondents: "Who is the worst Fox News personality," with these results: Glenn Beck (47%); Sean Hannity (27%); Bill O'Reilly (19%); Shepard Smith (3%); Greta Van Susteren (2%); Neil Cavuto (2%).

CONCLUSION: PREDICTABILITY

So, if "the bold fresh guy" is by definition fiercely independent, why are his FNC-ish views so predictable on all these issues?

Gung-ho cheerleader for wars; opposition to TARP; unemployment insurance; cuts in Pentagon budget; homophobia; START treaties; American exceptionalism; global warming; dismissive of Human Rights organizations; dismissive of spiritualities not part of a religion; anemic criticism of Enron executives; apologist for bloated CEO salaries; increased spending on education; foreign aid; Exxon Valdez disaster; species extinction; $=measure of success in life; global debt forgiveness; bailing out GM; anything to do with France; role of Comedy Central; academicians; Oliver North and arms-for-hostages; explanation for Communism's collapse in 9 of 13 countries; the American Empire; cultural relativism; judicial activism; the United Nations; affirmative action; nobility of Cold War; Feminism=Nazism; capital punishment.

Obamacare; Racial profiling; multilateralism; mainstream media bias; Obama the Socialist; sending US troops to the border; euthanasia; immigration policy; English-only policy; sufficiency of common sense; The Dream Act; progressive taxation; US as God's chosen nation; Vietnam Era chicken-hawks; questioning wars as self-evidently unpatriotic; draft dodgers in Canada; the faith/policy nexus in American politics; waterboarding; The Patriot Act; Guantanamo Bay detainees; liberals as Communist sympathizers; self-reliance necessary-and-sufficient condition for success in today's America; political correctness; anti-bullying programs in schools; C-SPAN; NPR; PBS; lapel flag indicative of patriotism; reflective thought respected; endnotes are for nerds.

CTS enables rank-ordering criteria-laden variation; therefore, below find my FNC stars (past and present) according to BRAGGADOCCHIO PARALINGUISTICS: [lxxv]

BRAGGADOCCHIO PARALINGUISTICS:

The Big O (self-described "bloviator;" a.k.a. Bill O'Reilly)

Arizona wannabe (a.k.a. Lou Dobbs)

"Obama is a racist and a socialist" (a.k.a. Looney tunes; a.k.a. Glenn Beck)

Informed viewers 12 times in three months "I'm a Catholic," (a.k.a., High-T Alpha male; a.k.a. Sean Hannity)

"Baseball bat only way to converse with Libs" (a.k.a. Neil Cavuto)

Fear-voice maestro (a.k.a. Shepard Smith)

Obesity on steroids (a.k.a. Rush Limbaugh)

Bush II's lonely surrogate brain (a.k.a. Karl Rove)

"Why didn't Timothy McVey finish with the NEW YORK TIMES building?" (a.k.a. Ann Coulter)

Second-wife wants him neutered (a.k.a. the Newt-Meister)

"Don't retreat, reload" (a.k.a. Sarah Palin)

"I've never, ever sexually harassed anyone" (a.k.a. Pinocchio; a.k.a. Herman Cain)

"Iraqi oil will pay for the war" (a.k.a. Darth Vader; a.k.a. "I just shot my friend in his face")

"You're either with us or against us" (a.k.a. Chicken-hawk In-Chief; a.k.a. "I'm the DECIDER)

"People keep saying I'm similar to Margaret Thatcher" (a.k.a. Michelle Bachmann)

Luxuriant facial-hair overachiever (a.k.a. Geraldo Rivera)

July 4th Resurrections (a.k.a. Oliver North)

Low-Testosterone (LT) liberal (a.k.a. Alan Colmes)

Best female fear voice (a.k.a. Megyn Kelly)

Fair and balanced (a.k.a. Greta Van Susteren)

Hindenburg-sized suspenders (a.k.a. Bob Bechel)

Does he still have a pulse? (a.k.a. Brit Hume)

"Corporations are people, my friend" (a.k.a. Mitt Romney)

"Whiter than vanilla," (a.k.a. John Gibson)

Right-leaning oral facial-tick (a.k.a. Dick Morris)

Bevy-bleached-blonde-babes (N=9)

The Big O's title sweats egocentricity: *A Bold Fresh Piece of Humanity*, and overall, I'm underwhelmed by his shameless wallowing in ignorance. Most poignantly, he utterly lacks the most important quality necessary to appreciate the sublime richness of the human experience: *Paradox*. Yin and yang represent alternating faces of our species that need each other to exist, and his simple-minded reductionism possesses no clue about the bounty of nuance.

Finally, the tunnel-vision Catholicism that I found suffocating lacks perspective; and his prose consists of serial choppy sentences, sloppy paragraph transitions, endemic redundancy, zero scholarship, sophomoric logic, and overuse of the verb "to be" (passive voice).

lxi. WIKTIONARY: Bloviator: "One who habitually bloviates; a pompous, opinion-ated, typically voluble commentator." : http://en.wiktionary.org/wiki/bloviator

lxii. WIKTIONARY: Paralanguage definition: http://en.wiktionary.org/wiki/paralanguage

lxiii. See Al Franken, *Lies and the Lying Liar's Who Tell Them: A Fair and Balanced Look at the Right (Plume Books, 2004), 421pp.*

lxiv. Theodor Adorno, THE AUTHORITRIAN PERSONALITY: STUDIES IN PREJUDICE (W.W. Norton and Company, 1993), 506 pp.; also, Robert Witkin, ADORNO ON POPULAR CULTURE (Routledge Taylor and Francis Group 2003).

lxv. WIKTIONARY: Sophistry: "An argument that seems plausible, but is fallacious or misleading, especially one devised deliberately to do so.": http://en.wiktionary.org/wiki/sophistry

lxvi. Michael J. Strada, *Benefits of Model Syllabi* (University Press of America, 2008), 246 pp.

lxvii. West Virginia Consortium for Faculty and Course Development (FACDIS):

lxviii. LIST OF FALLACIOUS ARGUMENTS: "Fallacy of the Excluded Middle,":http://www.don-lindsey-archive.org/skeptic/arguments.html

lxix. Michael J. Strada, *Through the Global Lens: An Introduction to the Social Sciences* (Prentice Hall, 3E, 2009), pp. 1-2.

lxx. *Ibid.,* pp. 259-266 (paraphrasing world religions).

lxxi. Howard Kurtz, "Bill O'Reilly, Producer Settle Harrassment Suit: Fox Agrees to Drop Extortion Claim, *Washington Post* (29 October 2004):

      http://www.washingtingpost.com/wp-dyn/articles/A7578-2004Oct28.html

lxxii. Irving L. Janis, *Groupthink: Psychological Studies of Policy Decisions and Fiascoes* (Houghton Mifflin, 1983), 351pp.

lxxiii. Caitlin Flanagan, "The Hazards of Duke: A Now Infamous Power Point Presentation Exposes a Lot About Men, Women, Sex, and Alcohol—And About

How Universities are Letting Their Female Students Down." *The Atlantic* (January/February 2011), pp. 87-96.

lxxiv. See these books on Kindle: Eric Bohlert, *Lapdogs: How the Press Rolled Over for Bush* (2006), 352 pp.; Deborah Jaramillo, *Ugly War, Pretty Package: How CNN and Fox News Made the Invasion of Iraq High Concept* (2009), 272 pp.

CHAPTER FIVE:

"Literature on the Bush Dynasty"

BACKGROUNDER:

How often can scholars assess huge foreign policy decisions by father and son presidents of the United States? At age 66, I'll surely never have another one. Before I begin reading about the Bushes, let me state that I began this project believing that Bush I entered the presidency with very strong professional credentials, while Bush II surely did not. Kindle's deep scholarly pockets have led me to reassess assumptions elsewhere, but will they here?

Before delving into the robust literature on the two Iraq Wars, let's examine books on the Bush's Dynasty not covered elsewhere here. Millenialists a decade ago implored the rest of us to "Go Google It" when knowledge was on our minds; similarly, my mantra in 2011 is similar: "Go Kindle It."

BUSH I'S FRIENDS; RUSSELL BAKER; THE SCHWEIZERS:

I'll start with *All the Best, George Bush: My Life in Letters and Other Writings* (1999).

The title derives from Bush I's practice of closing his extensive correspondence with "All the Best." When his book appeared in 1999, who guessed Bush II would scale the political summit as well? Thus, his 1999 authorship casually omits his own middle names (Herbert Walker). A lifetime of letter-writing does not morph easily; therefore, he thanks profusely those aides providing logistical and editorial help. However, he dedicates it to wife Barbara Pierce Bush (Bar).

Sixteen chapters: 1.) "Love and War;" 2.) "Texas, Our Texas;" 3.) "Potomac Fever;" 4.) "International Waters;" 5.) "The Eye of the Storm;" 6.) "China; "7.) "Protecting Secrets;" 8.) "Fire in the Belly;" 9.) "A Heartbeat Away;" 10.) "The Rough and Tumble;" 11.) "The Long Home Stretch;" 12.) "Mr. President;" 13.) "On the Frontline;" 14.) "Peaks and Valleys;" 15.) "The Worst of Times;" 16.) "Looking Forward," plus a Glossary of Names with 1999 insights about key people in his life, including the son later to be abbreviated simply as 'W' or 'Dubya.'

This book about a delightfully naïve, earnest, and patriotic teenager bolting from his elite prep school (Andover) into the Navy's youngest WW II fighter pilot; distinguishing himself as a decorated war hero. The Editor's Note by Lisa Drew states that all letters and journal entries appear in original form with four exceptions: 1.) Some edited for length; 2.) Editing for clarity (i.e., typos corrected but grammar and punctuation not); 3.) Formatting of letters made uniform; 4.) Protecting participants' identities.

Bush's Preface appears as another dated letter (1 June 1999) and begins: "When I left office and returned to Texas in January 1993, friends suggested I write a memoir. 'Be sure the historians get it right' was a major theme. Another ran that 'The press never understood your heartbeat—who you really are'. But I was not persuaded." (p. 272).

The confluence of several factors convinced him to proceed, not the least of which was his friend and editor, Lisa Drew, working on him relentlessly to use his life-long penchant for letter-writing as a rich source of biographical information. Then he turned to his "trusted friend," Jean Becker, who had helped Barbara Bush complete her book on the Bush family.

Bush writes "Jean spent endless hours contacting people whom I had written, digging through endless boxes of letters now in archives at The George Bush Presidential Library (Texas A & M), going through my records from my United Nations and CIA days, listening to pathetic little scratchy tapes I had made for my spotty diary. She dug, and edited. She cajoled and pleaded for letters. She pushed me for ideas as what to include, what to leave out. She never gave up. I will never be able to properly express my gratitude to Jean Becker." (p. 292)

No surprise that many of his experiences stem from the 20th century's grandest transfiguration: World War II. He promises "a look at what was on the mind of an 18-year old who goes into the Navy and then at 19 is flying a torpedo bomber off an aircraft carrier in WW II; what runs through the mind of a person living in China (half-way around the world); or, what a president is thinking when he has to send someone else's son or daughter into combat." (p. 304)

Family members tried to convince young Bush to skip the war, enrolling instead at Yale University (a cherished Bush tradition); however, as soon as he turned 18, he enrolled in the Navy's flight training program as a seaman second class. Most of his wartime letters avoided specificity to wend through the military's censorship bureaucracy. Also, they sound like you would expect any young man to write mostly to his parents; not a glimmer exists here to suggest that might ever become an American public figure.

Bush's Preface reveals elite America's priggishness at that time. It comes off like a badge of honor alien to most of Americans. I felt empathy for his character, courage, and above all else—his relentless ambivalence: falling in love with young Barbara Pierce at the most inconvenient of times. This young man wanted desperately to do the right thing, complicated by "The Big One." Bush's prospects as a naval pilot worried him; yet he passed each new test, boosting his confidence.

This noblest of 20th century wars, this teenager managed to see through the gung-ho drivel lapped up by some peers; despite his being viewed in each new group as "the kid." Writing to his parents "They hand out so much crude propaganda here that it is really sickening. Many of the intelligent men and officers realize it. Stuff like 'Kill the Japs—hate—murder' or 'you are the cream of American youth.' Some fellows swallowed it all. Many of whom possess below-average intelligence, two of my room-mates, for example, get a big kick out of hearing it. Maybe it is necessary, but the smart fellows know why they are here and don't require being brainwashed." (p. 369)

The first letters about buddies' training near-misses rivet the reader. Most begin "Dear Dad & Mum," "Yesterday a friend of mine cracked up. His motor cut on him and all landing sites were poor. He managed to get it fairly well down but then he nosed over, flipped onto his back, and was hanging by his safety belt—his head was hanging about one foot from. The tail was wiped right off the plane, but luckily he unhooked his belt and slipped out. Poor Ed, he hasn't been doing too well anyway and this may be just what he doesn't need. Motors are apt to cut on cold days." (p. 468)

Bush refers to his fiancé as Bar, and addresses his bitter-sweet ambivalence pervading their relationship: "I miss Bar(bara) something terrific but I suppose it's only natural. Feels like agony being so close yet so far away. I think of her every minute and know that I will be completely happy when I am with her again. I will be so pleased when she is mine for keeps, but when that will be is hard to guess. I certainly hope we can get married before she finishes at Smith. As far as her wanting to, that's settled. We both want to be married but clearly our wants are not the determining factor in this case. What do you think I should offer her before we get married? She does not expect us to have a thing, but I wonder if it would be fair for her to get married with what I have saved, say in a year after I get back I will have over $2,000 by then." (p. 782)

His job as a Torpedo Submarine Bomber (TSB) meant repeated take-offs and landings on a moving target (aircraft carrier), still a high-risk endeavor in 2011. His first carrier was called the San Jacinto and these words describe his first landing on it:

"We TSBs landed first. The ship looked really swell steaming along in her battle camouflage. We made a few practice passes down wind and then she swung around into the wind and we came aboard. She was moving at a good clip and the air was nice and smooth, facilitating landings. We each made three landings and then cut our motors on the deck. We taxied into position before cutting the motors. On carriers it is necessary to utilize ever inch of deck space. Therefore, the linemen taxi you right up to the very edge of the deck. They put me right on the starboard bow and I thought I was going to fall over any minute, with the water rushing by it is quite scary. Putting planes where they want them is called spotting." (p. 801)

I have to close with his sketchy letter explaining the flight for which Bush become both famous and infamous. His gripping letter runs to six pages, and attributes misspellings to a lame typewriter, not ignorance. His explanatory note sent home:

"I was shot down off the island of Chichi Jima, in the Bonins, and rescued by the USS Finback. I am still humbled by how lucky and blessed I was that an American submarine was patrolling the area and picked me up before the Japanese. I will always be grateful to fellow pilot Doug West, who stuck with me as long as he could, strafing the Japanese boats and pointing his wing at my life raft so the Finback could find me. Years later we learned from the Japanese report of the incident that two parachutes were seen leaving the plane. That means a great deal to me—that at least one of my crewmates made it out of the plane—although he was never found. Right after the war, the Japanese Commander in charge of Chichi Jima was tried and executed for eating the livers of captured American pilots. I like to tease Barbara that I almost ended up as hors d'oeuvre."(p. 1145)

Not only during the War Years, but after as well, the writer of these letters comes off as a sincere, responsible, courageous, unselfish, humble, competent, honest, respectful, ethical, and religious person.

RUSSELL BAKER:

A decidedly different tone emanates from noted journalist Russell Baker's *Family of Secrets: The Bush Dynasty, America's Invisible Government, and the Hidden History of the Last Fifty Years* (Bloomsbury Press, 2009).

Baker's 24 chapters: 1.) "How Did Bush Happen?"; 2.)"Poppy's Secret"; 3.) "Viva Zapata;" 4.) "Where Was Poppy?"; 5.) "Oswald's Friend;" 6.) "The Hit;" 7.) "After Camelot;" 8.) "Wings for W;" 9.) "The Nixonian Bushes;" 10.) "Downing Nixon;" 11.) "The Interregnum;" 12.) "In from the Cold;" 13.) "Poppy's Proxy and the Saudis;" 14.) "Poppy's Web;" 15.) "The Handoff;" 16.) "The Quacking Duck;" 17.) "Playing Hardball;" 18.) "Meet the Help;" 19.) "The Conversation;" 20.) "The Skeleton in W's Closet;" 21.) "Shock and Oil?" 22.) "Deflection for Reelection;" 23.) "Domestic Disturbance;" 24.) "Conclusion."

The Foreword by James Moore describes his reluctance to delve into a topic (The Bushes) oft-studied by Texas journalists. When governors runs for president, the issue-framing often derives from local scribes. Moore says he "spent about a decade trying to find accurate information on Bush II's record in the Texas National Guard. My curiosity was prompted by his failure to adequately answer a question I had asked him as a panelist in a televised debate with Ann Richards during the 1994 gubernatorial campaign." (p.47)

Moore also assumed the famous Bush loyalty would preclude any new investigatory discoveries, even from bitter Democratic rivals. He also believed that he and his fellow locals had looked under every rock for anything significant. He even admits to a "dismissive attitude" when Baker first approached him about new research.

"Baker, however, was undaunted; he was convinced the full story was untold. He went after the National Guard puzzle with vigor that I had long since abandoned because I was convinced the Bush team had scrubbed the files in a manner leaving little room for new revelations. Baker, however, chased down new witnesses; he dug deeper into the details of Bush's friends in the 'champagne unit' and uncovered close relationships with Saudi financiers that appeared to turn the unlikely into the possible for Bush and his broad protectorate. He found inexplicable money trails in the Permian Basin oil patch of West Texas and followed them wherever they led, which was not too distant from the bin Laden family and several Saudi royal families. Baker also does a much more comprehensive job of documenting Bush's irresponsible behavior in his youth than did every journalist in Texas that had heard stories of pregnant girlfriends, secret abortions, drunk driving, and walking away from an officer's commission in the Texas National Guard." (p.65)

However, Moore was even more impressed with Baker's scoops regarding untold back stories about Bush Is implausible rise to power; his secret involvement with the CIA long before publically taking over its directorship; decades nurturing dubious but lucrative foreign associations (including Saudi oil interests); ties to the bin Laden family—all of which

Baker describes as "foundational to almost every public achievement of the Bush family." (p. 74)

Baker begins chapter one: "This is the true story of a family we thought we knew—and a country we have barely begun to comprehend. George Bush, father and son, are vastly more complicated, and their doings vastly more troubling than the conventional wisdom would have it. This book reveals the story behind their story, documenting the secrets that the House of Bush has long sought to obscure." (p. 119)

Toward the end of Bush II's year in office, 81 percent of the populace disapproved of his performance, which Baker attributes mostly to the lame one-liners that came to typify each of Bush's disasters: Hunt for Osama ("Wanted: Dead of Alive"); the Feds and Katrina ("Hechuva-job-Brownie"); Mishandling Iraq ("Mission Accomplished"); Collapse of housing bubble and the Great Recession ("We're creating an ownership society.")

Concerning these serious debacles, Baker contends "It was becoming clearer to many that this wrongness was a matter not just of flawed policy decisions, but more fundamentally, of W's personal limitations. Which raises an obvious question—so obvious that almost everybody passed it by: How did Bush II happen? Why was this particular man out of all possible aspirants encouraged, and even propelled, to the top?" (p. 137)

Baker describes astute Republican observers such as John Dean warning about unprecedented abuses of power early in his first term. The well-documented human tendency to abuse power over-achieves early on.

Specifically "The fanatical secrecy, proclivity for police state tactics, contempt for democratic safeguards, the blatant determination to advance the interests of those already possessing so much, efforts to politicize government services from top to bottom—all representing evidence of a mindset rarely seen in American politics. Above all, the deception at the root of the decision to invade Iraq and the disastrous occupation that followed only confirmed my feeling that the assumption of power by Bush pointed to something deeper than a callow and entitled president surrounded by enablers and Iagos with dark schemes." (p. 149)

Baker traveled widely interviewing hundreds of people, including "Washington insiders, Texas muckrakers, Bush's old friends, dedicated foes, tycoons, and typists." (p.161) He then read everything he could find on the Bushes, ending up with about 500 books in his home library.

He approached this broad subject from every angle, such as their history, family dynamics, business relations, social circles, as well as associates, employees, and especially funders of Bush, Inc. Baker challenges many conventional wisdoms about how the Bushes became such scions of privilege.

Baker opines "Although George W. Bush styled himself something of a family maverick, and the media echoed this self-serving portrayal, to a remarkable degree W. has followed a path laid out for him by his forebears. He went to the same schools, joined the same secret societies, and benefited from similarly murky financial arrangements. He had made the same kind of friends and surrounded himself with people closely associated with his father, grand-father, and eve great-grandfather. Despite all the talk about his 'Oedipal' relationship to his father, the younger Bush clung close to the trunk of the family tree." (p. 185)

The author also describes a fundamental paradox concerning the Bushes. They have long served "forces that operate best in the shadows;" yet, they have wanted badly to occupy center stage. He characterizes this schizoid role as "living what amounts to double lives." (p. 204) In the Bush inner circle Bush I is referred to as "Poppy" and Bush II as "W."

Baker's scholarship produces many unique opinions about Bush, Inc, as privileged scions going back to America's founding and likely to remain so in the future. As money comes to dominate American politics increasingly (e.g., Super-PACs), the author argues that the Bushes' self-serving deception imperils the very integrity of American democracy.

Chapter two, "Poppy's Secret," took decades to materialize, with Baker performing the coup de grace regarding the machinations of the secrecy-obsessed CIA lurking in the shadows. At the time of President Kennedy's assassination, documents later revealed that there were two George Bushes simultaneously on the CIA payroll, and Baker presents solid evidence that the "other" George was a part-time minion on the payroll to provide cover for the "real Bush," if the latter's CIA links became public.

The CIA said that it attempted to locate the other guy (George William Bush) but told reporters that they failed. Nevertheless, additional investigators tracked down the "other Bush" still on the CIA payroll, with scribe Joseph McBride finding pay-dirt.

McBride wrote an article for the *Nation* magazine challenging Bush's many denials, and shortly thereafter this liberal magazine ran a follow-up op-ed "where evidence was provided that the CIA had foisted a lie on the American people." (p. 309) The media failed to follow up on it and "The George William Bush diversion was never understood for what it was: one in a long series of calculated distractions and disinformation episodes that run through the Bush family history." (p. 311)

It took roughly a decade after Bush I's 1988 inauguration before another declassified government memo cast new light on this latent matter. However, it was also very slowly that similar declassified documents shed light further back into Bush's morphing with the CIA before 1963, and another decade before declassified documents were found, read, and reveled publicly. The evidence? Bush I shows up in CIA memos as early as 1953, with Baker tracing them even further back.

Baker establishes that Poppy's letters aren't the full story. In 1942, Bush was trained in Norfolk, VA, not only as a torpedo bomber pilot, but also "as a photographic officer, responsible for crucial, highly-sensitive aerial surveillance. On his way to his assigned ship, Bush stopped off in Pearl Harbor for meetings with military intelligence officers assigned to the Joint Intelligence Center for the Pacific Ocean Areas (JCPOA)." (p. 447). Baker considers undeniable that Bush's unit involved both combat and spying: the spy program was called "Operation Snapshot."

The author is even more brutal going after Bush I for multiple contradictory descriptions of what happened on that fateful day that morphed him into a war hero. Myriad accounts had already been challenged by both journalists and protagonists. For example, Bush I has claimed that his plane was completely crippled.

In *Looking Forward,* a 1988 campaign book co-authored with staffer, Victor Gold, Poppy writes "The flak was the heaviest I'd ever flown into. . . . Suddenly there was a jolt, as if a massive fist had crunched into the belly of the plane. Smoke poured into the cockpit, and I could see flames rippling across the crease of the wing, edging towards the fuel tanks." (p. 499)

Eyewitness, Chester Mierzejewski, however, tail gunner in the plane ahead, has disputed all of the reported news accounts. Troubled, he tried in vain communicating with Bush I several times. Eventually, he took his eye-witness recollections to the *New York Post,* who quoted the tail-gunner "Only Bush himself bailed out that day and his plane was never on fire. I think that he could have saved those lives if they were alive. I don't know that they were, but at least they had a chance if he had attempted a water landing." (p. 505)

THE SCHWEIZERS:

I picked Baker's labor-intensive book as a counterpoint to the naïve portrait emanating from Poppy's own letters. My third selection consists of a journalistic couple, Peter and Rochelle Schweizers' book aiming for relative objectivity on Bush, Inc. *The Bushes: Portrait of a Dynasty* (Anchor Books, 2008.), impresses for its comprehensiveness, spanning an unbelievable 48 chapters.

The Introduction delves into ironies on family dynamics complicating the family's two most public figures: W and Jeb, deciding independently in January to run for governor of their states (W in Texas; Jeb in Florida.) They both claimed that no family agenda, or joint strategy, underlay their decisions. The Schweizers adroitly analyze the extant "conventional wisdom among the Bush clan: that the more serious Jebbie would win, while the more mercurial W would go down to defeat by Ann Richards." (p. 60)

Why? Because Jebbie had been considering it for a decade, was better-educated, polished, and "so close to Poppy that he would drop everything whenever his father needed him. He actually read all of those briefing papers put out by Washington think tanks." (p. 62) Family members took it for granted that Jeb's Florida victory would grease the skids of a presidential bid in 2000.

The baggage plaguing his older brother, W, makes for swell copy. While W possessed street smarts and intensity, "he was also the rebel, edgy and unpredictable. Mother Barbara had told her eldest son point blank she considered his candidacy a big mistake." (p. 66) Relatives feared that his adroit Democratic opponent, Ann Richards, would exploit some aspect of W's dubious history to discredit both he and the family, resulting in defeat. "In an earlier family history, younger sibling Marvin Bush had referred to his brother W as a clown." (p. 69)

The Schweizers characterize the family mindset: "The results were stunning to most in the family. Jeb was going down to defeat in Florida and W was beating Ann Richards big. When W was over the top and Richards had conceded, he got a phone call in his suite; it was his father." (p. 70) W's aunt, Nancy Ellis, was present while the unlikely victor chatted with Poppy. She reports W's agitation after hanging up. Why? Because the conversation dealt mostly with disappointment over Jeb's defeat, not kudos for W's win.

Eight years later, the authors describe the rituals and rivalries present when "274 members of the extended Bush family converged on the nation's capitol, on a cold and dreary day, but that didn't matter because they were witnessing the second member of the Bush clan being elected president; one young cousin quipping 'two-and-counting'." (p. 77) But this was nothing new, for the Schweizers establish clearly how the Bushes had cohabited with privileged America for over 100 years.

Unlike the Kennedys or the Roosevelts, the Bushes prove unwilling to break the implicit code of silence about family matters by supplying tidbits to media outlets. Some have mocked it as "the quiet dynasty." Here the roots of disdain for the media is traced back five decades when Prescott Bush made his first bid for a U.S. Senate seat from Connecticut. The authors cite multiple sources suggesting that the Bushes consider introspection "dangerously close to self-centeredness." (p. 92)

The Schweizers document well their conclusion that the clan considers itself the "un-Kennedys" via frequently juxtaposing themselves as decidedly different, going all the way back to Senator Prescott Bush regarding Kennedy patriarch, Joseph, and his heirs for shamelessly courting the media.

The Bushes are similarly noteworthy for standing up against all such rivals who challenge intense clan loyalty. Kennedy galas always include lots of intellectuals and close confidantes like Ted Sorensen or Arthur Schlesinger, Jr. Conservative author Gary Wills labeled such personages as "honorary Kennedys." Bush cousin John Ellis had intimate experience with both clans and provided much fodder.

Also described well is "The Bushes' conscious effort to pass along its heritage. Just as the young John Quincy Adams would listen in on his father's conversations with Thomas Jefferson, the Bushes seek to train future generations as history is being made. When Poppy Bush was president, he insured that not only his children, but also his grandchildren became familiar with the White House's pageantry." (p. 163)

Genealogist Gary Boyd Roberts has demonstrated that the Bushes are related to 15 former presidents: George Washington, Millard Fillmore, Franklin Pierce, Abraham Lincoln, Ulysses Grant, Rutherford Hayes, James Garfield, Grover Cleveland, Teddy Roosevelt, William Howard Taft, Calvin Coolidge, Herbert Hoover, Franklin Delano Roosevelt, Richard Nixon, and Gerald Ford. (I surely had no inkling)

The authors opine that what results is a vital universe of friends and allies to be drawn upon. Many Bushes has gotten started in life by visiting a close friend of a grandparent, or foreign business partner. And it's almost always about business, pure and simple: how to maximize profits. Nary a physician, lawyer, academic, cleric, teacher, or social worker to be found among Bush, Inc. It also seems to me that the Kennedy clan trumps the Bushes for myriad altruistic endeavors. The Schweizers don't hesitate calling their subject-matter "the rise of America's most powerful family." (p. 188)

Chapter one, "Iron" chronicles early business successes a century ago in Columbus, OH, by Samuel P. Bush, referred to simply as S.P., whose father and grandfather were both Episcopalian ministers. S.P. also eschewed advice to experience his higher education at Yale, opting instead for The Stevens Institute of Technology, located on Long Island. The choice proved propitious since Stevens was one of the few places S.P. could learn new theories of scientific management, which he absorbed with alacrity.

Spotting an industrial niche in Columbus, S.P. worked his way into and up a marginal firm (Buckeye Malleable Iron and Coupler Company) which he renamed Buckeye Steel. The company manufactured automatic couplers joining railroad cars together. S.P.'s Protestant work ethic, cutting-edge theories gleaned at Stevens, and a supportive new wife named Flora, described as charming and elegant all helped.

However, the authors also describe sort a love/hate relationship between S.P. and Cleveland-based financier Franklin Rockefeller, younger sibling of John D. Rockefeller. Franklin and John D. amassed a huge fortune via Standard Oil, but later experienced a bitter parting of the ways. S.P. Bush and Franklin Roosevelt established a complex relationship that continues bearing financial fruit for both clans.

The Schweizers point out that "Stockholders of Buckeye Steel Co. agreed to give Rockefeller $15,000 worth of stock and a share in any future increase in proportion to these holdings. In return, Rockefeller promised to use his influence to persuade the railroads to buy Buckeye couplers." (p. 229) Accidents, many fatal, occurred regularly in this labor-intensive manufacturing of railroad couplers in the course of 12-hour shifts.

The skill-based and mental sport of baseball (original national pastime) was being forced to share the pitch with a more violent upstart, American football, which appealed to S.P. as nothing short of sublime. However, so frequent were gridiron deaths that Theodore Roosevelt appointed the first commission to regulate the sport, morphing into the NCAA.

Why Teddy's concern? His son and namesake got seriously injured in a Harvard tussle. S.P. not only played football, but sponsored a Buckeye Steel team and signed on as an assistant coach when the Ohio State Buckeyes fielded their first entry—one experiencing few victories early on, even though competing against smaller Ohio colleges. One note-worthy fact consisted of OSU's being one of the first teams to integrate racially.

S.P. and Flora Bush produced four children, and the eldest (Prescott) helped keep the others in line. His kids all attended pedestrian public schools decidedly multicultural for those days. Prescott later wrote about the Douglas High School: "We had a very large negro population, many German students, and representatives of almost every ethnic group at Douglas High." (p.266)

While S.P.'s kids performed well academically, he really cared much more about competitive sports after hours, and while he loved football, young Pres also excelled at hitting and fielding, baseball's requisite skills. Later, Poppy Bush captained the Yale baseball squad as a first-baseman. Typical of the Bushes, Flora stayed home raising the teenagers while Dad made money forging bonds via travel.

Fearing that teenager Pres might not realize his considerable potential, the parents sent Prescott off to Newport, RI, where he enrolled at an Episcopal school named St. George's—which was known for solid academics coupled with serious discipline. There he played three sports and liked the debating process offered by its civics club. Owing to S.P.'s vaunted frugality, Pres worked as a caddy at an exclusive country club working for stars like Douglas Fairbanks. Apparently, S.P.'s parents' Episcopalianism bordered on Puritanism.

Chapter two is called "Bones," and includes interesting information about how Prescott Bush's life trajectory would unfold. The authors link contemporary Bush clan themes with S.P. Bush's most successful child. While S.P. had turned his back on a Yale education in favor of Stevens Institute, Pres reverted to the path taken by his grandfather and great-grandfather in that citadel of the American aristocracy located in New Haven, CT.

I like how they contextualize Pres at Yale: "Pres Bush fell between two distinct groups that tended to dominate campus life. The wealthy north-easterners from prominent bloodlines lived at a leisurely pace. They did not yearn to win at anything because they had, by definition, won already. Simultaneously, campus life featured upper-middle class sons who had made it into this university by virtue of their academic skills and intellectual gifts. Young Pres found himself awkwardly in the middle. He possessed more drive than the rich, but more wealth and style than the sons of the middle class; both accordingly regarded him with some level of suspicion." (p. 387)

While he studied history, literature, and politics, he was S.P.'s son and sports mattered most as the great symbolic democratizer with success both easily measured and available to all. Pres much preferred baseball and golf to football and the Schweizers write that "More than anyone else, it was Pres who would make baseball and golf the games of choice for generations of Bushes." (p. 392)

At Yale, he continued the family tradition of accepting an honored invitation by responding "yes" to the question: "Skull and Bones:" "Accept or Reject?" He then received a message wrapped in a black ribbon sealed in black wax. Embossed on it he discovered the number 322. Two of F. Scott Fitzgerald's novels tapped into the secret society's mystique. Schweizers refer aptly to Skull and Bones as "an elite within an elite, an incubator for members of future generations who would rise to power in their respective professional areas." (p. 407) Located above its crypt, these words appear: "Who was a fool, who a wise man, beggar or king? Whether poor or rich, all's the same in death."

Formally known as The Russell Trust Association, founded in 1833 by William Huntington Russell, each year a mere 15 Yale gentlemen are tapped for this honor. Similar societies, like Scroll and Key, are based on family prestige but Skull and Bones is generally considered to represent a meritocracy. Our authors argue his prowess on the ball diamond was likely most responsible for his being tapped. Pres was the first of many Bushes honored with Skull and Bones.

As a harbinger of Poppy's WW II letter-writing travails, Pres Bush wrote his parents about his experiences at the European warfront. He said that during a German offensive he had performed bravely, but also jokingly said he had saved General Pershing from a .77 mm artillery shell, deflecting it with his bolo knife. But nowhere in this missive did he state that this part of it was a joke. Proud as punch, Flora Bush relayed the story to a local newspaper, which ran it on the front page. His relationship with his parents never healed sufficiently after the war.

L. E. Cooper; Jacob Weisberg; Mickey Herskovits:

A surprising 2004 book taken from a series of Books on U.S. Presidents goes back 6,000 years to contextualize the Bush clan as extremely well-connected not only in America, but globally as well. Anthropologist L. E. Cooper relies on the latest kinds of DNA research to trace the family trees available to the general public via this DNA website:

http://www.qksrv.net/click-1539901-9289009. Cooper's book is called: *House of Bush: House of God* (2004), and counter-intuitively also traces the Bush lineage back to both Jesus and Mohamed. (I report, you decide!)

Cooper provides extensive family trees verifying alleged power from U.S. Christianity to global Islam. He states "Such a global single family could not occur, but for the Hand of God. And, that single global family includes not only U.S. Presidents but all kinds of people." (p.53)

I can hypothesize only three interpretations: 1.) His research is legitimate and should be followed up; 2.) He's a fundamentalist true-believer making stuff up and should be peer reviewed; 3.) Its some kind of satirical joke.

His chapters: 1.) "General Bush Family Trees;" 2.) "Descent from Jesus;" 3.) "Descent from Mohammed;" 4.) "Descent from Kings of Jerusalem;" 5.) "Descent from Pendragons;" 6.) "Descent from Kings of Iraq;" 7.) "Descent from Kings of Persia;" 8.) "Descent from Egyptian Pharoahs;" 9.) "Descent from Indian Emperors;" 10.) "Descent from Chinese;" 11.) "Descent from European Leaders;" 12.) "Descent from Russian Czars;"

13.) "Descent from Friesland;" 14.) "Descent from Ancient Heroes;" 15.) "Descent from U.S. Founders;" 16.) "Descent from Attila the Hun;" 17.) "Ancient Enemies;" 18.) "Descent from Early Americans;" 19.) "Descent from Joseph;" 20.) "Conclusions."

Most Americans know that the House of Bush went from patrician New England roots to the plebian Texas' oil business after Bush I's service release in 1945, with some side forays into Ohio during the interim. Cooper, however, goes back to Richard Bush in Dedham, MA (1666-97); Timothy Bush in Bristol, RI (1728-1815); Jonathan Fairbanks in Bristol (1623-1712); Jeremiah Fairbanks in Bristol (1674-1735); Deborah Shepherd in Bristol (1631-1705); Mary Fairbanks in Bristol (1699-1743); Samuel Penfield in Bristol (1653-1675); Mary Penfield in Bristol (1678-1735); Timothy Bush in New London, CT (1766-1850); John House in Rochester, NY (1742-1819). That comprises about one-quarter of the early House of Bush, and Cooper does the same for the Bush first ladies: Barbara Pierce Bush and Laura Welch Bush.

A nice pictorial family tree going back eight generations appears in journalist Jacob Weisberg's book: *The Bush Tragedy* (Random House, 2008). I like titles characterized by economy, and with only three words, Weisberg's title works for me. It includes seven chapters: 1.) "The Bushes and the Walkers;" 2.) "Father and Sons;" 3.) "The Gospel of George;" 4.) "The Shadow;" 5.) "The Foremost Hand;" 6.) "Án Amiable Monster;" 7.) "Dead Precedents."

Weisberg's Introduction, "Prince Hal in Houston," opens: "If you had to explain the second Bush Presidency through the lens of a single day, the day of choice would be 1 May 2003, when George W arrived by fighter jet on the deck of the USS Abraham Lincoln. Pulling off his white aviator's helmet and hopping down onto the deck of the aircraft carrier, he embraced wounded soldiers just returned from Afghanistan and Iraq." (p. 42) In equally-trenchant prose "Nearly everything he did in his youth was an attempt to emulate his beloved and successful father, with unimpressive and some times farcical results." (p.52)

Failing to match up as a student, athlete, soldier, businessman, or politician, Bush II finally nailed it by successfully landing his fighter plane on an aircraft carrier, similar to his Dad. And, even idiots couldn't miss the symbolism of the banner "Mission Accomplished," referring not only to major combat in Iraq, but also unfinished family business with Saddam Hussein (whom his Dad had called "the worst dictator since Hitler," and had plotted Bush I's assassination).

Weisberg's words about the aircraft carrier episode sting "Every gesture of the President that day spoke to his feeling of personal as well as national vindication. The mission he thought he had accomplished was not just vanquishing Saddam Hussein, but overcoming his father's shadow. For that brief, shining moment, righteous purpose and psychological need were fully joined. "(p. 57)

Finally, someone willing to delve into obvious psychological dynamics of one President settling unfinished family business! Both Bushes have always pooh-poohed the pertinence of psychology to their behavior. The former referred to it dismissively as "putting me on the couch," and the latter as "psycho-babble."

Given weighty decisions like going to war, even their critics have given them a pass in this regard. Scribes typically respond to such issues with, "I'm not a shrink." How utterly preposterous! Pundits seldom have studied economics, but that never stops them from hypothesizing about those matters. Why the taboo against using a legitimate social science's concepts and research here. The author nails it, arguing it's not up to the Bushes to determine how we interpret their key decisions.

Weisberg notes that they chafe even more at questions about the privileges of a dynastic clan going back two centuries. For Bush, Inc., however, even worse than Freudian or Skinnerian interpretations are pseudo-Marxist-class accusations about the interlocking directorate of elites oppressing the masses so cleverly: "Since deciding to run for President W has understood that he assumes leadership of a political clan, and the Bush past, as well as the Bush future rested on his shoulders." (p. 98)

Journalist Mickey Herskowitz's *Duty, Honor, Country: The Life and Times of Prescott Bush* (Kindle, 2003) has a Bush Family Tree, Foreword by Bush II, and 11 chapters: 1.) "Passing the Torch;" 2.) "Faith of His Fathers;" 3.) "God and Man at Yale;" 4.) "They Remember Mama;" 5.) "The Businessman;" 6.) "Giving Something Back;" 7.) "The Honest Broker;" 8.) "Red Rover;" 9.) "Alfalfa Party;" 10.) "End of Camelot;" 11.) "For All Things a Season."

The author captures the moment when Prescott Bush was sending his son, George, off to war: "They might have the PR models for a recruiting poster. One was a tall, handsome man in his mid-forties. The other, not yet out of his teens, looked so boyish you'd have trouble picturing him behind the wheel of a car, much less in the cockpit of a torpedo bomber." (p. 9)

Likewise, "There was only the slightest conversation between them, words about letters and phone calls and doing the Right Thing, as the older man knew the younger one would." (p. 10) And, "All around them was the chaotic concert of a railroad station: hissing steam engines, hundreds of hurried footsteps, the rumble of baggage carts, urgent shouts from families and train crews, and more quietly but equally urgently, loved ones clinging to their soldiers." (p. 11)

The Foreword written by Bush I about his Dad, Prescott, is touching and observant. Bush I sounds credibly humble "I knew then how proud Dad was of me;" and, Bush I also works in a little baseball lore relating to the "Splendid Splinter" (Ted Williams) who had hit an astonishing .406 batting average for the Boston Red Sox in 1941. Why? Because Bush I and Ted Williams were prepping together at a North Carolina training facility.

In June 1943, Prescott and Dorothy Bush travelled to Corpus Christi, Texas as their son George was receiving his Navy pilot wings. To mark the occasion, they presented him with gold cuff links, and must have worried since within six months he'd be battling the Japanese over the Pacific. The author states boldly that "Ensign Bush did not see war as a stepping-stone, his history tells us so. He did not fantasize about being elected leader of the Free World." (p. 37)

Those gold cuff links came in handy when Bush I gave them to Bush II after the latter's swearing-in as Texas Governor in January 1995. The inveterate letter-writer, Bush I and wife Bar, also gave their first son a touching letter expressing their pride in a W. A. prayer breakfast followed in the state capitol, Austin. W later recounted how tears rolled down his cheeks as he listened to the minister's sermon, not because of what was said; but rather what Poppy and Barbara had written.

Focusing on Prescott Bush, author Herskowitz writes: "Across the years, from hand to hand to hand, destiny reached out to them. Prescott Sheldon Bush carried the flame first, and he was a contradiction in terms, a modest politician who strived to remain discreet and trustworthy. If he did not always succeed, he came closer than most." (p. 44) Herskowitz wouldn't have written this book about Press unless he was a prescient harbinger of things to come.

The 1950s, when Prescott entered politics, featured an internecine rivalry with the Soviets, and the Senatorial scourge was anti-Communist witch hunter, Wisconsin's Senator Joseph McCarthy. Contemporary historians treat Press mostly as an affable but not highly-respected member of the Senate. The Bushes, however, point out that Prescott co-sponsored the bill creating the interstate highway system, JFK's Peace Corps, and criticized the belatedly-censured Joseph McCarthy.

And how are scribes able to get the Bushes apoplectically defensive? Mention the "D" word—in this case "Dynasty." "Ask that one and your interview will end abruptly and awkwardly. They are public servants, not politicians; generous contributors to charities; etc. Talk about name recognition: Herskowitz describes a poll taken after Bush II's nomination for President, in which 40 percent of respondents thought this was the same man who won Operation Desert Storm." (p. 76)

BILL MINUTAGLIO; THOMPSON/WARE:

Another book morphing Bush II into the family clan: journalist Bill Minutaglio *First Son: George W. Bush and the Family Dynasty* (Three Rivers Press, 2001), who inhabits the same West-Texas hill country as W. His chapters: 1.) "Reality Day;" 2.) "Deep Money;" 3.) "The Core;" 4.) "Style;" 5.) "The Arrogance;" 6.) "The Heaviness;" 7.) "Flying;" 8.) "Primogenitor;" 9.) "Despair and Capital Sins;" 10.) "Someone Really Political;" 11.) "The Big Elephant Field;" 12.) "Behavior Modification;" 13.) "Amazing Grace;" 14.) "Dog with a Bone;" 15.) "Giant Killer;" 16.) "Dynasty."

The detailed Preface provides us with lots of insights regarding Bush essentially between time in the Texas State House, and the U.S. White House, roughly one decade ago. While not an "official" biography, Minutaglio interviewed more than 300 people, including friends and relatives.

He points out the import of these first father/son Presidencies since John and John Quincy Adams so long ago. The "first son" phenomenon rife with Freudian implications is similarly analyzed by the author. One interviewee inquired as to whether the author was "pro or con" about Bush, and I think was accurate in responding "neither;" the scholarly response.

"This is about a political person in one of the most acutely political families in American history. Toward that end, and after 21 years as a journalist, I knew that the same rules would apply in Texas as in Washington: some close family members and staffers were helpful, even when others refused. I met with George W Bush in his second-floor office at the Texas State Capitol for two highly-insightful occasions in 1998 to convey my intention to do a fair, thorough book. It took him 11 months to consent." (p.91) Minutaglio performed research in West Texas, Austin, Dallas, Houston, Connecticut, and Massachusetts.

The political backdrop at that time consisted of Clinton's impeachment investigations. Also, he was contacted by scores of people when an article appearing on page one of the *Wall Street Journal* probing the evolution of rumors pertaining to W's reputed past drug abuse. The author is careful to defend his responses as consistent with journalistic ethics; i.e., he didn't jump on the bandwagon, similar to journalist David Maranniss resisted in his biography of Bill Clinton.

"Instead, this biography is meant to serve as an introduction to an exploration to the place and state of mind called Texas; as well as even-handedly examining what it means to grow up in an influential political family's legacy—both embracing and resisting it." (p. 110) Most of his extended-family relatives believed that W was driven mainly by the desire to not damage that legacy.

Bush II, seems compelled to have a cute nickname for everyone, and Minutaglio mentions those for other famous Texans such as: Willie Nelson, Lyndon Johnson, computer billionaire Michael Dell, Midland oil-buddy Joe O'Neill III, Ann Richards, Molly Ivins, speaker of the Texas House Pete Laney, Dallas Cowboy owner Jerry Jones, football guru Darrell Royal, Bill Moyers, Lee Atwater, originator of concept "compassionate conservative" for Bush I (Ron Kaufman), Laura Bush, adviser Karen Hughes, etc. Bush II later reverted to Ron Kaufman's slogan when seeking the presidency.

Concerning the milieu known as the Texas Hill country and its denizens, he waxes poetic with statements like, "The same loping country that LBJ retreated to, bouncing along in his huge Lincoln along the banks of the Pedernales River, near where Willie Nelson and his aging coterie of snaggle-toothed mad dog musicians like to claim as their outpost." (p. 150)

Another "Sometimes the Midland good-old-boys remind him: Back in '75 his West Texas friends would yodel and snort when they saw him. Here comes the Bombastic Bushkin, George W, that S.O.B... George Dubya. Out beer drinking one night he and his buddies decided to walk onto the stage while Willie Nelson was performing nearby when Willie was scheduled to sing 'Whiskey River take my mind' with the singer as usual in his goggle-eyed way looking otherworldly into the cosmic beyond." (p. 155)

Minutaglio had researched Dubya thoroughly.

The author's reportage of the victory celebration when Bush II became the first governor elected to consecutive terms in Texas follows suit. Bush steps to the microphone, energetically intoning:

"It's been a long and difficult campaign, but I'm glad Reality Day is here (he yelps into the air); yesterday was Speculation Day, today is Reality Day! (after which he bobs in a bantam rooster strut across the hand-laid bricks in the circular driveway). His head is tilted back, all chinny defiance. He's done 23 press conferences in the last seven days: Dallas, Austin, Waco, San Antonio. His caffeine-sucking press handlers, saggy faces, bad skin, and droopy shoulders are all dragging, but Dubya's up at 6 A.M. still crackling to jump on the King Air campaign plane." (p. 186)

But the first order of business on that date was a decades-long tradition by calling his father the morning after an election: "They talked about the same things they had talked about face-to-face several weeks before, during the almost-giddy annual retreat at the family's seaside resort in Kennebunkport, MA." (p. 197)

However, 25 years earlier, he had a very different conversation with his father. That night he was drunk and out driving with his 15-year old brother, Marvin. After he had rammed through the garbage cans with his car and walked into the front door of the house, he was ready, if it was going to be that way, to fight his father.

"He was beery, he had no real career, it was late, and for most of his life, he (more anyone else in his family), had been measured against his father, his grandfather, the Bush legacy. That night, he'd stood in front of his father, in the den, and asked his father if he was ready to fight: I hear you're looking for me, you want to go 'mano a mano' right here?"(p. 207)

"For all of 1998, Bush II used lessons learned about the media when his father's loyalty monitor, media monitor, and direct arm to the Hard Right, the Christian Right. He was stationed in his father's 1998 campaign command post, his little office in the Woodward Building, next door to his mentor, Lee Atwater, the founding prince of wicked political spin. It was Atwater's successor, Mary Matalin, who labeled the first Bush son a political terrorist." (p. 343)

Concerning W's role at the elite Philips Academy "He was the head cheerleader and people fed off of his energy, the way he was always just there, just remembering peoples' birthdays, habits, parents, brothers, sisters. He wasn't very good at baseball, his father's sport at Andover and Yale. When he got on stage with a rock band, his singing was lousy, unlike his august, bow-tied grandfather, who liked to croon masterfully with his Whiffenpoof singers at Yale. But he memorized everybody's name instantly, and it pleased them that he did so. Neither his father nor grandfather could duplicate that skill; plus, he also coined nick-names for each." (p. 368)

And for the wife who rescued him from a life of over-indulgence, Laura, Minutaglio says: "They married three months after they met; he was 31 and a bachelor with a reputation in the middle of a race for Congress—by then 'I'd lived a lot of life, and wanted to settle down.' They never really had time for honeymoon. They began campaigning the day of their wedding." (p. 422)

Knowing when this next book was published matters because its title in 2011 suggests a parody-laden tome; however, in 2003 it was anything but: Carolyn Thompson and James Ware *the Leadership Genius of George W. Bush: Ten Commonsense Lessons From the Commander-in-Chief* (Wiley and Sons, 2003). In The Preface:

"As longtime consultants in the area of leadership, we were fascinated by George W Bush. How does a guy who seems so much like your neighbor next door succeed as the most powerful leader in the world? People underestimate him, but time and time again he rises to the occasion; yet his style of leadership seems to contradict almost everything we thought we knew about leadership. Our task in writing this book has been to discover the secret that makes Bush a leadership genius. We examined his leadership style from what we considered a fairly well-rounded perspective. Our research duo consists of one male versus one female, one liberal versus one conservative, one Christian versus one nontraditional, and one right-brained versus one left-brained. And yet we both came away with the same admiration for Bush's leadership abilities." (p. 18)

The authors are mired in the self-fulfilling prophecies of the corporate profit-motive's utilitarianism. Their effort involves almost no pertinent research, relying on personal anecdotes via their consulting careers. They inhabit the dubious slippery slope that historical case studies from politics and business are interchangeable. If any scientific evidence exists for this hypothesis, they fail to present it. Plus, don't consulting gigs entail fooling gullible publics? The psychological ploys of corporate marketing, to me, represent worst-practices.

They boldly claim "The reality is that all business is politics and all politics business. The only difference is where we get our operating capital from. The rest—negotiating one's way through shifting alliances, hiring people, gaining trust, being disciplined, is all the same. George W. Bush is an easy first study because his career as a leader involves both the business and political arenas. We learned an incredible amount that we've already applied to our own businesses, and we know you too will benefit from studying his tactics and applying them to yourself and your organization." (p. 36)

The Preface ends with the "God card" "Finally, of course, thanks to the One who makes all things possible for us—God. For "without that hourly guidance," we'd never have been able to keep our focus." (p.55) God's hourly guidance? How does he/she/it keep tabs on 7 billion fickle humans simultaneously. All monotheistic religions exude anthropomorphism.

Their selection of chapter titles reveals much: 1.) "What Do You Stand For? Identify Core Values; "2.) "Where Are You Going? Inspire Through Vision;" 3.) "Can I Trust You? Become Credible;" 4.) "Bring In the Right People 101: Hire People Smarter Than You;" 5.)"Bring In the Right People 201: Leave Them Alone;" 6.) "Encourage Collaboration: Build Alliances;" 7.) "Communicate By Giving It To Them Straight;" 8.) "If It's Noon, I Must Be Jogging: Be Disciplined and Focus;" 9.) "Intuitive Wisdom: Trust Your Instincts;" 10.) "Getting Results: Hold People Accountable."

This flimsy bit of pamphleteering begins with these simplistic bromides to explain Dubya's leadership genius, conveniently dovetailing with any contemporary Republican national platform:

CORE BELIEFS:

1) Compassionate conservatism;
2) Individual responsibility;

3) Promoting limited government;
4) Opposing governmental controls over business;
5) Free markets.

Why are so many Republican fundamentalists: 1.) Allergic to endnotes; 2.) In love with lists; and, 3.) Believe that common-sense represents an unimpeachable public good?

CONCLUSION:

This genre of CIA-war-mongering, merged with sleazy politics endemic to the Bush Dynasty, is epitomized today by Karl Rove, whose deep Texas roots were begun by this master of dirty tricks with Bush I back in the 1970s, then Bush II as Texas Governor, followed by Bush II as President.

A recent documentary interviews Democratic Texas Governor Ann Richards, Texas journalist Molly Ivins, ex-Senator Max Cleland, numerous ex-officials in Texas government, John McCain's 2000 campaign manager, and several academics, called aptly, "Bush's Brain," a.k.a. Karl Rove.

If you ascribe to ex-football coach Bear Bryant's dictum that "Victory is not the most important thing, it's the only thing," then you'll exit from "Bush's Brain" convinced that God is in her heaven, and all is right with her world. However, if you are comfortable with the idea that a victory stolen represents a pyrrhic victory, then you'll probably leave this film seething anger.

However, both good and bad karma matter more distally than ephemerally. Like FNC, you can fool a gullible minority indefinitely, but eventually the rest humanity sees through sophistry.

CHAPTER SIX:

"Kindle Books on the First Iraq War"

INTRODUCTION:

My chapters five, six, and seven represent an intellectual troika: Five focused on the scholarly literature concerning the famously-secretive Bush dynasty, and indirectly to understanding FNC's American soap opera; six examines the First Iraq War; and, seven the Second Iraq War. Both six and seven rely heavily on memoirs from former decision-makers and analysts.

AMERICAN AND BRITISH PERCEPTIONS OF FIRST IRAQ WAR:

Let's begin our examination of the First Gulf War with a recently-completed official Army summary: *War in the Persian Gulf: Operations Desert Storm and Desert Shield (August 1990-March 1991)* (Washington DC, Center of United States Army Military History, 2010.) My Kindle e-reader is geared for text-laden serious readers, but underachieves regarding map-and-diagram laden tomes such as this. While many contributed to this book, authorship is attributed to Dr. Richard Stewart, the Center's Chief Historian.

Its chapters include: 1.) "The Army on the Eve of War in the Gulf;" 2.) "The First Deployments"; 3.) "Support of the Deployed Forces;" 4.) "Host-Nation Support and Contacts;" 5.) "Transportation;" 6. "Defogger;" 7.) Mobilizing the Reserve;" 8.) "Planning the Offensive;" 9.) "Operation Desert Storm;" 10.) "Attack on Khadafi;" 11.) "The 100-hour Ground War;" 12.) "Day One;" 13.) "Day Two;" 14.) "Day Three;" 15.) "Day Four;" 16.) "Cease-fire;" 17."Analysis."

The Introduction discusses events two decades earlier about the complexities of U.S. foreign policy in the Persian Gulf region. Unprecedented was America's deploying ground forces to an Arab ally (Saudi Arabia); also new was the first major combat U.S. missions since the Vietnam War; similarly, America and its allies had spent most of their time and money since WW II deterring an advance westward by the Soviet Union's huge Red Army. This study concludes that "The overwhelming success of those endeavors (Operation Desert Shield and Desert Storm) renewed the confidence and assertiveness of the U.S. in the Middle East and the world." (p. 47)

An American regional presence was needed for the next 20 years to contain a resurgent Saddam Hussein. I was pleased to see this official Army study argue that "The coalition partnerships cemented in that initial operation and in the regional peacekeeping operations that followed provided the basis for a growing series of multinational efforts characterizing the post-Cold War environment." (p. 51)

It also suggests that the first Iraq War established unprecedented interoperability between America's three military branches, raised the bar considerably regarding new electronic technologies, and created a new military gold standard copied by many countries. Describing itself as a "short account of a conflict that 20 years ago captured the attention of the world as the first test of the U.S. Army since Vietnam, and its first large-scale armored engagement since WW II." (p. 56)

On 2 August 1990 Iraqi dictator Saddam Hussein launched a major campaign against tiny, oil-laden neighbor, Kuwait. Dr. Stewart opens thus: "The United States Army, reveling in the end of the Cold War, on the verge of downsizing, faced a unexpectedly new challenge. The fall of the Berlin Wall on 9 November 1989, had changed the strategic equation, not only in Europe but throughout the world" (p. 62)

And "The sudden collapse of the Soviet Union left America as the sole remaining superpower in a new, unsettled world. The United States assumed more responsibilities globally and more strategic maneuver room to intervene in foreign crises with less risk of confrontation by another superpower." (p. 79)

In the post-Cold War era, author Stewart describes how one former Soviet client-state, Iraq's Ba'athist dictator, Saddam Hussein, certainly "felt empowered to press his luck here. (p. 81)

The 1990 U.S. Army was qualitatively superior to the one that lost in Vietnam, thus self-absorbed by the daunting task of redesigning itself from pillar to post. For the first time, a strictly volunteer Army without any conscriptees struggled to find its soul. What emerged were more real-world training venues, professionalism, new fighting doctrines (such as "counter-insurgency"), and shaking up the sclerotic military bureaucracy. Inevitably, more thinking outside the proverbial box ensued. (p. 86)

It set out to handle two simultaneous conflicts around the world on a strictly volunteer basis. Higher pay, benefits, and family outreach services were certainly required. The report savages those political advocates of a "peace dividend" as short-sighted, naïve idealists failing to comprehend what a dangerous world we inhabit. This report praises those sober realists eschewing rosy future scenarios of comity. (p. 91)

As for Saddam's motivation here, of course, oil is always discussed, as are Saddam's pan-Arabic delusions, a stale-mated eight-year bloody war with Iran, and the absence of strong warnings from the U.S. The third of these motivations is emphasized by Stewart:

"Hussein's desultory war with Iraq (1980-88) accrued enormous debts; leaving him a large and battle-hardened Army but an economy in disarray. The wealth of Kuwait, in his mind could fix this problem." (p. 97) Hussein's Army had grown ten-fold during the Iran-Iraq War to more than one million soldiers.

In Saudi Arabia, on 6 August 1990, King Fahd bin Abdul Aziz al-Saud, formally accepted American troops on native soil to defend the imperiled Kingdom. This controversial short-term decision would come back to haunt the King in the future. The Saudis possessed cutting-edge military equipment purchased from America, while former Soviet client-state Iraq was saddled with inferior weapons and training.

Let's look at *Gulf War One* by British Gen. Sir Rupert Smith (Random House, 2010), who commanded British Armored Divisions in Iraq. Smith says his views were shaped largely by three forces: "1.) Acquiring, organizing, and training the forces allocated to me so as to defeat the enemy in ways playing to our strengths; 2.) Given the isolation of a desert setting, I had little opportunity to interact with politicians, media representatives, or the general public; 3.) My position in the chain of command was firmly linked and subordinate to the Americans concerning tactics. I commanded about 15,000 men and 7,000 vehicles." (p. 42)

Upon reflection, had any of the coalition forces been poorly prepared, they never could have produced such stunning results so quickly. However, he does suggest that NATO's emphasis had remained askew for too long; that is, "Our training had become too narrowly focused on the anticipated defensive battle in north-west Germany that dominated Cold War-era deterrence. "(p. 71) Furthermore, to keep NATO defense budgets as low as possible, supplies and equipment become out-dated.

Consequently, those who served in the First Iraq War were faced with serious problems. However, Smith sings high praises for the rank-and-file called upon at short notice to deploy to the Middle East. For example, "To their great credit, the men and women deployed rose to the occasion. Considerable initiative and imagination was shown, old lessons were relearned, and necessary adaptations made. The professionalism and resourcefulness of those was very high, as amply illustrated in this book." (p.76)

In what was a conventional land battle, he praises the unsung naval forces providing logistical, communications, and the British Royal Navy that "Led the combined Fleet based on the U.S. Naval Carrier Battle Groups up the Persian Gulf towards Kuwait." (p. 80)

One-half of the Iraqi Navy was neutralized by these armed naval helicopters. He also praises the artillery power which proved more decisive than anyone could have imagined. The author says that sometimes chains-of-command become too hierarchical and stifle the dissent encouraged in democracies, commending his soldiers and others for keeping the dialogue bilateral.

Would the U.K. likely make contributions comparable to the First Iraq War? Probably not, he fears, since its forces have shrunk by one-third, and as he is writing, the British Parliament is considering a "defense review" portending huge defense slices to be lopped from Britain's budget. The Great Recession (2008-10) hurt everyone globally and the current recovery appears weak indeed. (p. 93)

He also commends the First Iraq War for liberating Kuwait, defeating Saddam's Army, yet failing to extricate him immediately, ceasing only after Bush II's invasion in 2003. In the meantime, humanitarian crises occurred in Kurdistan, UN Sanctions were enforced, and no-fly zones enforced over both northern and southern Iraq.

Author Gen. Smith later decries some senior politicians as unwilling to comprehend the way this war had been planned and fought on the ground. Even a few senior military leaders seemed clueless, according to Smith, Their problem? Thinking that "this was the war that never happened," Much ado about nothing; rounding up mega-armies sitting around; rag-tag troops of "old men and young boys." (p. 101)

In reality, this represented "The first war of the new technological era, and possibly the last tank war, in which the coalition fielded and fought the largest armored formation in military history with 400 more tanks than the German expeditionary force at Kursk in 1943." (p.111)

Saddam Hussein's 1968 coup d'etat via his secular Ba'athist Party, and in 1979, he became President and Head of the Army's Revolutionary Command Council. The United States had supported Western-leaning neighbor Iran under the Shah of Iran, but all that ended when a Mullah-run Islamic state under Ayatollah Khomeini emerged (America's worst-case scenario.)

Therefore, for the decade before Bush I decided to invade Saddam's Iraq, the dictator experienced cordial relations with America, simultaneously receiving trade and military aid from both Russia and France. The U.S. also supplied him arms to fight a bloody war with Iran with Iraqi deaths exceeding one million. (p. 124)

His bloody regime also possessed chemical/biological weapons, which Saddam had used against a Kurdish village in Northern Iraq (with Ronald Reagan not only looking the other way, but also blocking UN sanctions); plus, coming close to developing a nuclear weapon then, causing policy-related ripples in Western capitals to the present day. However, by 1990 Hussein's well-oiled Republican Guard led a battle-hardened land

Army unrivaled in the region. He had invaded Shi'ite Iran soon after the Ayatollahs took over that rival country in 1979 (pgs 200-04).

In General Smith's incisive analysis, "Emboldened by continued American support, and funded by oil revenues, Saddam's Ba'athists developed the idea that Iraq could become the leader of the Arab world, with, for example, a seat on the U.N. Security Council. His Ba'ath Party preaches secularism but has Marxist origins, preaches Arab unity, and is also very strong in Syria." (p. 211)

He chronicles what American journalists labeled "the April Glespie Affair," wherein this female U.S. Ambassador to Iraq "Telling Saddam that if he invaded the less-than-democratic rich neighbor (Kuwait), America would not interfere. One prevalent explanation for American behavior in this situation: "America was slowly losing its influence in the Gulf, and so desired a crisis from which it could rescue the oil states." (p. 227)

Chapter one "From Ally to Adversary," follows Bush I's trusted Secretary of State (James Baker) piled up frequent-flyer miles establishing a labor-intensive coalition truly worthy of the name. The UN acted within hours of the Iraqi invasion of Kuwait on 2 August 1990. It didn't hurt that Bush I understood the importance of the international body located in Turtle Bay, NYC, from his days representing his country there. The UN was a forum generally mistrusted by Republicans generally (and Ronald Reagan & Bush II specifically).

That September the U.K. promised to send an armored brigade which Bush I called "icing on the cake." Still haunted by ghostly memories of Vietnam, its prospects hinged significantly on contributions by the other half of the "special relationship," and fortunately for Bush I the British "Iron Lady," Margaret Thatcher, was still in office across the pond. Smith regales over Thatcher's adroit leadership producing a "resounding victory" 8,000 miles away in the Falklands Islands.

Applying his similarly-sophisticated analysis of Britain's readiness specifically and NATO's generally, Smith writes: "However, despite Prime Minister Margaret Thatcher's enthusiastic war leadership, Britain's armed forces were a very long way from combat preparedness. After four decades of increasingly unrealistic pretense of being ready to fight off the hordes of the equally notional Soviet Third Shock Army." (p. 261)

Who was Hashim Ali in this war? Smith calls him a courageous "Iraqi freedom fighter." "I was a freedom fighter, but I was not fighting against Iraq. I'm not Kurdish, but Arab. My group believed we could fight the Iraqi regime desiring that it collapse from within. The majority of opponents to Saddam's regime were Kurdish parties, forces, and militias. But several communist, democratic, and Arab nationalists represented a broad spectrum of opposition to the hated regime. Saddam's propaganda claimed that only his Ba'athist Party existed—but that was simply false." (p. 285)

Furthermore, citing Hashim Ali: "I was approached often to join the Ba'ath Party, but declined saying I had no interest in politics. They required that I sign documents saying I belonged to no other party; I was constantly under severe pressure, with my closest friends arrested and detained. We heard what was happening to people in the detention centers we called 'boxes,' found all over Baghdad." (p. 309)

Hashim's brother was released after a two-week detention, a broken man. He experienced torture by anyone's definition: with steel rods placed up his rectum, followed by electrical discharges shot through that rod. The guards referred to the process as "sitting on a bottle."

He was a member of the Ba'athist Party, so when another detention occurred several months later, he was never heard from again. So in 1987, Hashim left Baghdad for northern Iraq, where he broadcast populist messages exposing the regime's brutality. There he was near the sight of Saddam's poison-gas attacks, which he describes horrifically. (p. 323)

Another interesting person was Irish physician, Dr. Mary McLaughlin, experienced at hospital work in poor countries. In September 1989, she signed up for Baghdad duty, at a time the ravages of the stalemated Iran-Iraq War still wreaked havoc in the shops and writes "Month-by-month, life was slowly improving for the Iraqi people, and our ability to move around the city helped us do our jobs more effectively. They were beginning to spend money again and seemed to be loosening after an awful war." (p. 337)

Having completed her medical contract in Iraq, Dr. McLaughlin, took her ticket to the airport where she learned Saddam had just invaded Kuwait, and it was seven months before she caught another flight.

GULF WAR SYNDROME; GULF WAR NURSES; ANDY HOSKINSON DIARY:

Next, I'm curious about a topic on which I've never read beyond newspapers: Gulf War Syndrome. For that purpose, I turn to the most recent scientific update on the subject, *Gulf War and Health: Volume Eight*, produced by the Committee on Gulf War Health Effects, and published by the National Scientific Academies' Institute of Medicine Press (2010 update). Committee members were selected for their scientific expertise.

The Committee is presently chaired by Stephen L. Hauser, Professor and Chair of Neurology (California University at San Francisco); other medical experts include Epidemiology Professor Alvaro Alonzo (University of Minnesota); Robert Brown, Jr., Chair and Professor of Neurology (University of Massachusetts); Douglas Drossman, Professor of Psychiatry (University of North Carolina); W. Dana Flanders, Epidemiology Professor (Emory University); Matthew Kiefer, Professor of Occupational Medicine (Washington University); Francine Laden, Environmental Epidemiology (Harvard University); Jennifer Peck, Epidemiology Professor (University Oklahoma); Beate Ritz, Epidemiology (UCLA); Rebecca Smith, Psychiatry Professor (Mount Sinai Hospital); Ezra Susser,

Epidemiology (Columbia University); Christina Wolfson, Clinical Epidemiology (McGill University).

Such a major health issue requires lots of expertise, and this is one VERY detailed report; the list of Acronyms alone runs to 11 pages. Plus, the list of reviewers is equally sophisticated as the Investigatory Committee itself. Blind peer review represents the gold standard in scientific endeavors, and it permeates efforts to understand what the baffled public describes loosely as "Gulf War Syndrome." I paraphrase from the Summary.

The Preface runs eight pages, opening with the significant debt American society owes to courageous veterans of Operation Desert Storm; however, it must be countervailed by the best scientific methods brought to bear on sundry problems reported by soldiers and civilians. CTS/science require constantly tweaking what we know about "Gulf War Syndrome," in this eighth attempt to flesh out the details thoroughly (especially via blind peer review.)

"There is no doubt that many of the veterans deployed to the gulf region during 1990-91 continue to experience troubling constellations of symptoms involving multiple body systems; these have been variously termed multi-system illness, or Gulf War illness, and as such are emblazoned in the public mind as a consequence of military service in this battleground." (p. 181)

Especially notable? The prevalence of seemingly-unrelated symptoms, such as persistent fatigue, chronic fatigue syndrome, irritable bowel syndrome, memory problems, headache, bodily pains, sleep disturbances, in addition to other emotional disturbances. Diagnosis proves challenging because of the multiplicity of symptoms. Without putting words into its mouth, the report suggests that we still cannot explain the causative factors here. Consequently, treatments remain hit-and-miss.

Fully 81 million Americans today live with chronic pain, yet comparatively little research money goes to unraveling those baffling processes,

"It is beyond dispute, however, that the prevalence of various symptoms such as joint pain, headaches, and difficulty concentrating is higher in Gulf War veterans than veterans from other theaters." (p. 191)

This report seems to get us somewhat closer to our best approximation of the truth. For example, in 2006, despite higher than normal symptoms reported, "No associations with any specific exposures could be identified." However, two years hence, the experts concluded that Gulf War syndrome "resulted from exposure to pyridostigmine bromide, pesticides, and possibly other exposures." (p. 197) But the most recent report in 2008 is less convinced that this chemical was responsible, concluding, "The current evidence is inadequate to determine whether a causal exposure/symptom link exists here." (p. 203)

So the scientific debate remains robust. Not only does the accumulated body of knowledge keep growing, both study team experts and study team reviewers turn over quite rapidly. The social dynamic of every group varies significantly, especially regarding the scientific and political leadership roles. If a facile explanation existed, scientists would have discovered it long ago (See social psychologist Irving Janning's fascinating works on "groupthink.")

The two-page Conclusion here also warrants attention. Iraq invaded Kuwait on 2 August 1990 after which America constructed a military alliance; air attacks began on 16 January 1991, and a four-day ground offensive ended on 28 February 1991, with a cease-fire signed in April 1991. From about 700,000 troops initially deployed to the Persian Gulf, only 50,000 remained by June 1991. (p. 224)

During and after the war, many complained about symptoms now referred to as "Gulf War Syndrome." Exposure to oil-well fires, anti-nerve-gas agent prophylactic pyridostigmine bromide, and currently about one-third of all soldiers deployed continue complaining about debilitating symptoms such fatigue, musculoskeletal pain, sleep disturbance, cognitive dysfunction, and moodiness. These problems plagued not only Americans, but Canadians, Australians, British, and Danish natives as well.

Next, editor Patricia Rushton provides personal entries from nurses in both Gulf Wars: *Gulf War Nurses: Personal Accounts of 14 Americans, 1990-91and 2003-10* (McFarland Publishers, 2011.) The 16-page Introduction by editor Rushton is sufficiently eclectic, articulate, and personal to encompass nurses' diaries from both Gulf Wars. She begins by refuting the pervasive myth that nurses generally don't lead, merely follow, obeying the commands of more prestigious health practitioners.

As Director of the Nurses at War Project, Rushton's 14 case studies come from the diaries of heroic nurses serving in both Iraq Wars, refute this common myth with alacrity. And while this volume deals only with the Iraqi Wars, "I wish to assure the reader that nurses in every war have made important decisions greatly impacting themselves, their colleagues (and more importantly) their patients and families." (p.17)

She describes the same kind of rustiness referred to by General Smith regarding the U.K. military establishment as applicable to American nurses. But this was really to be expected, for America had not experienced major warfare since the Vietnam debacle, in the case of the U.K. they had the Falklands Islands War to develop pertinent skills.

Rushton joined the Navy Nurses Corps reserve in 1967, serving in Vietnam at the Naval Hospital in Philadelphia, PA. After Vietnam, her responsibilities were not very challenging for many years. She describes unwillingness for most of her reservist colleagues to imagine that Iraq's invasion of tiny, oil-rich Kuwait might result in their being called-up from the week-end duty to which they had become so accustomed. However, she writes that "I understood that the reason the Navy was paying me to drill was that I would be prepared to go to war, if necessary.

With talk of war dominating the news media, it seemed highly probable to me that I would be recalled and mobilized." (p. 26)

This sense of denial also permeated top administrators at the hospital where she then worked. Even when she and others pointed out the high percentage of reservists working there, most of her superiors reacted dismissively. Exactly that scenario came to fruition, of course, and it took time for these head-in-the-sand administrators to procure sufficient replacements.

She also notes that the "shock-and-awe" of real-life war overwhelmed many of her disbelieving associates. "Even for those of us who knew it could happen, the actual reality left us stunned." (p. 36) Many reservists' lives were abruptly interrupted with orders to report for active duty in a day or two. Compounding things was the fact many reservists were placed into positions they had little or no expertise. Furthermore, "All of us were distressed and frustrated by the dearth of information available to us in a rapidly-changing milieu, with decisions made several pay grades above ours, taking time to trickle down." (p. 39)

Like Britain's ill-prepared forces, the editor repeats this mantra: "U.S. nurses in the Gulf Wars have all done what they needed to do, providing medical assistance for soldiers in harm's way. She says that the nurses she interviewed were decidedly self-effacing, while routinely and literally saving lives of injured soldiers. In fact, by doing what was expected of them, considerable suffering had been alleviated. She hopes that the 14 stories "provide lessons of commitment, hard work, creativity, service, and honor from which we can all learn." (p. 56)

Let's examine one story, Navy Nurse Patrick Amersbach, because he personifies the versatility and flexibility at the core of exemplary wartime nursing. With 14 diverse stories to be told, nurse/editor Rushton faced several challenges. But with Amersbach's presented first, I think that the piece could have been tweaked for greater relevance to the title of her book. Maybe the Nurses at War Project lacked such ancillary services. A snippet of Amersbach's chapter pertains to either Iraq War; also, the prose seems sophomoric, and substituting more active verbs for repeated usage of the "verb to be," would add some punch.

Amersbach's story includes interesting experiences in venues as diverse as Bahrain, Yemen, and Iraq, yet only the final two pages treat the latter setting. Amersbach's recounting directly refutes the stereotypical myths that nurses "never lead," by nature "not good decision-makers," or "averse to assuming responsibility." Also implicit in these stereotypes lurks considerable sexism: these stereotypes persist because the bulk of nurses, both military and overall, are females (Amerasbach excepted.) (p. 79)

Next let's peek at soldier Andy Hoskinson's story: *Gulf War Diary* (Kindle, 2011). Pertaining specifically to Gulf War One, the author dedicates it to "The brave men and women who served honorably with the First Cavalry Division during Operations Desert Storm and Desert Shield from September 1990 to May 1991, especially those making the ultimate sacrifice by giving their lives for their country. May they rest in peace." New technologies enable authors to communicate in ways heretofore impossible; his email: andy@hoskinson.net (he welcomes respondents.)

Hoskinson's first-hand account of the Gulf War emerges from his serving as commander of Battery C, 3rd Battalion, 82th Field Artillery, a 155-mm self-propelled field artillery battery in America's famous First Cavalry Division. His unit in turn supported direct artillery assistance to the First Cavalry Divisions 2nd Blackjack Brigade, and was recognized for serving with distinction on many occasions.

Hoskinson's first chapter, "Change of Command," describes his assumption of responsibility on 1 August 1990 for 118 soldiers, eight M109A3 howitzers, and sufficient ammunition and support vehicles "to keep everybody shooting, fueled, and fed. C Battery historically stood ready to deploy to Germany for any possible Warsaw Pact invasion." (p. 63) His prose sounds much like U.K. General Smith's description of preparation for the wrong war, marvelous adaptations by coalition forces to Iraq, and heroes galore in the process.

Hoskinson's unit had also experienced a 50 % turnover rate in the prior six months and it had been a year since C Battery was last rotated to the U.S. National Training Center's desert setting. He believed that his main challenge consisted of months of preparation for a war-game exercise scheduled for the Mojave Desert. He reports that his unit performed admirably when bellicose events in the Persian Gulf presented wholly different sets of challenges. (p. 71)

Chapter two "The Alert That Would Never End," opens with him watching television on 2 August 1990 at 5:30 AM, tuning in to CNN (a self-admitted "news junkie"), where he first heard about Iraqi troops mobilizing on Kuwait's border. His father was a U.S. Army Officer with extensive Middle Eastern experience, contributing to his own fascination with the region. The author realized that if Saddam decided to invade Saudi Arabia as well, he would control fully 40 percent of the world's oil. He also briefed all lieutenants beneath him about the importance of combat-readiness. (p. 84)

As if August 1st and August 2nd hadn't been eventful in Hoskinson's life, August 3rd proved significant as well. Why? Because that date is set aside for "Battalion Organization Day," to commemorate historic accomplishments of that unit. He calls it "The Army's equivalent to a country fair for a battalion's soldiers and families, featuring athletic events, equipment displays, and a picnic lunch." (p. 101) He was promoted and then working out of Fort Hood, in central Texas, later famous for tragic events to transpire in 2011.

The author describes the ambivalence hanging in the air during Battery C's Organization at Belton Lake, near Fort Hood: "Everybody had a great time: the weather was perfect, food plentiful and delicious and athletic events well-organized; however, a strong sense of tension hung in the air among the soldiers and their families alike. What would be the conclusion of the Kuwaiti crisis?" (p.107)

Then on 8 August 1990, one of his platoon sergeants picked up on his portable FM Radio that President Bush had just directed the 82nd Airborne Unit, based at Fort Bragg, NC, to deploy to Saudi Arabia. Simultaneously, the 24th Mechanized Infantry Division at Fort Stewart, GA, was placed on alert.

"Upon hearing this news, I felt a mixture of pride, sorrow, and envy: pride because my country was doing something about this outrage; sad because U.S. forces were once again in harm's way, and envious because I was not there with them." (p. 122) This is one smart human explaining the "emotional roller coaster a professional military person rides regarding his chosen profession." (p. 124)

ORTHODOXIES: WEST POINT REMEMBERS; SO DOES DONALD KAGAN:

The next title grabbed my attention as useful for my survey of books on the First Iraq War: *Leaders in War: West Point Remembers the 1991 Gulf War*, edited by well-known military historian, Donald Kagan and Major Chris Kubik, as part of the Cass Military Studies Series, containing more than 30 books (Frank Cass Publishers, 2005.)

Kagan, Professor of Military History at West Point, and author of several books; one co-authored with Frederick Kagan, *While America Sleeps; The Military History of Tsarist Russia and the Soviet Union,* another co-authored with Robin Higham; and, *The Military Reforms of Nicholas I.* For more than two decades, Major Chris Kubik has held varied Army leadership posts, for example: duty in Panama, Persian Gulf, and Bosnia/Croatia. Now he works alongside colleague Donald Kagan at West Point.

Their book contains 12 chapters: 1.) "The Battle for Norfolk;" 2.) "Attacking the Republican Guard;" 3.) "Airborne Unit Operations;" 4.) "Theater Logistical Support;" 5.) "Military Police Support;" 6.) "Strategic Military Intelligence Support;" 7.) "The Battle of 73 Easting;" 8.) "Fratricide at Ar Rumayiah;" 9.) "Tactical Logistical Support;" 10.) toon Leader Challenges;" 11.) "Tactical Engineer Support;" 12.) "Training Individual Ready Reserve Soldiers."

The 6-page Foreword, by Dennis Showalter, touches on several themes relating to the U.S. Army's post-Vietnam funk. Eminently thoughtful, Showalter begins his analysis with these alluring words: "The Gulf War of 1990-91 is likely to be recorded by historians as an incomplete process that employed a steam hammer to crack a nut producing disappointing results given the elaborate preparation involved." (p. 121) He also traces the shock effect of the Cold War's silent denouement as problematic for the U.S. in several ways.

Reliance on revolutionary high-tech weapons, professionalization, favoring elite Special Forces over economies of scale, characterized a naval-gazing Army during these transitional years. What options should career soldiers be exploring in a down-sized, marginalized institution? For one, "to go or to stay?"

Reprise-like, "The one thing the U.S. Army of 1990 didn't expect was to pick itself up at short notice from its long-established bases conducting large-scale, high-end conventional campaigns in a significantly underdeveloped infrastructures" (p. 143) Showalter closes thus: "The narratives in this book combine to tell the story of an accomplished mission that only appeared easy in hindsight." (p.148)

Frederick Kagan's lengthy Introduction follows the Foreword impressively, providing essential background information. Then he shifts to its aftermath: "For the next 12 years, America/allies used air-strikes and ground-demonstrations trying to press Saddam into compliance with the provisions of several U.N. resolutions after combat ended in 1991, but to no avail. In March and April 2003, the coalition again assaulted Saddam's regime from the air, ground and sea, utterly destroying the Iraqi Army and his government in three weeks." (p.157)

Fredrick Kagan labels this as one of history's most successful military campaigns, right up there with the 1967 and 1973 Israeli victories, as well as the Nazis' blitzkrieg campaign leveling France and Poland. He also finds eloquence concerning the U.S. Army's patient professionaliza- tion in the 1970s and 1980s, to ever greater heights thereafter. However, he does take issue with the conventional wisdom that high-tech weapons of "shock-and-awe" constitute the principal explanation.

He does, however, describe how painful lessons were gleaned via post- Vietnam soul searching, as well as from Arab-Israeli Wars leading the Army to create five new weapons systems: M1 Abrams tank; M3 Bradley Infantry Fighting Vehicle; AH64 Apache Attack helicopter; the UH60 Blackhawk transport helicopter; and, the Patriot Anti-missile system. Plus, "the perfection of stealth technology led to the fielding of F-117 stealth fighters and their use in the First Gulf War, and the B-2 Bomber thereafter." (p. 183)

Finally, the Multiple-Launch Rocket System (MLRS) used in both Iraq Wars, far exceeded Iraq's out-dated Soviet weaponry. Something I didn't know before? The First Iraq War represented America's initial experience with an all-volunteer force.

Also, after Vietnam, services created their own combat training centers. The Air Force in 1965 at Nellis Air Force Base; soon, the Navy followed suit developing the Fighter Weapons School (Top Gun) at Miramar Base; in 1978 the Marines replicated these efforts via their Air-Ground- Training-Center at 29 Pines, CA; finally, the Army unveiled its National Training Center at Fort Irwin, CA.

What distinguishes these centers? Force-on-force simulated exercises. Kagan describes them as "invaluable in a number of ways." So he concedes the obvious point that cutting-edge high-tech weapons represented a necessary-but-not-sufficient condition to own the battlefields.

The book itself is broken down into four parts: 1.) "Senior Ground Force Commanders;" 2.) "Stories of Senior Combat Support Officers;" 3.) "Junior Combat Support Services;" 4.) "Junior Quarter-Master and Engineering Officers." They intend to diversify the requisite reporting processes.

The main conclusion? "That the two Gulf Wars were remarkably similar yet remarkably different." Both were decided by a large-scale mechanized maneuver (albeit smaller ground force against a weaker enemy in 2003); air campaigns were conducted simultaneously with ground offensives (much longer in 1991 than 2003); new weapons systems were used (but not as much in 2003); and, intelligence information assisted victory (but not as decisively in 1991). (p. 23)

Kagan states "The 2003 war did not end until American tanks drove through the streets of Baghdad, having destroyed Republican Guard armor units maneuvering to defeat them, just as they had in 1991. The fears and tensions of the battlefield were just as great. Those fears were even greater among the combat service support elements in this war because of the guerrilla attacks launched by the Saddam Fedayeen." (p. 281)

Chapter One is called "The Battle for Norfolk," and relies heavily on Brigadier General John S. Brown, also sporting fine credentials. His 2nd Armored Division brigade left its base in Germany to become the 1st Infantry Division's 3rd Brigade in the Persian Gulf. It provided additional tank capability to the expanding US VII Corps. Its role in Iraq is described as "uniquely" charged with punching straight through clearing safe lanes for other units rumbling around Iraqi fortifications.

In the wastelands of Northwestern Kuwait, General Brown participated in fierce battles against Saddam's highly-experienced Republican Guard. General Brown's tankers faced several tough missions: breaching, fighting, passage of lines, long range advancements through enemy lines, and multiple shared objectives.

He provides snippets of action, insights, and strategic analysis germane to modern combat. The General's unit's faced big challenges requiring near-perfect tactics and strategies in a desert milieu. Discipline, attention to detail, and honest assessment provide vital edges for the good guys in harm's way. The editors write poignantly that "leaders of character build units of character," although it seems to me that "a culture of obedience" gets more at the crux of what he describes.

Like his father, he has chosen the life of a soldier. On 26 February 1991 he describes what was happening around him: "At the 73 easting, the brigade's leading M1A1 tanks rolled into a fierce exchange with dug-in Iraqi tanks and soldiers. The bloodiest single engagement of the Gulf War (the battle for a goose-overlay code-named Norfolk),' was on. The patch of trackless desert being contested may have possessed a name other than Norfolk, but the Americans fighting for it certainly did not know it." (p. 322)

Fleshing out Operation Norfolk's details, Brown tells how the Americans attacked easterly at night from the barren desert with task forces three abreast totaling eight companies in the first wave via frontages of 1,500 meters per company and 100 meters per tank. Within companies, vehicles spaced at 50 meters apart, with several times that distance separating companies, and over a kilometer between task forces. (p. 342)

Enterprising M1A1 gunners knew that thermal sights detected temperature differentials from land mines buried beneath shallow sand. These gunners talked drivers through the mine-fields, enabling other lucky ones to follow precise path. Eleven A1M1 tanks fell into ditches or Iraqi bunkers, from which they were all extricated by intrepid M88A1 Recovery Vehicles, but "the most dangerous aspect of the obstacles and recovery efforts was the close proximity of Iraqi infantry soldiers." (p. 357)

Then, "As dawn broke in the desert, the Iraqi will to resist snapped. Maybe daylight provided their first full appreciation of the mass of armor facing them. Starved as they were for all supplies, perhaps they were discouraged by the businesslike refueling/resupply unfolding before them, but just out of range. Unlike soldiers the Brigade captured elsewhere, at Norfolk they were particularly well-fed, well-led and proud of the fight they had put up." (p. 378)

He stresses the complexity of the Brigade's maneuvers, executed during darkness without notice on the heels of a 10-kilometer front requiring 19 separate actions at the Battalion level. It propelled a Brigade-size front measuring 10-kilometers through six individual passage lanes; followed by linkups after blackouts. As for the soldiers involved, "They may not have known each other personally, but they knew the mission and its detailed coordination necessary to carry it out." (p. 402)

FIRST-WAVE REVISIONISM: STEPHEN PELLETIERE AND OIL:

Stephen Pelletiere takes on conventional wisdoms in *Iraq and the International Oil System: Why America Went to War in the Gulf* (Kindle, 2001). Its six chapters include: 1.) "The Birth of the U.S. Oil Industry and It's Movement Overseas;" 2.) "A Handful of Companies Gain Control of the Industry;" 3.) "The Fall of Mosadeq and the Triumph of the Oil Cartel in America;" 4.) "The OPEC Revolution and the Clashes Between;" 5.) "Second and Third Shocks and the 1987 Reflagging;" 6.) "Iran-Contra and Iraq: The Media Campaign that Took America to War."

Author Pelletiere argues that both the media and the American public have failed to analyze rigorously the real cause for the First Gulf War:

both asleep at the wheel, he suggests. Few observers ascribe causation to the real culprit: corporate oil interests deliberately designed to guarantee benefits to the lucky few by denying them to the masses.

To wit, "The explanation as to why the Gulf War occurred seems untenable. It was fought with such ferocity, and so many resources were expended, that there must have been something great at stake. Since Iraq has oil, and took over Kuwait, which also has oil, and since oil is so vital to the smooth functioning of the world's economy, it appeared natural that oil would have something (if not everything) to do with why this war took place." (p. 16.)

Pelletiere's thesis differs: "Insufficient evidence that a global oil system exists, unfurled in the 1920s by three corporations creating what classical capitalists claim to loathe: cartels (domestically= monopoly; internationally=cartel)." (p. 72) A major U.S. Senate investigation in 1952 provides the paper trail explaining the evolution of this powerful organization. Conventional journalistic wisdom believes that sometime between those 1952 hearings, and the start of the first OPEC revolution in 1973, the cartel merely managed to limp along until lady luck shone again in 1979 and then 1988.

Conversely, Pelletiere says that Saddam Hussein was looking to grow his influence in the region, which explains his Saddam's bloody/expensive 8-year war with Iran ending in 1988. Saddam's game plan: to head OPEC (providing both political and economic clout); control over OPEC pricing would constitute a major coup. He criticized America's extant 2001 policy towards Iraq (Dual Containment) as self-contradictory and likely to produce a bellicose reprise in the Middle East. In 2001, Pelletiere says he was warning U.S. policy-makers against dismissing the 1991 war as aberrational.

He peeks at big oil in America and how it morphed into a global phenomenon; and also details the formation of the greatest of all cartels, introducing serious scrutiny of how big oil became a "system," in the narrow social science sense well developed by many scholars. (Systems theory migrated from physical sciences to the social sciences)

The author also examines the U.S. government's mixed-bag of efforts to, if not regulate, at least influence big oil (the words influence and regulate apply here, but to see the government in any sense "controlling" big oil he considers delusional. Also, the combative relationship between various Iraqi regimes and OPEC (including Saddam's Ba'athist Party). Furthermore, the 1973 OPEC coup and its ramifications; and, analysis of the U.S. administration's PR selling the war to an ambivalent public.

Elsewhere, he answers everything you always wanted to know about both the economics of Big Oil and its history. Many families besides the Rockefellers' Standard Oil became deliriously wealthy. According to Pelletiere, however "the oil industry always tended toward glut." (p. 58) Which must be countervailed.

Why? Because of America's property ownership laws: Owners can claim not only above-ground legal rights, but below-ground as well. Also, "the rule of capture" enables one to own whatever migrates to your turf (including black gold). Also, once tapped, rigs can proceed to extract right up to the point of exhaustion. Thus, quickly huge amounts of oil supply are produced, reducing demand, leading plunging oil prices. (p. 63)

Could this occupational hazard of market gluttony be overcome by some kind of collective intervention via public or private actors? Yes, with such gargantuan resources at stake, humanity usually devises sleazily creative solutions. Somewhere along the line oil's flow needed to be interdicted. The refinery stage seemed a likely prospect, because they held onto the oil longer than anyone else.

While refiners typically were maverick characters, they were relatively few in number. Pelletiere says that the solution lay in what came to be known as "drawbacks," or coercions imposed on the refiners by the railroads, "who created conditions whereby the industry was made to behave." (p. 71)

This is how regulation was achieved; and surprise, surprise: The railroads somehow picked the Rockefeller group above other "competitors" for preferential treatment. Their first refinery was established in Cleveland in 1865; rebates were a favorite form of reciprocity then. Please identify the vaunted free spirit of competitive capitalism in this picture?

More importantly, how does this relate back to Schweizers' book on the Bush family's old-boy networks with the Rockefellers and other economic elites? Be prepared for facing the epitome of greed if you read Pelletiere. It's now all a well-documented greed-atorium historians have painstakingly unraveled. (p. 80) No wonder my favorite Rockefeller, Senator Jay (Dem-WV) goes by that name rather than his real one: John D. Rockefeller, IV.

My final entry for Iraq War One consists of an exciting memoir by two pilots named Braxton Eisel and Jim Shreiner, *Magnum! The Wild Weasels in Desert Storm* (2009).

It has 17 chapters, three Appendices, and lots of photos and maps. It's based on a personal journal kept by Jim Shreiner, the public record, and recollections by other members of the F-4G Wild Weasels aircrew.

In their Introduction, "When Iraqi President Saddam Hussein sent his military forces to invade and occupy the tiny neighboring country of Kuwait in August 1990, his actions and the actions of the American-led coalition that stood against him created a global chess game. The pieces on the board were controlled by those with the 'big picture.' The pawns in that game doing the fighting and dying consisted of hundreds of thousands of men and women who left their homes and families for a seemingly endless desert, while the world stage-play unfolded. At times, the war was scary; at other times funny as hell. If you survived the former, it turned into the latter." (p.56)

Also, "Remembering all of the war movies that I've seen, the thing that struck me the most about last night's cacophony was the absence of sound. The barrage of anti-craft fire seemingly all around my aircraft looked intimidating but was completely silent. Although it was probably much farther away than I thought, it definitely caught my attention!" (p. 62) The authors also go into the evolution of Surface-To-Air-Missiles (SAMS) as serious threats to American pilots.

It was on 1 May 1960 that Francis Gary Powers' 1,000+ mile route over the Soviet Union was rudely interrupted. Flying a CIA Lockheed U-2 reconnaissance jet at 70,000 feet, an altitude where previous Soviet MiG jets had failed to threaten him. However, on this day Soviet technology trumped America's as their new V-750 Dvina rocket sent Powers parachuting to hostile turf. This occurred late in Dwight Eisenhower's second term; shortly thereafter, John Kennedy defeated Ike's V-P (Richard Nixon) using to great advantage a supposed "missile gap" between the two superpowers. (p. 71)

Captured and humiliated by Soviet propaganda, Powers was sentenced and imprisoned in Moscow. "The SAM operator, under intense pressure from Soviet leader Nikita Khrushchev, fired the instant Powers was in range. With a cloud of noxious fumes and a bright orange glow, the V-750 Dvina salvo of three missiles quickly leapt from their launchers and rocketed skyward. From that day on, SAMs have become a major threat to Allied aircraft." (p. 82) Powers survived his landing, and the authors continue tracing Soviet SAMs role in the hands of the North Vietnamese in their Civil War.

Much of the book traces the arc of conflict in Desert Storm between Saddam's Soviet technology and Allied American military hardware. In other words, by 1990, the U.S. and its Allies had a long history of proving their superiority over the Soviets and rendering Francis Gary Powers' fate a glaring aberration; jargon-laden technologies spice up the Cold War vocabulary.

CHAPTER SEVEN:

"Kindle Books on the Second Iraq War"

INTRODUCTION:

A dozen years passed between the First and Second Iraq Wars, but the qualitatively different nature of each warrants using the concept of light years rather than calendar years. Before surveying the literature on the Second Iraq War, *New York Times* journalist Michael Schwartz has raised a frightening specter echoed by three other serious foreign policy analysts: Andrew Bacevich, Matthew Galbraith, and Matt Taibbi. Namely, George Orwell's nightmarish world of superpowers so heavily invested in war's self-fulfilling benefits as to render them incapable of imagining pacific solutions to conflicts.

NEW THESIS: WAR WITHOUT END ?

Michael Schwartz, *War Without End: The Iraq War in Context* (Kindle, 2008), includes 19 chapters: 1.) "The Oily Origins of the War in Iraq;" 2.) "Toxic Economics;" 3.) "The Neoliberal Project in Iraq;" 4.) "Struggle for Iraqi Oil;" 5.) "Collective Punishment;" 6.) "Insurgent Strongholds;"

7.) "Torture, Death Squads, and the Second Battle of Fallujah;" 8.) "The Human Toll;" 9.) "Creating Slum Cities;" 10.) "Saga of the Al-Fatah Pipeline;" 11.) "Degradation of the Iraqi Infrastructure;" 12.) "Downward Spiral;" 13.) "Tidal Wave of Misery;" 14.) "Who's Sovereign NOW?" 15.) "Creation of Shia City-States;" 16.) "Semi-Sovereign Kurdistan;" 17.) "Rebellious Sunni Cities;" 18.) "The Battle of Baghdad;" 19.) "Ending: How Washington's Dream Foundered in Iraq."

I like how Schwartz imbeds the 2003 Iraq War into proper historical context. Just how did Bush II hoodwink so many to accept his absurd article of faith: 9/11 changed everything so fundamentally that a new paradigm demanded radically new thinking? Bush II condescendingly referred to his rare critics as "mired in pre-9/11 thinking." Why did so few liberals defend Bill Clinton's pacific affluence sans bellicosity?

But since Bush II's neo-con "shadow" brain trust during the Clinton years blasted the Democrats for wasting "America's uni-polar moment," it should have been clear that Bush II's chicken-hawks neo-cons would prove more bellicose; but who have predicted the alacrity with which Bush II would exploit 9/11 so shamelessly?

Going after Osama bin Laden's Al Qaeda after 9/11? Of course: no brainer for any administration, Democrat or Republican. Getting Al Qaeda was the top-level law enforcement goal for which America's 17 secret services receive hundreds of billions of dollars. But an overkill War On Terror (WOT) inconsistent with democratic principles?

Give me a break!

The Democrats apparently feared looking weak on defense, caving in to Bush II's rationalizations to kill the Al Qaeda fly with mega-baseball-bats. Schwartz's title exposes the disquieting "business-as-usual" nature of GOP bellicosity.

Authors' Introductions often tap into the essence of their message. For Schwartz: "In the days just after 9/11, as the United States rallied behind President George W. Bush and his newly-initiated global War On Terror, many people visualized the use of America's military might as a fast and efficient way to cut through the Gordian knot of international intrigue that protected Al Qaeda and its terrorist cohort." (p. 18)

America's unparalleled military might struck the neo-cons as their perfect storm for two reasons. First, depose autocratic rogue regimes spurring our perennial goal of democratizing the world; Second, obliterate safe-havens in rogue regimes harboring terrorists ("state-sponsored terrorism.") Scholars writing about "state-sponsored terrorism" limited these miscreants to about 15 out of 190-some countries. Bush II, however, identified around 60.

What seemed initially like a quick military victory, with few casualties, and a public- support scenario consistent with the First Iraq War, success was hubristically taken-for- granted. A slam dunk in feeble Afghanistan, then a year later in Iraq. Bush II's true-believer neo-cons, especially Donald Rumsfeld, Dick Armitage, Dick Cheney, and Paul Wolfowitz, made it sound so easy.

However, in 2010 we were still mired in both Afghanistan and Iraq with soldiers routinely serving multiple tours of duty resulting in unprece dented rates of PTSD and suicides. I consider Bush's Polyannish prophesies sufficiently grave to warrant criminal proceedings of the kind advocated by ex-Prosecutor Anthony Bugliosi in chapter two.

Schwartz asserts that "The migrating goals for the continuing war in Iraq were telltale indicators that none of the publicly-stated justifications was fundamental to Washington's intransigent determination to conquer Iraq." (p. 51) Schwartz says his extensive research enabled him to dig beneath to the subtext of Bush's catchy one-liners as not only irrational, but often self-contradictory.

I liked his section on "The Paradox of Shock-and-Awe," the term U.S. military strategists used to describe "a fireworks show, featuring spectacular visuals of explosions in and around Baghdad." (p.73) The author attributes inspiration for this phrase to Navy Commander and National War College Professor Harlan Ullman. Elsewhere, Ullman is quoted analogizing "shock and awe" to the 1945 nuclear attack on Hiroshima.

Schwartz characterizes Baghdad "shock-and-awe's" similar to the impact on the civilian population as comparable to the infamous WWII Blitzkrieg of London. Demoralization represents a significant part of the game plan. He questions the wisdom of this strategy in the 2003 Iraq setting on several scores.

He also references Canadian journalist Naomi Klein's explanation of this phenomenon among U.S. policy-makers in her recent *Shock Doctrine.* Critics have a field day explicating several obvious downsides to the strategy; not least of which its disregard for the "just war" prohibition against confusing military and civilian targets. While Bush II made no effort to incorporate "just war doctrine" in 2003, his father cited the concept repeatedly in 1991.

Schwartz also contends that while 2003's "shock- and-awe created much damage to the Iraqi infrastructure, it fell well short of being considered profound in nature." (p. 128) He maintains that "shock-and-awe's" limited success in Iraq reduced displays of "overt bitterness" when American forces occupied all of Iraq's major cities. He attributes the well-documented but-preventable "looting" of historical treasures to forces unrelated to the invasion.

What went so fundamentally astray in Iraq? Schwartz fills many pages, but I especially like this paragraph "To understand the powerful resistance that emerged after that first quiescent period, and then continued to amplify for years afterwards, we must search for complex non-military factors energizing the revolution of social chaos into a guerilla war aimed at expelling the U.S. military from Iraq. We must in particular ponder the size and resilience of the insurgency, which persisted and grew magnitudes stronger despite the escalating application of overwhelming firepower." (p. 155)

And no surprise that he holds the American infotainment media guilty of dereliction of duty as quiescent lapdogs. They lacked the courage to dig beneath surface politics (many subsequently admitting so). They bought into what Naomi Kline so compellingly describes from economic development circles as "neoliberal structural adjustment theory," deriving mostly from "Chicago School economists" aggressively advanced for many decades, as a conduit for American imperial ambitions. (p. 160)

By 2006, Iraq's vital agricultural sector had been gutted, cities bulging with unemployed migrants, manufacturing weakened, and oil resources mismanaged contributing to a populace "mired in a downward spiral of poverty and desperation." (p. 164) All of this "real war" in Iraq occurred after Bush II's "Major combat operations in Iraq have ended" speech.

Schwartz also cites former FED chairman Alan Greenspan's words that: "I am saddened that it is politically inconvenient to acknowledge what everyone knows: that Iraq is largely about oil." (p. 171)

ISIKOFF'S HUBRIS; NIKOLAEV/HANEKIN'S GLOBAL MEDIA DEBATE; DISSECTORVILLE:

More excoriating, however, is Michael Isikoff's dense book wherein numerous eye-witness expletive-laden quotations are attributed to Bush II prior to the 2003 Iraq War. In the Introduction to *Hubris: The Inside Story of Spin, Scandal, and the Selling of the War In Iraq.* (2009) Isikoff cites several eye-witness sources describing frequent secret meetings between Vice President Dick Cheney and CIA officials responsible for intelligence concerning Iraq.

FOXYMORON

He copiously recounts V-P Cheney brow-beating CIA analysts to find any hint regarding two of Cheney's mistaken beliefs: 1.) Saddam Hussein possessed a robust nuclear weapons program; 2.) Hussein's Ba'athist Party was in cahoots with Osama bin Laden's Al Qaeda conspiring against the U.S. Methinks only one term accurately describes an obsessive mistaken-belief clung to tenaciously: paranoia. If the foo shits, wear it, and here it does.

CIA operative Valerie Plame Wilson, and her husband, Joseph got tangled up in knots pressured by Cheney's self-fulfilling prophecies. The "iron-cake uranium" rumors sniffed out by the U.K.'s M5 were lapped up by Cheney, Bush, and even Secretary of State Colin Powell at the UN (describing a wild rumor as confirmed fact). Furthermore, Bush II even inserted it into his 2006 State of the Union speech. Of Valerie Plame Wilson, Isikoff writes: "Her job was to find the evidence of clandestine efforts that Bush and Cheney desired." (p. 266)

Similarly, "From CIA Director George Tenet on down, everyone in the intelligence community realized it was crucial to do whatever they could—probe every corner, chase any lead—to penetrate Saddam's Iraq for information." (p. 276) Relentless effort went into recruiting any disgruntled Iraqi scientist with bribes/blackmail (carrots/sticks), but nothing panned out. The CIA possesses a vast bureaucracy of analysts and agents charged with separating the wheat from the chaff for consideration by policy-makers; however, a bizarre twist here consisted of Cheney demanding often to see "raw intelligent reports." (p. 131)

Scholars know how sleazy results occur when well-intended CIA agents take an assignment too personally, or become true-believers precluding sound judgment as objective analysts. Many books already document such abuses. However, in this case, Isikoff's extensive research leads him to defend good-faith efforts by CIA agents asked to fit a round peg into a square hole.

Ergo, "The operating premise of the CIA in this case was that accurate intelligence mattered. It was their duty to obtain truthful information (however possible) and get it into the hands of policy-makers. Spies, eavesdroppers, and analysts collected and processed information intelligence so that senior government officials, especially the commander-in-chief, could render the best decisions possible. However, these officials were convinced they possessed sufficient information about how to handle Iraq." (p. 323)

Isikoff quotes an expletive-laden, out-of-control comment about Saddam as something historians cannot ignore in explaining Bush II's magnetic honing in on Saddam, a man his father once called "the worst dictator since Hitler;" exclusive company indeed. Mining the endless Oedipal implications of this context, the author writes "The President's gut instincts and a powerful antipathy toward the dictator who had plotted to kill Bush I, and whom his father had defeated then left in place. Saddam also represented an all-too-easy target in the days after 9/11." (P. 338)

While the U.S. media were co-opted, that was not the case internationally. Two books I recommend highly: The first is called *Leading to the 2003 Iraq War: The Global Media Debate* (2008), edited by journalists Alexander Nikolayev and Ernest Hakanen, featuring media scholars around the world. They focus on the debate whether to go to war. In their Introduction, the authors refer to the bewildering barrage of rationales, and suggest the domestic news media were partially responsible for massive subterfuge.

Their 15 chapters include: 1.) "A Debate Delayed Is a Debate Denied;" 2.) "Strange Bedfellows;" 3.) "The Whole World is Watching, But So What;?" 4.) "Their Morals are Ours;" 5.) "Postmodern War in Iraq;" 6.) "Orientalism Revisited;" 7.) "A View From Australia;" 8.) "Le Monde on a Likely Iraq War;" 9.) "The Germans Protest;" 10.) "The Sheer and Opaque Screens;" 11.) "The American-Israeli Dialogue;" 12.) "Russia's

Failure to Support;" 13.) "Chinese Press Coverage;" 14.) "Zimbabwean Debate;" 15.) "Chilean, Mexican, and Spanish Coverage."

Nikolayev and Hakanen dwell on the uniqueness of any nation-state invoking the bogus legal doctrine of "preventive war," and supremely ironic that its perpetrator is bookmarked between Canada and Mexico. Why? Because our violent history makes even our allies skeptical about both motives and veracity. Nikolayev and Hakanen also contend that Bush II's rush to war seriously demeaned the international community's most potent voice for peace: the United Nations, which Bush I employed deftly but Bush II deceived intentionally.

Soon after 9/11, in his January 2002 State of the Union speech, W portrayed the "Axis of Evil" as his version of Ronald Reagan's "Evil Empire," advancing the legitimacy of "preemptive attack" against U.S. enemies. Stoking 9/11-related fears, he said: "I will not wait on events, while dangers gather. I will not stand by, as peril draws closer and closer." (p. 36) These authors repeat Isikoff's account of Bush II's full-court-press to fabricate phantom links between Al Qaeda and Saddam Hussein.

They cover the "hawks versus doves" dynamic found in many U.S. Administrations.

In Bush II's case, the hawks numbered four (Dick Cheney, Donald Rumsfeld, Paul Wolfowitz, and Condoleezza Rice); while the doves, in this case more properly called "internationalists," numbered three (Colin Powell, Richard Haase, and Richard Armitage). "The President, of course, sided with the hawks. However, the evidence favoring a 2003 War in Iraq proved so specious that a high-pitched drone of incredulity lasted not weeks or months, but many years." (p. 53)

Nikolayev and Hakanen, however, concentrate on the crucial pre-war months: Why? Because as William Dorman explains in chapter one, "The myth of war, once a war starts, has a power to overwhelm culture and public discourse, thereby taking over thought." (p. 63) He explains how typically once war ensues, serious media debating ceases. The preceding months normally witness considerable diversity of opinion.

They try to ferret out the "real reasons" why various countries either supported or opposed the 2003 Iraq War. And where better to discern cogent answers than via each nation-state's public media. These journalists believe this constitutes the motivational royal road in each country studied.

Subtext analysis contributes profounder understanding why various actors acted in a variety of ways. Actually, it appears to me that the edited treatise's level-of-analysis consists as more accurately regional than national. They do so in order to avoid a traditionally Eurocentric vantage point. Scholarship should aim at getting beyond ethnocentrism.

Some of the countries reluctantly supporting Bush II: United Kingdom, Spain, Australia, and Israel. Those in opposition were led by China, Russia, France, Germany, Mexico, and most Arab states. The authors also assure the reader that their endeavors possess "no political agenda." (p. 76)

Part I emphasizes America, the United Kingdom, and Australia ("the coalition of the willing"); whereas Part II hones in on the sizeable non-English speaking world. They also hold the domestic media as eager contributors to the drums of war (raising TV ratings.)

William Dorman writes "There is no action of the state that can have a more immediate or dramatic effect on the lives of its citizens than the use of military force against an external foe (real or imagined.) Consequently, in a democracy, public debate matters most over the question of whether to wage a war." (p. 105) Then he proceeds to explicate two theses: 1.) Once guns commence, CTS take a hiatus; 2.) The press is the only institution capable of even bringing CTS to the table regarding foreign policy generally, and war specifically.

Also, "You can count out the gullible general public almost completely on this score, unless a war is lost (e.g., Vietnam), or drags on too long (e.g., Iraq and Afghanistan.) Such public awakenings, however, occur after obscene amounts of blood and treasure have been expended. Therefore, this book fixates laser-like on those months before the spring of 2003. Dorman contends that so weak were Bush II's rationales de jour as to mislead Congress thoroughly, the sole question being whether he had done so knowingly." (p. 127)

"When people discuss the media in America, they mean TV news, like a daily textbook on world affairs, providing an agenda, and a vocabulary to describe various players on the world stage. Mistaken beliefs often overwhelm reality during such crises." (p. 138) A "belief versus knowledge gap" becomes embarrassing at such times. Research suggests that the most fallacious "misperceptions" consisted of a link between Osama bin Laden and Saddam Hussein.

After this war, writings and interviews with Bush II advisors and experts such as Richard Clarke, David Kay, and Hans Blix did little to correct popular misconceptions about key issues. How does this occur? Easily, because once a war is considered won, it becomes psychologically uncomfortable for denizens to contemplate their having been duped. Dorman's elegant explanation relies heavily on the theory borrowed from social psychology called "cognitive dissonance theory." (p. 154)

Weisberg maintains that not since JFK has America witnessed such a complex family drama. In each case we find the behavior of a "preexisting family dynasty," and clearly family expectations drove Bush II to enter politics. "But unlike Kennedy, Bush II has "always acted as a prickly nepotist." And one chapter addresses the question of Bush's relationship to God, and another to his complex relationship with Karl Rove, arguing that Rove get Bush II on the wrong path straight away. He also considers Bush more intelligent than the conventional wisdom, but rather defiantly anti-intellectual and incurious. (p. 166)

He concludes about Bush II's presidency "I came to think of his story constituting a tragedy because of the way that the president was unable to master his feelings for his father drove decisions with terrible consequences not just for him, but also for America and the world." (p. 178) Weisberg laces his prose with references to Shakespearean literature's profound understanding of human tragedy.

Another book comes from by ex-insider turned-outsider, free-lance journalist and filmmaker, Danny Schechter, the iconoclastic CTS practitioner that Bill O'Reilly only claims to be. Schechter's book and award-winning documentary film deal with the "Other WMD," *Embedded: Weapons of Mass Deception: How the Media Failed to Cover the War in Iraq* (Prometheus Books, 2003), Schechter says he "imbedded himself with his TV" to make specific comparisons to specific news media, both here and abroad.

According to Schechter, simultaneous wars involving WMD occurred: 1.) Military actions fought to neutralize Saddam Hussein's supposed Weapons of Mass Destruction; and 2.) Shadow war fought with cameras, satellites, and imbedded journalists via sophisticated propaganda. He writes: "The war coverage sold the war even as it claimed to be merely reporting it." (p. 10)

The clever process whereby Bush II's Administration "embedded" journalists with fighting forces was really unprecedented. The Pentagon learned from Vietnam the risks inherent in allowing journalists to roam free. Bush I nailed it in 1991 when stunning new technologies created the first "shock-and-awe" effects converting that slam-dunk war into kind of a living room "sports spectacle," and Americans lapped it up.

Schechter details how sordidly Bush II financed the embedding process, accuses the national media of "appearing comatose" concerning embedding. It took one investigative reporter from *Milwaukee Magazine* and a courageous editor to embarrass the national media into understanding that the American taxpayers picked up the hefty costs of this rabid infotainment. For example, training media personnel, transportation costs, and highly-sophisticated equipment proved costly.

Schechter lampoons the networks, contending "American TV networks saw the war coverage as 'their finest hour' giving it non-stop attention with new technologies revealing close-up access via embedded reporters. And not only did viewers in different world regions see different coverage, but so did Americans according to which channels they watched. For example, Fox News unabashedly provided 24/7 jingoism and repetition of Bush's story line." (p. 244)

FNC's ratings always skyrocket during wars, especially 2003. Schechter cites university research indicating that Fox viewers ranked highest on "frequency of misperception" (80%); whereas PBS scored lowest (23%) with CNN falling in between (55%) on this crucial variable.

CIRCLE IN THE SAND; WAR ON MILITARY FAMILIES; SHEER INCOMPETENCE:

The title of our next book caught my eye, Christian Alfonsi's *Circle in the Sand: Why We Went Back to Iraq* (Kindle, 2003), which claims intellectual dibs as the first book analyzing exactly why America rushed to war in 2003. Kindle's biggest weakness consists of relatively poor graphics, such as maps, diagrams, and photos (central to Alfonzi's book.)

He opens with these intriguing words: "This book will overturn much of what you know, or think you may know, about the two Bush presidencies and their respective wars against Saddam Hussein." (p.33) Being first always counts for something, but I think the author has better reasons to toot his own horn here.

Such as, "The book uncovers the hidden reasons why many of the same senior officials, serving in two Bush Administrations, came to hold radically different views about Iraq and Saddam Hussein the second time around. *Circle in the Sand* traces the shifting foreign policy beliefs of the Bush inner circle over these dozen years, revealing how the 'lessons' of the first Bush Administration directly impacted decisions on Iraq the second. The over-arching theme here relates to how the worldview of American leaders can undergo drastic changes in response to unexpected political setbacks—and the perceived mistakes of previous leaders." (p. 42)

The Cold War's symbolic end occurred with the fall of the Berlin Wall on 11/9/89 (an odd numerical juxtaposition to our 9/11/01), Alfonzi lauds the way Bush I went out of his way to not gloat, act hubristically, or embarrass Mikhail Gorbachev's rapidly-imploding Soviet Empire, as many Conservatives in America desired. After all, they reasoned, we won the big one and many Republicans were quick to take the credit. In reality, however, Democrats had decidedly different, subtler explanations for the USSR's demise. However, the author contends that while Bush I's team did not act hubristically, it was nevertheless thinking that way.

More specifically, "George H.W. Bush and the national security team surrounding him believed that they possessed an intuitive knack for foreign policy, and reveled in that fact. Like the self-assured cadre of Democratic officials who had gravitated toward John F. Kennedy in an earlier era, the Bush national security team seemed to represent 'the best and the brightest' of Republican foreign policy hands." (p. 75)

He also describes the similarities of both Bushes' Iraqi wars going well militarily, followed by dithering, neglect and political naivete about sectarian strife predicted by many regional experts (such as Fuod Ajami.) "Then came 1992, the *annus horriblis* of the Bush dynasty, a year that I now know continues to haunt the councils of the Bush inner circle to this day." (p. 85)

When Alfonzi interviewed key Bush personnel from the 1991 war several years later, he's convinced of their candor, because they considered the first Iraq War an historical issue, but surely not a political one, since no one could have anticipated either a second Bush presidency or a second Iraq War. Also, the American protagonists in 1991 left a considerable paper trail revealing their thinking. Each cared about getting his/her historical interpretation on the record.

Also, the author states that newly-declassified documents in the Texas Presidential library numbering in the hundreds constituting a treasure trove about these two GOP Administrations. Among these luminaries were Paul Wolfowitz, Colin Powell, Dick Cheney, Donald Rumsfeld, Brent Scowcroft, Richard Haas, and Condolezza Rice. None of whom could have anticipated decidedly different stories a decade later.

It took me a while to come across a scathing attack against Bush II by journalist Ian Williams: *Deserter: Bush's War on Military Families, Veterans, and His Past* (Kindle, 2004). Including a useful TIMELINE and 25 chapters:

1.) "Why Beat the Bush?" 2.) "Twelve Inches of Power;" 3.) "Timing;" 4.) "Wrapping the Flag;" 5.) "Potemkin Village;" 6.) "Soldier of Fortune;" 7.) "Quantum Vietnam;" 8.) "Old Money;" 9.) "Odious Comparison;" 10.) "The Military Tradition;" 11.) "Roll Alabama Roll;" 12.) "Evasive Action;" 13.) "The Harvard Years'" 14.) "Bayonets and Ballots;" 15.) "Commander-in-Chief;" 16.) "Why Iraq?; 17.) "Neglecting the Troops;" 18.) "Give Us the Tools, We'll Finish the job;" 19.) "Sticky Ends;" 20.) "Volunteers of America;" 21.) "Then and Now With the Guard;" 22.) "Well Done Good and Faithful Servant—Now Get Lost;" 23.) "Veterans and the Administration;" 24.) "Because Our President Lied;" 25.) "If He Were Not Serious, He Would Be a Joke."

The acerbic TIMELINE functions in this manner: 1.) Identify a key date; 2.) Cite vital events in the real world; 3.) Juxtapose what the Bushes were doing then. For instance:

12 June 1942: Bush I leaves Andover for the Navy; Bush I's father is trading with Nazis

January 1966: Bush II arrested for stealing Christmas wreath; USAF drops 600,000 tons of bombs on Vietnam

25 December 1967: Bush uses vacation to apply for National Guard; John Kerry starts Vietnam duty as ensign on a frigate

May 1968: Friend of Bush (FOB) Sidney Adger contacts Brig. Gen. James Rose to get Bush II in National Guard; LBJ announces he will not seek re-election

16 March 1968: Bush passes dental exam for the Guard; Hundreds die in My Lai Massacre

27 May 1968: Bush II's Guard application responds to qualifications by writing "none,"

Yet he is accepted as one of four out of 500 applicants in Texas, and a waiting list of 100,000 nationally

28 May 1968: Bush II graduates from Yale, becoming eligible for the draft with U.S. troops dying at rate of 350 per week

September-November 1968: Bush II granted inactive duty to work on Florida campaign of Edward Gurney

October 1970: Bush II application to Texas Law School rejected; Moratorium Day results in millions of war protesters taking to the streets

16 April 1972: Bush takes last flight as National Guardsman; Air Force introduces substance abuse tests for pilots

August 1972: Bush II travels with Dad to RNC in Miami; Bush II named RNC Chair

18 September 1973: Bush II granted early discharge to attend Harvard Business School

(Throughout this TIMELINE the author frequently contrasts what Bush II was doing, and what fellow Yale grad John Kerry was doing; especially volunteering for the navy and two terms of duty in Vietnam while wining three medals)

Caveats about America's Empire often come packaged as unsustainable and ultimately self-defeating. This theme is explicated by Peter Galbraith, *The End of Iraq: How American Incompetence Created a War without End* (Kindle, 2006). His chapters include: 1.) "The Appointment in Samarra;" 2.) "Appeasement;" 3.) "He Gassed His Own People;" 4.) "The Uprising;" 5.) "Arrogance and Ignorance;" 6.) "Aftermath;" 7.) "Can't Provide Anything;" 8.) "Kurdistan;" 9.) "Civil War;" 10.) "The Three-State Solution;" 11.) "How to Get Out of Iraq."

Most regional experts understood that considerable sectarian tension underlay Saddam's repression. With his ouster, Iraq's constitution, approved by its public, was intended to encourage political consensus by requiring a two-thirds parliamentary majority in order to form a government. However, as early as December, 2005, Sunnis blew up a Samarra Shiite mosque unleashing months of brutal religious violence. The Americans were unprepared to deal with such complexities, says Galbraith.

Plus, "As civil war accelerated, Iraq had only a caretaker government. In December 2005, Iraq held its third national in that calendar year, choosing the country's permanent parliament under its new constitution. Intended to cap a year of transition to a new democratic Iraq, the elections served to intensify Iraq's religious and ethnic divisions. Shiites voted for Shiite religious parties, Kurds for Kurdish nationalist parties, and Sunni Arabs for Sunni religious parties. Fewer than one-in-ten Iraqi's had voted for parties crossing ethnic or religious lines." (p.81)

Not even Iraqi existence as a nation-state could be taken for granted as a consensus-producer. Post-election haggling required four months to choose a President, two Vice-Presidents, Parliamentary Speaker, and Prime Minister. The author explains how and why America got stuck in the middle of these constituencies. Sunni Arabs believed that the U.S. intentionally delivered the Shiites and their Iranian brothers, failing to get involved in the February 2006 pogroms.

Shiites, conversely, accused America of having chosen the Sunnis shortly before the Samarra mosque was attacked. Abdul Aziz al-Hakim, leader of the largest Shiite party charged that "The U.S. Ambassador to Iraq (Zalmay Khalilizad) had given the terrorists a green light when he criticized the human rights record of Iraq's Shiite-led security forces." (p. 91)

Khalilizad, a Sunni Muslim from Afghanistan later naturalized as a U.S. citizen, is reverentially referred to as "Abu Omar," the second Sunni Caliph, considered by Shiites to have usurped the legitimate line of succession to the prophet back in the 7th century. Furthermore, radical Shiite cleric Moqtada al-Sadr, who heads the Mahdi Army, held American troops responsible for destroying the Askiriya shrine, making them worse than Saddam Hussein.

During these days, Galbraith was staying in the Baghdad headquarters of Kurdistan President Massoud Barzani, located strategically in the middle of Baghdad's highly-fortified green zone. Iraq's frustrated leaders were meeting there as well. Author Galbraith writes: "As they discussed the crisis overtaking their country, it was clear they saw it as a civil war, with many using that phrase in their conversations with me. As if to underline the point, three nine-foot Katyusha rockets landed in close proximity to Barzani's house while I was busy writing. Fortunately, the closest one to me was a dud buried three feet into the asphalt parking lot." (p. 101)

Unaware of these events were American policy-makers in far-off Washington, DC. However, Secretary of State Condoleeza Rice was in

Egypt doing an interview with journalist Mervat Mohsen, with Mohsen presenting the Sunni perspective as "excessive American meddling has brought the Shiites in Iraq to power. The neighboring Iranians are Shiite and the Sunnis compromised and America's trusted Arab allies are Sunnis. There is a civil war brewing in Iraq. WHAT HAVE YOU DONE?" (P. 106)

Galbraith is all over Rice's continued denial that these dysfunctional events in Iraq were outweighed by democratic processes there fully on track. Rice: "Well I don't think there is a civil war brewing in Iraq. I think what you have there is a country that has thrown off the yoke of a horrible dictator, who by the way, created all kinds of instability in this region with his wars against his neighbors. Now that the dictator is gone, you have the Iraqi people, who come from many different sects, many different ethnic groups, trying to use a political process of compromise and politics, to replace repression." (p. 111)

The author covers many examples of Bush II, Inc. substituting wishful thinking for CTS in its Iraqi policies, especially CIA ones. In July 2004, the Agency prepared a well-publicized National Intelligence Estimate (NIE) on Iraq, "generally considered to represent the collective judgment of America's most experienced analysts based on the best intelligence available to the U.S. government, the NIE warned about the possibility of civil war." (p. 171) Yet, when Bush II was asked by reporters three months later, he merely dismissed it outright.

On 4 June 2004, Galbraith attended the inaugural session of the Kurdistan National Assembly in the city of Erbil, alongside Iraq's President (Jalal Talabani, a Kurd) making him the initial freely-elected Head of State in this fledgling democratic experiment. A source of intense national pride for the minority Kurds, one thing completely absent from Erbil was any semblance of the Iraqi national flag. He quotes U.S. Embassy official Anne Bodine, saying the U.S. is committed to backing "the new Iraq, democratic, pluralist, and unified."(p, 121)

In fact, the Kurds never had it so good. It's diaspora of 25 million people has never matched up well with the arbitrary nation-state system. Promises made by varied Empires could be called anything but promises kept. The American invasion afforded Kurdistan considerable *de facto* sovereignty. Winston Churchill called forcing the Kurds' subservience one of his biggest mistakes there. (p. 145)

And, "Insurgency, civil war, Iranian strategic triumphs, break-up of Iraq, independent Kazakhstan, and a military quagmire represent the unintended consequences of America's invasion of Iraq unanticipated by the Bush Administration." (p. 152) Galbraith argues that it's not surprising that Bush II continued in denial since he not only misread most of the important signposts, but all of them. He bought into the fantasy of "America as liberator," and set an extremely low bar for democracy's existence: regular free elections. In fact, none of the other aspects of civil society struck him as pertinent.

The author also provides perspective to Iraq's checkered history, "cobbled together by the British after World War I from three different Ottoman provinces, mostly Kurdish Mosul in the north, Sunni Baghdad in the middle, and Shiite Basra down south. The British mishandled things, especially by including the fiercely nationalistic Kurds; the Brits empowered a foreign Sunni Arab prince (Feisal of Hejaz), who maintained order via a Sunni Arab military bureaucracy. In 1958, a military coup overthrew Feisal's monarchy, killing his grandson in the process. (pp.160-61)

However, the brutal new regime maintained Sunni Arab control of Iraq. It proved very difficult for Sunnis to rule over a 55 percent Shiite majority, plus 20 percent Kurds thrown in. Then, of course, in 2003 the U.S. gave the boot to Iraq's last Sunni Arab dictator. In the process quashing the Iraqi Army, legally liquidating Saddam's military, and dismantling the secret police that had enabled minority dominance in Iraq for about 80 years. (pp. 164-66)

Galbraith's next summarize his main thesis throughout this book: "The Bush Administration assumed the transition from Saddam Hussein's Sunni Arab dictatorship to a stable new order in Iraq would occur easily. So easy, in fact, that no real planning would be required." (p. 169)

"Many of America's contemporary difficulties in Iraq derive directly from the failure to plan for the day after U.S. troops entered Baghdad. The professional military wanted to send more troops to secure Iraq than Pentagon civilian leaders were willing to commit. But even with the troops present, the governmental ministries, and treasured archaeological museums could have saved by proper planning." (p. 172)

He details exactly what went awry in the 14-month occupation totally mismanaged. Postwar occupations in both Japan and Germany run by the U. S. worked beautifully; But, Bush's belated decision to turn matters over to an interim Iraqi government surely did not. When Rumsfeld finally chose an administrator for Iraq, he picked a retired diplomat with zero in-country experience and provided him with two weeks to prepare for this daunting mission.

Galbraith describes L. Paul Bremer's dysfunctional interference via inconsistent policy decrees, in what was supposed to be an Iraqi-directed endeavor. Essential services like electricity were not restored; macro-level economic decline worsened; non-competitive jobs were given to GOP crony firms like Halliburton; untold billions of dollars were wasted; corruption flourished; and, Bush II failed to train badly-needed police and soldiers expeditiously. (p. 181)

Bush II took the politically-expedient path of too few troops for such massive nation-building, ignoring the advice of experts while relying on vested-interest amateurs, failed to plan, harbored a Polyannish vision of catalyzing long-overdue modernization and democratization in the Middle East (six years before it spontaneously combusted).

I was suckered in briefly by his optimism over Middle East democratization, thinking, "Maybe I'm being too cynical; give him a chance here; after all, a whole body of scholarly literature argues the theory of the Democratic Peace." Essentially: 1.) Democracies don't fight wars with other democracies, history teaches us; 2.) Evidence suggests democratization has been spreading globally for many decades. However, ironically the most glaring democratic fallout from the Iraq War was the election of religious hard-liners in Palestine and Iran.

KITTY KELLEY; ILAN PELEG; COLBY BUZZELL:

Our next book comes from popular biographer Kitty Kelley: *The Family: the Real Story of the Bush Dynasty* (Kindle, 2008), and is also accompanied by a family tree incorporating the Bushes, Walkers, Pierces, and Robinsons. It features scores of photos paying homage to the proper family gods spanning 25 chapters. Kelley also explains why it required four years to complete this research: the Bush history of ostracizing snitches, clan loyalty, threats, and the family love affair with secrecy. She had long-since grown a thick skin impervious to lawsuits and bitter denunciations by living subjects of her work—but none prepared her for the House of Bush.

Frank Sinatra sued her before the first words were written, arguing that only he or his heirs could authorize writers to tackle the crooner's colorful life. Kelley notes, however, that "The amount of resistance I encountered in writing this book about the Bushes was unprecedented, but perhaps that's what comes with writing about a sitting President whose family possesses a very long reach." (p. 130)

A few pages later, "Many people who know the Bushes: friends, ex-employees, classmates, business associates, and even a few family members, were skittish about speaking for attribution. I heard an endless stream of excuses and apologies, some comical, others disconcerting: 'You don't know that family . . . If they think I've talked to you, they'll never speak to me again.' "This country is too small to rile the Bushes." (p. 134)

Many referred to them as thugs, especially regarding the 2000 Miami recount where Republican activists were paid with Bush family money called by one observer a "Brooks Brothers Riot." (p. 135) I know I was quite suspicious while watching it live on the tube.

Kelley quotes freely from Bush I's compendium of missives discussed above: *All the Best: George Bush: My Life in Letters and Other Writings*, whose 25 July 1991 letter blasts her supposed negativity regarding all of her subjects. However, she corrects his misstatement by pointing out that she never considered a Bush book until the infamous 2000 Supreme Court decision of *Gore v. Bush*, convincing her that this made the Bushes into a "political dynasty." She claims to have gradually interviewed more than 1,000 people. The Bushes' status as a dynasty created a qualitatively new paradigm.

The clan was even hell-bent over Peter and Rochelle Schweitzers' extremely favorable content, which Bush I had his personal aide, Jean Becker, reprimand these young upstarts. In one part, Becker stated: "You put out in a press release that I quote George H.W. Bush as opposed to his son's plan to attack Iraq. The truth is, from the very first day, President Bush no. 41 unequivocally supported the President concerning the war in Iraq. He had absolutely no reservations of any kind." Kelley dismisses the Bush tactic here as absolutely typical. (p. 22)

Adding to Kelley's travails is what she calls the astonishing frequency with which "lost records, misplaced files, and registers mysteriously destroyed by fire over the years." Things like bankruptcy records from federal court files were impossible to track down, leading her to file 14 Freedom of Information Act (FOIA) requests, but very few were granted.

For example, on 18 September 2001 her FOIA request for information on the black-sheep uncle of Bush I was denied and the FBI claimed to possess no such files, however, Kelley already knew that James Smith Bush had required a security clearance to be named to the Export-Import Bank in 1959. It took six months for her lawyers to finally receive those records. (p. 121)

One ex-insider providing a wealth of on-the-record information for the author was Sharon Bush, Neil Bush's ex-wife. She recounts how the family disowned her, making it very difficult for her to find Houston lawyers to represent her against Neil. Husband Neil had an affair with a woman working for the family, which George and Barbara not only knew about but had entertained at their home.

To which Sharon asked, "What kind of family values is that?" She blames Barbara for running things behind-the-scenes in the clan. Sharon also claims Barbara hated her for allowing daughter Lauren to become a model: "It was just too glitzy for the family values the Bushes purport to represent." (p.249)

Sharon talked freely about the hardships experienced by Bush family women, such as her husband's regular use of prostitutes during Asian trips, his sexually-transmitted diseases, Jeb Bush's history of affairs, drug abuse by several of her brothers-in-law (such as cocaine by Dubya and Marvin at Camp David when their Dad was President), alcoholism, and hidden cases of schizophrenia. The author states "Sharon will probably become one of the invisible ex-wives on the family tree, no longer even a footnote to history. She has learned the hard way that little room exists for a divorcee in the Bush family dynasty." (p. 270)

In chapter one, the crucial role of Prescott Bush setting the stage for future generations is dissected carefully. For example, he opened Yale's doors of exclusivity and privilege for several generations, including his four sons, three grandsons, two nephews, and finally in 2001, his great-granddaughter. Prescott was preceded at Yale by his paternal grandfather (Reverend James Smith Bush), and his maternal uncle (Robert E. Sheldon).

In the summer of 1908, 13 year-old Prescott spent his vacation at a tennis-oriented camp in New Jersey with a classmate and his family. Why? Mainly because this was the chosen sport for Prescott's father (Samuel). To her astonishment, however, Prescott's mother (Flora) discovered that Prescott was sent home by his friend's mother (Mrs. Dods). Flora's haughty mother-in-law (Harriet Fay Bush) encouraged Flora to demand not only an explanation but an apology from Mrs. Dods. But Flora demurred.

Prescott's fiery father (Samuel) was similarly upset, mainly because he hypothesized that Prescott must have misbehaved in their absence and it might preclude the lad's acceptance at St. George's school in September. In a letter to her husband, Flora writes "Prescott was pleased to return to us again. But he misses the sport at Osterville (there are no tennis courts here but poor grass ones) and Prescott said if he had some clubs he would play golf."

Furthermore, Mrs. Dods finally did end the confused uncertainty by writing a letter explaining Prescott's dismissal: she had become quite ill, thus unable to host young Prescott, and sent him home. Several days later, Prescott received his golf clubs establishing a family affinity for the sport. (p. 292)

That summer, the Bushes put the finishing touches on their 17-room, 3-story colonial style mansion in Columbus, OH, overlooking a bluff of Marble cliffs. Their letters that summer were filled with prideful excitement about seven-bayed windows, five dormered bedrooms, an upstairs ballroom, cedar-lined storage rooms, and an attached porch atop the first floor sunroom. (p. 301)

Kitty Kelley admires Flora Bush as ahead of her times in many respects, and also her husband's recognition of her considerable gifts, and "accepting her as his equal," which shine through the considerable correspondence between husband and wife when they were often in different places.

According to the author, "These letters, saved by Samuel and bequeathed to his heirs, reveal a vibrant partnership between parents who loved their children abundantly and cared for their welfare, although, truth-be-told, they write more of sons Prescott and James, than their two daughters, Mary and Margaret." (p. 381)

Yale was a very homogeneous milieu when Prescott matriculated at Yale with a class of 347 white Anglo-Saxon Protestant preppies, 58 of whose fathers were Yaelis. But only one Buddhist, nine Baptists, ten Jews, and 22 Catholics were accepted (all Caucasians). And, only 15 of 347 class-mates were tapped by the famed Skull and Bones.

He wrote these words on the eve of his 50th class reunion: "I am more than ever conscious of what Yale has meant to me since 1913. Wherever I found myself in war or peace, in business or politics, in sports or social life, always the fact of Yale seemed present. I make this acknowledgment with a grateful heart." (p. 437)

America's war declaration in 1917 saw Prescott heading for France, with his civic-minded father, Samuel, contributing his skills and experience serving as Chief of Ordnance, Small Arms, and Ammunition section of the War Industries Board under the highly-regarded Bernard Baruch. Progressive father Samuel was described as a "Jeffersonian Democrat" known for building housing units for his employees and lobbying for workers' rights legislation in Ohio. (p. 601)

Ilan Peleg's 2008 book seems a fitting conclusion to this chapter: *The Legacy of George W. Bush's Foreign Policy: Moving beyond Neo-conservatism* (Westview, 2008). His chapter headings consist of: 1.) "The Bush Legacy;" 2.) "America's Challenges in the Post-Cold War World;" 3.) "The Neoconservative Revolution;" 4.) "Varying Aspects of W's Personality;" 5.) "Complexities of the Decision-Making Process;" 6.) "Lessons for Future Presidents."

Writing at the time of the Obama transition, Peleg attributes Obama's fantastic approval ratings abroad in 2008 to one main cause: Bush II's foreign policy trampling all standards of good global citizenship. Peleg attributes the bulk of these problems to the recent ascendancy of Neo-conservatism among elite GOP intellectuals and policy-makers. Power realists, like Bush I, Henry Kissinger, and Brent Scowcroft became marginalized during the zeroes decade.

The author states, "If foreign policy prescription can be judged by its results, Neo-conservatism, as the ideational basis for the foreign policy of George W. Bush, ought to be regarded as a huge failure, an unmitigated disaster of historic proportions. Not only did his foreign policy not relieve the dangers associated with international terrorism, it aggravated them." (p. 58)

In order to avoid repeating Bush II's mistakes, Peleg argues that scholars should dissect every dysfunctional factor causing such weak outcomes. He says, "The bully days are over," and America's chances for re-emerging as a more constructive global presence depend on it.

Furthermore, "Neo-conservatism presented to the world the unattractive model of exceptionalism, militarism, and unilateralism by imposing its will while dangling its democratic values as justification for any means while pursuing selfish interests. No wonder that this policy was met with rejection, resentment, opposition, and eventually active resistance, and that the blowback is stronger than ever." (p. 77)

He also refers to ex-Columbia University social psychologist Robert Merton's studies on "self-fulfilling prophecies" as helpful to understand Bush II's decision-making. Peleg defines it thus: "The very prediction causes itself to become reality via the behavior of the party making the prediction." (p. 188)

I was glad to see Peleg address the relevance of psychological theories such as "self-fulfilling prophesies" when trying to explain the motivations of

Bush II trying to finish Bush I's family business. Most American analysts eager to opine on matters of economics or politics eschew valuable insights from psychologists.

Peleg rejects two conventional wisdoms about Bush II that I think should remain in the mix: 1.) Bush II's learning disabilities and low intelligence meant he was in over-his-head as President; 2.) His dearth of foreign policy knowledge/experience led him into a psychological comfort zone wherein Dick Cheney's impulses were trusted implicitly.

Recommended by Peleg: 1.) Demilitarize U.S. foreign policy; 2.) Reinstitute the diplomacy of consultation; 3.) Refocus on regional problems other than the Middle East; 4.) Guard against ideological blind spots via realpolitik; 5.) Embrace globalism and multilateralism; 6.) Set clearer policy goals.

Peleg quotes Neoconservative Robert Kagan from his 1996 *Foreign Policy* article chiding Bill Clinton for pussy-footing around: "Having defeated the evil empire, the United States enjoys strategic and ideological predominance. The first objective of U.S. foreign policy should be to preserve and enhance that predominance by strengthening America's security, supporting its friends, advancing its interest, and standing up for its principles around the world." (p. 313)

Author Peleg also criticizes American media for remaining ignorant about just how drastically American prestige has fallen in world public opinion under Bush II, which Peleg labels "unprecedented." A 2006 survey by Globe Scan's Program on International Policy Attitudes, found that 60 percent of respondents believed that the Iraq War increased the threat of global terrorism while a mere 12 percent believed that it decreased that threat. (p. 350)

The center of gravity of GOP foreign policy has typically been power realism, offered in juxtaposed to Democrats' Kumbaya proclivities. He quotes from Republican academics Stephen Walt and John Mersheimer who called it "an unnecessary war;" Brent Scowcroft, national security adviser under Bush I wrote an op-ed in the *Wall Street Journal* arguing that invading Iraq would de-fang Bush II's global WOT. Isolationist Pat Buchanan argued that the "preemptive war" doctrine represents a very slippery slope. Bush II's Neocons decimated bipartisan foreign policy since World War II.

A soldiers-eye view of the second Iraq War bleeds through Colby Buzzell's *My War: Killing Time in Iraq* (Kindle, 2006.) Gutsy, even profane prose dots this hard-hitting memoir. Down-time gets discussed here as much as prime-time combat, in a true story about an average grunt soldier in the Second Iraq War, including some comedic insights. He dedicates the book to all those who earlier served in Operation Iraqi Freedom.

First words matter, and here they border on snotty condescension about his Bay Area high schools peers too lazy or spoiled to do anything as stupid as volunteer for the U.S. Army. "Most of them either got their education at some big-name university, or lived in their parents' basement smoking pot and working a shit job like telemarketing." (p. 58) Only guys he knew joining the military were kids of career soldiers brainwashed into thinking it was somehow their sworn duty to follow suit.

Also, "There's a bar near my parents' I fucking hate going to it because it's always like a high school reunion. You can't even enjoy a drink without someone you barely knew act super-excited, saying Oh my God, what are you up to? I'd always say one of two things 1.) Same old shit; or, if I'd had a few drinks, 2.) A phony-baloney story that I was working part-time programming digital orbital satellite missions for NASA in San Jose. Either way, it didn't matter, since they always said 'Wow that's really cool!'" (p.68)

One friend, however, did impress Buzzell, and influenced him when the author bumped into him at age 23. They had played football together and both Dads had slogged through the rice paddies of Vietnam (his Dad with the Army, his bud's with the Marines).

The friend had completed a Marine Corps tour of duty in Iraq, the two got drunk together and Colby discovered how many close relationships his friend had forged in Iraq. Colby was impressed and vowed over a few Guinness' to become a jarhead; hung over the next day he figured he could discover the same pride and camaraderie in the Army, so he joined up. (pp. 81-85)

Buzzell next heard from the Marine when the author was doing monster duty in Mosul. Colby's Mom had given the Semper Fi guy Colby's email, and he wrote: "Glad you joined the service but why with the wrong one?" "Hope you're having a good stay in the holy land, been there and done that" . . . "My company led the march to Baghdad but we caused a lot of hateful discontent." . . . "I know it gets old over there and hope your time is short." (p. 97) His friend had subsequently turned Marine recruiter, and Buzzell complains often about lame Army ads compared to the spiffy "few good men."

After writing back from Mosul, his bud responded in part with: "How many kills have you had? I know you must have had a few. My confirmed count was in the thirties, but I know there were more because as a tank gunner you tend to blow shit up beyond recognition, so you can't tell for sure." (p. 103)

Looking back on his military service, Buzzell says "There were only two times that I had second thoughts about the Army. One was the time in Iraq when I definitely thought I was going to get killed, the second occurred on the first day of basic training, when they marched us all over to our barracks from the in-processing center at 30th Adjunct General, many miles away." (p. 355)

ANNE GARRELS; AWID ALAWI:

NPR foreign correspondent Anne Garrels' Iraq diaries are fittingly called *Naked in Baghdad* (Kindle, 2003), and dedicated to her Iraqi "guide" whom she refers to Amer, and to her husband Vint Lawrence; the former for keeping her alive, the latter for editing and reacting to her war correspondences. As a radio correspondent she was filing audio reports only.

Her first visit to Iraq, with no Arabic language training and insufficient appreciation for Baghdad's rich history, she struggled at first. Her first posting to Moscow helped prepare her for Saddam's brutal police state and the role of bribery if desiring to scratch below propaganda. Relevant analogies from her Soviet years were many. For example, part of her life in the Soviet Union consisted of chunky female floor spies (dezhurnaya) in Intourist hotels. I took ten student groups to Russia between 1985-95 when glasnost, perestroika, and demokratzia were both coming and going.

Addicted to authors' first words: "This is a chronicle of what I saw and heard during my visits to Baghdad, starting before the war in October 2002, until I left when U.S. troops finally entered the Iraqi capital in April 2003. Some is drawn from my reports for National Public Radio; other parts derive from notes and reflections scribbled at the end of long days. It's a personal account of the buildup, conduct, and aftermath that will be with us for a long time to come. Each reporter covering Iraq, whether embedded or not, had but one window on the conflict and conflicting views. My non-embedded window occurred in Baghdad." (p. 70)

Modern wars are increasingly reported via new mediums. Her book was impossible without email. As for husband, Vint, "one friend said that I reported the war and he reported on me with honesty, humor and, affection." (p. 77) In his missives, Vint refers to Anne as Brenda (after Brenda Starr, that intrepid comic book character constantly in and out of impossible scrapes); and, Vint morphs both characters to good comic effect.

Vint's epistle on 19 October 2002 starts out: "You might be forgiven for thinking that after Afghanistan, Pakistan, and Israel in the last Year, NPR could come up with, say, an in-depth series on beach erosion between Bordeaux and Biarritz, but the straws in this outfit all appear to be short."(p. 86)

He captures the angst-ridden ritual departures to which husband and wife have been accustomed: "Last-minute exotically-wrapped cartons of sophisticated new equipment arrive from NPR. Miniature satellite-phone antennae blossom briefly amid the dahlias. An hour before the taxi is due, she is still downloading a complicated NPR program with a cool competence that may keep her safe until she returns." (p. 100)

Before arriving in Baghdad, Anne spent three days in the Amman, Jordan airport awaiting the crucial-yet-elusive Iraqi visa required before flying to Baghdad. The word "fixer" seems to arise in every city; in Amman she paid $50 to the first fixer and $200 to the second.

When she arrived in Baghdad, the local buzz was all about a surprising release of thousands of prisoners by Saddam Hussein, so Anne's delay in Amman cost her that story. For a regime denying political prisoners even exist, observers were stunned. Human rights NGOs, such as Amnesty International and Human Rights Watch, had described cases earlier in Latin American during the contagion of "desaparecidos" shocked journalists. Some, however, described the release as a source of badly-needed manpower.

When Anne checked into the Al-Rashid Hotel with other foreign jour-nalists, she began hearing horrific accounts of prisoner abuse at Iraq's largest prison (Abu Ghraib). Chaos reigned as thousands of relatives tried to link up with their released loved ones (500 prisoners were being released per hour); fatalities were not uncommon in this milieu.

When you hear the term "free and fair elections" as the first step toward democracy's promised land, you can use Anne Garrels' facetious mockery of a vote held recently in which the regime claimed that Saddam had received 100 percent approval with 100 percent participation for a clean sweep in a referendum; the prison release was officially Saddam's thank-you gesture to his denizens.

Anne immediately felt at home in the Al-Rashid Hotel because she had watched television coverage of this huge place as pivotal in the First Iraq War. This is where she drew parallels between Soviet spooks and Iraqi spooks.

The Al-Rashid hotel contains a famous mosaic which she sees in person now for the first time. I also found interesting her comment that: "Everyone who enters or exits the Al-Rashid must walk over the scowling image of George Bush the elder with the words 'DOWN WITH USA' etched in tile." (p. 173)

Garrells explains how Western journalists in Iraq are controlled via rigorous monitoring procedures honed over decades. Its Information Ministry's goal is to limit the activities of journalists. Satellite phones in particular worry them and must be registered and stored in the Information Ministry; modern cell-phones are also much more difficult for Iraqi officials to bug. All reporters also have a specific handler assigned to them for the duration. One activity common activity in 2003 was taking observers to problematic water-and-sewerage treatment plants which the Iraqi government says were damaged by U.N. sanctions in place since 1992.

Almost all the traffic in Baghdad consists of ancient Chevys and Fords with broken windshields making the streets choked with snarly traffic. Charming is not an adjective that comes up when describing contemporary Baghdad; its cement buildings are spartanly utilitarian with very little public vegetation to interrupt a steady diet of beige-upon-beige.

Also absent from Garrells' account are the mysterious souks described in many other Arab countries. A 400-year rule by the Ottoman Empire ended the same year as the Bolshevik Revolution (1917). What stands out? A vast network of Saddam's palaces surrounded by crenellated walls, unreliable electricity, and over-crowded hospitals, while barefooted children play in fetid streets. The author states that while Iraq once ranked as high as 77th in the U.N.'s Human Development Index (HDI), in 2002 it had fallen to 127.th

Once her guide, Amer, has informed about SOP rules, Anne begins to push the envelope with a barrage of new questions. A schoolteacher unable to find work, he then switched to driving foreign journalists before landing higher status as a guide, helping to pay for three young children. Occasionally, Garrels manages to ditch her guide and wander around loose.

Next I peek at Ali A. Alawi's outstanding 2007 book: *The Occupation of Iraq: Winning the War, Losing the Peace.* With lots of maps, charts, photos and 25 ambitious chapters, this is a serious piece of scholarship reflecting both insider and outsider perspectives.

Chapter titles: 1.) "The Great Divide;" 2.) "Rise of the Opposition;" 3.) "Build-Up to War;" 4.) "Invasion;" 5.) "Occupation Authorities;" 6.) "Collapsed State, Ruined Economy, Damaged Society;" 7.) "Deepening Rifts in a Brittle Society;" 8.) "Dismantling the Ba'athist State;" 9.) "Formation of a Governing Council and Rise of Insurgency;" 10.) "The Shadow of Real Power;" 11.) "The Enigma of Ayatollah Sistani;" 12.) "Constitution in Waiting;" 13.) "Fires of Sectarian Hatred;" 14.) "Marshall Plan for Iraq?" 15.) "Turning Point: April 2004;" 16.) "Interim Government;" 17.) "Arabs and Persians;" 18.) "Showdown at the Shrine;" 19.) "Hold or Abort the Election;" 20.) "Corruption in a Potemkin State;" 21.) "Iraqi Society on the Eve of Free Elections;" 22.) "The Vote;" 23.) "Negotiating a Constitution;" 24.) "Crises and the Jafari Government;" 25.) "Into Uncharted Waters."

Alawi's Introduction begins: "In the history of conflicts and wars, there are few instances that match the invasion and occupation of Iraq for complexity of motive and ambiguity of purpose. A seemingly endless chain of causal events have been put forward to explain this most extraordinary episode in modern times, but none, it would seem, has provided a satisfying and comprehensive answer. Why did the world's only superpower see fit to marshal its huge military resources, cross oceans, and overthrow a tyrant and his brutal system of rule, in the teeth of overwhelming international hostility?" (p. 219)

He emphasizes the rapidity with which Saddam's brutal system was dismantled; when euphoria over the scale of the spanking lasted several weeks, followed by growing bewilderment as what to do next with this "prize." Alawi refers to Iraq as "this most complex of countries," none of which America's perfunctory pseudo-planning matched. He dislikes the term "Coalition" in this context, but can't identify a better moniker. He describes specific events creating an undeniable momentum propelling the U.S. toward bellicosity.

The *causus belli* (WMD) were conveniently forgotten; American officials made perfunctory salutations to elections as badges of democracy; living conditions deteriorated; popular religiosity got really ugly; serious mass looting occurred not only in Baghdad but elsewhere as well; burning public buildings: "None of this fit with the behavior of a grateful people liberated from tyranny." (p. 235)

Particularly valuable is the author's explanation of why Washington's policy toward Iraq long-derived less from bilateral considerations than from broader regional concerns. Throughout the decade of the 1950s, what trumped domestic considerations was the impact of the Baghdad Pact, the U.S.'s anti-communist alliance. Containment of communist expansion represented the crux of U.S. policy, not only in this region, but several others as well. (p. 249)

America's reaction to the coup overthrowing the Monarchy in 1958? Opposing the Iraqi Communist Party (ICP), and when the ICP had failed by the early-1960s, Alawi characterizes U.S. policy as "bordering on indifference," and by 1968 the Ba'athist Party had secured power and American policy changed little until Washington procured an unexpected new ally via the Shah of Iran in the 1970s. With Iraq marginalized, America's regional strategy sought to bolster the Shah of Iran's power and prestige in various ways. (p. 258)

This collapsed when the despised Shah of Iran was deposed by Ayatollah Khomeini's rabidly anti-American medieval theocracy in 1979, resulting in Jimmy Carter's worst nightmare: 444 Americans held hostage in Teheran, and his abortive rescue mission. "These events coincided with Saddam Hussein's subjugation of the Ba'athist Party, and for the next two decades the U.S. fell all over itself courting Hussein as a thorn in the britches of the Holy Ruling Mullahs in Teheran." (p. 269)

Furthermore, "The eight-year war that Iraq fought with Iran had as much to do with protecting and advancing the interests of the west as with local or regional considerations. The U.S. viewed Saddam's Iraq as the single most valuable (albeit indirect) bulwark against the spread of revolutionary Islam into the Gulf region. Post-war American policy once again turned passive regarding Iraq, stuck with a bloated Army, huge international debts, and an embittered leadership decrying its sacrifices on behalf of others being ignored." (p. 282) The author suggests, without saying explicitly, that Saddam invaded Kuwait largely to spite the Americans.

U.S. post-war support of Iraq's huge Kurdish minority in the north also drove Saddam crazy, and he was already half-way there. Bush I's Secretary of State, James Baker, plugged the war as "all about jobs, jobs, and jobs," but many scribes revamped it as "oil, oil, oil." As for the intellectual gurus underpinning Bush II's strain of Neo-conservatism, Alawi has read carefully the writings of Leo Strauss and Bernard Lewis as progenitors.

Strauss' Plato-based beliefs asserted that effective government depends on the crucial role of the "wise elite exercising power over the masses maintaining harmony and quietly propagating principles of the virtuous state and society." (p.291) Wise elites counsel discreetly the rulers sharing core values. The ignorant masses? Protect them from their own basest instincts. Liberal democracy's fragility regarding mass indifference or consumerism led Strauss to justify Cheney-like violations of civil liberties or civil rights (including water-boarding).

GOP theorists in the 1960s and 1970s kicked these ideas around, then the Reagan Administration used them to justify switching traditional détente with the Soviet Union to radical confrontation in the 1980s (The evil empire). This represented a perfect storm for Bush II. Reagan's Straussians were still in the building, buoyed by what they misinterpreted as Reagan's having won the Cold War single-handedly.

Islamic historian Bernard Lewis enters the Neo-con picture both more recently and more overtly than Strauss. "His particular slant on Islam's encounter with modernity ran counter to the extant conventional wisdom (that the Middle East's political repressiveness, social inequalities, and economic backwardness existed because western imperialism's legacy). The contrarian, Lewis, held that the region's backwardness derived from regional causes, not global ones. Specifically to Islam's inability to adjust to its diminished world status." (p. 302)

Lewis' essay, "The Roots of Muslim Rage," spelled out his thesis concisely and poignantly. Namely, neo-colonialism does not cause failure in the Muslim world; however, unable to accept marginalization by its traditional enemy (Christianity) Muslims are blaming the wrong causes. Well before American political scientist Samuel Huntington, Lewis had written ominously about the "clash of religious civilizations." (p. 307)

Alawi describes Lewis' ideas fit snugly with recidivists from Bush I to Bush II, and why they found him very attractive as their resident intellectual media star in the 2003 buildup to war. He became the mentor-of-choice for Bush II's Neocons since what came to be known as the Lewis Doctrine justified violence in putting Muslims in their proper medieval place. After all, it was they who were responsible for their problems, not Western colonialism.

Also, "Iraq was in the right place at the right time to start the region's make-over; Lewis and Strauss profoundly influenced in deep and subtle ways the nexus of advisers, policy-makers, and war-planners pushing the U.S. into Iraq." (p. 312)

Alawi explains how irrelevant these abstract macro-level theories were to more subtle micro-level realities in-country "The State Department, supposedly a citadel of Realist intellectualism had almost no first-hand experience in Iraq, relying instead on inference and analogous reasoning when trying to unravel the possible outcomes of the post-war period. The only certainty was that the American military knew it faced an inferior, dispirited, and ineffectual Iraqi Army." (p. 328)

Likewise, how and why Bush II reveled in debunking conventional wisdoms built up in academia over many decades. Key elements of the Iraqi émigré community provided access to Washington, possessing substantial vested interests in a U.S. invasion. He describes Neo-con "wish-fulfillment." How revelatory I found Alawi's insightful book. Ancillary post-war fallout included enhancing the power of Iran's Mullahs next door.

To crack the secrets of the Iraqi character, Alawi recommends the writings of Ali al-Wardi (1913-1995) whose work on the social-psychology of Iraqis and Iraqi social history represents an eminently controversial intellectual gift. Alawi bemoans that during al-Wardi's lifetime his valuable contributions were dismissed, but that subsequent scholarship reveals his considerable wisdom: "He was simply too awkward and too eclectic methodologically to have been taken seriously as an authority on Iraqiness." (p. 417)

Despite his working-class background, Al-Wardi matriculated at the prestigious American University of Beirut, followed by M.A. and Ph. D. degrees in the U.S., followed by academic tenure at Baghdad University, gaining local recognition for his voluminous writings. One methodological problem dogging him was his rejection of statistically-oriented social science in vogue in western universities; instead, he was inspired significantly by the writing of sociologist Max Weber, and Muslim philosopher Ibn Khaldun.

Al-Wardi notes the frequency and gravity of foreign invaders conquering the Iraqi people. The impermanence of foreign cultures led to a schizoid tendency in the Iraqi mindset: civilization versus tribalism; or, the city versus the desert. Exacerbating the Iraqi character's schizoid tendency was a complementary sense of ambivalence. Alawi says, "This cultural ambivalence has had serious consequences. The state (a defining feature of advancing civilizations), stands in sharp contrast to tribal solidarity as an organizing principle." (p. 435)

Alawi characterizes Al-Wardis thought as permeated by "visions of a conflict-strewn society," which could have disproven Bush II's Neo-con fantasies about a single-state Iraq without Ba'athist repression.

JEFFREY RECORD; ROBERT DRAPER:

I'm reporting all Kindle books from each Iraq War, and the next one's thematically similar to the others. Jeffrey Record's *Wanting War: Why the Bush Administration Invaded Iraq* (Kindle, 2010), sandwiched between a Preface and Epilogue are a mere five disquieting chapters: 1.) "A Mysterious War;" 2.) "The Neoconservative Imprint;" 3.) "Bogus Assumptions, Wishful Thinking;" 4.) "The Reasons Why;" 5.) "Consequences: An Iraq Syndrome?"

Academic Jeffrey Record starts his Preface "I decided to write this book because the U.S. invasion of Iraq made no sense to me;" furthermore on the same page, "A loose combination of sometimes contradictory arguments and expectations, none of them sufficient to justify war, propelled the Administration into Iraq. Indeed my research led me to conclude that the Iraq War was more about the United States than it was about Iraq. More specifically, the war was about the hubris of seemingly irresistible American military power." (p. 43)

He expresses his highest gratitude to the Air College's "fabulous Muir S. Fairchild Research Information Center," and academic colleagues Christopher Hemmer, Alexander Lassner, W. Adam Terrill, and Steven Metz. While millions of casual observers held similar opinions about the 2003 war, Record conducted painstaking research before passing judgment.

Chapter one begins with two pithy quotes; one from Robert Draper's book *Dead Certain: The Presidency of George W. Bush* describes how a "communicable disease" believing that Saddam Hussein's Iraq constituted a genuine threat to American security breathed life long before 9/11 (i.e., Paul Wolfowitz, Douglas Feith, Scooter Libby, and Dick Cheney).

The other from retired-CIA analyst Melvin Goodman's book *Failure of Intelligence: The Decline and Fall of the CIA* detailing how Bush II had provided a huge windfall for Osama bin Laden's Al Qaeda by invading Iraq and creating the WOT's ultimate self-fulfilling prophecy.

Professor Record relies on the term "Iraqi syndrome" analogizing it to one of America's profoundest debacles: Vietnam. Record also decries the near-futility of the new Administration's juggling two wars of convenience. He writes, "Regardless of when and how America leaves Iraq, it is critical that we understand how the U.S. came to invade and occupy Iraq, to improve future decisions about when and how to deploy American military power." (p. 74)

The author draws compelling historical parallels concerning what he brands as America's three unnecessary wars since 1945: Korea, Vietnam,

Iraq. "Alternative courses of action existed regarding Korea, Vietnam, and Iraq. His subsequent analysis of all three case studies provides cogent arguments for each. His point? All of these unnecessary wars were avoidable—if rational decision-making processes had been employed. And, of course, the fallacious Domino Theory undergirded Korea and Vietnam. (p. 123)

Having come of age in the 1960s, which started with sweet optimism only to end in bitter pessimism in a country torn asunder, no other war rivals Vietnam for dominating my consciousness. The kind of political schism that Bush II carefully constructed after 9/11 ("You're either with us, or you're with the terrorists") happened all by itself during Vietnam. The military draft exacerbated things, but there was simply no middle ground extant at the end of the 1960s.

I could quote many useful passages from author Jeffrey Record, but I'll settle for this one: "The Johnson Administration viewed the stakes in Vietnam in terms of the perceived domestic political consequences of NON-INTERVENTION. Vietnam was a Cold War struggle, a test of American resolve in containing the spread of Communism. It mattered little that Vietnam had no intrinsic strategic value to the United States or that it might be impossible to establish a viable non-Communist polity in the southern half of this politically divided country." (p. 216)

IRAQ AFTER AMERICA—AND VICE VERSA:

I am equally sanguine about my choice of Kindle books to end this series of three chapters examining the Bush Dynasty and its relevance to explaining a most unlikely fact; in 2011, 193 countries exist in the world; how in the hell did Bush I and Bush II end up attacking the same unfortunate one, and what do we Americans owe the Iraqi people? Noah Feldman, *What We Owe Iraq: War and the Ethics of Nation-Building* (Kindle, 2004).

Drawn to authors' first words, here are Noah Feldman's: "Late one night in May 2003, I was in a military transport plane somewhere over the Mediterranean, on my way to a stint as constitutional adviser to the American occupation authorities in Iraq. Most of the passengers were dozing, shivering slightly for the last time before we encountered Baghdad's heat. Adrenalin pumping through me, I was reading the best modern book on the Iraqi Shiite and hastily trying to teach myself some Iraqi colloquial dialect. When I looked around, a strange sensation came over me: they were not reading about Iraq, but rather about the post-WW II reconstruction of Germany and Japan." (p. 54)

The redundancy he experienced when looking more carefully at his brain-trust of colleagues shocked him. What in hell does it have to do with their mission? Couldn't be a mere coincidence because economic, political, and cultural conditions in Germany and Japan had nothing in common with contemporary Iraq; plus, that was 55 years ago and we were occupying Iraq in 2003 for wholly different reasons.

Gradually, it dawned on Feldman that such irrelevancies was anything but random. Qualitatively distinct strategic objectives call for qualitatively different tactics. Some other observers were beginning to question such disjunctions, but it seems our author was uniquely concerned about the ethical dilemmas of nation-building. One heard lots of talk about piety, faith, and morality under Bush II, but it seems like ethical dilemmas went on holiday.

In chapter one, Feldman addresses how nation-building can benefit the nation-builder's national interests; especially the argument that unstable failed-states harbor terrorists and in a world filled with relatively few homogenous (10 percent) states, there's no point in further encouraging heterogeneous Balkanization. Furthermore, powerful democracies have a vested interest in furthering the global trend toward democratization by supporting regimes perceived by their citizens as legitimate.

Chapter two sees Feldman taking on the concept of "paternalism," emanating from the rationalizations for empire dominating prevailing wisdom concerning historical nation-building. His main contention here: "Nation-building can be salvaged ethically only if stripped down to the modest proposition that the nation-builder exercises temporary political authority as a trustee on behalf of the people being governed, in much the same way that an elected government does. Nation-builders must authorize alternative means for the people they govern to monitor their performance." (p. 81)

The third chapter assails over-emphasizing the existence of free elections as both a necessary-and-sufficient condition for democratization. He says: "I propose that elections should be considered the mid-point in nation-building, not the end of the nation-builder's obligations toward the country in question." (p. 98) A milieu of general security must be established in order to facilitate compromises between sects, ethnicities, and races. Feldman lambastes Bush II's team on these grounds.

Noah Feldman argues that the U.S.-led occupation of Iraq is filled with ethical problems that can't be rationalized away. Moreover, post-Cold War United Nations nation-building projects undertaken in Somalia, Bosnia, Kosovo, East Timor, and Afghanistan proved far less problematic. Also, determining the "will of the international community" proved more specious in Iraq 2003 than these others," since the "coalition of the willing" was in reality more a coalition of the bribed and threatened. (p. 121)

One of Feldman's closing arguments pertains to the significance of ethics being taken seriously especially regarding issues such as law, democratic theory, and moral principle. It strikes me that ethics in American foreign policy went AWOL during Bush II and Feldman bolsters that point with many examples deriving from his Iraqi experiences.

NICHOLAS DAVIES; COLONEL GERARD SCHUMACHER; DEXTER FILKINS:

Similarly guilt-ridden themes pervade Nicholas Davies' *Blood on Our Hands: the American Invasion and Destruction of Iraq* (Kindle, 2010), dedicated to his colleague, International Human Rights activist, Ben Ferencz,

His chapters include: 1.) "History of Regime Change;" 2.) "Desire for Regime Change;" 3.) "Planning Aggression;" 4.) "Imagining WMD;" 5.) "Full Legal Advice;" 6.) "Crime of Aggression;" 7.) "Shock, Awe, and Death;" 8.) "Misleading the Troops;" 9.) "Resistance;" 10.) "Torture and Impunity;" 11.) "Massacre in Fallujah;" 12.) "Sunnis and Shiites: History versus Propaganda;" 13.) "Launching the Dirty War in Iraq;" 14.) "Attackers in Police Uniforms;" 15.) "The Ethnic Cleansing of Baghdad;" 16.) "Bring the Civilians Home;" 17.) "Blood for Oil;" 18.) "Escalation and Genocide;" 19.) "Conclusion: Law not War."

Davies' Preface traces an impressive litany of good things in America's history, but argues that we have lost our bearings. Nothing shabby about the Declaration of Independence; popular sovereignty; inalienable rights; being on the right side of two world wars; Nuremburg Trials; Woodrow Wilson and FDR sponsoring international legal institutions; United Nations Charter Leadership; Security Council Role for collective self-defense; Bush I hypothesizing a post-Cold War "new world order;" numerous U.N. Peacekeeping Operations; bringing various war criminals to trial. The rule of law internationalized is what the author honors most. And under Bush II America lost its way as Imperial Wannabe.

He describes the traditional international corollary to the liberal-conservative analytical motif domestically: Idealism versus Realism. While Democrats have felt more comfortable cohabiting with Idealism, and Republicans with Realism, nevertheless considerable wiggle room has existed in a country where consensus-based bipartisan foreign policy existed for many years.

While Davies concedes that we live in a complicated world where national security cannot be taken for granted, he's clear about the most deleterious recent trend: Bush II's Neocons completely rewriting the Republican foreign policy script. While he doesn't use the words "natural governor," he does hope Neocon delusions about Empire contain a silver lining forcing us to live within our means, avoiding the pitfalls of what Yale historian Anthony Kennedy so elegantly labeled "Imperial Overstretch."

One poignant episode consists of Davies' recounting the 2004 publication of the "Downing Street Papers" by reputable British newspapers, which "Established a systematic, deliberate conspiracy to deceive the American public about WMD in Iraq for an ill-conceived overthrow of Saddam Hussein." (p. 71) He notes that presumptions of innocence exist in democracies, but the monumental nature of Iraq 2003 consequences behooves responsible policy-makers to come clean afterwards, something Neocons remain in denial about. Watergate contributors John Dean and Charles Colson survived their serving of humble pie.

I like Davies' words: "Corporate-funded think-tanks have played a crucial role since the 1970s in developing the ideological and theoretical groundwork for these dysfunctional policies, promoting militarism in American society and manufacturing public consent for policies that would otherwise just seem unnecessary, irrational and dangerous. This present form of myopia isn't just an accidental feature of bureaucratic institutions; it is driven by commercial interests defining success by near-term corporate profits." (p. 307)

As Deep Throat said so eloquently 40 years ago, "Follow the money." A recent documentary on CNBC television interviewed eyewitness explaining how roughly ten percent of $400 billion of Iraqi redevelopment money was lost by the Neocons. And, how Cheney's former colleagues at Halliburton Security somehow received the most lucrative contracts on a "no bid basis," only to reward American taxpayers with gross negligence and inhumane behavior toward Iraqi citizens.

More broadly, Davies writes "Western reporting on the war was corrupted from the start by the Pentagon's 'embedding' program, quickly degenerating into a stenographic exercise orchestrated by the Cent-Com press office. The echo chamber of the U.S. corporate media fleshed out this artificial narrative creating an imaginary, virtual Iraq in the mind of the American public, feeding a public debate bearing no relation to the real war being waged, including the killing of innocent civilian victims." (p. 318)

He contends that America's Imperial delusions resulted in our outspending all other 192 countries globally with troops in more than 120 countries, while buckling with staggering debt, can learn much from the post-imperial Europeans U.K., France, Spain, and Netherlands. Why? Because they were smart enough to follow their years of hegemonic intoxication with sustainably constructive roles based on universal international law/ethics. (p. 324)

The author opines that the success of a few early post-WW II CIA covert operations (in Japan and Italy) created unrealistic expectations and unsavory tactics wholly inconsistent with American values. For example, when freely-elected Iranian Prime Minister Mohammed Mossadegh was overthrown in 1953 by a military coup engineered by the CIA and Britain's MI6, rendering "regime change" all too convenient. A year later, CIA operatives worked up considerably more of a sweat in deposing the elected government of Jacobo Arbenz in Guatemala. Motives undergirding each endeavor stank out loud. He asks the reader to identify any CIA covert action conducted admirably.

Next the Agency turned up the heat even further with arms depots and airstrip construction in Nicaragua, Honduras, and the Panama Canal Zone. In each case lovely tactics such as bribing senior military officials, planting false propaganda, unfair accusations of "Communist," planting caches of Soviet weapons, training small armies of mercenaries, providing U.S. pilots to fly surreptitious missions, sinking a British ship loading

Guatemalan coffee and cotton. The U.S.'s heavy-handed measures regarding the boat sinking was unsavory enough for Secretary-General Dag Hammarskjold to threaten resignation. (p. 468)

American policy-makers found covert actions far preferable to the politically risky decision to send in the Marines. U.S. newspapers were easily co-opted by specious national security claims.

Subsequent Congressional hearings were needed to expose this dark under-belly; also the author recommends William Blum's book *Killing Hope* (1995) which details additional failed coups in Haiti (1961 & 1991), Algeria (1960), Dominican Republic (1958 & 1960), Chile (1970), Costa Rica #2 (1971), Seychelles (1979 & 1981), Suriname (1982 & 1983), Angola (1992). (p. 497)

CIA mischief in Iraq began in 1958 with the revolution toppling the British-backed Monarchy and brought General Abdul Qasim to power. Pentagon interference soon included plans for a U.S.-Turkish invasion, called off reportedly because of Soviet threats to intervene. Qasim convinced other Arab states to protect their oil interests by forming what evolved into OPEC. Declassified CIA memos later revealed that the Agency quickly undertook efforts to kill Qasim, but failed. (p. 528) He was eventually toppled by the Ba'athist Party gestating Saddam Hussein.

Another scholarly tome brutalizing Bush II: *A Bloody Business: America's War Zone Contractors from the Occupation of Iraq,* by Retired Army Special Forces Colonel Gerard Schumacher (Kindle, 2010). His Preface begins "One would think that civilians who have taken jobs to work in Iraq would anxious and open to discussing their experiences. They are anxious but most are not open. Although many want to express themselves, the media has not been kind to these young men, women and firms they work for. They are warned by employers to steer clear of the press, and are often restricted by their contracts." (p.35)

Two exceptions to the rule consisted of Crescent Security and MPRI; neither requested editorial review or present any prefabricated "Dog and Pony Shows," and the author praises with these words, "They were accommodating, candid, and honest. Their employees were permitted to speak freely, and I sincerely appreciate their help and respect the risks they took on our behalf." (p. 50)

Especially MPRI media relations person, Rick Kiernan, and MPRI employee Larry Wood (Retired Army Col.) who runs their Team Viper training sessions on the Iraq-Kuwait border. Col. Schumacher also thanks the wife of a KBR contract truck driver (Renee Taylor) for tireless research efforts, since such efforts require inside help.

While many American citizens don't like the concept of private for-profit companies operating on the battlefield, the author disagrees with them, largely because the prevalence increased presence of insurgency armies, complexities of nation-building, new battlefield technologies, and the willingness of volunteers to sign up for a downsized military without a national draft any longer. (p. 82)

Since the First Iraq War, the ratio of private forces to professional soldiers has more than quadrupled, and current estimates of Pentagon-employed private contractors runs to 700,000 personnel. "When the political environment is not conducive to deploying U.S. regular forces, our government hires civilians to execute its foreign policy. This makes them more than a surrogate army indirectly supporting U.S. combat operations; they represent a virtual surrogate government." (p. 90)

Aristotle was one of the first philosophers to argue that what we call something matters significantly. Historically, the most prevalent term has been *mercenary,* however, few professionals today apply that term of opprobrium.

Colonel Schumacher describes contemporary mercenaries as burdened by a "Wild West hired-gun stereotype," inaccurately depicting today's more sophisticated skilled civilians. However, he admits that the mercenary stereotypes were largely justified regarding their progenitors. "They have always represented a quick and dirty way to build an army." (p. 96) Carthaginians, for example, employed mostly Libyan mercenaries to fight their battles against Roman soldiers in the Punic Wars.

The prevalent form of legitimized political rule for the past 350 years has been via the nation-state system begun in 1648 by the "Peace of Westphalia", ending the bloody Thirty Years War. Patriotic duty increasingly replaced a paycheck as the incentive for doing something our species is normally loath to do: kill other humans. Two huge bodies of international law have slowly developed: 1.) The Laws of Peace; 2.) The Laws of War. The latter was intended to "civilize" this kind of uncivilized behavior.

Colonel Gerard Schumacher says that one constant has been that money, or slavery, or personal freedom, or land have and will continue to motivate private citizens to sell their various skills on the battlefield. He also discusses how the proliferation of nation-states from 54 in 1945 to 193 in 2010; every large nation (e.g., 25 million Kurds) would love to have its own state, but that encourages Balkanization.

He analyzes the skill-sets required for each of these types of private contractors: 1.) Construction contractors; 2.) Trucking contractors; 3.) Training contractors; 4.) Technical-assistance contractors; 5.) Security contractors. Schumacher also describes this privatization tendency adopted by other countries as well. They are conveniently viewed as "temps."

"Uncle Sam is by no means the only employer of war-zone contractors, contracting agencies offer services to companies and allied governments around the world that require their expertise in executive protection, hostage rescue, language translation, strategic defense planning, airborne security operations, building oil pipelines, securing African diamond mines, and in the case of Sierra Leone, ousting a renegade government from power." (p. 174)

High-paying contractor jobs entail considerable risk, and the author details cases like an unfortunate Turkish beheaded, or contractors in Fallujah burned-then-hanged from a bridge, or 30 contractors blown up in a car-bomb attack; more than 300 American contractors died in Iraq, and the author bemoans one question asked is, "What would we do without them?" He claims that the book encounters everyday moral dilemmas faced by the contractors he met.

Next we look at *New York Times* foreign correspondent Dexter Filkins' *The Forever War* (Kindle, 2004), expressing themes already cited. His engaging Prologue begins at 2 AM in Fallujah during November of 2004:

"The Marines were pressed flat on a rooftop when the dialogue began to unfold. Minarets were flashing by the light of airstrikes and rockets sailing on trails of sparks. First came the voices from mosques, rising above the thundery guns."

"The Americans are here howled a voice from a loudspeaker in a minaret. The Holy War, The Holy War! Get up and fight for the city of mosques! Bullets poured without direction and without end. No one lifted his head. Nothing is being done here violates God's law, they repeated this refrain."

"This crazy, one marine yelled to his buddy over the din. Yeah, the Buddy yelled back, and we've only taken one house." (p. 47)

The embedded Filkins then reports that he saw a group of Marines stand up at the foot of gigantic loudspeakers while the Aussie heavy metal band, AC/DC, belted out the words to their song, "Hells Bells," the band's guitars celebrating satanic power echoing over the battlefield with church bells tolling thirteen times. All the while, from the mosques came, "Allah Akbar, God is Great, nothing so glorious as to die for God's path!"

The Jihadis held Fallujah for six months, but now the Marines were taking it back (6,000 strong) while Filkins rumbled along with Bravo Company, stunned by the high drama; for example, "I'd seen mortars in the movies and also in Iraq, but never this close or this huge; their booms, their booms were crushing and I imagined the shards of metal exploding with each shell, and felt surely we would die if we didn't move immediately." (p. 74)

Chapter one flashes back to Filkins' reporting in the Afghan capitol, Kabul, in September 1998. Again, the identical professionalism of U.S. Marines operating in Fallujah, Iraq: Highly dangerous duty again for Filkins and his platoon of Marines. Except that in Afghanistan, after the battles the author witnessed a surreal scene at a soccer stadium, as the place filled to capacity.

As a foreign journalist Filkins was placed front-row center; "Come sit with us, they would say, you are our honored guest. A white Toyota Hi-Lux drove up and four men wearing green hoods hopped out of the back, while a fifth man, a prisoner, remained unhooded, whom they lay on the grass and surrounded, with zero struggle occurring between the hooded and un-" (p. 144)

The miscreant was a pickpocket, the voice over a loudspeaker intoned. His already-severed hand was held up for all to see, as an indication this was not his first violation of Sharia law. Filkins suspected the thief had been drugged, for he protested not. The author figured that would end this thief's public humiliation; however, another Hi-Lux pulled up (a vehicle much praised by the Afghani Taliban), on which rode a Sharia judge named Mulvi Abdur Rahman Muzumi, was required because the thief had committed a more serious crime (murder in an irrigation dispute). (p. 165)

The judge intoned, "The Koran says the killer must be killed in order to create peace in society," and the wheels of justice consisted of Kalashnikov-wielding brothers of the murdered man riddling the body with scores of bullets. Again, Filkins took close note of the fact that once again, officials announced that "nothing against the laws of God have occurred here today." (p. 196) The author refers to the social milieu that day as similar to a college football game. Interviewing spectators later he found most people agreed with the verdict.

The entire subtext of Filkins' book strikes me as clear: His extensive reporting from both Afghanistan and Iraq leave him with two decidedly ambivalent impressions: 1.) America's grunt soldiers perform overwhelmingly bravely and honorably under extremely difficult circumstances in both wars; 2.) Both civilian policy-makers and military officers up and down the chain-of-command considerably less so; therefore, much tragically unnecessary violence occurs in Bush II's WOT, in what Filkins and other observers now see as an unsustainable state of war from which many rich people become richer.

CHAPTER EIGHT:

"Millennial Generation Blogosphere"

BACKGROUNDER:

Chapter one examined the merits of CTS trumping common-sense; chapter two reviewed the literature on American politics and addressed my personal politics; Chapter three sketched a brief-but-dense history of Foxymoron, including all biographies on Murdoch; chapter four featured my review of Bill O'Reilly's recent fallacy-laden autobiography.

Then, chapters five-seven delved into scholarship on the Bush Dynasty, plus orders of magnitude differences in how Bush I and Bush II handled their respective Iraq Wars. When the media continue referring to these as the Gulf Wars, they truly misspeak: these were both Iraq Wars through and through.

Here I inspect the political blogosphere of the Millennial Generation. As a Baby Boomer, all other such designations strike me as startlingly recent; especially the most recent one dissected here: Millennial Generation (Mil Gen), with which I interface so little I must research it aggressively

These 20-something, multi-tasking techies have dominated the blogosphere since the turn of the Millennium. Featured below are 24 rank-ordered, letter-graded, recent blogosphere book reviews by me according to these criteria: quality of *scholarship;* and, relevance to *public policy* (five others are rejected below).[lxxiv] *Wiktionary* defines blogosphere as "The totality of Internet blogs, especially the unique jargons, cultures and shared interests created by their interconnection."[lxxvii] Therefore, FNC's paralinguistic braggadocchio takes a brief holiday.

BLOGOPHILIA:

Five Highly-Recommended "A" Grades:

1.) Grade: A++: Blogging the Political: Politics and Participation in a Networked Society, by Antoinette Pole (Kindle, 2009).

2.) Grade: A+: *Blogging America: The New Public Sphere* by Aaron Barlow (Kindle, 2008).

3.) Grade: A: *Blog Wars* by David Perlmutter (Kindle, 2009).

4.) Grade: A-: *Boom and Bust in the Blogosphere: Case Studies of the Blogging Industry* by Dan Morrill (Kindle, 2008).

5.) Grade: A–: *Cyber War: The Next Threat to National Security and What To Do About It* by Richard Clarke and Robert Knake (Kindle, 2010).

Six Recommended "B" Grades:

6.) Grade: B++: *Rise of the Blogosphere* by Aaron Barlow (Kindle, 2007).

7.) Grade: B+: *Bullets and Blogs: New Media and the War-fighter* by Deirdre Collings and Rafal Rohozinski (Kindle, 2008).

8.) Grade: B: *The Master Switch: The Rise and fall of Information Empires* by Tim Wu (Kindle, 2010).

9.) Grade: B: *Millennial Makeover: MySpace, YouTube, and the Future of American Politics* by Morley Winograd and Michael Hais (Kindle, 2008).

10) Grade: B-: *Cause-Wired: Plugging In, Getting Involved, Changing the World* by Tom Watson (Kindle, 2009).

11) Grade B—: *Using Internet Primary Sources to Teach Government, Economics, Geography, and Contemporary World Issues* by James Shively and Philip Van Fossen (Kindle, 2001).

Five Mildly-Recommended "C" Grades:

12) Grade: C+++: *Born Digital: Understanding the First Generation of Digital Natives* by John Palfrey and Ure Gasser (Kindle, 2010).

13) Grade: C++: *The Myth of Digital Democracy* by Matthew Hindman (Kindle, 2008).

14) Grade: C+ *Grown Up Digital: How the Net Generation is changing Your World* by Don Tapscott (Kindle, 2008).

15) Grade: C-: *Living and Learning with New Media: Summary of Findings from the Digital Youth Project* (MacArthur Foundation) by Mizuko Ito et al. (Kindle, 2009).

16) Grade: C–: *Citizen's Handbook to Influencing Elected Officials: a Guide for Citizen Advocacy in State Legislatures and Congress* by Bradford Fitch (Kindle, 2010).

Three Very Marginal "D" Grades:

17) Grade: D+: *Digital Citizenship: Participation and Exclusion in the E-Society* by Ruth Lister and Graham Murdock (Kindle, 2011).

18) Grade: D: *The Internet and Democratic Citizenship: Theory, Practice, and Policy* by Stephen Coleman and Jay Blumier (Kindle, 2010).

19) Grade: D: *Digital Citizenship: The Internet, Society, and Participation* by Karen Mossberger, Caroline Tolbert, and Ramona McNeal (Kindle, 2007).

Five Failed "F" Grades:

20) S..A. Morse, *Blogging Basics for Beginners: Catch Up on the Blogosphere for the 21ˢᵗ Century* (Kindle, 2004);

21) Dwayne Conyers, t*he Best of the Blog (Kindle, 2006);*

22) Davis Whiteman, *Learning to Blog at Word Camp* (Kindle, 2005);

23) Manuel Braschi, *Blogging for Beginners: Decisions and Strategies to Set Up a Blog* (Kindle, 2003);

24) Rick Ricker, *Blogging for Beginners* (Kindle, 2005)

ASSESSING THE FIVE "A" GRADES:

Let's look first at the highest rated book (A++), *Blogging the Political: Politics and Participation in a Networked Society* by Antoinette Pole, whose book is dedicated to kindred-techie husband, Scott Simock.

This e-book has been optimized for Mobil Packet PDA format and includes scores of illustrative tables, figures, and boxes, dotting six chapters: 1.) "Political Blogging: Politics and Participation;" 2.) "Rainbow Bloggers: Race and the Blogosphere;" 3.) "Gender and Sexual Orientation in the Blogosphere;" 4.) "Blogging Among Congressional Members;" 5.) "Blogging for Red and Blue States;" 6.) "The Future of Political Blogging in Politics and Civic Engagement;" All accompanied by extensive end-notes. More than 80 political bloggers were interviewed by author Pole. Much of it was "conceived, discussed, and written at the CUNY Graduate School's Management Center." (p. 7)

Her chapter one begins with these words: "New technologies often change our lives in dramatic and unexpected ways. The Internet has perhaps transformed our public and private lives more quickly than any other technological innovation in the 20th century. How we conduct business, maintain relationships, and participate in politics has been altered because of the Internet." (p. 18)

With the maturation of the Internet, online communications have been significantly transformed from the early days of e-mail and chat-rooms to today's widespread use of social networking sites like *Facebook* and video sharing sites such as *YouTube*.

Among the emerging technologies facilitating online communication, political blogs represent a prominent agent driving many of these rapid changes. Blogging has changed the American political landscape, fundamentally transforming politics and civic engagement. Political bloggers were credited with unseating Senate Majority Leader Trent Lott in 2002 and assembling 20,000 demonstrators marching on behalf of the Jena Six defendants in 2007. (p. 26)

Pole writes "Checking the major media outlets, political bloggers unearthed falsified documents produced by CBS in 2004 revealed enhanced news photos depicting 'plume of smoke' from the Iraq War in 2006. Indicative of their influence, political parties and the main-stream media have been obliged to accommodate bloggers. Both political parties credentialed bloggers in 2004 and 2008, permitting coverage of the nominating conventions, while major media outlets like the *Atlantic* magazine the *New York Times* integrated bloggers into their regular coverage, thereby legitimizing the role of political bloggers." (pp. 139-40)

The author says the absence of books on this subject motivated her to systematically assess it. As to the perennial question whether new technologies bode good or ill for humanity. She initially takes the agnostic position (a given for the scientifically-minded) paying homage to both those who "fear debilitating polarization" (cyberbalkanization) and those who laud the realization of a "popular empowerment" (globalization) challenging the traditional privileges of political elites; in the end gravitating toward the optimistic latter over the pessimistic former.

While the blogosphere thus far has been dominated by white males, it has the potential to empower countless others: "I argue that political blogging improves the prospects for participation of minorities and other underrepresented groups. One's race, gender, occupation, or political affiliation presents few, if any, barriers to political blogging." (p. 161)

Also, "Drawing upon several literatures from political science and communication studies, this book investigates political blogging. Divided into two halves, the first examines specific groups of political bloggers based on gender, sexuality, race, and ethnicity, it inventories the individuals engaged in political blogging providing a demographic profile of each. Specifically, considering whether and how political blogging facilitates civic engagement and mobilization among minorities traditionally experiencing lower rates of participation." (p. 151)

The second half of Pole's book investigates how elite political actors (members of Congress and candidates for election) utilize political blogs. "I argue that political elites use their blogs in fundamentally different ways than other political bloggers: they blog as a means of informing specific political constituencies of interested readers, rather than appealing to a wider readership. Features found on most political blogs are absent on congressional and campaign-centered blogs." (p. 163)

Most political blogs contain archives, whereas congressional and campaign blogs generally do not. Also, comment sections are commonplace on political blogs but do not often appear on campaign blogs. "Despite differences between these two categories of blogging, I suggest that the former (elite blogs) have transformed American politics, particularly political campaigns.... and, "Voters have greater access to candidates and their campaigns, while candidates can issue updates through their blogs circumventing negative media" (p. 172)

Then the author's ground-breaking work explains empirically and theoretically how and why it (political blogging) is more of an asset than a liability to the American political system, and how her research points to a need to re-examine several contemporary bodies of literature relating to civic participation and political discourse: "To date, a majority of studies about political blogging focus on blogging as a new media form or they highlight noteworthy political events that arise because of elite misconduct or error. In contrast, this work explores how political blogging affects politics and civic engagement on a day-to-day basis." (p. 183)

Some observers note that change remains the only constant. She speaks directly here to this theme of change, change, change quite powerfully and directly: "Communication and political information used to be the sole domain of the media—be it radio, television, newspapers, or magazines. While most political bloggers do not provide breaking coverage of new events, a majority link to important articles and/or provide commentary on politics, public policy, and current events. Disseminating news has been altered, in that bloggers highlight articles they deem important, thereby diminishing the power of giant media corporations. Readers might otherwise miss or pay less attention to these articles if not for bloggers." (p. 240)

Specifically relating to campaign blogging, Pole lauds the extant literature describing how these types of blogging split into two groups: 1.) How blogs can be used to improve participatory democracy. For example, authors Kerbel and Bloom studied how the Howard Dean campaign used its *Blog for America* to increase participation. Also, authors Lawson-Borders and Kirk suggest that within campaigns blogs serve to offer a social narrative, organizing tool, and participatory journalism.

2.) Use of blogs by candidates: Benoit et al. in *Theory of Political Campaign Discourse,* examined whether campaign blogs rely primarily upon claims, attacks, or defenses. "Results from these analyses indicate that candidates frequently mention their opponent and rely upon attacks. Incumbents tend to attack more frequently than do their opponents." (p. 274)

My first serious exposure to the "new media" versus "old media" dynamic was Ken Auletta's *Googled.* Pole augments eureka moments, such as: "Typically, the study of the media is approached through a historical lens, emphasizing the emergence of new technologies. This is especially useful for students of the media because it offers an overarching framework detailing specific technologies. Reviewing this evolution contextualizes subsequent chapters, underlining how blogs fit within the media, especially new media." (p. 277)

Printing presses, radio, and television all evolved gradually enough for the masses to wrap their collective heads around their political implications. The revolutionary Internet, however, differs widely in this respect. "Some contend that Tim Berners-Lee created the first weblog in 1991, and Jon Barger first used the term in December 1997 for a log of links chronicling visits to various websites. Peter Merholz coined the term blog, shortened from weblog in 1999. As a joke, he divided the word weblog into two words (we blog) on the sidebar of his blog Peterme.com in the spring of 1999.

"At that time, blogs developed their signature look of multiple daily entries displayed in reverse-chronological-order, blog-roll or links to other favorite blogs, archives of past content, and sometimes a comment section." (p. 360) Creating websites required considerable programming knowledge, thus they remained uncommon until the appearance of a free-software package called *Blogger*. Via the Internet, domain name blogspot.com was available for the first time.

A 2008 study estimated about 184 million blogs globally, with 25 million in America. But Pole says volume of usage "fails to capture accurately the sheer diversity of political blogs." The most widely read blog in America in 2010? The Huffington Post by journalist Ariana Huffington. Three years later, AOL chief Dan Case announced AOL's purchase of it for several million dollars. That study also found political blogs "highly polarized" with few respondents reporting reading the alternative philosophy (liberal/conservative). (p. 396) Finally, "blogging's software is relatively easy to use, based on What You See Is What You Get (WYSIWYG), enabling users unable to write code." (p. 440)

I found that straight letter grades (A, B, C, D, F) sans plus/minus deprived students of full disclosure with their analytical writing. Many instructors use the "I'm overworked" defense in not assigning undergrads analytical writing projects. Therefore, I created a full-page set of holistic grading criteria so explicit and detailed that I began writing about them in several places, including *Benefits of Model Syllabi* (University Press of America, 2007).

My holistic grading approach enabled me to provide qualitative-feedback to students without the tedium of quantitative feedback experienced by students in their English courses. I proposed (unsuccessfully) adding plusses and minuses to letter grades as not only beneficial to students, but also teachers in cases of grade appeal.

Furthermore specific, clear and detailed holistic grading criteria foster CTS as my teaching/learning philosophy. Academia possesses today a rare consensus that the main goal for undergrads consists of teaching them CTS for life-long learning in an age of flux. And while such efforts prove labor-intensive on both sides of the lectern, they generally bear fruit.

Also, teaching students CTS is not expensive, but requires institutional commitment from the top. I rely on rank-ordering qualitative judgments since that process helps us to engage in CTS, such as my assessment of blogosphere books. The very high grade accorded above to the Pole book is almost matched by our second entry.

Aaron Barlow's *Blogging America: the New Public Sphere* (Kindle, 2008) has won high praise with a grade of A+. I find Barlow's book slightly less helpful than Pole's for two reasons: 1.) Much of it plays defense answering blogging's many critics; 2.) It deals only with personal blogging, skipping the sub-genre of commercial blogs almost completely. Nevertheless, it's still insightful and well-crafted.

The author includes six chapters: 1.) "An Introduction to the Blogs; 2.) The Blogs in Society; 3.) The Blogs from Within; 4.) The Blogs, Political Issues, and the Press;" 5.) "The Blog in Popular Culture;" 6.) "Online Community, Online Utilization: The Christian Blog."

His Preface addresses how he undertook this project: Barlow's previous book, *The Rise of the Blogosphere*, entailed an historical treatise on American journalism's gradual evolution into blogdom, and left both he and his editor feeling like the book left too much unfinished business, almost ignoring contemporary blogdom in the process. "Another book was needed, one with a new focus on what the blogs are doing today (2007), and why." (p. 13)

But describing 2007 blogs requires the retrospection found in *Blogging America: The New Public Sphere*. As to the parameters of his efforts, "It is impossible to cover all of the blogosphere. It is too big, too dynamic, and too responsive to change for anyone to say much about it beyond 'this is what I found in this particular place at this particular time'." (p. 21) Thus, he limited his inquiry significantly; in fact, the only blogging community he delves into is Christian Bloggers.

"One of the areas I have avoided is big commercial blogs. Even many of the small blogs, these days, do make a little money from advertising, but it isn't much. Some of the larger blogs, however, are commercial enterprises from start to finish. I do mention MySpace and Facebook in passing but do not delve into them. The intersection between the blogs and commerce, though fascinating, still hasn't shaken itself out into a form I am comfortable drawing conclusions on." (p. 26)

However, Barlow does comment about commerce and blogs: "Because blogs are not so tied to temporal immediacy and sequence, they are beginning to replace the phone connection between businesses and customers. No more waiting on hold! Simply place a query on the blog, and a response will come. This has advantages even over email, for its public nature proves useful to both business and user." (p. 31)

Regarding this sub-genre, "These blogs are the most interesting, for they show an aspect of individual relations to technology that could not exist until the advent of the World Wide Web and the rise of blogs. If blogs are changing our culture, it is because of the individual bloggers, not because of the other uses that have been found for blogs, no matter how fascinating these may prove. If nothing else, blogs change our relationships with technology, making them more personal and active than ever before—and not only in the political realm." (p. 37)78

His chapter one treks into communications theory pertinent to modern blogging, for example: B.F. Skinner, Walter Ong, and Jurgen Habermas. Here Barlow introduces the concept of "neteracy" skills and attitudes as prerequisites for interfacing with Web-related activities. In his analysis, the attitudinal-half of this intellectual walnut looms as large as the more obvious techno skill-half, including tensions over copyright/patent regulations.

Chapter two ventures into the oblique turf where blogs intersect with writers. He bemoans outsiders writing dismissively about blogs without really understanding them: "Because of their high media visibility, and impact on political discussion, blogs fall victim to descriptions having little to do with reality. Some of these descriptions arise from those who feel threatened by both blogs and the Web, since the Web doesn't increase dangers to anyone on its own." (p. 42)

Chapter three resets lenses viewing the blogs from within the blogosphere, to illuminate how the insiders perceive the outsiders. With analysts who dichotomize consciousness into "real" and "virtual" worlds, Barlow loses patience:

"Bloggers don't view themselves as entering a virtual world, but simply as the users of new tools to deal with situations in the 'real' world. On the other hand, their imagined expansionism sometimes is little more than a new way to talk to the same type of people they would be talking to anyway, the expansion being only in numbers and not in type. This does not mean that that the blogs do not have impact, but simply that rarely as a form of converting an audience to the blogger's belief." (pp. 48-49) This chapter ends "No blog exists alone, meaning that each is part of a greater conversation including comments, links, and other blogs." (p. 51)

Chapter four dives into the murky waters about the extent to which traditional journalism is threatened by the blogosphere: "Professional journalism certainly isn't going to die as a result of the blogs, but it will not remain the same as it has been for the last several decades. The same is true of politics. What is happening through the blogs is the carving out of a new place in the universe of organization and authority. Over the past century both have become increasingly hierarchical, top-down. The blogs, much more egalitarian in focus, are forcing recognition that the old model will no longer suffice." (p. 54)

Chapter five chronicles the relationship between a nation's popular culture and new communications technologies. His analysis consists of describing communications technologies five decades ago (one-way and centralized to passive recipients) contrasted with today (multilaterally decentralized with active recipients). "Today, those same individual audience members have become part of the creative process, taking more and more power each year." (p. 59)

The final chapter has an extended case study of one blogging community: Christian bloggers. "In some respects no different from other blogging communities, this one shows greater breadth and depth, along with a great desire to use the blogs for personal and community growth." (p. 60) As Barlow was writing a Eureka moment fired him up to defend against critics, for one, Andrew Keen.

Keen inspired these words, "I learned that blogs are boring. I learned that we need get beyond arguing about blogs versus *The New York Times*. But all anyone wants to discuss, it seems, is the well-trodden terrain of bloggers versus traditional news reporting. Enough of blogs and enough of bloggers! It's bad enough there are 70 million of them littering the Internet with fast-breaking news about what their authors ate for breakfast. But blogs are just one piece in the digital media revolution. They are boring to write (yawn), boring to read (yawn), and boring to discuss (yawn.)" (p. 65)

Ergo, "What would I prefer to discuss? The impact of Web 2.0 on truth, education, money, and power. I want to debate the increasingly Orwellian role of Google in our information economy. I want to talk about the way in which the Internet has unleashed a plague of pornography, gambling, and intellectual dishonesty on our youth. I want to discuss the future of the book." (p. 69) [lxxix] Among others, Barlow references Supreme Court Justice Lewis Brandeis's famous dictum that the antidote to bad speech is not to limit speech, but rather to increase it.

My grading comes up with another fine one for David Perlmutter's *Blog Wars* (Kindle, 2008). This Kansas University journalism professor provides a balanced assessment of political blogging while clearly articulating his own beliefs (two objectives I surely don't consider mutually exclusive). As to the "old media" versus "new media" paradigm this juxtaposition impressed me: "Blogs are always unfinished, their work always to be continued, revised, and extended later." (p. 71)

He describes researching/writing his book for four years as "similar to reporting on a modern NASCAR race with stone tablets. Much information will be dated, but that's not the point: a blogger's work is never done, nor, is that of a student of blogs. The implied point of ellipsis at the end of every essay or post in a blog is one of the crucial features of blog-style and content that makes it a joint enterprise rather than a monologue." (p. 98)

Like others examined here, Perlmutter devotes much attention to both the recency (mostly 2000-11) and raw, red passion of political blogging (ergo the title *Blog-wars*), which he says far exceeds political "pros" such as candidates, print journalists, or partisan consultants. He admits to liking the progressive blog called Daily Kos.

The passion exploding from political blogs stems partly from the absence of face-to-face interactivity, and pseudonym avatars to hide behind. He calls this feature ironically responsible for both the attraction and repulsion of political blogging. Perlmutter first began his own blog in 2005 (policybyblog.square-space) and followed that with several partisan *nom de guerre* guest blogs by invitation, and now edits a bipartisan Robert Dole Institute for Politics.

He describes the rapid increased use of blogging by political candidates (such as Hilary Clinton in 2008) and warns that such interactive strategies entail significant risks not found in old-school politics. Polls had long revealed that average Americans considered her too calculating, cerebral, and cautious. So she tried to add spontaneity via her blog "Let's talk."

Barack Obama is widely considered to have navigated those choppy waters better than his 2008 adversary. Perlmutter's pithy comment "The youthful future leaders of politics in America live in MySpace, see in YouTube, and write in blog." (p. 57) Obama is described by the author as "Perhaps the most techno-savvy presidential candidate of our time," pointing to his personal decision to address milbloggers (serving in US military) via video link to rally support for the Iraqi effort." (p. 52)

Perlmutter's book also comes in six chapters. One provides an overview of different kinds of blogs, sketches what we know quantitatively and qualitatively about current blogs, including both their audiences and participants. He also discusses the "major investigatory themes of political blogging, arguing they are special political media not because they are new but because they enable an old political impulse: reaching large numbers of people with personal messages and gathering together the like-minded and like-interested about political causes." (p. 159)

Perlmutter similarly reviews research about bloggers and blogging, exploring what he calls a "seeming paradox" concerning the simultaneity of aggressive partisanship counter-posed with a sub-theme: bridge-building a marketplace of ideas.

His second verse covers the pre-history of blogs, making this polemical point: "Blog-like entities and aspirations are very old and recur with new personalized, additive technologies, from the ancient Greeks writing letters up through Franklin Roosevelt's radio fireside chats." (p. 165) Ergo, scholars have debated the various upsides and downsides of blogging for two decades does not preclude our continuing that unfinished business (in the context of the "old media" versus "new media" conversation.)

Verse three takes a micro-strategy rather than a macro-one, teasing apart what he calls the "Year of the Blog-through" (2004) when it burst forth and influenced the 2006 midterms. "In particular I examine the presidential run of Howard Dean, who typified the advantages and drawbacks of blogging as a vehicle for political persuasion and organization." (p. 167) Also, "Blogs have become part of the media system not by accident but because of the particular qualities of blogging that allowed them to exploit opportunities that events afforded them." (p. 170)

Verse four lauds bloggers as "the citizen-press component" of the American political system. Possessors of influence without the power of elites, he includes bloggers as information reporters, collectors, collators, reviser and extenders of investigative journalism. Their efforts increasingly matter, in Perlmutter's judgment: "Bloggers progressively are being read as experts, analysts, and watchdogs on political events, issues, ideas, and persons." (p. 172)

Verse five argues that blogging increasingly becomes perceived as legitimate, shedding the stereotypical image of "amateurs over their heads." They land gigs as political consultants, marketers, or speech-writers as blogging becomes more mainstream. It takes time to blend into the rituals of American office-seeking. Among the serious perils of blogging for elite politicians he cites the "gaffe-prone nature of blog-style," plus the labor-intensive, humbling apprenticeship required.

Verse six includes both predictions and lessons learned about blog-wars in America. Specifically: 1.) blog-like forms will become part of almost every campaign; 2.) Whatever blogging morphs into will stimulate political participation producing more responsible citizens; 3) In one decade, analysts will describe the "blogged years from 2006 to 2008" as the vital turning point.

Our next entry classified with an "A-" grade is *Boom and Bust in the Blogosphere: Case Studies of the Blogging Industry,* by Dan Morrill (Kindle, 2008), which impresses with its scholarly depth, but struggles making this perplexing new world comprehensible to lay-persons. Dan Morrill's blogosphere mini-history pushes the calendar back to 2003, when he worked for Live Journal and then Blogger.com covering new technologies such as Nutch and Hadoop specifically, and more generally about interfaces between people, politics, and technology.

In 2006, he was recruited by Toolbox and became recognized as a glo-bally-syndicated blogger spanning 27 major Internet news sites. He also continues working on his own personal blog, and helps run Social Campus (extension of Web 2.0 into both university and corporate sys-tems). (p. 82)

The upside for Top Bloggers? They lead by example providing best-prac-tices footprints for novitiates. With Louis Gray and Robert Scoble, their mega-hits foster some unrealistic expectations for newcomers. In addi-tion, failed blogs often play out nastily via finger-pointing public vendet-tas. "For some, blogging turns into a tragedy of lawsuits, firings, public embarrassment, ridicule, and the exposure unleashed under court order when their blogs are used against them (blogging anonymity stripped away by court orders)." (p. 100)

Bloggers' decisions concerning acceptance of advertisements to cover expenses, or even make a profit, present thorny problems. For example, the two bloggers cited above (Louis Gray and Robert Scoble) differ com-pletely on this score, with Louis Gray refusing ad revenues and Robert Scoble welcoming them.

It took Google several years under new CEO Eric Schmitt to design a viable business model, consistent with its twin explicit benign goals: "do no evil" and "maximize the user experience." Morrill adds the concept of "signal-to-noise-ratio" from communications theory addressing the qual-ity control problem in the "infotainment" era.

Morrill notes "There are so many blogs on the Internet today that it has become difficult to separate the background noise from the independent signal. This signal-to-noise-ratio, made up of sites that scrape others' content without adding their own, sites that are spam blogs (splogs) or have no real value to add—against those churning out good content on a regular basis is one part of information over-load." (p. 141)

Morrill devotes less effort to the "bust side as opposed to the boom side" of the blogosphere. While diverse motives and practices exist, very many blogs provide good advice on blogging, with plenty of stellar role models out there. But equally apparent are failed bloggers who either lost interest or moved on to other challenges. "Many ways exist to get lost in the noise on the Internet. Some merely have lost interest in climbing the blogger hierarchy. For these people, fame is definitely not the issue, it is the very act of writing that drives them." (p. 183)

He concludes that they all share interesting stories often dramatic in nature, regardless of how successful by external standards. In a national landscape where reality TV is actually taken seriously by many viewers, blogs and social networks at least leave paper trails that can be studied by researchers (i.e., digital archaeologists) like him resulting in books on this novel subject-matter.

Getting more geeky, the author says, "A blog platform, such as Typepad, Blogger, Wordpress, and other software systems are considered Content Management Systems (CMS) allowing people to post information on the Internet without worrying about HTML or code to render the pages. The software will accept any input, with some simple formatting, post-information to the Internet when the blogger pushes the 'publish' button. Some blogs are built to look and feel like a newspaper, while many are more Spartan based on simple or two-or-three liners, still others feature nothing but podcasts or videos." (p. 215)

Furthermore, the flexibility of blogging software enables people to use the blogging CMS systems to deliver information to many kinds of readership. Some consist merely of static pages for content such as a Wiki. Some businesses rely on such static pages to keep employees and potential consumers apprised of new developments. The readership sometimes takes on a role as beta testers for new products or services. And, "the appeal is that real people are writing their own thoughts about a subject, without the polished spin of more formal information formats." (p. 248)

In chapter one I pitched CTS for quality-control regarding contemporary information overload. Morrill addresses the same concern: "Many of the automated systems we use to digest and collate blog-based information cannot yet tell good information from bad. Some deliberately inject false information (or biased information), apologizing later on. Many good examples exist for blogs doing bad things; like being repositories for malware, adware, or data others find objectionable." (p. 312)

He also warns against "bad boy blogs" cultivating reputations for contrariness as their modus operandi (like Bill O'Reilly as provocateur-in-chief at FNC). One good bad boy example cited by Morrill is called Valleywag.

Moving on, Richard Clarke is the most famous author in this bibliographic compendium. I saw him on TV in 2011 discussing his new book dedicated to Professor William Kaufmann. The Introduction describes a February 2009 memorial in which Clarke eulogized Kaufmann as the "man who had taught so many of us how to analyze issues of war and defense. Many of his former students, now in their fifties, drank toasts to their mentor who had just died at age 90." (p. 31) Kaufmann's teaching career included MIT, Harvard, and the Brookings Institution.

Clarke and his co-author jest about having referred affectionately to Kaufmann as "Yoda" for attempting to convey the vagaries of the "Force" to his trainees. They suggest parallels between the 1950s and today for undertaking revolutionary weaponry (nukes then); cyberspace war now) "Both of which occurred without public debate, media discussion, serious Congressional oversight, academic analysis, or international dialogue." (p. 51)

Also, the entire phenomenon of cyberspace war is shrouded in such government secrecy that it makes the Cold War look like a time of open transparency. The biggest secret in the world about cyber-war may be that at the very same time the U.S. prepares for offensive cyber-war, it continues policies making it impossible to defend the nation from cyber attack." (p. 61). Grade =A−.

In October 2009, a new General took over the U.S. Cyber Command charged with using information technology and the Internet as weapons, trumping similar efforts in Russia and China. "Given the unique nature of cyber-war, there may be incentives to go first, and the most likely targets are civilian in nature. The speed at which thousands of targets can be hit, almost anywhere in the world, brings with it the prospect of highly volatile crises. The force that prevented nuclear war (deterrence) does not work well in cyber-war." (p. 56)

And, "A nation that has invented the new technology, and the tactics to use it, may not be the victor, if its own military is mired in the ways of the past, overcome by inertia, overconfident in the weapons they have learned to love and consider supreme." (p. 61) Therefore, Clarke says he chose his co-author (Knake) carefully to countervail his 60-ish "neteracy" limitations with a 30-ish techie with whom he works well.

Their caveats to America come through loud and clear: "While it may appear to give America some sort of advantage, in fact cyber-war places this country at greater jeopardy than it does any other nation. Nor is this new kind of war a game or figment of our imaginations. Far from being an alternative to conventional war, cyber-war may actually increase the likelihood of the more traditional combat with explosives, bullets, and missiles." (p. 67)

The authors use a case study of deft cyber-war by the Israelis in April 2008 where they wiped out a North-Korean sponsored nuclear facility in Syria by tricking its pricey radar system purchased from Russia. How? By "owning" (taking over) superior Israeli cyber weapons bought from the Americans: "What appeared on the Syrian radar screens during Israel's successful attack was what the Israeli Air Force had put there, an image of nothing, as they absorbed this real stealth attack." (p. 174)

They discuss three probable explanations for this stunning Israeli achievement. All three reasons assume considerable credit goes to Israel's American sponsors. Clarke and Knake define cyber-war here as "actions by a nation-state to penetrate another country's computers or networks for the purpose of causing damage or disruption." (p. 189)

EXAMINING THE SIX "B" GRADES:

The first book under "B" Grades is the predecessor to Aaron Barlow's second book described above. *The Rise of the Blogosphere* covers this recent subject, grounded in deep American roots via 15 fifteen chapters:

1.) "The Concept of an American Popular Press;" 2.) "The Rise of Advocacy Journalism;" 3.) "Debate in the Early American Press;" 4.) "The Victory for Rights of the Press;" 5.) "Heyday of the Partisan Press;" 6.) "Rise of Professional Journalism;" 7.) "Creation of Press Empires;" 8.) "Domination of the Press by Electronic Media;" 9.) "Alternative Journalism;" 10.) "Failure of American News Media;" 11.) "Movement Toward Public Journalism;" 12.) "Birth of the Blogs;" 13.) "9/11 and the Rise of the Blogosphere;" 14.) "Research, Rather-gate, and the Power of Blogs;" 15.) "Political Reclamation and Citizen Journalism."

Barlow observes about himself, "I am one of those fortunate people with feet on both sides of the contemporary technological divide. From my early years, I was involved in printing, setting type by hand, running presses, melting lead for linotype pigs and pouring stereotype slabs for local newspapers. At the same time, I was beginning to get my first, small experiences with journalism by writing, editing, and mimeographing my own high school 'underground newspaper.' The worlds of job printing and small publications were my own." (p. 24)

This author credits the "citizen journalism" group ePluribus Media and its creation of an established online presence via its own blog and Internet journal. He describes the organization as both diffuse and possessing "deep netroots," now a professor at Kutztown (PA) University.

He warns against "techno-determinism" (technology possesses an onto-logical status prior to culture) which leads to a kind of "retro-determin-ism" (political history of a technology is converted into the unfolding nature of that technology.) Get used to encountering words not present in your dictionary via the expanding blogosphere. "We should never make the mistake of thinking that the blogs exploding on the scene in the last five years are nothing more than a function of technology. They are much more than that. In fact, political blogs have a pedigree even older than the United States." (p. 46)

He dwells at length on the 18th century as especially instructive: "The changes in newspapers in the 18th century underscores the extent to which news is a social construct, varying from era to era according to the social forces at work. News is a malleable compound, a synthesis of interests." (p. 72) This insight strikes me as helpful in assessing the role of FNC today. Barlow's Grade="B++."

A Grade of "B+" is earned by Deirdre Collingsworth and Rafal Rohozinsky's *Bullets and Blogs: New Media and the War-fighter* (Kindle, 2008). This brief book derives from a 2006 Department of Defense Quadrennial Defense Review (QDR) held at the U.S. Army War College in Carlisle, PA, attended by these two authors, which they refer to as "an analytical synthesis and workshop report."

Opinions expressed by others present don't reflect either authors' views, or the Army War College. It is divided into five parts: 1.) From informa-tion control to engagement: Winning in the new media battle-space; 2.) Leveraging and countering new media: Six requirements; 3.) Countering new media: Special considerations; 4.) Operations Security (OPSEC) in the age of radical transparency; 5.) Seizing the new media offensive: Priority issues. The list of illustrative boxes here consists of 13 serious ones cited in endnote five.[lxxx] Case studies and illustrative boxes intersperse the text.

The Foreword begins: "War is nothing if not a constant process of adaptation. Today, anyone armed with a digital camera and Internet access can become an information warrior, potentially reaching global audiences. Twitter, Facebook, YouTube and other blogs have become as important to the strategic outcome of military operations as bullets, troops, and air power. Appreciating the game-changing properties of new media are as important for today's war-fighters as are the skills, training, and tradecraft required to maneuver conventional forces." (p. 40)

They describe a "digital divide" in our armed forces wherein young "digital natives" follow orders taken from older officers classifiable as "digital immigrants." "For example, today's recruits come from a generation of 'digital natives' who have grown up with, and expect, 24/7 connectivity. They are consumers and users of new media, employing it ways often poorly understood by senior leadership, and which can inadvertently compromise Operations Security." (p. 62)

The authors consider the title for their report (Bullets and Blogs) illustrative of the symbiotic relationship between lethal and non-lethal warfighting today and call for a paradigm shift throughout the Pentagon.

They conclude six core competencies to underpin effective information engagement in the second decade of the 21st century: 1.) Speed; 2.) Authorities need to be powered down; 3.) Messages must possess consistency, persistence, and reflection; 4.) Media: If you aren't in their space, you are no place; 5.) Messengers must be trusted by audiences; 6.) Synchronicity fosters organizational speed and agility by empowering actors at all levels to act appropriately.

Considerable space is devoted to a 2006 case study in which the Israeli Army failed to achieve its track record for successful operations when essentially outsmarted by the non-state actor Hezbollah in their war fought in Lebanon, stating boldly "This conflict marked an important milestone for warfare in the information age. Hezbollah proved capable of thwarting Israel's primary war aims and forcing a battlefield stalemate." (p. 100)

And just how did Hezbollah pull off such a counterintuitive miracle against decidedly superior firepower? A strategic victory was achieved because Hezbollah used an "information-led war-fighting strategy leveraging new media to influence the political will of key global audiences, especially the Israeli public." (p.102)

Similarly, "Winning today requires effective information engagement, especially against irregular adversaries politically. The center of gravity is public opinion (often to multiple audiences). Effectiveness is based on the ability to engage those different publics—in the idioms and through the media that resonate. Increasingly, the expectations and communicative cultures of audiences in the 'information age' require a distributed presence on multiple and personalized media is imperative. It is also critical to maintain credibility at all times." (p. 121)

While tactics like taking down websites or wiping out satellite TV or radio from the air used to represent best-practices, that no longer holds true. Future efforts must effectively respond to any problematic messages rather than seeking to eliminate their source. "New media communications have also gone 'viral;' once the information has gone out on the Net, it is already mirrored to the extent that nothing can be done about it." (p. 178)

Finally, to "achieve strategic agility in the information age" the Pentagon should prioritize: 1.) Information engagement trumping information control; 2.) Embrace new media enabling the combative power of information; 3.) Prioritize research and development with flexibility; 4.) Educate digital immigrants; 5.) Exploit and nurture digital natives; 6.)

Enhance DOD's ability to better communicate with varied audiences. (p. 206)

A very respectable Grade of "B" in this fast company goes Silicon Valley journalist Tim Wu's (Kindle, 2010) *The Master Switch: The Rise and fall of Information Empires.* Wu's work consists of four parts and 15 chapters.

Immediately I'm struck by Wu's wit, comprehensiveness, and fiction-like prose. Seldom do I find illustrative quotations as apt as Wu's reference to playwright Tom Stoppard's *The Invention of Love:* "Every age thinks it's the modern age, but this one really is."

Wu's Introduction opens at a celebratory banquet in Washington, DC in April 1916, involving the reigning communications phenom then: The Bell Systems, personified by its legendary CEO, Timothy Vail. "Then 71 years old, his hair and mustache white, Vail was the incarnation of Bell, the Jack Welch of his time, who had twice rescued his colossus from collapse." (p.23)

Wu opines, "Few large institutions have ever borne the imprint of one person as thoroughly as Vail's at A T & T.' In an age when many industrial titans were feared or hated, Vail was widely respected. He styled himself as a private sector Theodore Roosevelt, infusing his imperial instincts with a sense of civic duty." (p. 65)

In 2011, Timothy Vail's world appears nothing if not antediluvian. Yet, Wu still wants us to appreciate the haltingly uncertain march of technology since 1916: "When we look carefully at the 20th century, we soon find that the Internet wasn't the first information technology supposedly changing everything forever. We see, in fact, a succession of optimistically open media, each, over time, became a closed and controlled industry like Vail's. Again and again, radical change involving information seemed, if anything, more dramatic than today." (p. 100)

Wu wants us not only to appreciate the forces working against high-tech revolutions, but also to ponder his new theory ("Cycles") about "open and closed" transformative technologies strictly run by one corporation (a cartel) oscillating back-and-forth. If true, why does it matter profoundly?" (p. 112)

Because Wu ambitiously posits this phenomenon as not merely a pattern, but a bona fide historical theory damned-near inevitable. "Sure, the Internet has truly become the fabric of our lives means we are sooner or later in for a very jarring turn of history's wheel." (p. 129) Clever as I find Wu's analysis, he over-reaches here.

Tim Wu's introspections include, "The inspiration for this book is my experience of the long wave of easy optimism created by the rise of information technologies in recent decades, a feeling of almost utopian possibility and idealism. I shared in that excitement, both working in Silicon Valley and writing about it. Yet I have always been struck by what I feel is too strong an insistence that we are living in unprecedented times." (p. 267)

He also describes the *Kronos Effect* (dominant companies consuming their potential successors during infancy) "Understanding the *Kronos Effect* is critical to understanding the Cycle, and for that matter, the history of information technology. It may sometimes seem that invention and technological advance are a natural, orderly process, but this is an illusion. Whatever technological reality we live with is the result of tooth-and-claw industrial combat." (p. 419)

A "B" grade also goes to *Millennial Makeover: MySpace, YouTube, and the Future of American Politics* (Kindle, 2008), by Morley Winograd and Mike Hais, divided into three parts: Part I: "The Cycles of American Politics"; Part II: "Transition to a New Era;" Part III: "The New American Political Landscape." These co-authors have chosen ambitious tasks.

Card-carrying Democrats, their day jobs reside in the private polling sector, and together they helped resurrect their beloved party in Michigan after a drubbing courtesy of Richard Nixon's landslide in 1972. They both recognize Bill Clinton as one of the first Democrats "to identify an entirely new constituency in American politics based on the impact of information and communications technologies on how our nation was beginning to work and live." (p. 28)

Morley Winograd had also co-authored with Dudley Buffa a 1996 book called *Taking Control: Politics in the Information Age,* studying what they call "wired workers" whom they introduced to the political lexicon during Clinton's presidency. Believers in a robust two-party system, Winograd and Hais also consult with suggestions for Republicans to improve their status after 2008's Republican debacle.

"This book attempts to illuminate the Millennial values and behaviors, as well as the technologies that help to create and enable them, for the Baby Boomers and Gen-Xers currently running America. In some previous eras, intergenerational misunderstandings and the failure to use new technologies wisely have had catastrophic consequences for our society." (p. 47)

Their book benefited from Frank Magid's Associates, a global leader in research for political consultation. In 2007, CEO Brent Magid celebrated its 50th anniversary as a firm with a massive project called "Magid's Millennial Strategy Program," advising corporations how to "communicate more effectively with the Millennial Generation," as detailed here. In January 2006, December 2006, and May 2007, Magid, Inc. sent out online questionnaires to samples much larger than the typical 1,000-ish magic number.

Their three target populations: 1.) Millennials; 2.) Gen-Xers; 3.) Baby Boomers; in order to compare/contrast their political attitudes and behaviors. Numerous technical assistants at Magid, Inc. helped with data collection, analysis, and conclusions. The authors also interfaced with the Center for Telecom Management (CTM) at USC's Marshall School of Business. They also thank Virgin Mobile CEO (Dan Shulman), Jibjab's CEO (Greg Spiridellis), their expert on digital music (Ted Cohen), Artist-Direct CEO (Jon Diamond), MySpace's Josh Berman, and YouTube's Jordan Hoffner.

Providing historical sweep, Winograd and Hais claim that "Each of the five major political realignments in U.S. history has been triggered by a crucial event, such as the Civil War or the Great Depression which in turn became the subject of extensive examination. But the real driving forces behind this constant and predictable shift in the fortunes of America's parties, institutions, and policy are underlying changes in generational size and attitudes with contemporaneous advances in communication technologies." (p. 134)

I recommend both this and the Wu book, but each possesses an excessive subtext of historical determinism. The present authors describe our political system facing another crucial test as a new generation of Millennials (born between 1982 and 2003) comes of age in large numbers. Their comfort level with "neteracy" confounds Baby Boomers who came of age politically in the 1950s and 1960s, when TV was the new "wow-factor."

The numerical superiority of the Millennials is also hyped, as is their unprecedented diversity and open-mindedness to the value of social tolerance via successive waves of civil rights progress. Millennials also buy into the optimism of "positive-sum games" (win/win) thinking, antithetical to the pessimism of "zero-sum games" (win/lose) thinking among Baby Boomers who continue culture wars from the divisive 1960s.

Winograd and Hais point to 2008 as a pivotal election year in which Democrats proved more adroit in cyber space, raising unprecedented money for Obama, significant chunks of which came from Silicon Valley. The authors discuss Obama's comfort level with "Netroots" campaign strategies alien to most Republicans, and they predict this dynamic to continue in future elections.

A lower but respectable grade of "B-" goes to journalist, blogger, media critic, and consultant Tom Watson for 2009's *Cause-Wired: Plugging In, Getting Involved, Changing the World.* His career includes stints at the *New York Times, Huffington Post, Industry Standard, and Inside.* He also serves as chief strategy officer for Changing Our World, Inc., and founder/editor of Newscritics.com., also holds an adjunct professorship at Columbia University.

A thoughtful Foreword by Jean Case, CEO of the Case Foundation (www. casefoundation.org), which invests in individuals, non-profits, and social enterprises catalyzing civil society. She writes "Today we find ourselves at a juncture where blended forms of civic engagement and business activity—supported and spurred by new social web technologies—are being used by both individuals and organizations to create and expand a rising culture of giving and mixing of ingredients that can create powerful opportunities for positive change." (p. 60)

She also discusses a new and different type of giver (*Net-native Millennials*) poorly understood therefore funded recently by the Case Foundation; and, relevant to *CauseWired's* basic premise: "that giving has in fact changed and will continue to do so before our eyes and in ways altering forever the relationship between, people and the causes that motivate them. Tom Watson has been there all along, exploring the nuances of what these new approaches might mean to the philanthropic sector." (p. 74) As well as describing these dramas, Watson prescribes ways to tap this new culture of giving.

Watson's Introduction: "Business pages are filled with stories of startup companies and massive valuations. Google grows ever more rapidly into a global powerhouse. The reach of social networks such as Facebook stretches every day. Americans are living more of their lives in public, creating vast lines of online 'friends' and professional colleagues, and sharing their experiences, their taste in music, their political choices, and even their personal lives." (p. 126)

The next creative wave will be establishing social networks as the next generation of life on the Web so uniquely facilitating real-time communication for everyone, but especially the Millennials who have never experienced life without the Internet.

He notes the ancillary effect of another vital phenomenon: globalization. Also, the "never again" mantra after the Holocaust continues online today concerning genocides such as Darfur, becoming in Watson's parlance "CauseWired." Grass roots videos from such places, and from the 2011 unraveling of Middle East dictators epitomize Cause-Wired, whose consumers are well-informed about corporate shenanigans, buy products according to social choice, and invest in firms identified as ethically responsible.

Watson's take on *CauseWired?* "You will be introduced to bloggers, media analysts, political operatives, and social activists experimenting with new forms of communications to raise both money and awareness and to support a wide range of causes. It is my belief that this core group of pioneers will change the way humanity views philanthropy and activism, in quest of improving life on Earth.' (P. 159)

As to its ephemeral nature, he notes "Writing this book has been like shooting at a moving target. When I began, Facebook was the darling of financial analysts and sociologists the world over, fat in both market cap and reputation as a game-changer. When I completed it, Facebook was still a giant but had lost some of its status as 'the next Google,' struggling with privacy concerns. By the time you read this book, Facebook may have been sold for billions. But that doesn't matter to the premise of *CauseWired.*"(p. 324)

The last book to escape the burn pile of "C" grades is *Using Internet Primary Sources to Teach Government, Economics and Contemporary World Issues* by James Shiveley and Phillip Van Fossen (Kindle, 2001). ,Grade=B—Their Introduction is titled "The Internet and the World Wide Web—Potential for Education."

Part I "Using Critical Thinking in the Social Sciences;" Part II "Using Primary Source Sites;" Part III "Secondary Source Sites." A disconnect exists between these few skinny Parts I, II, and III and endless headings dividing up Social Science content without chapters.

These authors also connect CTS with the complexities of 21ˢᵗ century civil society: "Citizenship education needs to promote understanding and appreciation of the multiple perspectives vital to democracy. A pluralistic democracy works when its diverse groups really believe that they and those around them are important parts of their society and culture. When multiple perspectives are infused into curricula, classrooms become more consistent with key democratic principles." (p. 135)

As to why so few social science instructors integrate the Internet for researching term papers, they posit three hypotheses: 1.) Few instructors are trained in classroom use of the Web; 2.) Many consider such endeavors too labor-intensive and suffering from the phenomenon of diminishing returns; 3.) Fear that way too much gunk floods naïve undergrads unprepared for information overkill.

This marginal book provides examples of techno-best-practices in education, deals with both primary and secondary research, books and relevant Internet sites, and multi-media resources online. The "neteracy" prerequisites for instructors are few indeed and stated clearly. Finally, they discuss the various complexities of "fair use" limitations of Internet materials. That is, "Generally, materials produced by federal agencies exist in the public domain and may be reproduced without permission." (p. 201)

The Digital Millennium Copyright Act (DMCA) of 1998 pertaining copyright law and digital technologies applies here.

EVALUATING FIVE MILDLY-RECOMMENDED "C" GRADES:

With a Grade of C+++, the best of this group consists of John Palfrey and Ura Gasser's *Born Digital: Understanding the First Generation of Digital Natives* (Kindle, 2010). Hyperbole seems to follow the Internet like a symmetrical sundial, and these two lawyers and Harvard professors are not immune.

For example, "Boomers may consider themselves so cool and forever-young to find themselves on the wrong side of a generation gap, but technology has created a great divide: Digital Natives (the Internet Age Generation) are so acclimated to cyberspace they verge on being another species." (p. 26) Metaphors about the Digital Revolution's

Digital Divide seem warranted to me, but talk about the process of speciation seems over the top. Admittedly, down-loading, text-messaging, multi-player online games, and YouTube watching possess profound implications.

Palfrey and Gasser's analysis does, however, exhibit sufficient cautionary notes about problems such as privacy rights, failure of the U.S. to regulate data-mining by search engines, controlling online medical and financial information, and the irretrievability of hasty words or actions later regretted, and cradle-to-grave dossiers on private citizens.

While harsh in their assessment of American laissez-faire policies toward data-mining search engines, other countries, especially European ones, receive high marks for best- practices leadership on this score. Social Scientists like me often fail to factor in the significance of revolutionary developments among business, but these authors do not: "Business can be done more quickly and over greater distances, often with much less capital required to get up and running." (p. 68)

They also say that "This narrative is about those who wear the earbuds of an iPod on the subway to their first job, not those of us who still remember how to operate a Sony Walkman or buying LPs or eight-track tapes. . . . This new generation didn't have to relearn anything to live lives of digital immersion. They learned in digital the first time around; they only know a world that is digital." (p. 86)

Furthermore, "Digital Natives are constantly connected. They have plenty of friends, in real space and in the virtual worlds—indeed, a growing collection of friends they keep a count of, often for the rest of the world to see, in their online social networks." (p. 101)

And, "They know how to use new software programs in a snap, seamlessly take, edit, and post pictures to share online in their sleep. They seem most creative when forging parallel worlds on sites like Second Life, after which they post a video on YouTube or Daily Motion." (p. 120). And concerning the cultural universal known as fear of the unknown, Palfrey and Gasser counsel us Boomers that "Fear is the biggest obstacle to getting started on that second path enabling us to realize the potential of digital technology the way Digital Natives use it." (p. 148)

Finally, they hit upon what I consider humanity's greatest challenge, the unsustainably widening gap between rich and poor both domestically and globally, which they refer to here as the digital participation gap. "The biggest concern that we highlight is the impact of the participation gap. The digital world offers new opportunities to those who know how to avail themselves. These opportunities enable creativity, learning, entrepreneurship, and innovation. Access to technology is vital, but the toughest dilemma is for learning digital literacy (skills needed to navigate this complicated hybrid world.") (p. 266).

Arizona State University political scientist Matthew Hindman's book also scores pretty well at C++: *The Myth of Digital Democracy* (Kindle, 2008). He challenges much of the conventional wisdom found in theoretical musings on this subject; specifically that life online expands the public voice, counters gatekeepers, and broadens swaths of civic engagement. He claims his work represents the first serious empirical study on the relationship between the Internet and participatory democracy, and provides both utopian and dystopian interpretations concerning the balance sheet on digital democracy.

He attacks this subject via seven chapters: 1.) "Internet and the Democratization of Politics;" 2.) "Lessons Learned from Howard Dean;" 3.) "The Link Structure of Political Web sites" (googlearchy); 4.) "Political Traffic and the Politics of Search; "5.) "Online Concentration;" 6.) "Blogs: The New Elite Media;" 7.) "Elite Politics and the Missing Middle." Followed by Appendices: Support Vector Machine Classifiers; Surfer Behavior and Crawl Depth; Hitwise's Data and Methodology.

In 1993, University of Illinois students led by Marc Andreesen posted software online called Mosaic (world's first graphical web browser). Prior to that the Internet invented by an English physicist working in Geneva changed everything. "Prior to that, the cumbersome text-based programs preceding Mosaic made the Web a colorful and inviting medium navigable by everyone, soon transformed it from a haven for techies and academics into the fastest-growing communications technology in history." (p. 65)

Hindman traces how Mosaic's release, commercialized via the Netscape browser in 1995, triggered the Internet Revolution and rapid Internet stock market bubble resulting from Netscape's public stock offering. "That the Internet makes public discourse more accessible finds expression in case law. In striking down the Communications Decency Act, the U.S. Supreme Court emphasized the potential for the Internet to create a radically more diverse public sphere," and he quotes from the Court:

'Any person or organization with a computer connected to the Internet can publish information.'" (p. 90).

The author's mission? Studying more rigorously the Internet's impact on politics, covering many case studies on the nexus between these two variables.

Journalist Don Tapscott's 2008 book comes in slightly lower at a C+: *Grown Up Digital: How the Net Generation is changing Your World.* Tapscott's qualitative data base derives from more than 11,000 interviews with young people between ages 16 and 29 internationally. Funded by a $4 M grant from several corporations, Tapscott takes on five big questions: "1.) How the brain of the Net Generation processes information; 2.) Seven ways to attract and engage young talent in the workforce; 3.) Seven guidelines for educators to tap the Net Gen's potential; 4.) Parenting 2.0: No place like the new home; 5.) Citizen Net: How young people and the Internet are transforming democracy." (p. 27)

Tapscott's sizable team of researchers also limited their references to sources readily available online, making it "completely accessible to any reader, not just the cognoscenti." (p. 209)

The same generational trifecta appears here as well: Boomers; Gen-Xers; Net-Gen. He tries to relax hyperactive Boomers to get over our egocentricity and tap into this new generation's multi-tasking skills: "Chances are you know a person between 11 and 30. You've seen them doing five things at once: texting friends, downloading music, uploading videos, watching movies on a tiny screen, and doing who knows what on Facebook or MySpace." (p. 214) Yes, my three grandsons fit that profile.

The author's work is divided into three parts 11 chapters: Part One (*Meet the Net Gen*): chapter 1.): "The Net Generation Comes of Age;" chapter 2.) "A Generation Bathed in Bits;" 3.) "The Eight Net Gen Norms;" 4.) "The Net Generation Brain; Part Two" (*Transforming Institutions*):

chapter 5.) "Net Generation as Learners;" chapter 6.) "Net Gen in the Workforce;" 7.) "Net Generation as Consumers;" 8.) "Net Gen and the Family; Part Three" (*Transforming Society*): chapter 9.) "Net Gen and American Politics;" 10.) "Making the World a Better Place Bottom Up;" 11.) "In Defense of the Future. "

His Introduction starts: "It's amazing how far kids have come in the dozen years since I wrote my previous book (*Growing Up Digital*), inspired by watching my two children use complex technologies like computers, video games, and VCRs with seemingly no effort. By 1993, my son Alec (seven) played sophisticated games, typed class assignments on a Mac, and sent an e-mail greeting to Santa at Christmas. My daughter Nicole (ten) figured out how to communicate with friends using computer chat lines. She was always pushing the envelope on technology in our home, even more than her brother. When Mosaic appeared, they took to it like ducks to water, becoming more proficient surfers than me or my wife Anna." (p. 233)

Tapscott considered his kids prodigies until he witnessed their peers behaving similarly. The title for his first book includes the words "growing up digital" while his sequel changes it to "grown up digital" (a fait accompli). His first book luxuriated on the *New York Times* best-seller list for many months (explaining his scaring up such killer funding for the sequel).

In a section called the "dark side," the author dissects ten Net Gen criticisms: "1.) They're dumber than we were at their age; 2.) They're screen-agers, net-addicted, losing their social skills, and have no time for sports-related healthy activities; 3.) They have no shame; 4.) Because their parents have coddled them, they remain adrift in the world afraid to choose a career path; 5.) They steal; 6.) They bullying acquaintances online; 7.) They're violent; 8.) They posses no work ethic, making poor employees; 9.) This constitutes the latest narcissistic "me-generation;" 10.) "They don't give a damn." (pp. 294-308)

To examine these myths, his project undertook the most complete research effort to date. If we can challenge such ideological assumptions with data (both hard- and soft-) then even we Boomers can tap into this vast resource more productively, as I did here.

The book by Mizuko Ito et al., scores lower at C-: *Learning and Living with the New Media: Summary of Findings from the Digital Youth Project*, funded by the John D. and Catherine T. MacArthur Foundation (Kindle, 2009), whose moniker on the PBS News Hour I love ("In search of a more just, verdant and peaceful world.") An ambitious three-year ethnographic study of young people at home, in-school, after-school, and online. While the Tapscott effort above blended both hard-data and soft-data, the Ito book sticks almost exclusively to the former. A humanities research scientist at Berkeley, Ito also directed a huge staff under the title Digital Youth Project. This is actually a truncated version.

The Foreword fits the Ito book broadly in the MacArthur Foundation Reports on Digital Media and Learning (MIT Press), all focusing on "present findings from current research on how young people learn, play, socialize, and participate in civic life." Annual MacArthur funding for these efforts averages about $50 million with all results initially published openly online. Why? To stimulate more research on this rapidly-changing subject.

Graded slightly lower at C–, but recommended, is a 2010 book by journalist Bradford Fitch: *Citizen's Handbook to Influencing Elected Officials: Citizen Advocacy in State Legislatures and Congress.* Its functions he describes as three-fold: research studies; interviews and focus groups; experiential. Heavy on manual-like practical advice such as: persuasive letters to the editor; sending emails to officials; planning/preparation to meet with elected officials; effectively interacting with legislators face-to-face; plotting off-the-record interviews; and, understanding the decision-making process for officials. If it weren't already sub-titled, another good choice might have been: a best-practices compendium.

Its Table of Contents includes two parts, seven chapters, and four Appendices. Part I (*How Government Really Works*): chapter 1.): "How Congressional Offices Work;" chapter 2.) "Congressional Culture;" chapter 3.) "How Legislators Make Decisions;" 4.) "People Who Can Influence Legislators and How They Do It; Part II" (*How to Influence a Legislator*): chapter 5.) "Strategies for Influencing Legislators;" chapter 6.) "Face-to-Face Meetings;" chapter 7.) "Varied Communications."

I like his Introduction's finish: "Once you recognize that most of the decisions legislators make are not front-page news, yet still have a profound impact on impact on your life; once you see that those decisions are not only influenced by lobbyists and special interests, but also by regular citizens; once you master the crucial basic skills to influence undecided lawmakers, you will be ready *to participate* in the most important conversation humankind ever conceived: the democratic dialogue. This book shows you how." (p. 191)

THREE "D" GRADES MARGINALLY-RECOMMENDED:

Ruth Lister and Graham Murdock, *Digital Citizenship: Participation and Exclusion in the E-Society* (Kindle, 2011): Grade=D+.

Stephen Coleman and Jay Blumier, *the Internet and Democratic Citizenship: Theory, Practice, and Policy* (Kindle, 2010): Grade=D.

Karen Mossberger and Ramona McNeal, *Digital Citizenship: The Internet, Society, and Participation* (Kindle, 2007): Grade=D.

FIVE "F" GRADES (NOT RECOMMENDED):

S.A. Morse, *Blogging Basics for Beginners: Catch Up on the Blogoshere for the 21st Century* (Kindle, 2004);

Dwayne Conyers, *The Best of the Blog (Kindle, 2006);*

Davis Whiteman, *Learning to Blog at WordCamp*(Kindle, 2005);

Manuel Braschi, *Blogging for Beginners: Decisions and Strategies to Set Up a Blog* (Kindle, 2003);

Rick Ricker, *Blogging for Beginners* (Kindle, 2005)

Concerning Internet and Technology magazines he cites only four: 1.) Tech Review; 2.) PC Magazine; 3.) 2600 Magazine: The Hatcher Quarterly; 4.) Information Week. However, on the subject of political blogs the N=3,061. Here the top ten consist of: 1.) Kindle Books; 2.) Free Books on Kindle; 3.) I Love My Kindle; 4.) Sexy Stories; 5.) Popsci. com; 6.) Tech Crunch; 7.) Gizmodo; 8.) Kindle World Blog; 9.) The Street; 10.) The Kindle Reader.

Finally, regarding North American best-selling newspapers, Kindle lists 97 with the top ten being: 1.) New York Times; 2.) Wall Street Journal; 3.) USA Today; 4.) Washington Post; 5.) The Onion; 6.) Financial Times; 7.) International Herald Tribune; 8.) Los Angeles Times; 9.) Boston Globe; 10.) San Francisco Chronicle.

BEST- PRACTICES: THE WEBBY AWARDS:

Other competitons exist; such as the Golden Web Awards (GWA)[lxxxi] but the real action for the past 15 years has surrounded the gradual expansion of the Webby Awards. Another free recent web competitor called Stand Out Awards (SOA) has ambitious plans, describing its missions: "To serve as a source of inspiration to those looking to see some of the best web work from around the world." SOA touts itself as more international than the English-language-intensive Webby Awards.[lxxxii]

Information about the Webby Awards derived from three main Internet sources.[lxxxiii]

It commenced in 1996, initially sponsored by *The Web Magazine* meeting in San Francisco (1997); it was produced by Tiffany Shlain. However, this magazine shut down in 1998 with ceremonies continuing on an independent basis.

That same year, the International Academy of Digital Arts and Sciences was founded and has run the show capably since. Among the Academy's most famous members we find David Bowie, Martha Stewart, Harvey Weinstein, Arianna Huffington, Matt Groening, Biz Stone, Vinton Cerf, Richard Branson, and Bob Greenberg.

In 2005, ownership and administration of the Webby Awards moved to Recognition Media (also in charge of the Telly Awards). Always seemingly in a state of flux, The Webby Awards in 2006 established categories rewarding interactive advertising, as well as original film/video premiering on the Internet; and, the next year started a new category honoring mobile Websites. By 2009, the 13th Annual Webby Awards fielded nearly 10,000 entries from every state in America. Simultaneously, more than 500,000 public votes were cast in the Webby People's Voice Awards.

Procedures affect perceptions of any award's credibility, and both the nomination and evaluation processes here haven't changed much, and they strike me as pretty rigorous. The number of entries has risen to impressive levels, again speaking volumes about the award's significance. Several thousand responses to the "Call for Entries" are rated by Associate Members of the Academy; those receiving the highest marks during this first round of voting make it onto *category-specific shortlists,* then examined by prestigious Executive Members of the Academy.

Thereafter, Executive Academy Members with "category specific expertise" evaluate the short-listed entries based on explicit criteria for each of four separate award categories. Their ballots determine Webby Honorees, Nominees, and Webby Winners. I like the fact that Price Waterhouse Coopers handles all of the auditing.

Currently, the Webby Awards include four entry categories: Websites; Interactive Advertising (banners, rich media, viral, etc.); Online Film and Video; and Mobile (phone-generated). The Academy selects five (5) nominees per category with one (1) winner chosen for the coveted Webby Award. I like even better the Public Vote by the online community resulting in a second Webby in each category. Entrants choose the appropriate categories to enter.

From their "Frequently Asked Questions" we learn the following. Can aspirants enter more than one category? Yes. Are entrants limited to the United States? No, however, "sites must be accessible to our predominantly English-speaking judges." Also, foreign language films/videos must be dubbed or subtitled. What claims are made by critics and how do the Webbies respond? See below:

The most vocal criticism centers on what amounts to a "two-fer" regarding payment: 1) To enter; and, 2) To attend the ceremony. Ancillary to this is a charge of discrimination against the vast majority of small sites unable to compete under these circumstances. Webby Award Executive Director David-Michael Davies is quoted by the *Wall Street Journal* saying "entry fees provide the best and most sustainable model for insuring that our judging process remains consistent and rigorous; not dependent on things like sponsorships that can fluctuate from year to year."

To me, the significance of all awards relates to rewarding/encouraging best-practices by separating the wheat from the chaff. CTS pervade such selection and promote the integrity and credibility in awards competitions. In academia, we have blind peer-review as the intended fail-safe mechanism for quality control.

I suggest comparability between the Webby Awards for excellence and traditional print journalism awards such as the Pulitzer Prize or the Emmy Award. For the 2010 Webby Award Nominees are led by the

New York Times with 15 nominations, followed by **BBC** (9), the Harvard Onion (6), and College Humor (6).

WIKIPEDIA cited in endnote #6 generalizes about the most frequent past winners, citing: "Amazon.com; eBay; Kayak.com; Yahoo!; iTunes; Google; FedEx; **BBC News**; **CNN News**; MSNBC News; New York Times; Annie Lennox; **NPR News**; Salon Magazine; Facebook; Meetup; Wikipedia; Flickr; ESPN News; **Comedy Central**; **PBS News**; The Onion News Network; The Office Webisodes; My Damn Channel."

The above honor roll consists of supposed "elitist" sources often criticized by FNC as unjustly privileged; however, I believe that proven excellence is nothing to feel embarrassed about. For more information, go to: http://www.webbyawards.com/webbys/current.php you can review all annual Webby Nominees and Awards from 1997-2010. Trust me, you'll need an electron microscope to find traces of FNC, Newscorp, or Rupert Mordoch's other pseudo-news clones.

2009 Emmy Award Nominees and Winners ("News and Documentary Category"):

As I expected, the FNC enemies' list shines even brighter in the 2009 Emmys for a category officially called "Over-the-Air, Cable, Satellite, and Internet Broadcast Nominees." The Emmys possess a much longer and prestigious pedigree than the more recent Webbies. The Emmy is often described as the television corollary to Academy Award Oscars for feature film or the Grammy Awards for music. All are considered to represent the pinnacle of best-practices.

FNC is MIA for 2009 (0 nominations); Table 5.1 cited below lists all" 2009 News & Documentary Emmy nominees" rank-ordered with two or more plus winners:

Table 5.1: 200984
"Over-the-Air, Cable, Satellite, and Internet Broadcast Nominees"

Network	Nominees:	Winners:
PBS=	36	5
CBS=	31	7
HBO=	20	1
Nat Geog=	19	2
NBC=	17	6
ABC=	9	2
CNN=	6	0
History=	6	2
CNBC=	4	1
Sundance=	2	2
New York Times=	2	1
Planet Green=	2	2
BBC=	2	0
Reuters=	2	0

FNC=MIA

CONCLUSION:

Ignorant about the blogosphere congenial to my grandsons, I was pleased to discover many fine books in 2011. As always, Kindle works wonders for me. I favor using rank-ordering as a process catalyzing CTS by making numerous qualitative judgments about the relative value of competing ideas.

Some writers bug me when they over-use the adjective "great" serially, rendering it meaningless. With English providing so many wonderful options to "great" why drive it into the proverbial ground?

With results for both the Webbies and Emmys ("News & Documentaries"), FNC is once again exposed as intellectual imposter. Finally, Internet Age information overload renders best-practices quality control absolutely vital. Good reasons undergird academia's consensus that our most important goal consists of teaching CTS to undergrads.

lxxv. Not recommended were the 5 following "F" Grades: *Blogging Basics for Beginners: Catch Up On the Blogosphere in the 21ˢᵗ Century* by S.A. Morse (Kindle 2004); *The Best of the Blog* by Dwayne Conyers (Kindle 2006); *Learning to Blog at WordCamp* by Davis Whiteman (Kindle 2005); *Blogging for Beginners: Decisions and Strategies To Consider When Setting Up a Blog* by Manuel Braschi (Kindle 2006); *Blogging for Beginners* by Rick Ricker (Kindle 2008).

lxxvi. WIKTIONARY: *BLOGOSPHERE: http://en.wiktionary.org/wiki/blogosphere;* This Wiktionary site also defines many of the colorfully esoteric jargon of the blogosphere. For example, Afrosphere: Faye Anderon's blog dealing with African-American politics; kulterberikare: Used by far-right bloggers to demean the Swedish welfare state; leftosphere: left-wing blogs taken collectively; rightosphere: right-wing blogs taken collectively; netroots: grassroots political activism on the Internet, especially blog activities; Kossack: derived from Kos, nickname of the progressive blog's founder (Markos Moulitsas); vlog: a weblog, commonly known as a blog, using video as its primary vehicle; wingnutosphere: the community of bloggers perceived to emanate from the political right; blogmaster: one who maintains a blog. The history of civility traditional among academics is noticeably absent in the blogosphere. Wiktionary defines around 100 other colorful examples of jargonista.

lxxvii. Neteracy: "A new set of skills not replacing literacy but increasingly necessary as more and more human activities acquire Web-connected aspects." (p. 37)

lxxviii. See Andrew Keen's own book on this subject: *The Cult of the Amateur: How Today's Internet is Killing Our Culture.*

lxxix. Boxes listed: 1.) Six characteristics of new media; 2.) New media and the 2006 Israeli-Hezbollah War (three takeaways); 3.) Strategic information wins: Hezbollah's attack on the Israeli ship *Hanit;* 4.) DOD and information engagement: Cultural and organizational change; 5.) Operation Valhalla: US Special Forces neutralized for a month by cell phones; 6.) Lessons from Lebanon (speed matters); 7.) U.S. strategic communication win in Iraq (decentralized authority); 8.) Engaging Al-Jazeera and other media; 9.) Encouraging soldiers to speak (LTG Caldwell's four Es); 10.) Third party validators in the Israeli-Hezbollah War (Lebanese bloggers and Internet watchdogs); 11.) Lesson from Lebanon:

Bombing the delivery system doesn't stop the message; 12.) Negative operational consequences of kinetic action against communications nodes; 13.) Lessons from Lebanon: New media and OPSEC in the Israeli-Hezbollah War.

lxxx. GOLDEN WEB AWARDS (GWA) is presented annually by the International Association of Web Masters (IAWMD) for "sites whose web design, originality, and content have achieved levels of excellence deserving recognition." This totally-free service criticizes the more prominent Webby Awards for its costs:

http://www.goldenwebawards.com/

lxxxi. STAND OUT AWARDS: www.standoutawrds.com/

lxxxii. WIKIPEDIA: "Webby Awards:" http://en.wikipedia.org/wiki/Webby_Award; "Webby Award:" http://www.webbyawards.com/webbys/current.php; "Colbert, Galifianakis Top List of 2010 Webby Award Nominees,": http://articles.cnn.com/2010=04-13/tech/webby_awards_1_webby-awards-five-accep...

lxxxiii. "2009 Emmy Award News Nominees and Winners:" http://wwwemmyonline.org/mediacenter/news_31st_winners_data.html

CHAPTER NINE:

"FNC Antidote: Humor on Steroids "

BACKGROUNDER:

Chapter one introduced well-researched core concepts pertinent to this topic. For example: common sense; Critical-Thinking-Skills (CTS); scientific method; suspension of disbelief; alpha male stereotypes; authoritarian personalities; infotainment; journalistic ethics; best/worst practices benchmarking; and blind peer review.

The second chapter assessed contemporary American politics, especially the reality of mean-spirited bifurcation, as well as juxtaposing highly-ranked conservative and liberal Kindle books found under those rubrics. The remainder consists of truth-in-advertising (personal politics), simultaneously describing my ideological proclivities and commitment to scholarship.

Then chapter three undertakes a relatively objective account of Foxymoron's history. While writing this book, vituperative polemics characterized the left-versus-righ incivility. Both progressive and conservative diatribes excoriate the "other" as not merely misguided, but demonic. Political pundits and politicians alike are trampling the spirit of civil society; therefore, I wonder whether a more scholarly effort might prove helpful?

No contemporary examination of politics can avoid the huge impact of technology. The role of the political blogocracy among the Millennial Generation (Mil Gen) had already impressed me among my three grandsons, all possessing "Neteracy" skills making me drool with envy. This constitutes the stuff of chapter four.

Following all of these relatively atomistic chapters, a triple-header revolves around what can only now be called the Bush Dynasty. In chapter five, an extensive scholarly literature digs into the deep historical pockets of the resilient Bush family, especially interfacing the CIA and shady economic practices for centuries.

Chapters six and seven delve into my opinion that Bush I entered office well-prepared while his son did not. That perception ties gets tested in case studies about how each Bush handled his particular Iraq War. My conclusion? Bush I's multilateral planning, careful execution, and reasonably-modest cleanup to the First Iraq War should be seen as exemplary; whereas Bush II's responsibility for the worst American foreign-policy disaster since Vietnam must be considered severely flawed. Case studies invite hyperbole, but I think that the former approaches best-practices benchmarking, while the latter flirts with worst-practices.

INTRODUCTION:

The current chapter consists of three sections. First, the blended concepts of humor, mirth, and laughter are explained and analyzed. This cultural universal has produced impressively comprehensive philosophies and psychologies of humor in academe. Also, an informal history of political satire in America entertains.

Second, John Stewart, Stephen Colbert, and Comedy Central have already inspired several interesting books, not to mention numerous Emmys and other awards indicative of television and internet best-practices. Why does FNC always go AWOL during awards? And, who exactly was it that inspired FNCs comedic debacles? Third, the philosophical transfiguration from classical to modern to contemporary neo-liberalism is dissected as an assertive new identity (the Newest Neo-Liberalism.)

The dilemma facing the three networks and CNN (how to maintain their dignity given FNC's infotainment model) was solved by MSNBC coming to the rescue (the left's assertively not-aggressive answer to FNC). At MSNBC, the newest neo-liberal brand is epitomized by Rachel Maddow, Lawrence O'Donnell, Ed Schultz, Chris Matthews, Dylan Ratigan, Andrea Mitchell, Chris Hayes, Alexis Witt, and Rev. Al Sharpton. On the outside, KOS, Alternet, Bill Maher, Michael Moore, Moveon.org, Dany Schechter, Keith Olbermann, and Al Gore's Current TV channel, have also contributed to non-aggressive assertiveness (a significant distinction.)

HUMOR, MIRTH, LAUGHTER EXPLAINED:

USEFUL ACADEMIC PSYCHOLOGY:

As a cultural universal, humor warrants serious scholarship, including a systematic psychology of humor. Academic author Rod Martin's 2007 book impresses with its comprehensiveness: *The Psychology of Humor: An Integrative Approach.* It consists of an Introduction, Epilogue, eleven meaty chapters, and several neat Appendices.

In the Introduction, we learn what everyone intuitively understands: the visceral nature of humor: when "someone tells a joke, relates an amusing personal anecdote, makes a witty comment or an inadvertent slip of the tongue, we are suddenly struck by its humor. Depending on how funny, responses range from smiles, chuckles, or peals of convulsive laughter.

Our response includes feelings of emotional well-being and mirth." (p. 709)

But while innately familiar, the author cites myriad ways in which studying humor/laughter empirically produces interesting counter-intuitive results. In other words, research reveals many surprises. And, because of its assumed universality, the discipline of psychology is replete with scholarship on humor.

Some of the intriguing questions motivating author Martin include things like what: mental processes contribute to "getting a joke?" Or, what makes us perceive someone or something as funny? Or, what is the nature of the interface between laughter and humor? Or, how does it affect our brains physically? Or, why is humor so pleasurable? Or, how does it develop in children? (All tantalizing musings indeed.)

Similarly, does humor help physical and/or mental health? Despite such undeniable pertinence to the human experience, the author claims that only fairly recently has the professoriate begun giving it the scrutiny it deserves. His book seeks to fill that void, by dividing the psychology of humor into four categories: 1.) Social context; 2.) Cognitive-perceptual processes; 3.) Emotional responses; 4.) Vocal expression of laughter.

Just as the various social sciences differ regarding vital concepts such as power, race, economic productivity, or ethical environmentalism; psychology and anthropologists clash fundamentally regarding the concept of cultural relativism: an article of faith to anthropologists, but incompatible with psychology's belief that it can uncover cultural universals such as humor. Essentially, anthropologists consider psychology's assumption about universals as tainted by self-serving ethnocentrism.

The author also discusses the close relationship between humor and irony/paradox. Spontaneous conversational humor falls into 11 types which he defines and explains:

1.) Anecdotes (personal stories); 2.) Wordplay (witty responses); 3.) Irony (literal and intended meaning vary); 4.) Satire (aggressive social commentary); 5.) Sarcasm (aggressive personal commentary); 6.) Overstatement/ Understatement (exaggeration); 7.) Self-deprecation (targeting oneself); 8.) Teasing (targeting the listener's foibles); 9.) Rhetorical Questions (no response expected); 10.) Clever replies to straight questions; 11.) Double entendre (dual meanings often sexual in nature); 12.) Puns (homophones involving different sounds). (pp. 765-71)

In his first chapter, Martin examines scientific research on humor's universality and evolutionary (biological) origins: laughter is also found in other primates (such as bonobos, chimpanzees, orangutans and gorillas). He concedes that among all primates, humor/laughter performs an integrative function binding social groups together while simultaneously creating the dynamics for "out-group hostility." This chapter is entitled "Introduction to the Psychology of Humor" and includes a brief history of humor, relationship between humor and mirth, humor's social context, jokes, positive emotions of mirth, coping with adversity, and wit versus humor.

Committed to empirical research on humor's universality (disputed by anthropologists), the second chapter is called "Theories and Early Research I: Psychoanalytic and Superiority Theories." Like all other serious 21ˢᵗ century scholars in his field, the author is saddled with recognizing two facts: 1.) Psychoanalysis doggedly dominated the public discourse throughout the 20ᵗʰ century; and 2.) The scientific evidence supporting Freudian Psychoanalysis is virtually non-existent. About all one need do is watch any Woody Allen movie to glean the futility of Freudian verbal masturbation. Like another pioneering 19ᵗʰ century eclectic genius (Karl Marx), Freud cannot be ignored due to his historical impact.

It comes as no surprise, then, that chapter three is called "Theories and Early Research II: Arousal, Incongruity, and Reversal Theories." Less familiar to the casual reader than Psychoanalysis, these three successor theories are defined carefully. And guess what? The empirical evidence here is vastly more exciting, and suggests the need for further research.

Chapter four specializes in dissecting "The Cognitive Psychology of Humor," expressed in more engaging prose than his two previous chapters. Here we learn to discern humor from incongruity and schemas, applications of schema theory to humor, linguistic approaches to humor, semantic priming techniques, effects of humor on cognition, creativity, memory, and computational approaches to humor.

Next we encounter "The Social Psychology of Humor" in the fifth chapter. Here emphasis is placed on social controls, status and hierarchy maintenance, norm violation, ingratiation, discourse management, interpersonal attraction, friendship and mate selection, humor and prejudice, humor and gender, and teasing.

Chapter six, "The Psychology of Humor and Laughter" also includes lots of fascinating insights. For example, the acoustics of laughter, laughter respiration and phonation, facial expressions like smiling, visceral concomitants of youth, laughter among other primates, the play face, pathological laughter, tickling, humor and brain injury, EEG studies, and evolutionary theories of laughter.

Novel topics continue to appear in each chapter. For instance, in chapter seven, "Personality Approaches to the Sense of Humor." Individual humor appreciation, theoretically-based approaches, early factor-analytic studies, Ruch's factor-analytic work, existing humor questionnaires, humor dimensions, sense of humor and intelligence, professional humorists, types of sense of humor, and personality correlates with sense of humor.

Developmental psychology earns a chapter in every textbook, here in the eighth chapter: "The Developmental Psychology of Humor." Look for smiling and laughter in infancy, smiling and laughing in early childhood, humor and aging, McGhee's Four-Step Developmental Model, humor and cognitive mastery, humor as emotional coping, sarcasm, social influences on humor, genetic factors in sense of humor, family environmental factors, and teasing among children.

Chapter nine is called "Humor and Mental Health." Interesting topics include things like humor and emotional well-being, experimental research studies, healthy versus unhealthy humorous behaviors, stressors and coping mechanisms, correlation studies between trait humor and emotional well-being, humor in coping with varied life stressors, and interpersonal aspects of coping humor.

The penultimate chapter (10) proceeds under this moniker: "Humor and Physical Health." Highlights not expressed in previous chapters feature topics like: popular culture myths about humor and health, the relationship between humor and immunity, correlation studies in this area, humor and pain, humor and blood pressure, humor and heart disease, humor and illness symptoms, and humor's contributions to longevity.

Despite the diversity of research questions covered in chapters 1-10, the author saves some intriguing surprises for chapter eleven, entitled "Applications of Humor in Psychotherapy, Education, and the Workplace." Such as, distinctions between psychotherapy and counseling as appropriate to humor, humor-based therapies, humor as the prime therapeutic technique, the skilled therapist's use of humor, empirical research studies in this domain, pedagogical research concerning humor, studies of textbook humor, student learning interfacing humor, and caveats concerning forced humor in textbooks.

However, this fails to deliver a subtext message pervading the book: The discipline of History is officially classified by the National Endowment for the Humanities (NEH) as one of the humanities, along with philosophy, religion, and studies of the arts. As a interdisciplinary practitioner of the social sciences (anthropology, economics, politics, sociology, and psychology) I know how important scientific method is to social scientists.

Humanities like history pose fundamentally different questions, answer them qualitatively rather than quantitatively (i.e., scientifically), and place great faith in experiential insights via rigorous logical analysis. While I consider the author's rudimentary history of the psychology of humor excellent as a first step in the right direction, it lacks the nuanced subtlety a humanities scholar might bring to it.

Martin does argue well that the psychological lexicon regarding humor requires refinement; Why? Because too much ambiguity exists around key concepts; for instance, I particularly like his passage: "Humor is essentially an emotional response elicited by the particular types of cognitive processes discussed above. However, the pleasant emotion associated with humor familiar to us all, represents a unique feeling of well-being that is also germane to such terms as *amusement, mirth, hilarity, cheerfulness, and merriment.* Like joy, it contains exultation plus a feeling of invincibility." (pp. 769-70)

My favorite paragraph on this subject follows: "From the 17th to the 20th centuries, popular conceptions of laughter underwent a remarkable transformation, shifting from the aggressive antipathy of superiority theory to the neutrality of incongruity theory, to the view that laughter could sometimes be sympathetic, eventually to the notion that sympathy is a necessary condition for laughter. These changing views were also reflected in the prevailing social norms. As recently as the 1860s it was considered impolite to laugh in public in the United States." (pp. 792-93) Today, on the contrary, humor and laughter find themselves courted in almost all social settings.

MORE USEFUL ACADEMIC PHILOSOPHY:

I prefer another scholarly book: John Morreall, *Comic Relief: a Comprehensive Philosophy of Humor* (Wiley-Blackwell, 2009), whose dedication to son Jordan says, "Your generation will probably cure cancer and Alzheimer's before these issues get solved." The pithy Foreword is written by veteran

New Yorker cartoon editor, Robert Mankoff. He opens with: "I take cartoons, and the humor they represent, very seriously—or at least semiseriously, because surveys reveal that 98 percent of our readers view the cartoons first, while the other 2 percent are lying." (p. 257) Also, this quote illustrates the fact that key human insights get revealed by literal untruths.

Mankoff quotes author E. B. White: "Analyzing humor is like dissecting a frog; few people are interested and the frog dies from it." (p. 297) Yet, Mankoff notes that a 2011 Google search resulted in an astonishing 25 million hits for "humor analysis." He also lauds humor's recent recognition by academicians as warranting copious research; and, abandoning the dysfunctional "aggression versus depression model" as motivators for humor's place in the human drama. Mankoff marvels that humor's many overt upsides have remained unappreciated for so long. He has many kind words about humanities scholars' disputation of social science colleagues perpetuating negative myths concerning humor's multifaceted quality.

I knew from an interdisciplinary body called FACDIS (winner of two national awards, one regional award, and one statewide award during my involvement) that quality control matters. Ditto for my book catalyzing academic best-practices via syllabus enhancement where a robust literature praises smaller institutions for bucking the trend of specialization at mega-universities. Why? Because class size, phantom scholars, reliance on TA's, and rewarding research over teaching result in a perfect storm for failure on academe's consensus goal for undergrads: teaching CTS. Bigger is often better for graduate education; however, small is inherently superior for undergraduate education.

Back to Mankoff's Foreword calling John Morreall "an inter-disciplinarian nonparallel" for the same reasons I chose philosophy as un undergraduate minor: seeing the holistic picture via rigorous analysis, today known as CTS. "John is a philosopher by training who combines the temperament of a scholar with the timing of a stand-up comedian. This book entertains as it educates us in what we find funny, and why." (p. 291)

As an Assistant Professor looking for a niche, Morreall pondered a statement from Aristotle piquing his curiosity on a conundrum: "Why is it that no one can tickle himself?" He began reading everything on humor and laughter and was struck by a disconnect between their importance, yet producing so little scholarship.

His first book, *Taking Laughter Seriously* (1983) and its sequel, *The Philosophy of Laughter and Humor* (1987), generated sufficient publicity for invitations from medical and business groups for consultancies on humor's benefits. Interested parties included AT&T, IBM, and the IRS, and another practical tome *Humor Works* (1997). Along the way, he began creating courses on humor in Zen and a humanities-based fourth book: *Comedy, Tragedy, and Religion* (1999).

Morreall's current book, praised by John Mankoff's Foreword, opines humor produces a sudden change of mental state, a cognitive shift disturbing under other circumstances (taking it seriously). "However, disengaged from ordinary concerns, we take it playfully and enjoy it. Only humans are linguistically-trained and apes can't do this. Why? We are the most rational animals." Long concerned with all manner of ethics, he wants his colleagues to comprehend "comic disengagement as the key to understanding both harmful humor and beneficial humor." (pp. 305-06) *New Yorker* cartoons dot the landscape of this book.

Early in chapter one, Morreall pens these words: "Of all the things humans do, laughing may be the weirdest. Something happens or someone says something, and our eyebrows and cheeks lift as muscles around our eyes tighten. The corners of our mouths curl upward, baring our upper teeth. Our diaphragms convulse in spasms, expelling air from our lungs making staccato vocalizations. If intense, our entire bodies are overtaken, we bend and hold our stomachs, our eyes tear, and liquids ingested dribble out our noses. We may even wet our pants, since all bodily parts are involved: But none with any purpose." (pp. 340-41).

Equally intriguing is laughter's anomalous nature. Social conventions get routinely broken, including insulting elites. Exaggeration becomes routine and we luxuriate in it. Deception pervades the entire process. From Ancient Rome to Medieval Europe to diverse modern settings, sacred taboos get violated. Scholar Paul Grice emphasizes five social conventions, and the author provides examples aplenty on their transgression in chapter one: 1.) Say only what you believe to be true; 2.) Avoid claims made insufficiently evidenced; 3.) Avoid obscurity; 4.) Avoid ambiguity; 5.) Be brief.

The previous psychology book traced Western Civilization's about-face transfiguring humor from miscreant, to neutral, eventually to contemporary hero. Given the anti-establishment nature of much modern humor, prior to two centuries ago, it was regarded with great suspicion by the wealthy and powerful. The "Superiority Theory of Humor" took a very long time to loosen its grip on social consciousness, which literally considered humor as inherently anti-social, with it's perpetrators considering themselves more intelligent than the low-lifes characters on the receiving end. Equally anathema to social status: undisciplined loss of self-control endemic to laughter.

More eclectically related to my efforts here, an entrant from the "Psych 101 Series" by Mitch Earleywine entitled *Humor 101* (Springer Publishing, 2011) works for me. This psychology professor at SUNY-Albany possesses roughly 100 peer-reviewed articles, as well as three books with Oxford University Press, and has performed stand-up comedy at the Comedy Store, Ice House Comedy Club, and Ha Ha Comedy Club in Los Angeles while teaching at USC.

His seven chapters include: 1.) "Models—Funny in Theory;" 2.) "Laughing Together;" 3.) "Linking Personality to Sense of Humor;" 4.) "Practical

Humor;" 5.) "Humor and Health;" 6.) "Humor and Psychological Well-Being;" 7.) "Bringing Humor to Everyday Life."

Earleywine addresses general questions such as "What makes something funny? Can a joke help sell a product or negotiate a bargain? Could a witty story ease tension on the job? Can comedies prevent the common cold or spread a good mood? Can humor find you a partner for life (or the night)?"

Professional comedians who tutored and prodded were Brett Siddell, Derick Jackson, Rob Smith, Michael Buzzelli, and Henry Senecal. James Kaufman, Series Director of the "Psych 101 Project," encouraged Earlywine's participation. He admits to liking the feeling of assessing the humor literature as trained both in social science and humanities (music to my interdisciplinary ears.)

He introduces the strategy known as "Calling the room," when jokes produce deadening silence. Rather than dozing through undaunted, "experienced comedians such as Johnny Carson change the dynamic by responding with comments like, 'this is really a tough crowd!' or, I guess it's late in the week!" leading the audience to rescue the comedian (subconscious reverse psychology)." (p. 13) Jay Leno has built a schtick around berating his writers in front of his audience. It humanizes the exchange between performer and audience that can become dehumanized if lacking spontaneous interaction. Once after following a very sophisticated act, Mitch mocked his failures; truthfulness can win over ambivalent hearts.

INTERDISCIPLINARY WORK:

Paul McGhee's recent *Humor as Survival Training for a Stressed-Out World: the Seven Humor Habits Program* (Author House, 2010), builds on both his academic as well field experiences aimed at infusing a lighter tone in the American workplace. To wit: "The goal of this book is to improve your sense of humor to the point that it does not abandon you when you are having a bad day! It teaches you how to use your sense of humor to cope with stressors in your life. And it does this by building on some basic humor habits on good days." (p. 324) Specific tips permeate this action-oriented book.

His humor good habits consist of:

1) Reinforce more humor habits in your daily life;
2) The above consists of cultivating a playful attitude in yourself;
3) Laugh more often and more heartily than normal;
4) Practice playing with language creatively via jokes/stories;
5) Search for the lighter side of life's weird events to cope with stressors;
6) Embrace self-effacement (laugh at yourself);
7) Access core skills in creating verbal humor.

McGhee relies on motivational speeches, varied workshops, videotaping and other A-V venues, as well as performance feedback. One of his signature techniques consist of "Personal Humor Logs" for each participant. A variety of workbooks accompany McGhee's consultancies are assessed thoroughly and transparently (including humor pre-and-post tests).

Patty Gellman's gripping personal account also warrants attention: *Humor after the Tumor: One Woman's Look at Her Year with Breast Cancer* (Prometheus Books, 2004). The book resulted from a trail of emails Gellman used to inform friends and family about her journey through what she refers to as "Cancer World." Not enthused to see many people during that difficult time, or to rely on individual phone conversations alone, she exploited the email update instead. I'm never surprised when I hear anecdotally about "writing-as-therapy" reports. But then, breast cancer, is such a challenging diagnosis that my interest piqued about "humor-as-therapy."

She already enjoyed life in a family adept at softening the edges of life's challenges (even breast cancer) with graceful humor. All of the royalties from her book go to searching for the elusive cure. Coincidentally, my mother died from melanoma after receiving expert treatment at the same stellar hospital: Roswell Park Cancer Center in Buffalo, New York. Her account is detailed, candid, self-effacing, and humble, and courageously funny. I recommend both highly.

As denizens of the professoriate, Diana Loomans and Karen Kohlberg's authorship of *The Laughing Classroom: Everyone's Guide to Teaching with Humor and Play* (H.J. Kramer Books, 1993) spoke to me on several levels. The Foreword by Steve Allen (yes, that Steve Allen) didn't hurt anything. Allen states that three teachers stand out in his memory: all humanistic souls capable of personalizing learning via humor.

Allen opines, *"The Laughing Classroom* is a humorist's happy hands-on book because it entertains, educates, and celebrates; making it delightful to read." (p. 459) The ancient bromide that good teaching consists of about one-half art and one-half science contains much wisdom, and Steve Allen amplifies on that solid theme (invoking a head/heart duality metaphor in the process).

The authors' Introduction is lean but meaty and describes how one of them experienced a rare epiphany in 1983 while attending a one-week Disneyland seminar called" The Healing Power of Laughter and Play." She describes that week as "forever enriching both my personal and professional lives." (p. 480) The seminar tapped into a rich experiential base during childhood when she and her siblings "used to induce fits of laughter by contorting the goofiest of faces, singing the silliest songs, and acting out outlandish characters." (p. 489)

In the "Disneyland Seminar," participants are strongly encouraged to engage in laughing fits, artless falls from chairs into aisles, heckle-absorb ent instructors, wearing weird props to sessions, and circulate the room at will. Instructors included legendary jokesters Ike Skelton, Steve Allen, and Joel Goodman. As for the head/heart analogy, participants were also exposed to latest research findings how attitude, humor, and good health correlate seamlessly. She was then "on fire" for several weeks experimenting with this pedagogical goldmine in her own already-creative environment (including best-practices pedagogies such active learning, writing across curricula, and simulations).

She already had absorbed the most important insight about undergraduate education: the lecture method involves no risk to the instructor, places students in a passive state, feeds faculty egos, and constitutes worst-practices pedagogy among the professoriate. Their book seemed like inevitable serendipity, and it has impacted every conceivable subject-matter and level-of-education.

I love the intriguing way their book ends:

Identifying "50 Common Excuses for Not Laughing," for example:

"Tried it once, but it didn't work;" "Our school is too academically-oriented for that;" "Is this another right-brain experiment?"; "I'm not trained for that;" or "Maybe after I receive tenure:" etc.

JEWISH HUMOR:

I like the opening joke to Simcha Weinstein's *Shtick Shift: Jewish Humor in the 21st Century* (Barricade Books, 2008) from film director Paul Mazursky: "The goyim don't know how to laugh because they haven't suffered enough." (p. 3) Coming of age in a blue-collar Manchester, U.K. neighborhood, Simcha was both diminutive and nerdy, resulting in lots of gentile bullies mistreating him. However, in high school everything changed for him: Why? Humor's many paradoxes.

"During high school, however, I made a life-changing discovery. Beneath my nebbish exterior, I possessed a hidden 'superpower' of my own: the power of humor. Suddenly, I became the class clown, cracking up my teachers and classmates alike. Now that the cool kids liked me, the mean ones were less prone to beat me up. And I learned that I was in good company—many famous Jewish comedians had emerged as class clowns as well." (p.21) Unaware of this subculture's existence, Simcha had somehow tapped into it.

After finishing college, Weinstein became more religiously observant and argues that more than most religions, Judaism fosters a paradoxical sense of the absurd. Many Hebrew parables rely on split-second reversals of fortune; for example, the festival of Purim, inspired by the Biblical Esther, celebrates Jews in ancient Persia being saved from genocide. "The inherently serious nature of Purim makes it a great taproot of Jewish humor." (p. 33) Irony works well in Jewish humor (and beyond).

He says that while pogroms have dotted European history, America represented something of a "safe-haven" for Jews. The shadow side of relatively benign treatment of Jews in North America, however, consists of "rampant secularization and assimilation." (p. 42) Both of which matter to him since he has become a U.S. citizen recently. Witnessing serious vandalism in Brooklyn Heights after hostile anti-Semitic Iranian President Mahmoud Ahmadinejad spoke at Columbia University, his point is this: despite many challenges facing American Jewry, counterintuitively, plenty of useful fodder still exists for 21st century Jewish comedians.

Editor Leonard Greenspoon's *Jews and Humor* (Purdue University Press, 2011) similarly both entertains and enlightens. Greenspoon serves as Purdue University's Klutznick Chair in Jewish Civilization, and edited this volume. He notes "I guess I should admit it: I'm pretty good at identifying (and appreciating) good humor when I hear, see, or read it. None of this makes me a particularly funny person or a humorous one (if a real distinction exists between the two). Fortunately, it allows me to benefit, and derive great pleasure from my role as editor of this volume." (p. 355) His Introduction capsulizes each author's unique chapter faithfully.

Charles David Isbell's chapter is entitled: "Humor in the Bible," and focuses on the prophet Elisha's track-record for miraculous deeds (even after his death). "Elisha died and was buried. Then Moabite robber barons entered the same cemetery and came upon Jews performing another burial, leading them to throw the body into Elisha's grave and depart. When the other man's bones touched Elisha's they came back to life standing on his feet." (2Kgs 13:20-21)

Who can remain unimpressed by such power? Yet, what remains unsaid here unlocks the humor for one character in the story (the resurrected one): He has just died without gaining consciousness, comes back to life tightly wrapped in shroud immobilizing him. Proximate to him is a rough band of grave robbers, and he will die again of fright, thus resurrection at best turns into a mixed blessing.

In Eliezer Diamond's piece, "But Is It Funny? Identifying Humor, Satire, and Parody in Rabbinic Literature," she performs similar interpretive tasks. Moses is standing at Mt. Sinai and God says: "You shall not boil a kid in its mother's milk;" to which Moses replies: "So you are saying we should not eat milk and meat together?" God's impatient reply: "I said, you shall not boil a kid in its mother's milk;"

A still puzzled Moses says: "Do you want us to wait six hours after a meat meal before consuming dairy products? Is that what you mean?" God reiterates: I said, "you shall not boil a kid in its mother's milk." Still befuddled, Moses asks: "You want us to use separate tablecloths for meat meals and dairy meals?" With resignation, God says: "You know what, have it your way."

A contemporary example here resonates from Jason Kalman's imagination, called "Heckling the Divine: Woody Allen, the Book of Job, and Jewish Theology after the Holocaust." Here's the dialogue: Woody Allen: "So that leaves Job's wife, my favorite woman in all of literature. Why?" Because when her cringing put-upon husband asked the Lord, why me?

And the Lord told him to shut up and mind his own business, and that he shouldn't even dare ask, Job accepted it. But the missus, already in the earth at that point, had previously scored with a quotable line of unusual dignity and one that Job would have been far too obsequious to have come up with: "Curse God and die" was the way she put it. And I loved her for it because she was too much her own person to be shamelessly abused by some vain and sadistic Holy Spirit. (p. 355)

Rabbi Joseph Kalushkin's *Jewish Humor: What the Best Jewish Jokes Say about the Jews* (Harper Collins, 2010) taps into similar wisdom. His chapter titles ooze creativity: 1.) "Oedipus, Schmedipus, as Long as He Loves His Mother" (Inescapable Hold of the Jewish Family; 2.) "Two Men Came Down a Chimney" (Jewish Playful Intelligence); 3.) "So How Do You Make a Hurricane?" (The Jew in Business); 4.) "The Doctor is Three and the Lawyer Two" (Loathing, Praise, and Other Jewish Neuroses); 5.) "Pardon Me, Do You Have Another Globe?" (Persecution and Jewish Homelessness); 6.) "And I Used to be a Hunchback" (Assimilations Delusions); 7.) "If I Could See Just One Miracle" (Poking Fun at God); 8.) "Better To Be Late in This World Than Late in the Next One" (Why Are Few Funny Israeli Jokes?) 9.) "Why Is This Knight Different From All Others?"

Rabbi Kalushkin uses the Introduction to disabuse readers of simple answers to complex questions, both generally, and, specifically regarding Jewish-ness; any attempts to do so misses the key point about Jewish humor: it's articulate way of frustrating impatient listeners. No fans of reductionism need apply here.

The author begins recounting first-century Rabbi Hillel's response to a potential convert requesting that the Rabbi explain the essence of Judaism while standing on one foot, the Rabbi said "What is hateful unto you, do not do unto your neighbor. The rest is commentary, now go and study." (p. 62) Both metaphorically and polemically, Rabbi Kalushkin intones that "I hope to make apparent that Jewish humor reveals a great many truths about the Jews, but not any one particular truth. Indeed, 150 years of Jewish jokes, two millennia of folkloric witticisms have the uncanny ability to reveal truths missed by academicians." (p. 64)

In addition to deriving from Jewish people, Jewish humor must also express a Jewish *sensibility*. "Merely giving individuals in a joke with Jewish names, or ascribing the joke to Jewish characters, does not a Jewish joke make." (p. 67) Also, Jewish sensibilities coalesce around key issues such as: anti-Semitism; or financial success; or verbal aggression; or assimilation. Known as independent thinkers, Rabbi Kalushkin says that anti-Semitism may constitute the only issue claiming Jewish unanimity.

In societies where Jews have been allowed to compete fairly, the author says, much evidence backs stereotypes about high education, professional success, affluence, and liberal politics. A major contributor to this phenomenon consists of the Jewish mindset valuing them highly. Anxiety also permeates the Jewish mindset, since anti-Semitism often impedes such successes. The author deserves credit for pointing out that using humor to cope with anxieties is not a Jewish monopoly.

The author describes numerous jokes pertaining to America as Jewry's paradoxical, ironic mixed blessing where relative freedom and longevity create a perfect storm for rapid assimilation. A subtext tension always part of their history is their miniscule percentage among world religions, and future minority status in Israel because of proliferation of Arabic populations regionally.

He also muses about Jewry's second holy book (The Talmud) as training for what we call today CTS (logical solutions to seemingly insoluble legal and ethical conundrums). Special attention is devoted to the most popular of its 63 tractates (BAVA MEZIA) opening with this paradox: "Two men enter court clutching a document; each asserts his first dibs to it, with no witnesses. The Talmud devotes considerable space to finding a logical method for assigning ownership of the garment. What other culture devotes such energy to solving such vexing problems? Naturally, offshoots of Talmudic creative logic often find their way into Jewish humor." (p. 116)

While conscious of Jewry's impact on America's performing stage, I was surprised by this quote from the author: "During the last four decades, 80 percent of the country's leading comics have been Jews, indicating broad-based appeal for Jewish humor." (p. 132) He dissects complexities of the American JAP (Jewish-American-Princess) stereotype depicting them as materialistic, nagging, and frigid. He describes a diminution of this kind of JAP stereotype for a variety of reasons, and that "the perplexing issue is whether one can tell ethnic jokes of any kind without dehumanizing the joke's subject." (p. 184)

Considerably less impressive, but still useful, is how I would describe freelance journalist Nichole Force's tripartite tome about humor's contemporary "hidden powers:" Nichole Force, *Humor's Hidden Power: Weapon, Shield, and Psychological Salve* (Braeden Press, 2011).

Her 16 chapters: 1.) "Humor as Weapon, Shield & Psychological Salve;" 2.) "Humor's Physiological and Psychological Effects;" 3.) "The Subversive Power of Humor;" 4.) "Gender Differences;" 5.) "The Way of the Comedian;" 6.) "Neuroplasticity;" 7.) "Depression;" 8.) "Anxiety and Fear;" 9.) "Rejection and Divorce;" 10.) "Stress;" 11.) "Illness;" 12.) "Financial Loss;" 13.) "Self-Esteem;" 14.) "Anger;" 15.) "Aging;" 16.) "Death."

Force cites books claiming health benefits of humor, but says hers updates latest scientific discoveries, includes historical case studies of movers and shakers, and wades through the literature on behalf of lay readers. Chapters 1-6 review the research relating to humor's therapeutic powers. While 7-16 recommend specific therapeutic regimes to attack what she calls mental hygiene's ten challenges: anxiety, depression, heartbreak, work-related stress, illness, financial loss, low self-esteem, anger, death/

dying. Counter-intuitively, while nothing is funny about these problems, humor has an ameliorating track-record to run on.

COMEDIC BEST-PRACTICES: JOHN STEWART, STEPHEN COLBERT, AND COMEDY CENTRAL:

Quality control via best-practices bench-marking exists in almost every profession. Take films, for example: I watch few of Hollywood's dollar-driven formulaic clones. My exception? Oscar nominees and winners. Why? Professional critics contextualize many thousands of movies viewed to separate the great from the mediocre. Words exist for good reasons, so note the comity here between the word for guardians of quality control (film critics) and academia's consensus goal for undergraduate education (CTS).

I watch mostly independent films (indies) on the Sundance Channel, Independent Film Channel, and LOGO because of their unpredictability compared to Hollywood formulaity. Indies also celebrate their own annual "Oscars" called "Independent Film Awards," some of which also win Oscars. Methinks predictability among humans possesses a relatively short half-life.

Humans like the division-of-labor because we want trained experts to wade through the prosaic popular culture so that we don't have to. This cultural universal pervades our consciousness. Many websites have arisen challenging both the veracity and ethics of FNC; my favorite is called: "We Watch Fox News So That You Don't Have To!"

Similarly with music, where I rely on experts via the Grammys, in television its Emmys, and with college football: pollsters (since that sport lacks the equivalent of hoops' March Madness, which funds the majority of college of sports by itself.)

In academe, we rely on blind peer review of scholarship, as well dueling experts to assess the relative value of our intellectual labor. Why? To apply CTS as our *Modus Operandi* for quality control. Assessing our faculty consists of combining three criteria: teaching/learning; research; service. Theoretically, in that order of emphasis; however, since teaching is inherently subjective, the more verifiable realm of research usually trumps everything else in the reward structure.

Many academic awards include all three variables (teaching; research; service). For example, the West Virginia Political Science Association (WVPSA) does so and chose me as its 2003 recipient. In 2008, I finished as runner-up for Statewide Professor of the Year among 4,600 tenured faculty members. I wrote FACDIS' two national-awards: Theodore S. Hesburgh Award for International Education (1989) from TIAA-CREF; then, in 1995, the G. Theodore Mitau Award for Innovative Education from AASCU (1995). In 2003, I received my institution's first and only Meritorious Professorship (teaching, research, service.)

When it comes to political satire, American liberals have always run circles around literal-minded conservatives (easily verifiable via awards.) Yet my motivation for choosing humor as this chapter's motif arose from completely different circumstances: my personal nadir in American politics; namely, the astonishing re-election of Bush II in 2004 despite a mendacity-laden, disastrous first-term. Jon Stewart, Stephen Colbert, and Comedy Central all aided and abetted my keeping my sanity from 2005-08.

Editor Jason Holt pervades a recent book from the "Blackwell Philosophy of Popular Culture Series" entitled, *The Daily Show and Philosophy* (Blackwell, 2007). The Introduction boldly asks the question: "Great Book or the Greatest Book?" Editor Holt writes: "You already know *The Daily Show* with Jon Stewart is funny, really funny, and that the performers and writers are pretty smart. You also realize it doesn't qualify as run-of-the-mill TV comedy. In its decade-plus run *The Daily Show* has achieved an undeniable, potentially disturbing, cultural significance, as fit for ranting blogs as for academic treatises." (p.34)

Editor Holt waxes us via pretty prose morphing through the subtext themes of each contributors' chapters (here labeled appropriately "Senior Philosophical Correspondents") one-by-one. Since *The Daily Show* inherently touches upon all of the following contemporary issues: "news media, politics, religion, science, truth and a host of other topics." (p. 37) According to the editor, it performs all the essential functions of contemporary Critical Thinking.

Holt delivers under five headers: 1.) How fake news fiction, such as *The Daily Show,* contribute meaningful insights (truths via fiction); 2.) Jon Stewart is cast here as a quasi-philosopher drawing parallels with the classical Greek philosophers Plato, Aristotle, and others tapping into sagacious "bath-tub living and joke-making cynics;" 3.) Emphasis on the relationship between CTS and relentless bullshit-testing by Stewart; 4.) The show's philosophy of religion via segments such as "This week in God," or "Evolution, Schmevolution." 5.) Contiguous topics beyond the show itself, such as Stewart's book *America*, and spinoffs like Stephen Colbert's truth-laden neologisms.

The first chapter by "Senior Correspondent" Gerald Erion strikes me as particularly erudite for explicating the importance of NYU Emeritus Professor Neil Postman's book *Amusing Ourselves to Death,* who in turn pays tribute to progenitors Britain Alodus Huxley and Canadian Marshall McLuhan (the medium is the message).

Erion writes "I like our editor's reference to Postman's concept of the deleterious nature of 'smoke signals' in public discourse: While the medium of smoke may communicate relatively simple messages over intermediate distances, many other types of messages can't be transmitted this way. Philosophical arguments, for instance, would be especially difficult to convey with smoke signals since "Puffs of smoke remain insufficiently complex to express ideas on the nature of existence." (p. 153) Postman graduated with my father from SUNY-Fredonia in 1948, and I followed his fine career. All authors mentioned above help aid comprehending the vagaries of television's profitable "infotainment" genre.

Elaborating further, the author opines "On television, thoughtful conversations are reserved for only the lowest-rated, least profitable niche markets," and, "Just as ventriloquists and mimes play poorly on radio, so does thinking on television," plus "TV loves the sort of gut-based discourse celebrated by Stephen Colbert's character," as "amusing ourselves to death." (pp. 161-62)

I saw a CSPAN piece interviewing a group of *The Daily Show* writers, and my impression was similar to author Gerard Erion's: "Now, as far as I know, the writing staff of *The Daily Show* doesn't acknowledge Postman's influence. It's even possible they've never heard of him. Nonetheless, it's clear that these general ideas about television news, whatever their sources, can aid in understanding the significance of its wittiest and most inspirational jokes." (p. 177) Bill O'Reilly disagrees, having dubbed Stewart's devotees as "stoned slackers who get their news from Jon Stewart." (p. 180)

It's clear that Stewart wants ALL of the lazy journalists to wake up, elevate the discussion, and stop insulting public's intelligence. The author also highlights areas in which Postman and Stewart operate via wholly different prisms: e.g., Postman considered attempts to bolster the integrity of television news hopeless the moment it adopted the boob tube; Stewart, however, clearly believes that TV can be cajoled into doing better. In that sense, Postman comes off as a pessimist, Stewart an optimist. As a retired professor, however, I see another dynamic at work here: Professors' gloomy or rosy opinions produce few direct consequences, leaving us more detached. Political activists' raison d'etre presupposes greater impatience.

Pertinent factual background about Jon Stewart comes from George Andersen's *Jon Stewart: a WikiFocus Book* (Wiki, 2010), whose cover photo comes from The "Rally to Restore Sanity And/Or Fear," 30 October 2010. Born Jonathan Stuart Leibowitz on 18 November 1962 in New York City; this writer, TV host, author, political satirist, and stand-up comedian has won so many professional accolades (including an unbelievable 14 Emmys) that one has to wonder what kind of kool-aid was being consumed by his competitors. (pp. 6-11)

While best known for hosting *The Daily Show* (ironically convening only four times weekly), on Comedy Central, his career really began as a stand-up comedian in clubs and then moved to MTV, including one called "You Wrote it, You Watch it;" and another called "The Jon Stewart Show," before Comedy Central's mega-hit *The Daily Show*, including huge spin-offs like Stephen Colbert ensued. Envious critics suggest Stewart benefits from a gross double-standard: he ridicules "real news" with his "fake news" from his safe Olympian perch. (pp. 24-28).

He and his brother (Larry Leibowitz) were raised in a supportive Jewish family in NYC; little bro now inhabits the position of New York Stock Exchange Operating Officer. His parents were both educators (father Donald a professor of physics) and (mother Marian a teacher and consultant). The couple divorced when Jon was 11 years old. Part of his youth included mean-spirited bullying by anti-Semites and his political inclinations were decidedly leftist.

After graduating from William and Mary with a psychology degree (while playing varsity soccer) his jobs were many and varied, but he maintained personal contact with W & M classmate Congressman Anthony Wiener before the latter became infamous. His stand-up comedy act debuted at the same place as his youthful idol, Woody Allen, "The Bitter End." When David Letterman retired, Stewart was a finalist, but the coveted slot went to Conan O'Brien.

His first show on MTV proved an instant hit and finished second on that year's MTV rating to a slouch known as "Beavis and Butthead;" then, when Paramount yanked the plug on "The Arsenio Hall Show"

and Viacom acquired that studio, it launched a full-hour syndicated late-night "Jon Stewart Show. "David Letterman was always impressed enough with Stewart to continue assisting in various ways. (pp. 120-132).

Blending right into best-practices bench-making, let us turn to *Is He America (And Should You Care)*, a biography of Stephen Colbert by Jim

Nikel (Minute Help Press, 2011). The Introduction performs well, "A Satirical Conservative Pundit Taken to Absurd Extremes," intended to skewer the inherently ridiculous American partisan politics. A superficial take on The Colbert Report might think it's only intended to insult conservatives, but Nikel's subtext analysis reveals a pox on both of your self-righteous houses. Author Nikel describes satirical humor as the only logical response to the prevalence of the pseudo-news infotainment genre targeting the lowest common denominator (I concur)

Nikel contends that Stephen Colbert's TV persona is "Overly enthusiastic about what he does, who he is, and especially what he stands for. His character is loud, ambitious, and downright preachy. . . He's unlike any conservative pundit you've ever met; in fact, he's all of them combined and then some." (p. 47) Accordingly, Colbert parodies all superficial journalistic imposters, not just the low-lying FNC fruit. Of course, Colbert's huge hit grew as a sidebar to Jon Stewart's *The Daily Show* and still appears immediately after on Comedy Central. Nikel sees Stewart as an intellectual attack on the right's fallacies, while Colbert's is more subtly emotional rather than rational. What do you think?

Most observers believe they understand Jon Stewart's progressive politics, because his show involves him being himself; however, we're not sure about the extent to which Colbert really believes his bullshit, or is sufficiently co-opted by the permanent war establishment to act as its unpaid lobbyist. Therefore, author Nikel asks: "who is this guy, and what makes him tick?" (p.50) Again what do you think?

Author Nikel traces carefully "Colbert's surprisingly rich personal history tempered by the tragic premature loss of both his father and brother," Colbert's early years as a precarious improvisational comedy artist, and an undying love for the various performing arts. In several ways, Colbert's was the prototypical Catholic family (e.g., eight siblings), he the last.

"Outside the Colbert Report show, he is known for his wild politi-cal stunts. In 2008, he ran for President from his home state of South Carolina. Two years later, he participated in a Congressional hearing on migrant labor. Many observers wonder if Colbert is just doing this to further his comedic brand or should be applauded for taking a stand on controversial issues. For a 'fake' newsperson, he sure is involved in the American political process to an astonishing degree." (p. 61) However, the same observation also works in spades for Jon Stewart.

Back to my Kindle, *The Stewart/Colbert Effect: Essays on the Real Impact of Fake News,* Amaranth Amarasingam, ed. (McFarland, 2011). This recent scholarly tome includes an Introduction by Josh Compton summariz-ing current literature on Jon Stewart and Stephen Colbert's monster hits. Compton suggests that satirical political humor has reached an unprec-edented peak in America, ditto for scholarly research on the same, includ-ing both networks and cable, viral online video clips, books, and even bumper stickers.

The author claims that "Analyses reveal that such programs influence viewers' evaluations of political candidates, viewers' perceptions of vari-ous institutions, their interest in campaigns, and their support for par-ticular policies." (p. 124) Similar specific empirical studies suggest that many people learn about politics via soft (fake) news. However, some other studies cast doubt about such hypotheses regarding real-world impact of Jon Stewart and Stephen Colbert's massively successful infotainment.

As if this project didn't have enough moving parts, a substantial 8-page Foreword comes from media expert Robert McChesney; University of Illinois Communications Professor, author of many books and articles, and co-founder of the media reform organization called "Free Press," and host of a weekly television show called "Media Matters."

McChesney updates comments made by Ralph Nader during his 2000 presidential campaign about an extended trip that Nader made to the now-defunct Soviet Union in 1962, his first chance to assess Soviet Communism up close. His main conclusion: in the USSR, there existed the best underground satirical humor he has ever witnessed; and, it was so strikingly well-received because official state journalism had been discredited by intellectuals as atrocious propaganda.

McChesney's paraphrasing Ralph Nader's Soviet observation grabbed me as erudite: "I have long thought Nader's Soviet assessment applied to understanding and situating the 'fake news' phenomenon of Jon Stewart and Stephen Colbert. While their humor clearly ranks as brilliant (to be sure) it remains based on how atrocious official journalism has become today, when mainstream media regurgitate whatever nonsense those in power utter." (p. 129)

Part I entails five chapters evaluating the state of recent literature exploring the social significance of TDS and TCR: 1.) "The Science of Satire;" 2.) "Making Sense of the Daily Show; "3.) "Stoned Slackers or Super Citizens?" 4.) "Is Fake News the Real News?" 5.) "Jon Stewart a Heretic?"

Part II consists of five more essays creating a theoretical models to contextualize these hit shows: 6.) "Irony and the News: Speaking Through Cool to America's Youth;" 7.) "Wise Fools: Stewart and Colbert as Modern-Day Court Jesters in America's Court;" 8.) "I am the Mainstream Media (And So Are You!) 9.) "It's All About Meme;" 10.) "Real Ethical Concerns and Fake News."

One of the authors refers to a famously disputatious exchange between CNBC's financial guru Jim Cramer and Jon Stewart, about which Fox-friendly conservative comedian Dennis Miller said to Bill O'Reilly on the latter's show, "Jon's a Mensch who doesn't like disingenuous people and I knew Cramer was headed for evisceration. Plus, Cramer hates the idea that someone as quintessentially cool as Jon Stewart calls Cramer a putz." (p. 13)

For a purveyor of fake news, Jon Stewart has lots of people taking him very seriously. For instance, a 2007 survey by the reputable Pew Research Center discovered that respondents ranked Stewart as fifth "most admired journalist, after Brian Williams, Tom Brokaw, Dan Rather, and Anderson Cooper." (p. 4)

THE NEWEST NEO-LIBERALISM: PROGRESSIVES REGAIN ASSERTIVENESS:

One American political paradigm, "the Pendulum Theory," posits that Americans slowly tire of each Duopolost, when its base rebels against the party's abandoning its principles. Obscene piles of money, of course, explain neither the Reds nor the Blues holding each other even slightly accountable; Bush II's Wars of Convenience warranted impeachment, but that's only for serious matters (i.e., Oval Office BJs); each side turns both rectal cheeks until its turn. New Super-PACs and the Supreme Court's "Citizens United" case exacerbate things even more.

Author Matt Taibbi was my first exposure to "America as duopolist."

European parliamentary systems can, at least, count beyond two, and much more representational pastiches result. Taibbi asserts that only dictatorial monopolies exceed our duopoly in boredom. Some scholars provide impressive data that democratization has taking over the world. If so, let's hope they choose parliamentary over presidential models. The Tea Party is the latest challenger to the duopoly, but they will also disappear. Why? Our rigid duopoly provides huge historical, structural, legal, and economic advantages to Republicans and Democrats.

Since neither party can win the presidency without the crucial one-third slice of moderate independents, both enrage their ideological base ad infinitum. Many Americans, including me, would love to see the kind of core-value consensus found in most of Europe. However, such wishful thinking borders on delusional when we factor in numerous empirical studies describing two incompatible visions of America: bifurcation.

When I operated among the professoriate, participating in a "civil society" of reasonable people advancing mutually exclusive policy preferences civilly inhered in the job description. Retirement, however, is different; more freedom to express opinions without working for a public institution.

It also strikes me that, in our center-right country, we liberals must evolve ethical imperatives to challenge the establishment, what I call here the newest, neo-liberalism. In a sense, conservatives make this process relatively easy by saying so many false things easily refuted via scholarship. We almost always have ethics, the facts, and CTS on our side. I see a new assertiveness emerging via spokespersons like Andrew Bacevich, Danny Schechter, Michael Moore, Al Gore, the Alternet website, KOS website, liberal blogocracy, and MSNBC having the cajones to take on FNC so adeptly. Damn ratings as anything meaningful!

And the ethical stylistic advantage we posses is countering Right-Wing aggressive rhetoric with non-violent assertiveness, as demonstrated elegantly throughout history by the likes of Mahatma Gandhi, Martin Luther King, and *Time's* 2001 Person of the Year (non-violent protesters from Cairo to Wall Street). And, no one had better predicted the karmic Blowback from American Empire and perma-war than Ex-CIA analyst, military adviser, and current academic Chalmers Johnson.

One of the most recent disturbing books is by Alison Dagnes, *Politics on Demand: The Effects of 24-Hour News on American Politics* (Praeger, 2011), a Shippensburg University Professor of Political Science, her Introduction is labeled "How the Media Are Failing American Government," begins with this trenchant quote from Joseph Levine: "You can fool all of the people all of the time if the advertising is right and its budget big enough." (p. 21)

She decries the diminution of professional journalism's ethical standards and the rise of web-based amateurs accountable only to themselves. While the amazing "Arab Spring" and "Occupy Wall Street" movements of 2011 impress for their tech-savvy grass roots micro-politics, stealing the ethical high-ground from sclerotic bureaucracies, Professor Dagnes is here to describe a considerable political downside accompanying these ebullient events.

What accounts for journalism's amateurization? 1.) Technological wizardry expanding political communication; 2.) Overkill of media outlets via cable TV, radio, and Internet; 3.) Proliferation of opinion shows rather than traditional journalism due to big time slots that require programs; 4.) Both politicians and journalists scrambling to fit r messages into infotainment sound bites; 5.) Corporate merger mania narrowing the cast of characters. (p. 52-54)

I experienced publishing merger mania: I went with Prentice-Hall in 1996 for my textbook because they were number one in sales with more and better-trained field agents. My first edition did pretty well, my second edition very well, and my third edition flamed out. Why? Because in the interim P-H was sold thrice, with the current British owner providing no useful services. So my globalization textbook was scuttled by the very processes it was intended to illustrate.

Back to author Dagnes, confirmed facts become endangered species in this overwhelming new political milieu. She states: "I don't suggest that we return to the age of horses and buggies, but rather that all these new media options make us more insular and misanthropic. So many selections make the media fragmented, polarized, and angry. This incentivizes specialized niche programming inconsistent with civil society." (p. 63)

Finally, the gold standard of best-practices television news against which contemporary journalism must inevitably be compared is written by one of the pioneers of CBS television news. Even today CBS' *60 Minutes* investigative journalism continues raking in Emmy after Emmy. The soft-spoken author present at the creation, Sig Mikelsen, wrote *Decade That Shaped Television News: CBS in the 1950s* (Praeger, 1998), explains why CBS in the 1950s represented journalistic best-practices.

Mikelsen tells this story elegantly in 20 diverse chapters: 1.) "Search for a Road Map;" 2.) "First Awkward Steps;" 3.) "New Star on the Horizon;" 4.) "Driving Television's Golden Spike;" 5.) "New Species of Documentary;" 6.) "Breaking New Ground;" 7.) "Blacklisting Exploits Fear;" 8.) "Not so Strange Bedfellows: Politics/TV;" 9.) "Television News Comes of Age;" 10.) "The Great Airplane Race;" 11.) "Corporate Cease Fire;" 12.) "Aftermath of Cease Fire;" 13.) "Spare the Rod, But Don't Spoil the Picture;" 14.) "Corporate Combat;" 15.) "Changing of the Guard;" 16.) "Filling the See-It-Now Void;" 17.) "The Happiest Couple: Pigskin and the Tube;" 18.) "Carrying the Olympic Torch to TV;" 19.) "Pursuing Dollars;" 20.) "Decade's End."

Mikelsen's history of CBS runs from 1946 until 1960, describing the prototypical success story for television news engineered with creativity, accountability, transparency, and hard work. TV production was on hold until World War II ended, and few industries better symbolize an affluent public's appetite to enjoy life than TV. CBS staff rose from six employees in 1946 to more than 400 in 1960. Other networks such as NBC had rudimentary plans for news but lagged behind.

The fall of 1948 witnessed both CBS and NBC launching the first five-night network news broadcasts. In that year only when only 400,000 television sets existed nationally, concentrated in the Northeast. That year also involved initial television coverage of the Republican and Democratic national conventions. However, by January 1950 that number of boxes swelled to three million and then to 46 million by 1960. He writes that "By 1960 the news-consuming public was apparently well-pleased with what it saw, and the start-up phase had concluded." (p. 36)

Furthermore, "Television was a key player in converting news from a mostly-local commodity to a national service. No national newspaper had yet emerged, although UPI and AP wire services had nationalized and internationalized. However, the chief source of news and information for most Americans was the local newspaper." (p. 41)

Heretofore, sports viewership consisted mostly of baseball; however, the national pastime changed to football very quickly. Viewership for the two sports most adult then played (golf and tennis) also benefited immensely. Ditto for the Olympic Games, totally opaque to American consciousness in between each of its quadrennial resurrections. The author marvels at the rapidity which the tube revolutionized all facets of American existence.

Mikelsen's signature-event for symbolizing the paradigm shift? The first nationally-televised presidential debates so beneficial to the young, photogenic John Kennedy, and sublimely deleterious to the twitchy, unshaven Richard Nixon. He touts the relevance bona fides of his book when published in 1999, and I second his description of best-practices broadcasting even more pertinent to America today: "It may also furnish tools for better understanding the communications revolution now underway." (p. 83)

Reinforcing the themes expressed by Mikelsen is Roger Mudd's *The Place to Be: Washington, CBS, and the Glory Days of Television News* (Public Affairs Press, 2008). This venerable journalist's ambitious Prologue runs to 13 pages including a serious history of journalism.

Here he speaks to the bitter-sweet rapid democratization of cyber journalists today while others had morphed far more slowly in the past. "Today (with the help of the technological revolution) almost anybody is taking a turn at journalism. There are web reporters like Matt Drudge, revolving-door journalists like Tim Russert, and talking-head journalists like John McLaughlin, plus bloggers of all stripes." (p. 74)

Similarly, concerning the best-practices thesis, "Technology improved throughout the 1950s, but not until 1963's expansion of the *CBS Evening News with Walter Cronkite* to 30 minutes, did the Golden Age of Television News really begin. For the next 20 years, CBS news set a standard for thoroughness, balance, credibility, commitment, and journalistic skill that has not been equaled. (p. 124)

Mudd recounts front-page headlines nationwide when CBS' revered anchor, Walter Cronkite, retired and was replaced by another veteran-journalist (Dan Rather.) After Mudd's 19-year career at CBS he was disappointed when he didn't receive the prized promotion at CBS. Instead, took the top spot at NBC, a fast-rising but still weaker network. Serendipitously, this disappointment turned out well for Mudd, whose tenure at NBC resulted in improved ratings, as well as some bad things occurring at CBS: encroaching infotainment, indiscriminate firings, draconian budget cuts, and "a greedy take-over maneuver by Larry Tisch." (p. `132)

But his book mostly dwells on CBS's Golden Age, where Mudd bore witness to events like the dawn-to-dusk coverage of the Great March on Washington in 1963; stellar treatment of all matters related to the assassination of JFK; Senate's civil rights filibuster in 1964; coverage of the Vietnam War; Watergate Scandal; and, the unelected president's (Gerald Ford) rise.

LIBERALISM: FROM CLASSICAL TO TRADITIONAL WESTERN:

Let's examine the literature concerning traditional definitions of American liberal philosophy, starting with Colgate University Philosophy Professor David McCabe's *Modus Vivendi Liberalism: Theory and Practice* (Cambridge University Press, 2010), in which he assesses what he calls "the Liberal Project."

I understand it as pursuing two distinct goals: 1.) It's pragmatic political methods; and, 2.) The inherent nature of the substantive argument." (p. 90) His purview includes nation-states considering themselves as liberal, and quotes Isaiah Berlin: "Liberal states create conditions in which as many individuals as possible can realize as many of their ends as possible." (p. 93)

McCabe also emphasizes John Stuart Mill's "harm principle" that personal freedom should extend to the point where it begins to harm equal rights of others. In addition to Mill's prohibition against "state paternalism," or state-sponsored interference with those freedoms. Both, he notes, represent "ideal types," to which states can be expected to fail often. Likewise, "The main idea here is that liberal theorists are committed to an account of political legitimacy which states that the fundamental principles structuring the political realm can be rationally conveyed to its citizen subjects." (p. 96)

I also like this key paragraph: "I believe that liberals have not adequately engaged with the conservative critics' concerns. Factor in here the author's endorsing contemporary scholar Michael Ignatieff's praise for Isaiah Berlin as the only thinker of consequence taking the trouble to enter the mental world of liberalism's sworn enemies." (p. 169) Michael Ignatieff represents a model all too rare as a (generalist), Renaissance Man among liberal intellectuals: this Canadian-native has impressed me with the diversity of his liberal roles as journalist, filmmaker, Harvard academic, and political activist.

McCabe's book considers the specific intellectual objections from liberalism's numerous critics, taking them seriously, by reading their writings carefully. As an eclectic humanities Philosopher, he outshines my narrower social science colleagues. What I attempted in my chapter four applying CTS to fallacy-laden look at Bill O'Reilly's recent retrospective *A Bold Fresh Piece of Humanity*. Unpleasant, but vital to my getting behind his eyeballs.

Having established credentials for taking conservative critics seriously, the end of McCabe's book develops what he calls an alternative way of defending liberalism, abandoning the impossibly high bar established by Isaiah Berlin and John Stuart Mill, advocating what he calls *modus Vivendi liberalism* (from the Latin mode of living). This realpolitik in a world far from ideal, thoughts from early philosophers helps in a bifurcated America: "A mode of living among citizens who remain deeply divided on the basic norms governing political life." (p. 208)

Alan Wolfe's impassioned plea for liberalism is called *The Future of Liberalism* (Alfred Knopf, 2009), with nine chapters: 1.) "The Most Appropriate Political Philosophy for Our Times;" 2.) "In Praise of Artifice;" 3.) "Equality's Inevitability;" 4.) "Why Good Poetry Makes Bad Politics;" 5.) "Mr. Schmitt Goes to Washington;" 6.) "How Liberals Should Think About Religion;" 7.) "Open Society's Friends;" 8.) "Why Conservatives Can't Govern;" 9.) "Liberalism's Promise."

British philosopher John Locke's insistence 300 years ago that "governments operate by consent of the governed," is singled out by Wolfe as the single most potent component of liberalism, and the significance of his declaration that "All the world is America," meaning that the center of gravity of human consciousness had crossed the Atlantic.

This American author also writes "Liberalism is a way of thinking and acting so easily taken for granted that one can easily forget how it struggled to exist, solved many of the problems it was asked to address, spread its influence globally, not through coercion, but owing to its universal appeal, and remains far more attractive than its alternatives." (p. 49) Respecting individualism, equality, and a passion for justice are touted here by Wolfe. He also bemoans that today appreciation for liberalism's hard-won battles may sit at its nadir in American history.

Wolfe also praises political scientist Louis Hartz's exemplary book *The Liberal Tradition in America* (Praeger, 1955) as holding up well to contemporary scrutiny, despite its insufficient treatment of racial politics in the U.S. Broader Lockean "self-evident truths" were also woven into the Declaration of Independence by Thomas Jefferson.

American presidential campaigns involve roughly 100 issues, and many books arguing what liberals should think about multiculturalism, religion, equality, free speech, affirmative action, and scores of others. Some writers implore liberals to abandon defensiveness around the idea that "the L-word implies unelectable," and take on conservatives more assertively, dispelling the myth that liberals are like Canadians (too nice for their own good). (p. 117) Sometimes these discussions involve the relative merits of our two main labels (liberals versus progressives). Should conservatives be allowed to monopolize verbal assertiveness? No.

ASSERTIVE LIBERALISM:

Author Wolfe advocates three traditions to create a more full-throated Liberalism: 1.) Substance: "Maximize extent to which persons control their destinies;" 2.) Procedure: "Inclusive participation;" 3.) Temperament: "Assertiveness." (p. 197) Separating liberals from civil libertarians, I like Wolfe's observation that modern liberalism promises a positive conception of liberty: leaving citizens alone is not good enough, because liberals want positive results from government.

Michael Walzer also has a track record for defending liberalism's noble causes. His recent work is *Politics and Passion: toward a More Egalitarian Liberalism* (Sage Publications, 20004). Walzer's Introduction is called "Liberalism and Inequality;" Six chapters include: 1.) "Involuntary Association;" 2.) "The Collectivism of Powerlessness;" 3.) "Cultural Rights;" 4.) "Civil Society and State;" 5.) "Deliberation and What Else?" 6.) "Politics and Passion;" Epilogue: "Global Equality."

The first paragraph from Walzer speaks to the perception I mentioned earlier: America is often described as a center-right nation: "Although the

L word (liberalism) was for a time pure poison in American politics, it has long represented the universal antidote of American political theory. Liberal democracy is the rule of the many without its dangers (minorities protected and human rights guaranteed). Liberal religion is a faith free of dogma, and a church notable for acknowledging the legitimacy of other churches." (p. 17)

To be improved in the future, he argues liberalism should incorporate several aspects of civil society that he labels the *communitarian correction* (a more passionate transcendence that stops relying so much on intellect and taps into humanity's equally important emotional side to further civil society). (p. 46) Grass roots civil society associations, empowered by new technologies are revolutionizing the essence of politics worldwide, as in the "Arab Spring" and "occupy" movements domestically.

Pulitzer prize-winner Chris Hedges' *Death of the Liberal Class* (Noonan Books, 2008) contains six chapters: 1.) "Resistance;" 2.) "Permanent War;" 3.) "Dismantling the Liberal Class;" 4.) "Politics as Spectacle;" 5.) "Liberal Defectors;" 6.) "Rebellion."

American journalist Hedges is comfortable using present-day case studies to amplify broader themes. One involves Ernest Logan Bell, 25-year old unemployed Marine Corps veteran conducting a six-day, 90-mile "Liberty Walk" in rural upstate New York, hoping to run for the local Congressional seat. Bell camped out for three nights and stayed in cheapie hotels the other nights. Like so many of his contemporaries, this veteran fears being trapped in serial unemployment.

Ex-Leatherneck Bell's heroes consist of: 1.) Ohio Rep. Dennis Kucinich for consistent opposition to America's lust for war; and 2.) Texas Congressman Ron Paul for a similar civil libertarian mantra ignored in Washington until. Author Hedges sees Bell as the "New face of resistance wary of what he has witnessed about not only the Federal Government, but the educated liberati as well, carrying deep pockets of anger around with him." (p. 57) Bell genuinely fears a total systemic nervous break-down prophesied for decades by Militia groups, now greased by totally unfounded Mayan-generated myths.

Long interviews with Bell provide Chris Hedges with lots of soft data to make his case that what he calls "the liberal class" (i.e., intelligent-sia, literati, dissident academics, defenders of human rights, naïve opti-mists about the future) has become an endangered species in America. Actually, I think the clarity of Hedges' hypothesis could have benefited from adopting any of these other labels, since the word "liberal" bears too much emotive baggage.

Posed more subtly, I would respond more favorably to legitimate obser-vations about post-Affluenza America. For instance, the author contends that "These harsh emotions spring from the failure of the liberal class over three decades to protect the minimal interests of the working mid-dle class as corporations dismantled the democratic state, decimated the manufacturing sector, looted the U.S. Treasury, waged unwinnable Imperial Wars, and gutted civil liberties." (p. 125) Hedges gets too fix-ated on the Fallacy of Single Cause. Young people like Bell to their anger, but singling out the intelligentsia ecreates no value-added for the politi-cal discourse.

Hedges relies on well-known philosopher John Gray's stipulation of four hallmarks of classical liberalism: 1.) Individualist rather than collectivist; 2.) Egalitarian rather than hierarchical; 3.) Universalist throughout our species; and 4.) Meliorist human progress via critical reasoning. (p. 134)

More importantly, "By the time Cold War liberalism shifted to embrace globalization, imperial expansion, and unfettered capitalism, the ideals characterizing classical liberalism no longer applied. And finally, some-thing few contemporary American liberals would quarrel with: Cold War liberalism, cornered and weak, engaged in the politically safe game of attacking Communism's barbarism (and later Islamic militancy) rather than fighting the mounting injustices and structural abuses of the corporate state." (p. 146)

Brandeis History Professor James Kloppenberg's entry is aptly-titled *The Virtues of Liberalism* (Oxford University Press, 1998), and features a history of American liberalism from the 18th century to the present. Its chapters include: 1.) "Rethinking America's Liberal Tradition;" 2.) "The Virtues of Liberalism;" 3.) "Knowledge and Belief in American Public Life;" 4.) "Premature Requiem: Republicanism in American History;" 5.) "Life Everlasting: Tocqueville in America;" 6.) "Democracy and Disenchantment;" 7.) "Deliberative Democracy and the Plight of America's Poor;" 8.) "Political Ideas in the 20th Century;" 9.) "Why History Matters to Political Theory."

Kloppenberg's Preface notes "All these essays deal with aspects of American political thought, but they do not present a single consecutive argument. They are arranged to proceed chronologically, moving gradually from a focus on the 18th century to the present." (p. 10) He muses over competing impulses facing authors publishing previous essays: Rewrite the essays completely to reflect current events and new scholarship? Or, Stick with the original text leaving it up to the reader to fill in the blanks? Kloppenberg has followed a middling strategy, revising a few essays.

Elsewhere the author writes compellingly, "Our nation has flourished because we have not permitted those with power to silence those who challenge them, whether the former brandished dogmas of religion, race, ethnicity, gender, culture, or economics. Madison insisted that force should never be the measure of right; we must not allow selfish fashionable doctrines to masquerade as virtue or rationality." (p. 76)

Liberalism's commitment to an America both rational and egalitarian (the proverbial shining city on a very high hill), leaves us open to charges of hypocrisy. For example, let's hope the author's well-reasoned case study of

Bill Clinton selling out liberalism in order to get reelected isn't repeated by Barack Obama. He also warns about a virulent strain of conservatism demonizing liberals today.

Seeking the essence today's definition of liberalism he emphasizes two main perceptions: 1.) New Deal, New Frontier, or Great Society policies for greater social equity via the Federal Government; and, 2.) Expanded tolerance for an inclusive diversity of all kinds of disenfranchised, impoverished, and abused peoples. (p. 174)

Kevin Mattson's *Intellectuals in Action: the Origins of the New Left and Radical Liberation* (Penn State Press, 2002), covers much intellectual turf very well mostly from the 1960s. However, this not a history book, and Mattson is clear about his purpose: "I emphasize the ideas that inspired the New Left, some of which live today, even if not fully recognized." (p. 6) Also, "The New Left Promised a non-Marxist democratic model of political change at a time of great historical possibilities." (p 78)

He identifies progenitors to the New Left, such as C. Wright Mills, Paul Goodman, and William Appleman Williams' dissatisfaction with 1950s complacency, including its Blacklist era. When he wrote this book Bush II has ascended to the presidency and he warned against anti-intellectualism and failing to recognize the potency of big ideas.

Historian Alan Brinkley is noted observing that while the New Left never developed the political infrastructure to create an enduring movement, much of its cogitation represented brilliance. The New Left had the sense to abandon any identity with symbols of the Old Left (Marxism's failed model). Mattson also wants to debunk many stereotypical myths as illusory.

Change in the 1960s was multi-faceted, however New Lefties deliberately chose to ignore the more abstract notions of "culture wars" and to focus exclusively on realpolitik as their field of dreams. Similarly, 1930s notions of Marxist analysis were virtually abandoned in favor of much more optimistic ideas of participatory democracy. Counter-intuitively, says the author, they relied on universal human rights norms embodied in the United Nations as ethical fuel to drive their politics.

Four hack-jobs demonizing liberalism come from conservative pundits Michael Savage, J. Gresham Machover, Conde Pallen, and Ann Coulter. Savage's is called *Liberalism is a Mental Disorder* (Thomas Nelson Publishers, 2005); Machover's come under the title *Christianity & Liberalism* (Fig Books, 2011); Pallen's rubric is *Liberalism is Sin* (B. Herder Publishers, 2004); and Ann Coulter's taps a similar theme with *Godless: The Church of Liberalism* (Liberty Books, 2004).

Noto Bene: This is not Jon Stewart making things up, or my fantasies. Check out Kindle for verification.

Proof that conservatives suck wind at humor oozes from James Delingpole, *365 Ways to Drive a Liberal Crazy* (Regnery Publishing, 2010), purporting to offer clever ways of discombobulating liberals only includes about half that many, since he uses each of the following at least 10 times: "start a rumor; explain why Obama has to go; prefer chairman to chairperson; call them libertards or regressives; tell a joke."

Others include: "reclaim rock music for conservatism; tell them you don't give a damn about polar bears; go hunting polar bears in Nunavit; praise Agusto Pinochet; next time it's cold, ask them what happened to global warming; say a prayer; serenade them with Ted Nugent's 'kiss my ass;' reclaim the language for conservatism; stand up for Joe McCarthy; cite the 'burqua' as great symbol of female liberation; demean multiculturalism; blame the BP oil spill on environmentalists; mow your lawn; quote G. Gordon Liddy."

CHAPTER TEN:

"Foxymoron's Cogent Critics Galore"

BACKGROUNDER:

American political bifurcation contributes to nasty hyperbole on both sides. The system incentivizes neither pundits nor politicians to apply CTS; fortunately, it does for the professoriate. I applaud liberal political scientist Kerwin Swint for maintaining his professional standards throughout his biography of Roger Ailes, whose ethically-challenged life jumps up and grabs you by the throat.

Similarly, Bush II's decade-long procedural and substantive worst-practices will take a long time to expose fully. His was the most secretive presidency in recent history, epitomized, of course, by Darth Vader (Dick Cheney). Like Bill O'Reilly and his ilk, it takes time to unravel all this sophistry, but amounts to cherry picking using CTS.

Endless liberal fodder ensued when Bush II stole the 2000 election; then, the John Roberts Supreme Court provides a fig-leaf along ideological lines; then, he's clearly AWOL throughout 9/11; then, he botches

Afghanistan via premature ejaculation letting Osama bin Laden escape; then, (worst of all) he invades Iraq against his generals' advice.

He tramples civil liberties with unprecedented domestic spying resulting in few prosecutions; then, "The Decider" looks the other way during Abu Ghraib, sanctioning illegal torture killing America's reputation abroad; and, most long-lastingly, eviscerates America's middle class via dysfunctional tax cuts for the 1% least needy, considered ill-advised by multi-billionaire Warren Buffett. Shame on the American media for willful gullibility!

My claim not readily-verified by scholars relates to 9/11. That requires much research, which I have done. Bush's 9/11 sin was one of omission, less egregious than sins of commission, according to Christian doctrine. All 9/11 required was Bush II asleep at the wheel (Richard Clarke's memoir says as much) when it mattered most. So maybe our true-believer, born-again Christian, deserves Purgatory not Hell? 9/11 represented the perfect self-fulfilling prophecy pined for in 1994's GOP's *Project for a New American Century* (i.e., Hegemonic Empire.)

The GOP ridiculed Bill Clinton for limiting American power-projection abroad to economics; wasting our Post-Soviet "unipolar moment." Neocons like Dick Cheney, Scooter Libby, Paul Wolfowitz, Fred Barnes, Charles Krauthammer, and Bill Kristol caricatured Clinton as a wonkish wimp. The subtext for their bolder vision? To resurrect Reagan's "Star Wars" (SDI) extending American military hegemony to the heavens.

Their favorite metaphor consisted of Pearl Harbor: only such a profound trauma could prevent the Post-Cold War "peace dividend" from shifting Pentagon dollars to trivia like education, infrastructure repairs, green energy, health insurance reform, middle class tax relief, and high tech R & D. Bush II was so emboldened by 9/11 that one Congressman jested that all the GOP needed to ram anything through was "to combine 9/11 with any verb of their choosing."

I have read much 9/11 literature and lots of goofy conspiracy theories proved untrue, thus rejected by reasonable critics relying upon CTS. However, a small coterie of "truthers" continues clinging to disproven hypotheses. Since Bush II never provided real answers to scores of 9/11 questions, naturally lots of wacky ideas proliferated. Scientific method and CTS enable us to separate fact from fiction, and that's what occurred for the most sentient among us.

Chapter two described ex-prosecutor Vincent Bugliosi's case for impeaching Bush II; similar turf is covered even more thoroughly by law professor Michael Haas' *George W. Bush's War Criminal?: The Bush Administration's Liability for 269 War Crimes.* (Praeger Publishers, 2009).

Haas specifies fully 269 war crimes committed by Bush II. Haas writes "Under American and international law, heads of government cannot be hauled into court for criminal offenses committed while in office. However, they can (and sometimes are) prosecuted after leaving office." (p. 171)

More biting, "George W. Bush does not have a law degree, so he relied on legal advice. When legal opinions differed, he relied on his own judgment. He is fully aware that he and others may have committed war crimes. As president, he could have had received the best legal advice in the world. But presidents who value loyalty over competence avoid appointing with independent judgment. Those who dissented from the White House consensus were marginalized from the decision-making process." (p. 174)

The author's Table 1.1 lists and categorizes Bush II's legal advisers; the most influential were Alberto Gonzalez and Harriet Miers, possessing zero international law experience. John Ashcroft and James Comey resigned when their legal opinions were rejected. Ditto for Colin Powell, hero of Iraq War I, whose advice to affirm the Geneva Conventions was ignored. Likewise for Jack Goldsmith, complaining that the legal opinions written by John Yoo and Jay Bybee conflated common law with international law in unconvincing memos. (p. 79)

Respected lawyer/journalist Anthony Lewis compared Bush's legal advice as "akin to mafia dons using mob lawyers to skirt the law but stay out of prison;" and international lawyer Philippe analogizing the conspiracy among Bush II's lawyers to "the clique of judges whose legal opinions were cited to convict them in the Nuremburg War Crimes Tribunals in 1948." (p. 126)

Furthermore, Haas calls the Bush Doctrine responsible for besmirching America's reputation, accomplishing a goal otherwise impossible for Al Qaeada: "Transforming America into a rogue nation feared by the rest of the world and loved by almost none." (p. 137)

INTRODUCTION:

Between published books, articles, and Internet contributions, FNC's shoddy history has generated myriad intelligent complaints. I think that all elements of this unholy triptych possess a short half-life and will implode slowly, which I said long before 2011's phone-hacking scandal erupted in London's *News of the World*.

Serious scholarship requires that we concentrate on FNC's book-length disputations first; and Kindle again comes through. However, let me first pluck the lower-hanging fruit from briefer articles. Rank-ordering into primary, secondary, and tertiary categories forces us to employ CTS unconsciously.

PRIMARY ARTICLES:

Case studies help to illustrate broader truths. *Newsweek* journalist Lara Franchella's 2009 article does so elegantly, titled "The O'Garbage Factor:

Fox News Isn't Just Bad, It's Un-American," which she milks for ironic effect. Her opening paragraph:

"Last week, when White House Communications Director Anita Dunn charged FNC with right-wing media bias, Fox responded the way it always does: Denying the accusations with a straight face while proceeding to confirm it with its coverage. Consider Fox's Web story on the episode in which it quotes five people, two of whom work for Fox, all of whom assert that Administration officials are either wrong in substance or politically foolish to criticize the network. No one cited supports Dunn's criticisms or saying that it could make sense for Obama to challenge the network's power. It's a textbook example of a biased journalism." (p.3)

The author also refers to the befuddled responses of Low-Testosterone (LT) token liberalette, Alan Colmes, on all issues; Likewise ,what I call the Big O's aggressive paralinguistics (Franchell "bullying"); or, declaring moot the argument over whether Rupert Murdoch's rightward tilt results from ideology or profits; finally, what I call Fox's 9 Bevy-Bleached-Blonde-Babes, and the author "platinum pundits." (p. 5)

But how would Franchella work Un-Americanism into her article? Via what I perceive as a European versus North American dichotomy, which she widens to an "Australian-British-Continental" model of politicized media different from 20th Century America's valuing of media independence as the ideal typology pioneered by CBS News.[lxxxv]

The next story impresses for its proximity to the action, an anonymous ex-insider. Eric Boehlert's ALTERNET title derives from a direct quote via the ex-insider, "We were a Stalin-esque Mouthpiece for Bush's Policies," where the prevailing culture demanded in order to survive, staffers were expected to tow the line according to daily briefings, but add lib the details when not directed specifically on an issue." (p.8) Fairness and fact-checking be damned.

The whistle-blower's interview was given to MEDIA MATTERS (one of the veracity police), leading MEDIA MATTERS editors to conclude what critics have been suggesting for years, namely, that "Fox news is run as a strictly partisan operation, virtually every news story gets actively spun by a staff whose goal is prop up the Republicans and knock down the Democrats." (p. 9)

The key element of this story consists of the thesis that gradually over time, FNC morphed from biased and sleazy journalism to being an active player on behalf of the Republican Party. For the biggest issues, such as Obamacare, or War in Iraq, carefully crafted sound-bites were to keep the network strictly on-message.[lxxxvi] (At which Republicans excel, anyway.)

It appears only I among Fox critics taps into the paralinguistic scholarship pertinent to FNCs' SOP. SLATE journalist Jack Shafer does analyze one obsession by the Big O: telling everyone ad nauseum: "Shut Up."[lxxxvii] Shafer's article refers to more than 100 scoldees whom the Big O has abused thus. "Recipients include Al Franken, Tom Daschle, Jimmy Carter, Rosie O'Donnell, gay people, atheist Boy Scouts, peaceniks, both parties, and scores more."

Shafer observes "On his TV show, O'Reilly uses 'shut up' as a place-holder for an idea still formulating in his brain. As a way to begin, punctuate, or end a sentence, sometimes saying it with fury, eyes bulging. While being dismissive, he delivers it off-handedly without real malice. Other times, he says it gently, with a minx-like twinkle in his eye, signaling that he's merely acting frisky." Sometimes he dumps on entire nations in the stereotypical alpha male *Modus Operandi.*.

Shafer doesn't use the word, but he's really talking about the Big O using it as an "audible pause," or as a "verbal tic." Given genetic and social reasons for human behavior, where might one look to explain the Big O's "shut up" fixation?

Shafer looks to someone arising often in O'Reilly's writings: his luke-warm, ambivalent, ambiguous, bitter-sweet, unassertive Dad: "My father didn't tell me anything. My father just said: 'Shut up, and eat your food, children are starving to death in Korea, but he didn't offer a lot of career counseling—but he never discouraged me." (p. 7) This kind of back-handed slap also appears often in the Big O's autobiography.

My favorite of Shafer's vignettes, exposing so much of O'Reilly's sophistry, while blasting a 2003 Iraq War Protester whose father died on 9/11:

Big O: "Shut Up, Shut Up."

Protester: "Oh, please don't tell me to shut up."

Big O: "Out of respect for your father, who was a Port Authority worker, a fine American who got killed unnecessarily by barbarians."

Protester: "By radical extremists who were trained by this government—"

Big O: "Out of respect for him."

Protester: "Not the people of America?"

Big O: "I'm not going to—"

Protester: "the small minority of the ruling class."

Big O: "Cut his mike, I'm not going to dress you down anymore because of your father, we will be back in a moment with more of the FACTOR."

Protester: "That means we're done?"

Big O: "We're done." (4 February 2003)

Next, ALTERNET writer Mark Howard reports on an extensive University of Maryland survey by its World Public Opinion project provocatively titled, "Study Confirms that Fox News Makes You Stupid."[lxxxiii] The subtitle also packs a solid punch: "A New Survey of American Voters Shows That Fox News Viewers Are Significantly Less Informed than Consumers of News from Other Sources." (p. 1)

The frequency of this conclusion popping up in reputable studies bleeds through Howard's opening sentence: "Yet another study proves that watching Fox News is detrimental to your intelligence." Howard refers to other research but points out that the 2010 investigation describes a cumulative effect is associated with Fox News: "the greater the exposure to FNC, the more misinformation increases." (p. 2)

This research followed the first election cycle after the Supreme Court's striking-down of campaign spending limits created by Congress, on the grounds that such limits represented an unconstitutional First Amendment proscription of free speech. Here nine out of 10 voters said that in 2010 they encountered information they believed to be bogus, a major increase over previous studies.

The poll was conducted from 6-14 November 2010, consisting of 848 participants, using a Web-enabled technology known as "Knowledge Panel," with a margin of error of 3.4 percent. The system purports validity as a national opinion survey. Initial screening uses telephone numbers and residential addresses, after which online participation is invited. For willing participants without computers, "Knowledge Panel" provides laptop and ISP connection.

Data supporting the main hypothesis here was found applicable to a wide variety of issues:

1) Stimulus Package: While the Congressional Budget Office (CBO) concluded that TARP had saved/created between two and

five million jobs, 68 percent believed it created/saved only a few jobs, and 20 percent believed it created no jobs.

2) Health Care Reform: While the CBO predicted that Obamacare would reduce the federal budget deficit by 53 percent, 53 percent of voters predicted it would increase the budget deficit.

3) Economic Recovery: While the Commerce Department concluded that the recession ended in the third-quarter of 2009, 55 percent of voters believed the economy still getting worse.

4) Climate Change: While most scientists overwhelmingly warn of problems, one-third of respondents considered scientists evenly divided. (p.5)

Additionally, "Those who watched FNC almost daily were significantly more likely than those who never watched it to believe that the stimulus caused job losses, that health care reform would worsen the deficit, that the economy is getting worse, that the stimulus package did not include tax cuts, that their income taxes had gone up, and the auto bailout occurred only under Obama." (p. 9)

All of which are incorrect. Furthermore, the effect is not simply a partisan one, since the study controlled for that variable. People who voted Democratic but also watched Fox News was considerably more likely to believe such misinformation.

FNC's worst-practices have resulted in boycotts; for example, Apple Inc., under Steve Jobs when then Fox-pundit Glen Beck was registering outrageous calumnies such as calling the President "a racist" and progressives "cancerous." A 2010 article by Michael Grothaus is called, "Apple Boycotts Fox News Because of Glenn Beck," including over 200 other companies, making it more difficult for FNC to sell ads. Coincidentally, these events occurred just as Apple was releasing its wildly popular iPad.[lxxxix]

Also, that same year, *Forbes* magazine reported that Glenn Beck made $32 million, citing his TV, radio, books, and touring. FNC pays him $2 million annually for his 5 PM talk show, and $13 million came from book sales, all gleaned from an article by Andy Barr.[xc] Another sneaky one escaping my consciousness was FNC conspiring with McDonald's Corporation. How so?

From 2008-10, journalists sought corroboration for a bizarre trend reported by McDonald's customers inquiring of employees why the large plasma TVs in McDonald's was set only to the Fox News station. Store managers kicked it upstairs reporting that this was company policy; however, when journalists talked to Regional Directors and to Danya Proud, spokesperson for McDonald's USA, she denied such a corporate policy exists, but that Regional Directors possess considerable discretion.

Since FNC relies on dirty tricks, critics are tempted to reciprocate. I've read about countless other Foxy freebies/bribes to intermediaries as a reliable growth strategy (At which Foxymoron excels). Scholarly ethics rise above such chicanery; however, I'll cite a little scrambler online called "TV-B-Gone" for $17.99 shutting off stealthy FNC sets.[xci]

McDonald's pseudo-food causes smart people to steer clear of the Golden Archers like poison ivy, but many Americans fail the smart test consistently. Michael Moore holds the patent on documentary films with heavy-handed socio-political messages, but I recently saw a work by a West Virginia native (Morgan Spurlock) doing a fine Michael Moore impression with his low-budget "Super-Size Me," which finished in Current TV's recent top ten ranking of all-time best documentaries.[xcii]

Playing filmmaker as guinea pig is not unique, but Spurlock trumps others by taking a hit for humankind: For one month he eats nothing but McDonald's fare. Beforehand, both he and his attending physicians assume that such a brief experiment will likely only bump up measurements moderately (e.g., blood pressure, heart, rate, cholesterol level, weight gain, and physical discomfort.)

However, his frequent check-ups prove that almost immediately really bad things start happening, and continue worsening rapidly, helping viewers comprehend shocking post-experiment numbers. Also, symptoms consisted not only of physicality, but emotional and psychological ones suggestive of addictive harbingers.

This low-budget experiment also produced other surprises, especially McDonald's, Inc, cancelling its traditionally profitable "Super-Size" program.

Jon Stewart's contributions were covered in chapter nine, but I also want to quote from a *New York Times* piece by Brian Stelter called, "Jon Stewart's Punching Bag: Fox News." It opens noting that in April 2010 Stewart's staff member called the White House to ask a factual question and received a prompt response; something FNC failed to do regarding a questionable story appearing on "Fox & Friends."

Stelter writes "On the subject of Fox, Mr. Stewart is pretty relentless, demonstrated by that crescent segment and dozens of others since Mr. Obama took office. In fact, he may well be television's pre-eminent fact-checker of FNC, the nation's highest-rated cable news channel." That's saying quite a lot when reputable fact-checking services such as factcheck.org and 'Media Matters' have impressed scholars. The latter's President, Eric Burns, opines "Stewart does a great job of using comedy to expose the tragedy that is Fox News, because he understands the seriousness of it." (p.3)

And the simple question FNC failed to ask, but Stewart didn't? Fox was spinning a crescent-shaped logo used by the nuclear security summit as an Islamic image chosen by Bush as an olive branch for good Muslims around the world. But FNC was dead wrong on this. In fact, the image was taken from the Rutherford-Bohr model of the atom, familiar to most scientists (but how often does that species appear on Fox?).

The hook for Stelter's article consists of: Having lost Bush II, Cheney, Rumsfeld, and Karl Rove to kick around, FNC provides endless fodder for Stewart's faux journalism, which continues salting away Emmy after Emmy for comedy. Also, Comedy Central has recently extended the political satirist par excellence's contract through 2013. When was the last time you saw FNC even nominated for any kind of Emmy? (Never) (p. 6)

The author describes Stewart's verbal parries reaching way, way, way beyond his devoted Comedy Central viewers, especially on blogs and other Web sites repeating his voice in something of an echo chamber. According to "Project for Excellence in Journalism" President, Mark Jurkowitz "Media criticism has become part of Stewart's brand, and the maestro has also aimed lengthy jabs at both CNN and MSNBC. Typically, Stewart allows his shows to speak for themselves, but occasionally he'll take on Bill O'Reilly directly." (p.22)

Stewart's staff laughs off criticisms that they are pretending to be journalists, but the maestro stated recently that "I have not moved out of the comedian's box into the news box, but the news box keeps moving toward me." [xciii] As the go-to infotainment network, FNC mimics Murdoch's other examples of journalistic worst-practices. One such instance occurred between the fall of 2010 and winter of 2011.

Sarah Palin, Newt Gingrich, Rick Santorum, and Mike Huckabee were all receiving hefty payments for appearing on FNC while considering running for president. At issue: how does a news organization cover a primary campaign when so many of the candidates are on its payroll?

How did FNC handle this conflict-of-interest quandary? By issuing contracts to these illuminati prohibiting their appearance on other stations, and producers at NBC, ABC, CBS, CNN, MSNBC, and C-SPAN were told to ask FNC for permission, which were denied. "C-SPAN Political Editor Steve Scully said that when he tried to have Sara Palin on for an interview, he asked FNC's permission which was denied. At that time, Mitt Romney was the only Republican not on the Fox payroll." (p. 27) Are Mormons real Christians?

The authors describe other fairness, professionalism, and propriety concerns whenever FNC acts irresponsibly. Also, "With Fox effectively becoming the flagship network of the right—and more specifically the Tea Party Movement—the four Republicans it employs enjoy an unparalleled platform from which to speak directly to primary voters determining the party's next nominee."[xciv]

As a social scientist, I'm always eager for the scientific method to assist us. Half way into this project, I came across an 11,495 word mini-book published by the "Center for the Study of the Presidency" chock full of data, released in 2008: "Who's the Fairest of Them All? An Empirical Test for Partisan Bias on ABC, CBS, NBC, and FNC." [xcv]

Owing to the subject' complexity, author Tim Groeling notes that while various generalizations about News media can be made "These efforts tend to be undermined by the inherent subjectivity of defining bad news; also, they find it hard to test for selection bias." (p. 3)

I appreciate that no discipline monopolizes wisdom; therefore, I'm not only an interdisciplinary social scientist, but also well-schooled in the Humanities (including several research grants from state and national humanities associations).

Early in my career, I hoped science could help us to study humanity more objectively. However, I soon learned that we humans represent a tough study, given our well-documented perfidy. Plenty of FNC-relevant quantitative statements exist in this "Center for the Study of the Presidency" project for me to better criticize Fox News. However, author Groeling wisely cites the utter subjectivity of news assessment.

What's needed most here is CTS, deriving from both philosophy (humanities) and psychology (social science), with the former's bounty of qualitative wisdom, and the latter's quantitative certainties.

SECONDARY ARTICLES:

Late in 2009, two key FNC executives were telling correspondents exactly how to frame the health debate and how not to frame it: the right way (government-run plan); versus the wrong way (public option). "Politico" journalist Jennifer Epstein explains how and why this occurred. [xcvi] And once again, we see "Media Matters" exposing Fox stealth adroitly.

V-P and Washington Managing Editor, Bill Sammons, sent a memorandum to all staffers beginning thus: "Friendly reminder: Let's not slip back into calling it the 'public option' when discussing Democrats' proposals for a government-run health plan, according to internal e-mails released recently. Instead, Sammons suggested several ways to describe it but emphasized the import of using the "government-run plan."

Within minutes of Sammons' note, Michael Clemente, Senior V-P for News, ramps up the pressure with his own memo that "Number 3 on your list (government-run option) is the preferred way to say it, write it, and use it." In releasing the memos, Media Matters, said "these memos give credence to allegations that news from Fox's Washington Bureau is deliberately distorted to benefit conservatives and the GOP."

Sammons defended his words in an interview with "The Daily Beast," "While the public option is vague, bland, and non-descriptive and likely to stir up tensions, the government-run plan is a more neutral term." Really? When asked if his phrasing was preferred by the GOP, he responds straight-faced: "I have no idea what the Republicans were pushing; it's simply an accurate, fair, and objective term." Wow!

The GOP generally, and FNC specifically, demean science's relevance to the collective public good; however, they do indeed take as many public opinion polls as do the Dems. What Sammons failed to mention in his interview was that two months before the Sammons and Clemente memos, Republican pollster, Frank Luntz, explained on air to Sean Hannity that "If you call it a public option, the American people are split; however, if you call it the government-run option the public is overwhelmingly against it." Finito, Benito!

Seth Ackerman's dense eight-pager in "Fair" relies on copiously wide-ranging interviews in "The Most Biased Name in News: Fox News' Extraordinary Right-Ward Tilt." His hook? Rupert Murdoch's famous taunt to "Salon" magazine: "I challenge anybody to show me an example of bias in FNC," to which Ackerman provides more than 50. Also, "Fox even has the audacity to argue that it is the ONLY unbiased network. So far, Fox's strategy of aggressive denial has worked surprisingly well; faced with its unblinking refusal to admit any conservative tilt at all, some commentators have simply acquiesced to the network's self-assessment." (p. 1)

Ackerman cites applicants who had applied to work at FNC then demurred when asked by management whether they were Republicans. For instance, Andrew Kirtzman, a respected New York cable reporter, refused to cough up the litmus test, and received the cold shoulder thereafter. The author also runs through Fox's entire prime-time programming and identifies near-unanimously conservative credentials.

Al Franken's 2003 book had already dispelled this myth when this ex-college wrestler challenged a verbally-abusive conservative talk-show host to a refereed public wrestling match and the pundit blithely ignored Franken. Ditto for Ted Turner inviting Rupert Murdoch to duke it out in the ring when FNC was ridiculing Turner's then-wife, Jane Fonda. Hell, I'd fight for Jane Fonda too!

Former CBS producer Don Dahler resigned from his FNC post after Executive Director John Moody ordered him to change a story playing down the overwhelming statistical evidence for a general lack of social progress among Black Americans. About the same time, several former Fox employees wrote to the *Columbia Journalism Review* about management changing stories in ways that cooked the facts. (p.4)

Similarly, longtime CBS Producer Jed Duvall who left Fox after one year told NEW YORK magazine that "I'll never forget the morning that one producer came up to me and, rubbing her hands like Uriah Heep, said Let's have something on Whitewater today. That won't happen in a professional news organization" (p. 5)

And with all things FNC, comparisons with CNN must be trotted out: "The difference between these cable news networks is that while some conservative-friendly fare airs on CNN, Fox has oriented its whole network around it. CNN and its other mainstream outlets is not liberal or conservative, but staunchly centrist. The perspectives they value most are those of the bipartisan establishment middle." (p. 8) [xcvii] I agree and applaud both CNN and the networks for not trying to out-fox Fox (excepting Iraq 2003.)

Next I look at Justin Berner's "It's Like, Almost a News Show: Fox & Friends' Stupidest Moments of 2010," "Media Matters."It's header: "2010 was quite a year for Fox News' serial misinformation on the curved couch regarding, the stimulus package, health care reform, the ground zero mosque, 2010 election returns, as well as other topics."

I'll cite a few of the goofiest ones:

1) "It's like almost a legal document, but it doesn't have a story!" Correspondent Brian Kilmeade after months of exaggerative complaints about specifics on Obama's health care reform law, Kilmeade imprints his own rave, that it's lengthy, hard to read,

and legalistic. His explanation? The Democrats intentionally did it that way to confuse the less-literate, intimating that America is better served if Democratic legislators wrote bills to read more like children's stories.

2) "The Buddy System," Fox's derogatory code-word for Barack Obama's multilateral strategy treating our allies like allies (trusted equals whose advice we seek, as opposed to Bush II's costly unilateralism (lives and treasure).

3) "I predict that the House Democrats will implement a secret plan that my sources say will propose health care legislation, if the Senate Democrats made changes to the bill in reconciliation," from Dick Morris, who leads every league in failed predictions. However, when he announced this brainstorm on 27 January 2010, Washington was already abuzz with similar reports.

4) "The crotch bomber," for the Christmas 2009 failure to blow up an airliner headed for the U.S. FNC used that moniker because his name is too hard to pronounce: Umar Farouk Abdulmuhfalab.

5) "Sorry global warming people—we have too many polar bears now." Correspondent Kilmeade broke a story about a large sculpture of an iguana arriving at the Ft. Worth zoo. He bravely declared himself "anti-polar bear" contextualized by his long history of dumping on preservationists as effete snobs.

6) "Roasting marshmallows on air by hand with a plastic spoon." In November someone had built a studio from ice outside News Corp headquarters, leading "Fox & Friends" three hosts to work from there during their weekly chat with Chris Wallace, but walking and chewing gum at once proved impossible for these dummies. Why? Because the fire pit in front of them burned down and their plastic forks melted while roasting marshmallows.

7) "Hawaiian birds have redone their chromosomes to coexist with football stadium lights." Their correspondent characterized stadium officials as solving their problem with sea gulls flying the lights by redesigning their genes by switching to day games, exposing their ignorance of fundamental genetic science.

8) Lastly, "the bogus claim about the symbol being used for the nuclear disarmament talks having been lifted from Bush II's symbol of recognition with Muslims" (in fact it still remains the symbol devised by scientists Rutherford and Bohr as the atomic symbol). Trying to link the Obama administration with radical Muslims routinely occurs at Fox.

GOP vulnerability concerning gun control, where the American public fears loose guns more than loose nukes, according to surveys. With 300 million citizens in the U.S., and the NRA pushing for more permissiveness in the world's most violent society, hundreds of thousands of persons are guaranteed to qualify best-case scenario as paranoid, and worst-case scenario as schizophrenic. Doesn't that even dent the consciousness of legislators scared-off by the NRA lobby? After all, Gabby Gifford was a legislator.

Compounding matters, most American mental hospitals were closed 30 years ago, creating a perfect storm for Tucson after Tucson after Tucson. I find pathetic FNC's ritual absurdities following each inevitable mass murder; and, what happened in Tucson, during 2010, played out as scripted for our outdated, dysfunctional gun culture.

I had been unaware of the "gun show loophole" whereby guns supposedly illegal here are sold by unlicensed dealers requiring no background checks. Several investigative journalists have proven how utterly easy it is to buy even the most lethal assault weapons, placing our police forces behind the proverbial eight ball, including *Current TV.*

Melissa McEwan's detailed 6-page expose especially compelling: "Let's Get This Straight: There's No Leftist Equivalent to the Right's Violent Rhetoric," with this sub-header: "The shooting in Tucson was not an anomaly. It was inevitable as long as we continue playing this foolish game of "both sides are just as bad, it will re-occur." (p. 1)

The author starts with the most recent Republican V-P candidate, Sara Palin, who regularly exploits imagery (e.g., rifle sights) and provocative language (e.g., "Don't Retreat, Reload") exhorting her libertarian rednecks to fix America's unsatisfactory politics violently. Alaska's latest Maverick appeals to FNC idiots looking for simple solutions to complex problems. (p. 2)

Next McEwan examines Glenn Beck, ditto for whom no leftie counterpart exists. His radical rhetoric includes poisoning Nancy Pelosi; comparing Al Gore to Hitler; condoning a fatwah against Michael Moore; accusing Philanthropist/Holocaust Survivor George Soros of collaborating with Nazis; equating immigration reform with burning U.S. citizens alive; comparing universal healthcare with rape; publically endorsing violent revolution here; and countless cases of exterminationist rhetoric. (p. 3)

Nor is there a progressive alternative to Fox contributor and syndicated columnist, Ann Coulter. Among quotes for which she is infamous: "We need to execute people like John [xcviii] Walker to physically intimidate liberals, making them realize that they can be killed, too;" plus, "My only regret with Timothy McVeigh was that he did not go to the *New York Times* building." (p. 4)

The Big O's simpleton braggadocchio inspires plenty of ink; however, McEwan settles for his lying about and then stalking relentlessly his critics. For example, claiming that the progressive "Air America" hosts were traitors and should be put in chains; or, liberal bloggers should be dealt with via hand grenades; or, to Al Qaeda: all of America is off limits for you, with one exception: San Francisco, go ahead, blow up the Coit Tower! (p.5)

On 13 January 2011 I jotted down these O'Reilly gems after the Tucson gun massacre: "I knew I would have to respond to the crazy blame-game by the Left, because the FACTOR is now the news program of record" (a title generally reserved for the venerable gray lady residing in NYC).

Speaking of the Big O, an exchange between him and two co-hosts of CBS's morning chit-chat called "The View," developed legs long enough to carry it worldwide in a nanosecond. This was a classic case of liberal versus conservative interpretations of 9/11. Many jocular exchanges between O'Reilly and Jon Stewart on both of their shows have enabled them to play to their respective bases, imprint their brands more deeply, but in a civil manner.

However, "The View" was different because two of its co-hosts walked off the set. On 14 October 2010 O'Reilly stated that "Muslims killed us on 9/11" in the midst of discussing the proposed mosque near Ground Zero.

He was there pitching his new book, *Pinheads and Patriots,* when Whoopi Goldberg challenged his contention that the proposed mosque was inappropriate by noting that 70 Muslim families were killed on 9/11, to which the Big O made his infamous retort. Always staking out the populist turf, O'Reilly's main argument was based on his belief that 70 percent of Americans oppose building a mosque there. To which Goldberg said "That is such bullshit."

Moderate octogenarian Barbara Walters chastised her co-hosts for walking off the set, offering an olive branch by suggesting that O'Reilly should recognize that it was only "Muslim extremists" who committed the terrorist act. Behar and Goldberg returned after the Big O said, "If anyone thought I was demeaning all Muslims, I apologize," quite unusual for this egocentric alpha male.[xcix]

Let me quote here from a book review of Peter Hart's scathing *The O'Really Factor: Unspinning Fox News' Bill O'Reilly,* by Timothy Scanlon, from Hyattsville, MD, one of those regular Joes for whom the Big O claims to speak. Scanlon calls his father-in-law "one of the world's greatest prudes," and dutifully read something written by O'Reilly and emerged completely underwhelmed by its boring predictability.

The reviewer wondered what inspired so many conservatives to get pumped up by this bully? Once he saw his first TV performance by the Big O on "The Factor," he got it. Scanlon doesn't refer to O'Reilly para-linguistics as I do, but that's essentially what he means by "loudmouth windbag," also O'Reilly's use of the term "Dummycrats," or describing O'Reilly as the "ultimate control-freak."

This prescient reader also notes how the Big O "has mastered the art of simply tuning out those who disagree with him," or, "Yet O'Reilly has the audacity to call his stands 'unspin' while that's all he does." I also concur that Al Franken skewers O'Reilly much entertainingly than does Peter Hart, but then the Big O really makes it so easy by aggressively spouting such nonsense.[c]

During the climate change talks in December 2009, "Media Matters" writer Ben Dimiero did a story about another an infamous leaked memo sent to staffers by Bill Sammons, Fox News Washington Bureau Chief, ordering underlings to debunk the science associated with global climate change; much like Bush II declared that the "science on global warning is uncertain." Technically, Bush had a point: no scientific information can be proven with 100 percent certainty; however, on global warming the scientific community was about 99.999% convinced.

Many other reputable FNC ex-insiders have expressed grave concerns about Sammons' using his powerful position to slant coverage rightward. In this memo's case, Sammons' words were these: "Refrain from asserting that the planet is warming (or cooling) in any given period without IMMEDIATELY pointing out that such theories are based upon data that critics have called into question"

Like Sammons' other infamous memo (on "government option"), this occurred after a propitious stimulus, namely, minutes after Fox correspondent Wendy Goler accurately pointed out on-air that the United

Nations World Meteorological Organization announced that "2009-10 is on track as the warmest decade ever recorded."

Further contextualizing this latest of Sammons' unsavory memos, other sources have reported that for about six months, he was behind the network's relentless promotion of the fabricated "Climate-gate Scandal," misrepresenting emails sent to and from climate scientists at the University of East Anglia's Climate Research Unit.

The scientific consensus at that time was simple: a bogus Climate-Gate Scandal in no way threatened the science on global warming. Several subsequent investigations found no basis for a Climate-Gate Scandal. [ci] Borrowed from the phenomenon of Holocaust Deniers, science's enemies here have been called Climate-Change Deniers.

Finally, the underlying problem keeping America from finding greatness once again, in my view is tackled head-on in a recent article in "Politico" by Joshua Holland, called "How a Trillion-Dollar Empire Causes Our Deficit Problems."

A total of 193 countries exist in 2011, and America continues to outspend all other 192 by a significant margin on defense, that really should be called offense, during our decade of perma-war (largely for economic reasons.) The Post-Col War Peace Dividend never materialized, and huge chunks of current military expenditures (like America protecting Europe from a defunct Soviet Union) seem superfluous. Of those 193 countries, the U.S. has bases in 120-some; how can that not be considered an Empire putting the Romans to shame?

Joshua Holland maintains that "America could eliminate its budget deficit and still fund Social Security/Medicare without raising taxes by outspending our biggest military rivals by threefold." (p. 1) Bureaucracies take on a self-sustaining life of their own, and despite GOP complaints about "big government," their beloved Pentagon leads the league.

Furthermore, the media have ignored the greatest expansion of government since the New Deal (Department of Homeland Security/ and other redundancies post 9/11).

Roughly one-fifth of the American budget officially goes to national security ($711 Billion) in 2010. "However, this is completely misleading because the American security state is covertly dispersed throughout the federal budget. When you include all of the extra dollars in hidden programs, the actual number rises to $1.45 Trillion in 2010." Furthermore, "With Washington in the grip of deficit hysteria, the elephant in the room never getting mentioned is defense spending." (p. 2)

Author Holland also cites recent OECD data covering the 29 richest countries, revealing that America places 26th (with 29%) while the five highest tax rates ranging between 40-46% (Denmark, Sweden, Belgium, Italy, and France) measuring tax rates as percentage of GDP. (p. 3) In other words, the relative tax burden upon Americans is much lower than among our peers.[cii]

Rush Limbaugh floats the inaccuracy that America's corporate tax rate ranks highest in the world. Actually, Japan ranks first with America second. But even that is very misleading, because of the furtive tax-loopholes crafted by corporations and gobbled up by a Congressional leaders hooked on corporate donations. Occupy Wall Street protesters in 2011 finally forced the majority of Americans to get it: America has adopted a welfare state, however not for the poor, but for the elite 1%—middle class be damned.

TERTIARY ARTICLES:

Ben Dimiero's piece for "Media Matters" cuts to the chase after a tour-de-force 12-page review of Glenn Beck's recent books: Beck's self-contradictory paranoid delusions are best explained thus: understanding that Beck is an old-style religioso/huckster always morphing into something different, and because of entertainment mileage trying to explain the inscrutable. Forget it, says Dimiero because no true core exists in Beck to discover; It's all about smoke and mirrors.[ciii]

Elsewhere, Mark Howard's "The Real Reason Glenn Beck Is Bashing Google," with a persistent campaign of calumnies is not that he resents Google's near-monopoly status, or disrespect for privacy right, which would be too logical for Beck. Sources say the main reason is simple: His boss, Rupert Murdoch, hates the search-engine giant's incursions on, and support for, critics of Murdoch's News Corp.

Glance at how Beck conflates fallacies into rationalizations for a lethal conspiracy: "May I recommend that if you're doing your own homework, don't do a Google search; seems to me that Google is petty deeply in bed with the government. Maybe this is explaining why Google is being kicked out of other countries? Are they just a shill now for the United States Government?" (p.12)

Quoting an anonymous ex-insider that "Murdoch has had it in for Google for more than one year, believing that Google is appropriating his content without paying for it: distributing a memo asking rhetorically, should we allow Google to steal all of our copyrights?"[civ]

Mark Howard's article speaks to successful boycotts against FNC over Glenn Beck, called "Number of Advertisers For Glenn Beck In the UK: Zero!" but it addresses the issue in the U.S. as well. First, in the U.K. Beck's show on Sky News ran five straight days with absolutely no advertisements. The author says "Besides losing money carrying an albatross freebie by Murdoch, the symbolic value is significant; no longer can he perpetuate the charade that he is a legitimate businessman, no he is a naked propagandist."[cv]

New York Times reporter, Jacques Steinberg, wrote an article on 28 June 2008 about "ominous trends in Fox News ratings," which someone important at Fox must have considered hostile. Why? Because five days later two FNC reporters referred to Steinberg, and his editor, Steven Radcliffe as "attack dogs," featuring pictures of them digitally-altered to make two handsome guys look homely. As the author describes it, "the journalists' teeth had been yellowed, facial features exaggerated, and portions of hair receded." Fox admitted to the deception.[cvi]

Insiders have reported that an aging Rupert Murdoch dislikes intensely facing hostile TV cameras, partly because of his inarticulateness. A 2010 report by Scott Wong and Keach Hagey, "Democrats Pounce as Rupert Murdoch Goes Live," "Politico" describes discomfort before American authorities maybe one percent as damaging compared to a veritable meltdown one year later in the U.K., which I watched live on CSPAN. He and his son James, now the heir apparent in many eyes, floundered badly.

The 2010 U.S. situation involved Murdoch and the House Judiciary Committee, "posing as a typical businessman," and recommending "America should undertake a broad immigration overhaul—including a path to citizenship for millions of illegal immigrants—as good for the ailing economy" (p.1) Yet, Murdoch is both Chair and CEO of News Corp, which many Democrats consider their "most powerful media nemesis."

Rep. Linda Sanchez (D-CA) accused him of hypocrisy, since Americans who watch Fox News are familiar with its steady drumbeat of negativity with its "anti-immigrant positions, including provocatively calling them "illegals," rather than more neutral words such as "undocumented immigrants." Ivan Roman, Executive Director of National Association of Hispanic Journalists, states: "The term illegals is used more frequently by FNC than any other network as part of the rhetoric employed by those hostile to immigrants." (p.3)

Sanchez's California colleague, Rep. Maxine Waters, also asked Murdoch why he didn't do more to publicize his immigration views at his many newspapers, now including the prestigious *Wall Street Journal*? Only

Republican Rep. Lamar Smith of Texas defended Murdoch by referring to mythic studies claiming Americans perceive Fox as the "fairest of all stations."

Journalists often turn to Michael Wolff, author of the densest Murdoch biography called *The Man Who Owns the News,* points out that the crux of the matter boils down to "Murdoch's being an internationalist, while Fox's Roger Ailes harbors considerable suspicions about internationalists." Plus, Murdoch's current wife is a young Chinese woman who worked for News Corp before marrying up in the world. (p. 3)^{cvii}

The U.K. *News International* phone-hacking scandal of 2011 is under investigation, both there and in the U.S.; however, given Murdoch's age, the leadership dilemma, and unimpressive track-record for son Michael, the current debacle seems to dwarf previous ignominies hard-won by Murdoch's tabloid portfolio, how can his personal empire not be headed for massive down-sizing? (of course growth matters most to him).

Every recent President failed to reform our moribund, corporate-and-investor friendly sham whereby we pay a higher percentage of GDP than our peers for health care. How to deal with FNC presents a conundrum for Obama: ignore it hoping they'll disappear; or, assertively take the offensive as MSNBC has done? Fox's alpha-male demographic is loyal, but a small minority nevertheless.

In March 2010, Obama employed what I'd call a "tweener strategy" by using reason with the beast in a Fox interview, which Josh Gerston attended, calling it "often testy." The key procedural issue revolved around if House Republicans would trot out a little-used ploy, "the deem and pass procedure," which would allow Speaker Boehner's restless Tea Party rebels "to avoid casting a vote in support of the current Senate bill that many of them dislike strongly, fearing it could be used against them in bids for reelection." (p. 1)

Public opinion favors Obama's beseeching the GOP "get on with the peoples' business," but Obama decided not to officially recommend this procedure, leaving it up to John Boehner, noting that the Senate bill included many revisions suggested by Republicans on this most vexing stalemate. (p. 2) Also, many Americans are going bankrupt or losing houses because of obscene health care expenses.[cviii]

Year 2010 kept the veracity police busy. Factcheck.org provides various services, like lesson plans for teachers to incorporate CTS. Its Introduction cites its complex role: "Here's the thing: Kids today grow up in a world of ceaseless information; as are we all, transmitted in huge helpings and in a virtual instant. Unfortunately, its quality varies tremendously, much of it failing to meet contemporary standards for critical thinking. Our aim is to help them become smart consumers." (p.1)

Factcheck.org's 2010 cheat-sheet is paraphrased below: 2010 represented an embarrassment of riches for fact-checkers, with Democrats fighting for control of both houses of Congress, and Republicans in attack mode, torrents of money amplified its predictable effect. Reps accused Dems of favoring cuts in Medicare, while Reps did the same concerning Social Security. Reps charged their opponents with plans for huge tax increases on families and small business; while Dems said their opponents sought a 23% national sales tax. Fact Check found fault with all such claims.

Health Care Reform: Serious Rep misrepresentations included scare tactics that Medicare patients would lose their personal physicians, or that Dems wanted to give Viagara to sex offenders, or that families would pay $2,1000 higher premiums.

Social Security Hyperbole: Dems in Nevada, Wisconsin, Michigan, Kentucky, and Colorado falsely accused Reps of wanting to privatize social security.

Stimulus Spin: Rep ads in Connecticut, Florida, Washington, South Dakota, Ohio, and Pennsylvania claimed that the economic stimulus package had failed to create jobs.

Bailout (TARP): Everyone jumped on Wall Street's bailout in 2010. Dems: Many who voted for the bailout lied their way out of it. Reps: Accused House Dems of voting to give huge bonuses to all Wall Street employees.

Taxes: Reps: Dems will unleash massive tax increases on middle class; Dems: Reps plan to increase small business taxes.[cix]

All Dem fact-checkers love chances to beat up on FNC's "War on Christmas Stories," in this year's case especially because Fox reporter Megan Carlson didn't even attempt to contact the school involved for corroboration.

Carlson claimed that a Florida elementary school banned traditional Christmas colors (red & green) from all classrooms, in her words "teachers are not going to let red & green in their classrooms." However, when "Media Matters" contacted Heathrow Elementary School officials on 29 November 2010 they heard: "There is no ban on the colors red and green at Heathrow Elementary."[cx] Thank you veracity police!

A comprehensive 10-pager comes from ALTERNET'S Michael Wolraich, "Why Glenn Beck Keeps Peddling Whack-Job Fantasies about Euthanizing Grandma, ..." delivers the promised goods.[cxi] Most of Beck's paranoid fantasies derive from his careful reading of Adolph Hitler's writings, even whipping out his Fascist *book du jour* on air.

Beck began his FNC shtick around Barack Obama's Inauguration, but it took a year for the conspiratorial object of his evolving paranoia to become undeniable. First, he borrowed freely from right-wing conspiritist Alan Skousen, whose bogeyman consisted of the kind of world government fantasized by scholars after World War II; then, Beck cooks up a Mex/ Amer/Can conspiracy to gobble us all up into an regional dictatorship, which he abandoned soon because of the "difficulty of correlating excessively wide highways in North America with Nazism."

Beck also demonized Al Gore's campaign against global warming with disinformation about: "An Inconvenient Truth;" Gore's finances; and both his Nobel Peace Prize and Cannes Film Festival Award. He characterized Gore as a naïve idealist trying to cram an Ectopian visions down our throats. "In presenting Al Gore as a cunning Hitlerian super-villain, Beck was warming us up for his future role as chief witch-hunter for the right-wing; comparisons between progressive bogeymen and murderous dictators would soon emerge as a standard part of his repertoire." (p. 1)

Jon Stewart loves citing the frequency of Hitlerian references, that "Beck suffered from "Nazi Tourette Syndrome," and author Wolraich suggests what psychologists call Freudian projection via this wall-to-ceiling paranoia: "Stoking fears that Al Gore was employing scare tactics by comparing him to the scariest fear-monger (Hitler). It's so twisted that it's brilliant" (p. 3) The *New York Times* did some articles on Beck tapping into pent-up feelings of alienation in downsized America.

But, Al Gore was either too nerdy or too pacific for Hitlerian imagery. Beck also adopted the buddy system at Fox by exploiting one of Bill O'Reilly's long-standing nemeses in philanthropist George Soros. The author says this was resented by O'Reilly, quipping "O'Reilly's a one bogeyman kind of a guy; everything he hates is somehow funded and controlled by Soros." (p.6)

Beck also exploited what critics have labeled his "Czar Wars," these Executive branch government bureaucrats not confirmed by Congress, therefore subject to corruption. Bush had countless Czars but Beck never complained about those (e.g., Abstinence Czar; Faith-Based Czar; Birth

Control Czar). Obama ditched some of Bush II's Czars, but Beck counted 32 under Obama. They fall under Beck's Shadow Government Conspiracy.

In Beck's words: "This collection of these Czars, they are evil people, simply wicked. How can you trust anyone who bypasses the constitutional confirmation process, and sit at the center of the Shadow Government." (p. 9) Author Walraich calls Beck "chief cook and bottle washer of the Czar scare." (Beck could also use a grammar coach)

But Walraich says all of this drama merely represented the prelude to Beck's grand finale: accusing President Barack Obama of being a subversive revolutionary out to remake America from the top down. He couldn't invoke Hitlerian imagery with Obama, but conflating Obama with two other supposed Black Revolutionaries helped immensely.

Namely, Rev. Jeremiah Wright (Obama's fiery ex-pastor in Chicago) and Anthony Van Jones (Special White House Advisor for Green Jobs, and called a Czar by Beck), thus closing the Black Radical Conspiracy circle neatly. Reporters at FNC have long been accustomed to referring to Van Jones as "the Green Jobs Czar."

Beck implores a dozing America to wake up? He opines, "These three devoted revolutionaries are doing exactly what Hugo Chavez did in Venezuela: get elected legally, followed by conspiring to fundamentally transform Venezuela into a Socialist State; however, when running Chavez neglected to tell Venezuelans his true intentions." (p. 10) Mr. Paranoia cries déjà vu all over again with Obama, Wright, and Jones.

Additionally, "Obama is wearing a mask, but he has surrounded himself with radicals and revolutionaries, and has done this for his entire adult life," then, this powerful jeremiad screeches on TV not merely that the President pals around with black nationalists and communist revolutionaries; rather, he is saying directly that *Obama is a black nationalist and communist revolutionary.*" (p.12) If other FNC pundits making better contact with reality had uttered their treasonous calumnies they would have been skewered; Maybe Beck's self-evident craziness gives him a pass as beyond the pale?

Robert F. Kennedy, Jr. lacks the charisma of his father and his uncles. However, he has carved out a respectable career among environmentalists who consider him their patron saint. When the sweeping energy and climate bill collapsed in 2010, stalling in the Senate, Kennedy emerged guns a blazing, and the title of journalist Robin Bravender's pensive article speaks volumes: "Robert F. Kennedy, Jr. Says FNC, GOP Killed Climate Bill." (p.1)

Some progressives blamed Obama for not pushing harder, but RFK, Jr. points out that Obama is merely human, and has been amazingly successful legislatively, therefore the real culprits should be scrutinized, namely: FNC, its bogus climate-gate scandal, with other journalists failing to challenge Fox falsehoods, Big Oil, and GOP House leaders who acted irresponsibly. Kennedy is also President of an environmental NGO called the "Water-keeper Alliance." He also praised Massachusetts Democrats John Kerry and Ed Markey for their valiant efforts. (p. 2)

Kennedy blasts Fox's Glenn Beck for dreaming up the bogus "Climate-Gate Scandal," subsequently proven sophomoric at best, and delusional at most by investigative panels on both sides of the Atlantic. RFK, Jr. was "Irked by the fact that climate skeptics with no scientific bona fides continue getting play in the news media who should be treated like those who claim cigarettes don't harm health, or the world is flat, or we never actually landed on the moon." (p. 3) [cxii]

Another 2010 article examines Fox's unintended role as exposer of GOP fissures through its expanding roster of presidential hopefuls, by Keach Hagey, "GOP's Struggles Play Out On Fox." When Fox chose to give birth to the Tea Party movement by covering its early days so enthusiastically, detractors accused FNC of crossing the line separating journalism and political activism.

However, 18-months later, ambivalence within Fox about the Tea Party movement's current star (Christine O'Donnell) are hard to miss. Why? "Because in the weeks leading up to O'Donnell's upset victory in Delaware, Fox provided an important platform for her supporters, according to analysis by POLTICO'S Eric Boehlert. And, "Michelle Malkin endorsed O'Donnell on Sean Hannity's radio show on 8 September, which Sara Palin repeated it the very next day, and three days later Greta Van Susteren aired Palin's endorsement of O'Donnell." (p. 1)

Plus, "by then, all hell had broken loose, dispelling any notion that FNC's opinionated prime-timers speak with a monolithic conservative voice. Karl Rove slammed O'Donnell as nutty, a day after listing concerns about her checkered background, to Sean Hannity." (p. 2) Eric Boehlert opines that this represents the first time he had witnessed such disarray concerning FNC. [cxiii]

Another piece explains why only rarely are we treated thus, by Sara Pavlus, "The Fox News Divide that Never Was."[cxiv] Essentially, she argues that the main divide necessary for responsible journalism (clear separation between covering news and opinion shows), which so clearly goes AWOL at Fox propagandized as "fair and balanced" incessantly. Such buffoonery works with a gullible public, but critical thinkers see through such sophistry. As the *New York Times* did in the previous story

She draws a fundamental distinction between the relatively benign misinformed gossip spread by supermarket tabloids (for example, Murdoch's), and serious real-world public policy consequences for any country purporting democratic credentials. For example, New York Congressman John Hall (member of House Global Warming Committee) refers to Bill Sammons' Fox memo as "not only regrettable but ideologically slanted."(p. 3)

Awards like the Pulitzer matter greatly, and the veracity police known as PolitFact, in 2010 selected as most egregious "Lie of the Year" as Fox's reporters consistent reference to health care reform as "a government takeover." (p. 4)

KINDLE BOOKS:

So plentiful are books by smart critics that I'll cover only the most important ones. We begin with a "twofer" by journalists Joseph Amann and Tom Breuer. First we'll examine the more recent one: *Fair and Balanced My Ass: An Unbridled Look at the Bizarre Reality of Fox News.* (Nation Books, 2007)

Its cover states: "This is a wide-ranging, irreverent, and humorous look at America's No. 1 cable news network. In addition to examining Fox's phony patriotism and piety, its dishonest crusades, and its well-defined agenda and ratings-driven techniques, the book delivers a hearty slap-down to the jewels of the Murdoch crown: Bill O'Reilly, John Gibson, Hannity & Colmes, Neal Cavuto, Brit Hume, et al. What results is a hilarious and bracing read: red meat for liberals and food for thought for anyone who is both amused and concerned about journalism's continually-eroding standards."

Their Introduction profiles FNC viewers, whom they call "an interesting lot," and they have come to know intimately via researching two separate Fox News books. Scores of rabid e-mails, enraged voice-mails, disputatious book signings, personal interviews, and online blogs have left strong impressions on Amann and Breuer. An early quotation from Ashland, OR, resident Brenda Watson to her patron Saint (Bill O'Reilly) whose track-record for maligning Canadians preens for our attention.

Watson: "I think you people up there are absolutely disgusting. I love Bill O'Reilly, and you're nothing but a bunch of Commies. You asshole Canadians let all of these people into your country because you don't give a shit about us; you're really anti-Christ: a bunch of atheists and assholes and I can't stand people like you. Freedom of speech, okay, thank you for my freedom of speech since I can't stand you. What the hell are you doing? I love Bill O'Reilly so fuck off." (p. i)

Brenda Watson hiding behind Christianity's ultimate imprimatur: fickle love for freedom of expression except when it involves people with whom they disagree; and, harboring deep suspicions about all foreigners, typifies FNC's niche demographic. However, name two countries on the planet which have enjoyed greater synergy economically, defensively, in foreign policy, or culturally than the U.S. and Canada. Maybe it's Canadians' trademark devil-may-care attitude responsible. (p. 4) The authors also paint FNC as merely symptomatic of a deeper malaise tantamount to mental illness (known as clinical insanity).

In December 2005, the *New York Times* disclosed that Bush II had approved warrant-less domestic wiretapping in apparent violation of the Foreign Intelligence Surveillance Act (FISA), and, of course, many Democrats criticized this as un-American. More surprisingly, in that post-9/11 milieu when Republicans dared not say boo to any presidential request, one very prominent Republican Senator did just that and more.

Pennsylvania's Arlen Specter, then chairing the Senate Judiciary Committee called Bush II' s wiretapping "highly suspect and quite possibly illegal." Amman and Breuer not only praise Specter for his courage, but also the legal reasons for Specter's objections over domestic wiretapping, calling them "compelling."

Amann and Breuer describe FNC's predictable overkill response: "In defense of what was pretty clear violation of both the spirit and the letter of American laws and the Constitution, Fox let loose a barrage of misinformation that would have made Joseph Goebbels soak in his Ubermensch Underoos." (p. 21)

They acknowledge traditional journalism's tendency to take the safe route with a "don't ask, don't tell policy" regarding correspondents' religion (an agnostic strategy). But not FNC, which the authors say "discusses religion incessantly, even when irrelevant to the news." Amann and Breuer identify seven times during 2005 in which Sean Hannity alone mentioned off-topic that he was a devout Christian. (p. 37)

FNC's religioso heavy-hitters (Bill O'Reilly and Sean Hannity) are both Catholics, however, Fox appears to favor only mainstream Christianities, but not "sects." How do they handle someone I consider a Christian (Mormon Mitt Romney)? In 2011, Romney was the only Republican presidential hopeful not on the FNC payroll, was it because he's a Mormon?

Amann and Breuer cite numerous historical instances in which Christians have failed to turn the other cheek by going to war with one another. Scholars identify a well-documented theory called "the Democratic Peace,"(democracies don't attack democracies), but not even an idiot has ever uttered a theory called "the Christian Peace."

They describe in detail some of Christianity's permutations: Catholics, Lutherans, Methodists, Baptists, Evangelicals, Pentecostals, Anglicans, Eastern Orthodox, Jehovah's Witness, Mennonites, Quakers, Amish, Seventh-Day Adventists, Mormons, Jews for Jesus, the 700 Club, and Gary Busey. (p. 39)

I alliterate over FNC's bevy-of-bleached-blonde-babes intended for alpha males to salivate over, raising another interesting FNC conundrum: What could be more inconsistent with Fox's across-the-board conservative philosophy, love affair with Evangelicals, prudity, and sexual abstinence campaigns of "just say no" than exploiting the female body to drive up ratings? Our authors note: "Those who study Fox know that you'll find more blond bimbos, gratuitous skin, and inappropriate middle-aged banter on this network than anywhere outside of NFL Sunday with the Texas Hooters." (p.77)

FNC also relies on Democratic Turncoats, but quality control suffers because "Fox loves to invite guests with Democratic pedigrees whose last liberal impulse was supporting Jimmy Carter's favoring the SALT II talks, or opining that kinky sex fetishes should remain a private matter between top campaign strategists and their prostitutes." (p. 189) This final reference, of course, relates to Fox's favorite Turncoat (Dick Morris).

Always introduced as a "Democratic ex-Clinton adviser," Fox omits a more apt tagline: Former Clinton adviser fired for having an extramarital affair with prostitute Sherry Rowlands; plus, Morris always overachieves as backstabber. And if you're tuned into both verbal and non-verbal cues like I am, he's fat enough to do childhood obesity commercials, decided ugly, and (best of all) looks like he had a stroke since he talks strictly from one side of his mouth. (p. 193) I'll bet you can guess which side?

O'Reilly continues pontificating *ex cathedra* (Papa-bili) refusing to even discuss sex on his prudish show. I expected that after he paid $10 million in 2005 to settle the sexual harassment lawsuit by an ex-co-worker that he might tone down his facile moralizing, but The Big O scores a zero on everybody's introspection test.

About homophobia, these authors say, "When the dazzling intellectuals at FCN weren't getting totally grossed-out over the thought of two boys kissing, they were doing their best to dismiss 'Brokeback Mountain' as merely an "agenda film" of no aesthetic merit. You know their shtick: "both of the effete, out of touch liberal U.S. coasts were heaping praise on a dreary little art film destined to languish in the red and purple states in between." (p. 229)

FNC neo-con foreign policy contributor, Charles Krauthammer, worked overtime in an interview on 2 January 2006, with Brit Hume, keeping his brilliant predictive record intact (a leading Chicken-Hawk coaxing Bush II to War in 2003), here the consequences of his wrong-headedness proved less damaging. He had just panned the Hollywood film "Brokeback Mountain," saying that "It only won the Academy Award because it was seen in theaters by 18 people, but the right 18 people, therefore it won." (p. 231) B.S. (Bad Science)

The authors refer to the Big O as "utterly uneducable for resurrecting a moribund War on Christmas" schtick shot down so often that he should be suffering from whip-lash, especially after an extremely brusque dust-up by late-night TV's David Letterman. In 2006, he was at it again doubling-down on this stupid theme in a new book, *Culture Wars,* which they label as "an absurdly Manichean manifesto."

Plus, they quote from more than 30 newspaper editorials ripping O'Reilly for beating this dead-horse into oblivion. They add perspective with these words: "No one denies that the ACLU regularly challenges religious displays and expressions (including those involving Christmas) that are sponsored by local governments, nor that some retailers prefer the more generic and inclusive 'Happy Holidays' to the overtly Christian 'Merry Christmas' The quarrel is about what this means, and we disagree totally with FNC." (p. 235)

Their Acknowledgments thank Al Franken and Keith Olbermann as inspirational, Especially by "stoking the fires of O'Reilly's insanity, from which we draw considerable warmth." (p. 236) Furthermore, his agent and publisher receive kudos, and for contemporary Internet researchers like me, he recommends MEDIAMATTERS.ORG and NEWSHOUNDS.US as exemplary cyber police.

I assume that the second book occurred because its predecessor did well: *Sweet Jesus, I Hate Bill O'Reilly* (Avalon, 2005), by the same two authors, who dedicate it to "That blind squirrel (Rupert Murdoch) who discovered our favorite nut (Bill O'Reilly)"

Its chapters are well-titled: 1.) "Like a Record, Baby Right Round Round Round;" 2.) "O'Reilly and the Art of the Impotent Boycott;" 3.) "Bill is Both Outraged and Lovin' It;" 4.) "See Bill. See Bill Jack. See Bill Jack and Call Jim;"5.) "Three-Dollar Bill: O'Reilly among the Queers;" 6.) "Who Hath Deceived Thee So Often as Thy Self;" 7.) "Bill Forgets About His Amnesia;" 8.) "Bill is More Popular Than You;" 9.) "Bill Just Don't Understand;"10.) "Mea Culpa Sorta: O'Reilly and the Half-Assed Apology;" 11.) "Hillary Versus O'Reilly: The Fake Race That Never Was;" 12.) "Million-Dollar Crybaby: O'Reilly and Hollywood;" 13.) "The ACLU Rat Pack: Hitler, Stalin and Chairman Mao;"14.) "Moore and Air America and Soros, Oh My!;" 15.) "Secularists at the Gate;" 16.) "The Elite Media: They Think They're so Damned Elite;" 17.) "The O'Reilly Factor for Kids;" 18.) "Who's Looking Out for You?" 19.) "The O'Reilly Factor: The Good, The Bad, and the Completely Ridiculous in American Life;" 20.) "The No Spin Zone;" 21.) "Those Who Trespass;" 22.) "How Thin Is That Splotchy Skin?" 23.) "President O'Reilly Goes Down Hard in the Big Easy;" 24.) Bill: Portrait of a Sociopath;" 25.) "The Future of This Book."

Their Introduction opens with a letter to Bill O'Reilly explaining they had to write this book because they really care about his mental health; given his proven track-record for unbridled fabrication, they believe that only a professional *intervention* can rescue him. And while that's scary, and Bill's not the brightest bulb on the tube, he should take heart from other celebs unable to handle the pressure of fame and benefitting by facing reality. If he completes his rehab program, Amann and Breuer will start working on a sequel with only word different: "substitute love for hate."

That tone pervades their tome: a beneficent therapeutic intervention for this mendacity addict. In one spot they write "More and more we observe cracks in your fragile psyche…. As a result it appears you are losing not only your grip on reality but on your audience as well.' (P.9) (precisely what matters to this egotist: ratings.) Elsewhere they note that "the man is as introspective as a legume." (p.14)

Concerning his stereotypes about "liberals as hippies with nose rings who bathe rarely using the illegal weed grown in their parents' basement to maintain their meager stocks of bean curds and Che Guevara t-shirts," the authors don't use the scholarly term of "cognitive dissonance theory" but it really fits here. They argue that O'Reilly simply-mindedly believes in his prejudices, otherwise even he would be couldn't live with himself. (p. 144)

Then the elite media he constantly refers to is epitomized, of course, by the *New York Times* and network television. However, he got his start working for both ABC and NBC TV in the 1970s, but has touted his show as not merely alternative media, but remedial media. (p. 175)

His definition suggests: "The *New York Times* is ground zero for the elite media, and you would think executives at that paper would understand how detached they have become from the real America. But they don't, in fact, before their music critic Thomas Rich gave a positive review to rapper named Ludacris. That's right: he gave a positive review for Ludacris while criticizing the "Passion of the Christ film." (p. 179)

Next Marvin Kitman's *The Man who Wouldn't Shut Up: The Rise of Bill O'Reilly* (St. Martin's Griffin, 2008), this ex-media critic for *Newsday* examines the main question behind O'Reilly's retrospective: What makes O'Reilly O'Reilly? Kitman and I arrive at completely opposite conclusions about the Big O. Kitman's book was written with O'Reilly's permission, but not approval. It seems to me that Kitman aimed at a relatively objective analysis of this controversial public figure.

The *New York Times* book review says "Kitman performed Boswelian prodigies of research to suggest that O'Reilly's struggle is less about passionate conservatism and more about parading his seething personal resentments to become that which purports to despise: a celebrity;" *Publisher's Weekly* taps some similar sentiments with: "It's difficult to imagine a better researched or less biased work about such a divisive figure as O'Reilly;" and, Keith Obermann said on his TV show: "Finally, someone has attempted to explain and contextualize Billo's charlatanism; I also liked the parts about me." (p. 7)

In his Preface, Kitman says he's a liberal ex-journalist trying to strike a balance in writing the first full-length biography of this conservative provocateur. One reason he seeks this role is the bifurcated literature on O'Reilly, very little of it positive (most of that written by The Big O.) The dismissive stuff is both more prevalent and more diverse. However, even this professional journalist aiming for tolerance completely loses patience with The Big O's narcissism.

Kitman says he's uniquely qualified to do a serious Big O biography: 1.) Kitman's long career as a media critic occurred on Long Island including five weekly columns at *Newsday*; 2.) Growing up in Levittown, O'Reilly considered Kitman his professional role model; 3.) While Kitman certainly qualifies as a liberal, his core professional identity consists of TV critic; 4.) Given O'Reilly obvious conservatism, Kitman has developed a unique theory about O'Reilly-as-publicity-whore; 5.) Kitman knows Bill personally, which always counters demonization. The latter sociologists call the "contact theory," also, Kitman believes he can live with his liberal comrades considering him stupid to take on this noble task.

His book is different, or "Fair and balanced· by that I mean it doesn't trash O'Reilly in the usual way. I seek an even-handed, in-depth examination of the man through the prism of his work as a journalist," (p. 13) I guess Kitman's research missed paralinguistics, but he does probe the Big O's "uniquely aggressive style" on the tube. However, get this: Kitman asserts that "O'Reilly's not really an ideologue by contrasting him with the right-wing's quintessential ideologue: Rush Limbaugh." (p. 15) A worse-case scenario is always feasible!

Kitman's biography runs 352 pages, including endnotes. Also, he interviewed The Big O in his NYC Fox office 29 times, as well as 62 interviews with friends, colleagues, college professors, and Long Island residents. Procedurally, at least, this book approaches best-practices status for unraveling the onion layers built up around controversial public figures. And he delivers on his promise to avoid taking cheap shots or coddle his friend: "While Bill O'Reilly is certainly not his own worst enemy, I can be." (p. 17).

Kitman wrote both an Introduction and a Prologue; in the former his thesis amounts to: O'Reilly is less an ideologue than a maverick; in the latter; perspective about how FNC/O'Reilly took off during a major journalistic crisis, partly self-inflicted. The pivotal year (2004) when the giants who had carried the burden of filling the shoes of long-time icon, Walter Cronkite, retired: namely, Dan Rather, Ted Koppel, Tom Brokaw, and Peter Jennings.

Lacking an obvious single cause for the networks' collective demise, he refers to 2004 as the "year of the meteorite," why? Because these anchors' mutually-reinforcing sclerotic style made network news predictably boring, and Kitman cites statistics tracing how badly the networks were bleeding decade-by-decade (it was anything but sudden, yet the mass exodus symbolized the key year). Then add into the mix killer communications technologies, and its crisis-management-mode nationwide.

Enter Roger Ailes and Bill O'Reilly (who also serves as V-P to Ailes besides his own show), fervently believing that network news lacks an explanatory narrative capable of simplifying an increasingly complex world for a weary, over-worked populace. "A revolution had already been taking place on FNC about the way news is presented on TV. Bill

O'Reilly has spearheaded that radical movement directed by Roger Ailes, his Chairman." (p. 3)

Furthermore, "O'Reilly is radical for TV journalism because he thinks he knows what all the news means. You may not agree with his analysis, point of view or values, but you always know where he stands; plus he never shuts up." (p. 6) So revolutionary does Kitman see Fox's story, that he calls it the first paradigm shift since Walter Cronkite. He refers to this new genre of loosey-goosey style of "media mud wrestling contest as yeller journalism" (p. 7) I think its better traced to Foxymoron's history practicing worldwide tabloid journalism.

In the Ailes/O'Reilly mutual admiration society, Kitman provides some new quotations never before recorded. For example, from Ailes' view-point, "Bill's absolutely fearless; I've never seen him afraid of any topic;" or, "Bill's authentic: He's an authentic prick but not just on air. He's a prick to his staff, to management, his family, and everyone else; that's what has enabled him to be so successful." (p. 8) Kitman's task in his book: explain how O'Reilly got so damnably authentic.

The Afterword is also candidly personal. However, for a media critic, his bar for deciding to write the book is rather low. The key here is the word "fearless," other synonyms might be "Maverick;" or "Feisty Irish;" or "Banty Rooster" all expressing what Kitman admires here: "Let me explain: I wrote a biography of Bill O'Reilly because I admired him. What I like most about him was the fearless quality of his journalism. He went after stories others were afraid to cover or otherwise ignoring." (p. 278)

Their interactions were pretty cordial until Kitman devoted a chapter to O'Reilly's phone-sex scandal, resulting in a sexual harassment lawsuit brought by ex-colleague Andrea Macris. "It's the kind of story O'Reilly would have covered on his cable news show, if he weren't the defend-ant. He was hypersensitive about the story. In his opinion, his phone sex problem should not have appeared in what the *New York Times* book reviewer called a definitive biography on him. But I disagreed completely." (p. 280)

Kitman elaborates, "His embarrassment was so enormous that he couldn't bear to think about it, no less read about it. He was so eager to flush the incident down the memory hole that he paid off the plaintiff, which Keith Olbermann reported at $10 million." (p. 283) What more elegant example of "cognitive dissonance" at work?

Also, "After the book I became aware of another new, very different Bill O'Reilly, whose motto should have been 'Often wrong, but never in doubt.' The author ends up taking a vow never again to write a biography of a living person, as much as admitting that he should have listened to his liberal friends issuing caveats.

Equally marvelous stuff comes from Peter Hart's *The Oh Really Factor: Unspinning Fox News' Bill O'Reilly* (Seven Stories Press, 2003), which reading seven years later informs about how little O'Reilly's schtick has changed. Reputed Communications scholar Robert McChesney wrote the Foreword, analyzing the concept of "irony" and how well FNC epitomizes its meaning.

McChesney states "Peter Hart shows us how preposterous is O'Reilly's claim to oversee 'a no-spin zone;' indeed, O'Reilly is the consummate spin-meister, the deft propagandist." (p. 2) A zone where the GOP gets treated with kid gloves, while adversaries get raked over the coals, where the double standard is utterly palpable. Bullying and self-absorption are two of The Big O's distinguishing features: good entertainment/lousy journalism.

The disconnect between O'Reilly/FNC high ratings and worst-practices reporting begs explanation, and McChesney asserts two contenders: 1.) Merger mania resulting in mega-corporations amplifying the bottom line as key (shows like O'Reilly's require little infrastructure; 2.) Contemporary conservatism bears little resemblance with its historical progenitors. "Today it stands for little more than crass opportunism wrapped in thousand-dollar bills." (p. 4)

Author Hart's Introduction is called, "The All-Spin Zone," and dissects the simple-but-potent marketing strategies employed by FNC, "enabling an O'Reilly brand, which manages to mold his don't B.S. me, folks next door persona, into a brand comparable to Nike." (p.3) Well, maybe Enron would make a better analogy.

Hart describes O'Reilly's last stint before moving to Fox as host for the network infotainment tabloid called "Inside Edition," where he helped begin the practice of paying stars to do interviews, labeled by critics as "checkbook journalism." Hart compares the unconvincingly desperate manner in which O'Reilly defended "Inside Edition" then and FNC today.

Peter Hart's Conclusion is called "Sheer O'Reillyness," meaning essentially hubris, or "Bill's sheer confidence in the righteousness of his pronouncements makes his words seem believable absent evidence. Hart first got this term from a rival network producer called on the carpet for failing to check out misinformation she described having been mesmerized by his sheer O'Reillyness," (p. 149) handing him a journalistic blank check.

Hart calls his examination of The Big O's garbled facts and twisted logic fairly superficial, suggesting there are many more books needed to flush out the truth. One final vacuous braggodocchio the author leaves us was uttered on 18 March 2003 when he issued this empty promise concerning WMD in Iraq:

"If the Americans go in and overthrow Saddam Hussein and that country is clean, no WMDs, then I will apologize to the nation, and I will not trust the Bush Administration again, all right?" (p.152)

And, on 7 July 2003 "If Bush lied—if he lied—I'll be the first one to hang him, all right?" However, when the Big O wrote his retrospective in 2008 (with Iraq's AWOL WMDs undeniable), he continued praising Bush's handling of Iraq. (p. 154) What about journalistic accountability?

A new Kindle gem entered my consciousness by career-U.S. Marine Clinton Sprauve, *All Hail the Messiah: Why Fox News Channel and the Conservative Clan Couldn't Crucify Him (Obama)* (Authors House, 2011) This young man came to America as a child immigrant with his family of loving parents and three siblings wherein Christianity was taken very seriously as a code of conduct.

Sprauve entered the Marines, serving multiple tours in war zones, which worried him, since he had started a family, including three children. This was a serious Christian Black man who regarded Barack Obama's election as nothing short of miraculous in America. To say he glorified Obama would grossly understate the obvious. So what incensed this Christian family man enough to take on FNC's deep pockets? His conscience.

Very simply, the demonization of Barack Obama by radical conservatives who portrayed his election as nothing short of a death sentence for America as they define it, and which author Sprauve characterizes as "much like a barrage on the battlefield." (p.11)

Also, "The Conservative Clan (CC) consists of highly educated individuals associated solely on the basis of their conservative ideology and mutual desire to prevent a President Obama Administration. Though unsuccessful, they still endeavor to torpedo his presidency daily. Some call themselves Libertarians or Independents, but remain in the Anti-Democratic Party. Members of this group number in the hundreds, therefore, only some of the nationally-renowned members are listed here." (p. 163)

Among those analyzed are: Rush Limbaugh, Karl Rove, Newt Gingrich, Charles Krauthammer, Bill Kristol, Bill Bennett, Sean Hannity, Glenn

Beck, Brian Kilmeade, Steve Doocy, Sarah Palin, Ann Coulter, Michelle Malkin, Bill O'Reilly, Laura Ingrahan, Rudi Giuiani, Fred Thompson, Fred Barnes, Pat Buchanan, Neal Boortz, Mark Steyn, Mark Davis, Bill Cunningham, Michelle Malkin, Kevin Wall, Jed Babbin, Brent Bozell, Lars Larson, Byron York, Laton Dawson, Tammy Bruce, Monica Crowley, and Michelle Bachmann. Whew! Among prominent spinster Think-Tanks: The Heritage Foundation; The Claremont Institute; The Manhattan Institute; The American Enterprise Institute; and, The National Review.

My next entry almost makes me feel sorry for contemporary conservatives: editor Clint Willis' *The I Hate Ann Coulter, Bill O'Reilly, Rush Limbaugh, Michael Savage, Sean Hannity Reader: The Hideous Truth About America's Ugliest Conservatives* (Thunder's Mouth Press, 2004), which is dedicated to their victims. Chapters are contributed by well-known liberals like David Corn, Eric Alterman, Richard Cohen, Charles Taylor, and Matt Bivens. Like others from this genre written more than five years ago, the analysis possesses a durable shelf-life.

Veracity police such as Eric Alterman cite words uttered by Ann Coulter on MSNBC's "Hardball With Chris Matthews:" "I haven't read the decision yet, but don't you expect that the judges who said the Pledge of Allegiance violates the constitution were appointed by Democrats, not Republicans? I'm just waiting to see if anyone will take me up with any bets as to which political party appointed those judges." (p. 114)

Only one judge was appointed by a Democrat, Judge Stephen Reinhardt, a Carter appointee. Alterman points out that the other Judge, Alfred Goodwin, was appointed by that reckless liberal named Richard Nixon. Such a cavalier attitude mixing fact and fiction into faction probably characterizes the FNC motif better than anything else. This case study with Ann Coulter also shows that FNC braggadocchio is not limited to its alpha males.

American journalist Justin Fox strikes far more broadly and deeply by exposing the right-wing delusion that magically, if just left alone, the market will get it right sans governmental meddling. This ideological myth first appeared during the Great Depression, and apparently the Great Recession (2008-10) was insufficient for needed systemic revisions. This GOP-inspired conventional wisdom since Reagan is dismantled in *The Myth of the Rational Market: A History of Risk, Reward, and Delusion on Wall Street* (Harper Collins e-books, 2011)

In his Introduction "On the fourth Tuesday in November 2008, 82-year old Alan Greenspan paid a visit to Capitol Hill admitting that he had misunderstood how the financial world works. The ex-Fed Chairman started by reading a statement explaining what had gone so wrong with the financial markets during the past year. When he finished, California Democrat Henry Waxman summed it up: In other words, you found that your view of the financial world, your ideology, was incorrect; it was not working, is that right?" (p.81)

To which Greenspan responded directly, "Precisely, that's precisely the reason I was shocked, because I had been operating for 40 years with considerable evidence that it was working exceptionally well." (p. 82) Almost half of that time Greenspan held the powerful position of the Federal Reserve Bank (Fed), as Wall Street became much more influential and less-fettered by the government. Fed bond markets exploded right along with the stock market. Wall Street whiz kids were simultaneously taking over mortgage loans, auto loans, and credit card debt. The most dizzying growth occurred in over-the-counter derivatives, custom-made financial instruments (options futures, swaps). (p. 87)

Derivatives (insurance against bad loans) grew from $866 billion in 1987 to $454 trillion in 2007. In a cautionary infamous caveat in 1996, Greenspan worried that the stock market was "losing itself in frenzy of irrational exuberance," when markets kept surging the lesson he learned was that "the market knew more than he did." (p. 86) Later in 2008, he testified that "the whole intellectual edifice collapsed last summer." (p. 93)

His successor, Ben Bernanke, and Treasury Secretary, Hank Paulson intervened in September to avert a catastrophic run on Lehman Brothers, with only a partial governmental take-over of the financial sector (also occurred in Europe), eventually restored approximated normalcy. Author Justin Fox labels Greenspan's ideology as the "Rational Market Theory," hypothesized at the University of Chicago in the 1960s, embraced by the GOP, and refined by Paul Samuelson and others. Critics, however, argued that various theoretical inconsistencies existed, as well as a dearth of the empirical proof economists love to see. (p. 113) lxxxv. Lara Franchella, "The O'Garbage Factor: Fox News Isn't Just Bad, It's Un-American," NEWSWEEK:

http://www.newsweek.com/2009/10/17/the-o-garbage-factor.html

lxxxvi. Eric Boehlert, "We Were a Stalin-esque Mouthpiece for Bush's Policies," ALTERNET:

http://www.alternet,org/story/149879%22_we_were_a_staline-sque_mouth-piece_for_bush...

lxxxvii. Jack Schafer, "Bill O'Reilly Wants You to Shut Up, Also Includes SLATE":

http://www.slate.com/toolbar.aspx?action=print&id=2087706

lxxxviii. Mark Howard, "Study Confirms that Fox News Makes You Stupid," (16 December 2010),ALTERNET:

http://www.alternet.org/media/149193/study_confirms_that_fox_news_makes_you_stupid/

lxxxix. Michael Grothaus, "Apple Boycotts Fox Because of Glenn Beck," TUAW:

http://www. Tuaw.com/2010/03/29/apple-boycotts-fox-because-of-glen-beck/

xc. Andy Barr, "Forbes: Glenn Beck Made $32 Million Last Year," POLITICO:

http://www.politico.com/news/stories/0410355551.html

xci. "TV-B-Gone," Safe, fun, effective $17.99: THINKGEEK:

http://www.thinkgeek.com/gadgets/electronic/755e/cpg=cj&ref=&CJURL=

xcii. "The McBoycott," BOYCOTT OF THE MONTH:

http://foxnewsboycott.com/featured/botm-april-2010/

xciii. Brian Stelter, "Jon Stewart's Punching Bag: Fox News," *New York Times:*

http://www.nytimes.com/2010/04/24/arts/television/24stewart.html?_r=1

xciv. Jonathan Martin and Keach Heagy, "Fox Primary's Complicated Contracts," POLITICO:

http://www.politico.com/news/stories/0910/42745.html

xcv. Tim Groeling, "Who's the Fairest of Them All? An Empirical Test for Partisan Bias on ABC, CBS, NBC, and FOX." CENTER FOR STUDIES ON THE PRESIDENCY:

http://www..amazon.com/fairest-empirical-partisan-News-SYMPOSIUM/dp/ B0001L2EM...

xcvi. Jennifer Epstein, "Fox News: Avoid Public Option in Health Care Debate," POLITICO:

http://www.politico.com/news/stories/1210/46186.html

xcvii. Seth Ackerman, "The Most Biased Name in News: Fox Channel's Extraordinary Right-Ward Tilt," FAIR:

http://www.fair.org/index.php?page=1067

xcviii. Melissa McEwan, "Let's Get This Straight: No Leftist Equivalent Exists to the Right's Violent Rhetoric": http://www.alternet.org/story/149470/ let%27s_get_this_straight3A_is_no_leftist_e...

xcix. Devon Thomas, "Bill O'Reilly on the View: Muslims Killed Us On 9/11, Co-Hosts Exit," CBS NEWS:

http://www.cbsnews.com/8301-31749_162_20019660-10391698.html

c. Timothy Scanlon," Book review of Peter Hart's *The O'Really Factor*, AMAZON BOOKS:

http://www.amazon.com/Oh-Really-Factor-Unspinning-Channels/ dp/158326601X/ref=sr...

ci. Ben Dimiero, "Foxleaks: Fox Boss Ordered Staff to Cast Doubt on Climate Science," MEDIA MATTERS: http://mediamatters.org/blog/201012150004

cii. Joshua Holland, "How Our Trillion-Dollar Empire Causes Our Deficit Problems," ALTERNET:

http://www.alternet.org/economy/149019/ how_our_trillion_dollar_empire_causes_the...

ciii.   Ben Dimiero, "The Glenn Beck Conundrum, MEDIA MATTERS:

http://mediamatters.org/columns/201006040059

civ.   Mark Howard, "The Real Reason Glenn Beck Is Bashing Google," NEWSCORPSE:

http://www.newscorpse.com/ncWP?p=3883

cv.   Mark Howard, "Number of Advertisers For Glenn Beck in the UK: Zero!" NEWSCORPSE:

http:www.newscorpse.com/ncWP/?p-=1561

cvi.   "Fox News Airs Altered photos of NYT reporters," MEDIA MATTERS:

http://mediamatters.org/research/200807020002

cvii.   Scott Wong and Keach Hagey, "Democrats Pounce As Rupert Murdoch Goes Live," POLITICO:

http://www.politico.com/news/stories/0910/42984.html

cviii. Josh Gerstein, "Obama-Fox Sitdown Gets Testy," POLITICO:

http://www.politico.com/news/stories/031034599.html

cix.   "Fact Check Articles": http://www.factcheck.org/

cx.   Janice Stein, "Exclusive: Fox Runs With Another Bogus War on Christmas Story," MEDIAMATTERS:

http://mediamatters.org/research/2010112990017

cxi.   Michael Wolraich, "Why Glenn Beck Keeps Peddling Whack-Job Fantasies About Euthanizing Grandma," ALTERNET: http://www.alternet.org/story/149456/why_glenn_beck_keeps_peddling_whack-job_fantasies...

cxii.   Robin Bravender, "Robert F. Kennedy, Jr. Says Fox News, GOP Killed Climate Bill,"

POLITICO: http://www.poltico.com/news/stories/1110/44957.html

cxiii. Keach Hagey, "GOP's Struggles Play Out On Fox News," POLITICO:

http://www.politico.com/news/stories/0910/42344.html

cxiv. Sara Paulus, "The Fox News Divide That Never Was," MEDIA MATTERS:

http://mediamattere.org/columns/201012170036

CODA:

"Global Best-Practices: Oh, Canada!"

Economic indicators such as Gross National Product (GNP), Gross Domestic Product (GDP), and Annual Growth Rate % rely solely on macro-level number crunching in which the underlying assumption is simple: Growth is not only very, very good, but all that really matters.

Such strictly quantitative indices ignore crucial qualitative issues; The United Nations' rank-ordering of all countries according to the Human Development Index (HDI) combines three quality of life variables. More enlightened economist, such as the University of Maryland's Herman Daly, call for the news media to wake up and discover the HDI as the superior yardstick.

One competition in which the U. S. never finishes near the top? Yup, that same HDI quality of life rank-ordered scale, on which Japan, Scandinavian countries, New Zealand, and Australia always score very high. The best-kept secret, however: Canada has finished first among 190-some countries six times in the last decade. We often take our northern neighbor for granted as virtually a 51st state. FNC generally, and Bill O'Reilly specifically, malign Canadians routinely.

However, many scholars document Canada's altruistic, beneficent, unselfish and multilateral role constituting Best-Practices Bench-Marking globally. This sense of "good global citizenship" stands in sharp relief against America's infatuation under Bush II with hubris, unilateralism, endless war, narrow self-interest, and disdain for world opinion.

Best-practices bench-marking, taken from Business, insures quality control concerning humanity's capacity for both good and bad behavior. A sampler-plate of quality of life morsels feasted on Canada is sketched via four themes: 1.) Content (idealism); 2.) Methods (multilateralism); 3.) Resilience (historical continuity); and 4.) Uniqueness (big influence/ small nation).

Greek academician Costas Melakopides' book on Canadian foreign policy since World War II states "The idealist component of Canadian foreign policy reflects the endorsement by its makers a set of interests conditioned by humane values. For example, justice, commitment to global human rights, duties beyond Canadian borders, moderation, and cosmopolitanism."[cxv]

Likewise, University of Alberta Political Scientist Thomas Keating points out that if the substance of Canadian foreign policy consists of idealism, so too its methods cohere around unselfish multilateral diplomacy: "Domestic economics have also helped shape the Canadian government's commitment to multilateral diplomacy, since the Canadian economy is unusually dependent on international trade."[cxvi]

The resilience of idealism and multilateralism is traced by many authors describing their historical continuity in Canada. For instance, in 1947, Foreign Minister Louis St. Laurent stated "We Canadians have a useful role to play in world affairs: useful to ourselves by being useful to others."[cxvii]

In 1956, Prime Minister Lester Pearson won the Nobel Peace Prize for designing the creative policy of UN Peacekeeping. In 1974, Canadian businessman David McTaggart founded the environmental NGO called Greenpeace. In 1995, Foreign Minister Lloyd Axworthy invited the international community to replace the Cold War fixation on "physical security" to a more enlightened emphasis on "human security," pioneering this entire paradigm shift.

In the 1980s, when Ronald Reagan was demeaning the role of human rights in American foreign policy, Canada responded by aggregating several "Like-Minded-Nations" to keep that flame lit in the international discourse. Other participants included India, Ireland, Australia, Netherlands, Sweden, and Finland.

Canadian policy has discomfited U.S. Presidents, including Johnson and Nixon by not only criticizing the Vietnam War, but also accepting American draft-dodgers. Liberal Bill Clinton, influenced, by Pentagon budget hawks, refused to sign the Canadian 1997 Land-Mine Treaty, cleaning up millions of post-war land-mines killing civilians (The majority U.S.-placed.) Finally, each successive Canadian Prime Minister ignored the U.S. trade embargoes against Castro's Cuban mini-state.

cxv.   Costas Melakopides, *Pragmatic Idealism: Canadian Foreign Policy Since World War Two* (McGill University Press, 1998), pp. 4-5.

cxvi. Thomas Keating, *Canada and World Order: The Multilateralist Tradition in Canadian Foreign Policy* (McClelland & Stewart, 2003), p. 22.

cxvii. Fen Osler Hamson, Michael Hart, and Martin Rudner, *Canada Among Nations 1999: A Big League Player or a Minor League Player* ? (Oxford University Press, 1999.)

APPENDIX A:

AMERICAN THINK TANKS

SOURCE WATCH

The American NGO SOURCE WATCH provides a useful introduction to the role of think tanks, as paraphrased below. A think tank (a.k.a. Policy Institute) is an organization, institute, corporation or group conducting research and engaging in public policy advocacy. Many have non-profit status, which in the U.S. and Canada entitles them to tax-exemption.

This website describes the role of think tanks with specificity. For example, think tanks are funded primarily by large businesses and foundations, and twice as many conservative ones exist compared to liberal ones; and, the former are generally better funded than the latter. Most think tanks possess a discernible political ideology.

After the re-election of Bush II in 2004, liberal supporters sought to bolster funding in order to countervail what had proven to be a powerful Republican political machine. Democrat Rob Stein organized these efforts via an organization called the DEMOCRACY ALLIANCE, who was quoted as saying: "During the last two years, dollars funneled to conservative think tanks totaled $295 million, whereas left-wing think tanks received only $75 million."

Many employ experts known as "Senior Fellows" or "Adjunct Scholars" who perform wide-ranging research and advocacy. While they have been called "universities minus the students," they also lack the quality control system of blind peer review found in academia. The American government also funds think tanks, especially relating to national security: like the Naval War College, National Defense University, and Institute for National Security Studies. See: SOURCE WATCH, "Think Tanks": http://www.sourcewatch.org/index.php?title=Think_tanks

C-SPAN'S MISSSION/THINK TANKS STUDY

A large 2010 study conducted by FAIR on behalf of the Center for Economic and Policy Research (CEPR) came up with some impressive results. Established for the express purpose of providing "balanced coverage concerning public policy," these data suggest otherwise. The entire C-SPAN archive constituted the vast data base here, and the study divided programming into five categories: Progressive; Center-left; Centrist; Libertarian; Conservative.

The study's main finding: "C-SPAN coverage of think tanks overwhelmingly favored conservative ones over left-of-center ones by startling margins: More specifically, Progressive (7%); Center-left (9%); Centrist (32%); Libertarian (7%); Conservative (42%)." See: http://www.cepr.net

I had fallen into the habit of accepting conservatives referring to America as a center-right country; however, this study, and others cited suggest that by 2010 this really was shifting to center-left. After examining many issues wherein progressives hold solid majorities, they fail to offer an overriding cause for this shift, but it seems to me that eight years of Bush running amok has placed conservatives into untenable positions on numerous issues.

APPENDIX B:

LIBERAL THINK TANKS

The liberal *Cleveland Plain Dealer* newspaper singles out several progressive think tanks which it recommends highly:

1) *Brookings Institution*: One of Washington's oldest think tanks, Brookings Institution conducts research and education in the social sciences primarily in economics, metropolitan policy, governance, foreign policy, and global development.

2) *Center for American Progress*: Begun in 2003 with funding from philanthropists Herbert and Marian Sandler, and led by President/CEO John Podesta, who headed Barack Obama's transition team in 2008, as well as ex-Chief of Staff for Bill Clinton.

3) *Center for Economic and Policy Research (CEPR)*: A Washington progressive economic policy think tank founded in 1999, which works largely on Social Security, U.S. housing bubble, Developing Countries (especially Latin America), and U.S. income inequality.

4) *Century Foundation:* A non-profit Washington liberal think tank public policy research institution founded on the belief that the security and prosperity of America depends upon effective government, open democracy, and free markets and is based in New York City.

5) *Tellus Institute:* A non-profit research and policy organization based in Boston and intended to bolster transition to a sustainable, equitable, and humane global civilization. Founded in 1976 by Paul Raskin, et al. Raskin continues to serve as the organization's President.

Appendix C:

Up-and-Coming Think Tanks in U.S.

PUBLIC POLICY'S identification of promising young think tanks categorized as centrist, liberal, conservative, and libertarian.

Centrist

1. Pew Research Center (2004);
2. Streit Council (2004);
3. Third Way (2005);
4. Future of American Democracy Foundation (2006);
5. Information Technology and Innovation Foundation (2008);
6. Hamilton Project (2006);
7. Global Financial Integrity (2006);
8. Center for a New American Security (2007);
9. Foundation for Excellence in Education (2008);
10. Center for Advanced Study of Communities and Information (2008).

Conservative

1. Committee for a Constructive Tomorrow (2004);
2. Let Freedom Ring, Inc. (2004);
3. Americans for Prosperity (2004));
4. National Policy Institute (2007);

5. American Enterprise Institute (AEI) Legal Center for the Public Interest (2007).

LIBERAL

1. National Security Network (2006);
2. Campus Progress (2005);
3. Roosevelt Institute Campus Network (2004).

LIBERTARIAN

1. Clemson Institute for the Study of Capitalism (2005);
2. Middlebury Institute (2005);
3. Show-Me Institute (2005);
4. Sam Adams Alliance (2006).

See PUBLIC POLICY, "Up-and-Coming Think Tanks,"

http://www.mastersinpublicpolicy.org/top-25-up-and-coming-think-tanks-in-the-us.html

APPENDIX D:

TOP 10 CONSERVATIVE MAGAZINES

About.com's Justin Quinn writes "We've researched over 100 online and offline publications to find the 10 most informative and insightful conservative perspectives anywhere. While some are familiar to all conservatives, a few may surprise the reader, because they represent some of the freshest minds out there."

1. *The Weekly Standard* (1995) Edited by William Kristol and Fred Barnes, appears 48 times annually offering vociferous opinions and insightful articles.
2. *National Review Online (NRO)* aimed at affluent, well-educated Republican readers, combining news/opinion and covers a wide range of issues.
3. *Taki's Magazine* (2007) the brainchild of journalist/socialite Taki Theodoroco- poulos for whom Elizabethtown humanities professor Paul Gottfried frequently contributes articles. It combines both conservatism and libertarian philosophies, recommending a peace-with-honor-strategy rather a surrogate-war-strategy for contemporary America and sprang from the bios of Bush II's privileged chicken-hawks.
4. *The American Spectator* (1924) covering everything from politics to sports with a decidedly conservative slant.
5. *The American Conservative* bills itself as the magazine for the disenfranchised modern conservative angered by pseudo-conservatives

straying from its historical givens, such as family, faith in God, and patriotism.

6. *The New American* is committed to the primacy of the U.S. Constitution and those traditions making America exceptional, published by The John Birch Society.

7. *Front Page Magazine* represents the online voice for The Center for the Study of Popular Culture, and seeks specifically to create more of a conservative presence in a decidedly liberal Hollywood culture.

8. *The Cybercast News Service* (1998), a.k.a. CSNEWS.COM, and operated by the Media Research Center, featuring stories often ignored elsewhere and presented relatively objectively.

9. *Christian Science Monitor* (1908) founded by Mary Baker Eddy is published five times per week internationally, and despite its misleading name, bears no religious imprint. Many consider it a uniquely independent journalistic voice.

10. *Human Events* was Ronald Reagan's favorite newspaper for its faithful protection of American freedom through strength, and deep faith in free enterprise.

See: http://usconservatives.about.com/od/gettinginvolved/tp/TopConservativeMagazines.htm?...

BIBLIOGRAPHY

Ackerman, Seth. "The Most Biased Name in News: Fox News' Extraordinary Right-Wing Tilt," (4 August 2001): http://www.fair.org/index.php?page=1067

Adler, Bill. *The Quotable George W. Bush: A Portrait in His Own Words* (Kindle, 2004).

Adorno, Theodor W. *The Authoritarian Personality* (W.W. Norton, 1993).

Ailes, Roger. *You Are the Message* (Dow Jones-Irwin, 1988).

Alfonsi, Christian. *Circle in the Sand: The Bush Dynasty in Iraq* (Vintage, 2007).

Alterman, Eric. *What Liberal Media? The Truth About Bias in the News* (Basic Books, 2003).

Anderson, Bonnie. *News Flash: Journalism, Infotainment and the Bottom-Line Business of Broadcast News* (Jossey-Bass, 2004).

Arden, John. *America's Meltdown: The Lowest-Common Denominator Society* (Praeger, 2002).

Asher, Ed. *Toward a Socialist America: What Socialist Action Stands For, with Speeches by James Cannon* (Penguin, 1997).

Auletta, Ken. *Backstory: Inside the Business of News* (Penguin, 2003).

Auletta, Ken. *Googled: The End of Life as We Know It* (Kindle, 2008).

Auletta, Ken. *Thee blind Mice: How the Network News Lost Their Way* (Random House, 1991).

Bacevich, Andrew. *The Limits of Power: End of American Exceptionalism* (Kindle, 2010).

Bacevich, Andrew. *Washington Rules: America's Path to Permanent War* (Metropolitan Books, 2011).

Barbanel, Josh. "Roger Ailes: Master Maker of Fiery Political Darts," *New York Times* (17 October 1989).

Barsiman, David. *The Decline and fall of Public Broadcasting: Creating Alternative Media* (South End Press, 2001).

Bageant, Joseph. *Deer Hunting with Jesus: Dispatches from America's Class War* (Broadway, 2008).

Baker, Russell. *Family of Secrets: The Bush Dynasty, America's Invisible Government, and the Hidden History of the Last Fifty Years* (Kindle, 2009).

Baum, Dan. *Citizen Coors* (Perennial, 2000).

Beck, Glenn. *Arguing with Idiots* (Kindle, 2008).

Beck, Glenn. *America's March to Socialism: Why we're One-Step Closer to Giant Missile Parades* (Simon & Schuster, 2009).

Beinhart, Larry. *Fog Facts: Searching for Truth in the Land of Spin* (Nation Books, 2005).

Bennett, Lance. *Civic Life Online: Learning How Digital Media Can Engage Youth* (MIT, 2007).

Berinsky, Adam. *In Time of War: Understanding American Public Opinion from World War II to Iraq* (Chicago Press, 2009).

Bishop, Bill. *The Big Sort: Why the Clustering of Like-Minded Americans is Tearing Us Apart* (Mariner Books, 2009).

Black, Lewis. *I'm Dreaming of a Black Christmas* (Riverhead, 2010).

Black, Lewis. *Me of Little Faith* (Riverhead, 2011).

Boehlert, Eric. *Lapdogs: How the Press Rolled Over for Bush* (Free Press, 2006).

Bolter, Jay. *Remediation: Understanding New Media* (MIT Press, 2002).

Bowman, John. *Socialism in America* (! Universe, Inc., 2005).

Brady, James. *Flyboys: A True Story of Courage* (Kindle, 2004).

Brawley, Edward Allan. *Speaking Out for America's Poor: A Millionaire Socialist in the Progressive Era* (Amazon, 2007).

Breuer, Tom and Joseph Amann. *Fair and Balanced My Ass: An Unbridled Look at the Bizarre Reality of Fox News* (Nation Books, 2007).

Breuer, Tom and Joseph Amann. *Sweet Jesus, I Hate Bill O'Reilly!* (Kindle, 2004).

Brock, David. *The Republican Noise Machine* (Crown, 2004).

Burbach, Roger. *Imperial Overstretch: George W. Bush and the Hubris of Empire* (Zed Books, 2004).

Burke, Bill. *Call Me Ted: My Life, My Way* (Business Plus, 2009).

Bush, George H.W. *All the Best: My Life in Letters and Other Writings* (Rutledge, 2000).

Bush, George H.W. *Heartbeat: George H.W. Bush in His Own Words* (Kindle, 2001).

Bush, George W. *Decision Points* (Kindle, 2010).

Bush, Laura. *Spoken from the Heart* (Kindle, 2011).

Chaitkin, Anton. *George Bush: The Unauthorized Biography* (Kindle, 2004).

Chenoweth, Neil. *Rupert Murdoch: The Untold Story of the World's Greatest Media Wizard* (Crown Business, 2002).

Colbert, Stephen. *I Am America and So Can You* (Kindle, 2009).

Collins, Scott. *Crazy Like a Fox: The Inside Story of How Fox News Beat CNN* (Portfolio, 2004).

Colford, Paul. *The Rush Limbaugh Story: Talent on Loan from God* (St. Martins, 1993).

Conason, Joe. *Big Lies: The Right-Wing Propaganda Machine Distorts the Truth* (Thomas Dunne Books, 2002).

Corn, David. *The Lies of George W. Bush* (Kindle, 2004).

Crainer, Stuart. *Rupert Murdoch's Way: Ten Secrets of the World's Greatest Dealmaker* (Kindle, 2002).

Crawford, Craig. *Attack the Messenger* (Rowman & Littlefield, 2005).

Davis, Richard. *Typing Politics: The Role of Blogs in American Politics* (Oxford, 2009).

Debord, Guy. *Society of the Spectacle* (Black & Red, 2000).

Demint, Jim (US Senator). *Saving Freedom: We Can Stop America's Slide into Socialism* (Kindle, 2010).

Devereau, Eoin. *Media Studies: Key Issues and Debates* (Sage, 2007).

Diamond, Edwin. *The Spot* (MIT, 1988).

Dimiero, Ben. "FOXLEAKS: Fox Boss Ordered Staff to Cast Doubt on Climate Science." MEDIAMATTERSFORAMERICA: http://mediamatters.org/blog/201012150004

Dover, Bruce. *Rupert Murdoch's China Adventures: How the World's most Powerful Media Mogul Lost a Fortune and Found a Wife* (Tuttle, 2008).

Ellison, Sarah. *War at the Wall Street Journal* (Houghton Mifflin Harcourt, 2010).

Engel, Jeffrey, ed. *The China Diary of George H. W. Bush: Making of a Global President* (Princeton, 2008).

Engelman, Ralph. *Public Radio and Television in America: A History* (Sage, 1996).

Epstein, Jennifer. "Fox News: Avoid 'Public Option' in Health Care Debate." POLITICO:

http://www.politico.com/news/stories/1210//46186.html

Esposito, Anthony. *The Ideology of the Socialist Party in America, 1901-1917* (Garland Studies of American Labor, 1997).

Fallows, James. *Breaking the News: How the Media Undermine American Democracy* (Vintage, 1997).

Foley, Michael. *The Civil Society Reader* (Tufts, 2003).

Forsberg, Randall. *Abolishing War: Dialogue with Peace Scholars Randall Forsberg and Elise Boulding* (Amazon, 1998).

Franken, Al. *Lies and the Lying Liars Who Tell Them: A Fair and Balanced Look at the Right* (Dutton, 2003.

Friendly, Fred. *The Good Guys, the Bad Guys, and the First Amendment* (Random House, 1976).

Gehring, Verna. *The Internet in Public Life* (Rowman & Littlefield, 2004).

Gelpi, Christopher. *Paying the Human Costs of War: American Public Opinion and Casualties in Military Conflicts* (Princeton, 2009).

Gingrich, Newt. *To Save America: Stopping O'Bama's Secular-Socialist Machine* (Kindle, 2010).

Giuliani, Rudolph. *Leadership* (Hyperion, 2002).

Goldberg, Bernard. *Bias* (Regnery, 2001).

Goldman, Wendy. *The Murdoch Mission: Transformation of a Media Empire* (Random House, 2001).

Gould, Stanhope, "Coors Brews the News," *Columbia Journalism Review* (March/April, 1975).

Gormley, Beatrice. *President George W. Bush: Our 43rd President* (Kindle, 2005).

Graber, Doris. *Mass Media and American Politics* (Kindle, 2008).

Graber, Doris. *The Politics of News: The News of Politics* (Kindle, 2005).

Gray, Jonathan. *Satire TV: Politics and Comedy in the Post-Network Era* (NYU, 2009).

Groeling, Timothy. *Who's the Fairest of Them All: An Empirical Test for Partisan Bias of ABC, CBS, NBC, and Fox News* (Center for the Study of the Presidency, 2008).

Grossberg, Lawrence. *Media-Making: Mass Media in a Popular Culture* (Sage, 2005).

Grossman, Lawrence, "Bullies on the Block," *Columbia Journalism Review* (Jan/Feb 1997).

Hagey, Keach. "GOP Struggles Play Out on Fox." POLITICO:

http://www.politico.com/news/stories/0910/42344.html

Hannity, Sean. *Censorship: The Threat to Silence Talk Radio* (Threshold, 2009).

Hart, Peter. *The O'Really? Factor: Unspinning Fox's Bill O'Reilly* (Seven Stories Press, 2003).

Hartung, William. *How Much Are You Making in the War, Daddy? Guide to War Profiteering in the Bush Administration* (Kindle, 2003).

Hastedt, Glenn. *The Presidencies of George Herbert Walker and George Walker Bush: Like Father, Like Son?* (Kindle, 2008).

Hickey, Neil, "Is Fox News Fair?" *Columbia Journalism Review* (March/April, 1998).

Hill, Annette. *Reality TV: Factual Entertainment and Television Audiences* (Routledge, 2005).

Hillyard, Joshua. "How Our Trillion-Dollar Empire is the Cause of Our Deficit Problem: We Could Make the Budget Deficit Disappear and Fully-Fund Social Security Without Raising Taxes, If We'd Only Outspend Our Closest Rival by Threefold." ALTERNET.

http://www.alternet.org/economy/149019/
how_our_trillion_dollar_empire_is_the_cause_of...

Holland, Joshua, ed. *Fifteen Biggest Lies about the Economy* (Independent Media Institute, 2010).

Hodgkinson, Virginia. *The Civil Society Reader* (Tufts University, 2003).

Holsti, Ole R. *To See Ourselves as Others See Us: Public* Perceptions *After 9/11* (Michigan Press, 2008).

Howard, Mark. "Study Confirms That Fox News Makes You Stupid: New Survey of American Voters Shows Fox Viewers Significantly More Misinformed Than Other Viewers." UNIVERSITY OF MARYLAND:

http://www.alternet.org/media/149193/
study_confirms_that_fox_news_makes_you_stupid/

Hudson, William. *American Democracy in Peril* (C P Press, 2009).

Huntington, Samuel P. *Who Are We? Challenges of America's National Identity* (Simon and Schuster, 2005).

Ikon Group International. *Infotainment: Webster's Timeline History, 1985-2006* (Digital Printable Version, 2009).

Ivins, Molly. *Bush-Wacked: Life in George W. Bush's America* (Kindle, 2007).

Jamison, Kathleen Hall. *Dirty Politics: Deception, Distraction, and Democracy* (Oxford, 1982).

Jamison, Kathleen Hall. *Packaging the Presidency 1968* (Oxford University, 1992).

Janis, Irving L. *Groupthink: Psychological Studies of Policy Decisions and Fiascoes* (Houghton Mifflin, 1982).

Jaramillo, Deborah. *Ugly War, Pretty Package: How CNN and Fox News Made the Invasion of Iraq High Concept* (Kindle, 2009).

Jenkins, Henry. *Convergence Culture: Where Old and New Media Collide* (NYU Press, 2008).

Jervis, Robert. *Why Intelligence Fails:* Lessons from the Iranian Revolution and the Iraq War (Cornell Press, 2010).

Johnson, Chalmers. *Blowback: Costs and Consequences of the American Empire* (Metropolitan, 2010).

Johnson, Chalmers. *Nemesis: The Last Days of the American Republic* (Macmillan, 2010).

Jones, Jeffrey. *Entertaining Politics: Satiric Television and Political Engagement* (Rowman & Littlefield, 2009).

Juhasz, Antonia. *The Bush Agenda: Invading the World, One Economy at a Time* (Kindle, 2007).

Jurgen, Ronald. *Infotainment Systems* (SAE International, 2007).

Kelley, Kitty. *The Family: The Real Story of the Bush Dynasty* (Stedman, 2004).

Kellner, Douglas. *Media Spectacle* (Routledge, 2008).

Kengor, Paul. *God and George W. Bush: A Spiritual Life* (Kindle, 2004).

Kennedy, George. *What Good is Journalism? How Reporters and Editors are Saving America's Way of Life* (Missouri University, 2007).

Kennedy, Paul. *The Rise and Fall of the Great Powers* (Vintage, 1989).

Kern, Jonathan. *Sound Reporting: The NPR Guide to Audio Journalism and Production* (Kindle, 2006).

Kimmel, Daniel. *The Fourth Network: How Fox Broke the Rules and Reinvented Television* (Ivan R. Dee Publishers, 2004).

Kitman, Marvin. *The Man Who Would Not Shut Up: The Rise of Bill O'Reilly* (St. Martin's, 2007).

Lamonica, Paul. *Inside Rupert's Brain* (Kindle, 2009).

Lawrence, Steve. *The Making of a Police State: The Socialist Agenda for America* (Kindle, 2006).

Leishman, Frank. *Policing and the Media: Facts, Fictions, and Factions* (Willam Publishers, 2003).

Lester, Paul Martin. *On Floods and Photo Ops: How Herbert Hoover and George W. Bush Exploited Catastrophes* (Kindle, 2009).

Levy, Bernard-Henri and Michel Houllebecq. *Public Enemies: Dueling Writers Take On Each Other and the World* (Random House, 2011).

Lilleker, Darren. *Key Concepts in Political Communication* (Sage, 2006).

Limbaugh, Rush. *The Way Things Ought To Be* (Pocket Books, 1992).

Lin, Carolyn and David Atkin. *Communications Technology and Social Change: Theory and Implications* (Routledge, 2006).

Lipset, Seymour Martin. *It Didn't Happen Here: Why Socialism Failed in America* (Amazon, 2000).

Lord, Donald. *Dubya: The Toxic Texan and Environmental Degradation* (Kindle, 2005).

Maher, Bill. *Does Anyone Have a Problem with That?* (Kindle, 2010).

Maher, Bill. *New Rules: Polite Musings from a Timid Observer* (Kindle, 2011).

Maher, Bill. *When You Ride Alone, You Ride with Bin Laden* (Phoenix, 2005).

Manovich, Lev. *The Language of New Media* (MIT Press, 2002).

Mansfield, Stephen. *The Faith of George W. Bush* (Kindle, 2004).

Marquez, Heron. *Biography of George W. Bush* (Kindle, 2001).

Mayer, Jeremy. *American Media Politics in Transition* (Mc-Graw Hill, 2008).

McAdams, Dan. *George W. Bush and the Redemptive Dream: A Psychological Portrait* (Kindle, 2010).

Mc Cauley, Michael. *NPR: The Triumphs and Trials of National Public Radio* (Columbia, 2005).

McClelland, Scott. *What Happened Inside the Bush White House and Washington's Culture of Deception* (Public Affairs, 2008).

McEwen, Melissa. "There is no leftist equivalent to the right's violent rhetoric: Shooting in Tuczon not an anomaly, but inevitable if we continue game of 'both sides are equal."

ALTERNET:

http://www.alternet.org/story/149470/
let%27s_get_this_straight%3A_there_is_no_leftist_e...

McGinniss, Joe. *The Selling of the President, 1968* (Trident, 1969).

Melton, Stephen L. *The Clausewitz Delusion: How the American Army Screwed Up the Wars in Afghanistan and Iraq* (Zenith Press, 2007).

Miller, Mark Crispin. *The Bush Dyslexicon: Observations of a National Disorder* (Kindle, 2002).

Mitchell, Jack. *Listener Supported: The Culture and History of Public Radio* (Praeger, 2008).

Moon, Robert. *Scam: The Liberal Misinformation Machine and its War on America* (Create Space, 2009).

Moore, James. *Bush's Brain: How Carl Rove Made George W. Bush Presidential* (Kindle, 2004).

Musa, Bela and Cindy Price, eds. *Emerging Issues in Contemporary Journalism: Infotainment, Internet, Libel, Censorship, Et Cetera* (Edwin Mellen Press, 2006).

Newsweek's Education Site, "The O'Garbage Factor: Fox News Isn't Just Bad—it's Unamerican":http:www.newsweek.com/2009/10/17/the-o-garbage-factor.html

Ornstein, Norman. *Second-Term Blues: How George W. Bush Has Governed* (Kindle, 2007).

Oulette, Laurie. *Better Living through Reality TV: Television and Post-Welfare Citizenship* (Wiley-Blackwell, 2008).

Oulette, Laurie. *Viewers like You? How Public TV Failed the People* (Columbia, 2002).

Palast, Greg. *Fortunate Son: George W. Bush and the Making of a Presidency* (Kindle, 2002).

Parry, Robert. *Secrecy and Privilege: Rise of the Bush Dynasty from Watergate to Iraq* (Kindle, 2004).

Phillips, Kevin. *American Dynasty: Aristocracy, Fortune, and the Politics of Deceit in the House of Bush* (Viking, 2004).

Philips, Lisa. *Public Radio: Behind the Voices* (Vanguard Press, 2006).

Prior, Markus. *Post-Broadcast Democracy: How Media Choice Increases Inequality in Political Involvement and Polarizes Elections* (Cambridge, 2007).

Public Broadcasting News: http:www.pbs.org/topics/news-politics/

Renshon, Stanley. *In His Father's Shadow: The Transformation of George W. Bush* (Kindle, 2004).

Renshon, Stanley. *One America? Political Leadership, National Identity, and the Dilemmas of Diversity* (Georgetown Press, 2001).

Richardson, John, "Okay Ailes, Fix Me!" *Communicator's Journal* (Nov/ Dec, 1983).

Robertson, Lori. "Quicker and Deeper: NPR's Ambitious Goal," *American Journalism Review* (1 June, 2004) p. 30.

Robschaux, Mark. *Cable Cowboy: John Malone and the Rise of the Modern Cable Business* (Wiley, 2005).

Rollins, Ed. *Bare Knuckles and Back Rooms: My Life in American Politics* (Broadway Books, 1996).

Sauer, Fred. *A Simple Guide: How Liberalism, Euphemism for Socialism Destroys People and Nations* (America's Cultural Studies, 2008).

Scheer, Robert. *Playing President: My Close Encounters with Nixon, Carter, Bush I, Reagan and Clinton and How They Failed to Prepare Me for George W. Bush* (Kindle, 2006).

Schlachter, Christina. *Newsless: How the American Media Are Destroying Democracy* (Create Space, 2009).

Schweitzers, Peter and Rochelle. *The Bushes: Portrait of a Dynasty* (Kindle, 2005).

Shannon, David. *The Socialist Party of America: A History* (South End Press, 1967).

Shawcross, William. *Murdoch* (Simon & Schuster, 1997).

Schechter, Danny. *Embedded: Weapons of Mass Deception: How the Media Failed to Cover the Iraq War* (Prometheus Books, 2003) + documentary film with same title.

Slotnik, Elliot. *Television News and the Supreme Court: All the News Fit to Air?* (Cambridge University, 1998).

Spiro, Peter. *Beyond Citizenship: American Identity after Globalization* (Kindle, 2006).

Stamberg, Susan and Cokie Roberts. *This is NPR: The First Forty Years* (Chronicle Books, 2011).

Stan, Adele and Don Hazen, eds. *Dangerous Brew: Exposing the Tea Party's Agenda to Take Over America* (Independent Media Institute, 2011).

Starr, Gerald. *Air Wars: The Fight to Reclaim Public Broadcasting* (Temple, 2001).

Stelter, Brian. "Jon Stewart's Latest Punching Bag, Fox News," *New York Times:*

http://www.nytimes.com/2010/04/24/arts/television/24stewar.
html?_r=1

Stewart, Jon. *The Daily Show with Jon Stewart Presents Earth: A Visitor's Guide to the Human Race* (Grand Central, 2010).

Stewart, Jon. *The Daily Show with Jon Stewart Presents America: Teachers Edition* (Grand Central, 2011).

Surhone, Lambert. *Randall Forsberg and Peace Studies* (Betascript Books, 2010).

Swint, Kerwin. *Dark Genius: The Influential Career of Legendary Political Operative and Fox News Founder Roger Ailes* (Sterling, 2008).

Swint, Kerwin. *Political Consultants and Negative Campaigning: Secrets of the Pros* (University Press, America, 1998).

Thussu, Daya. *News as Entertainment: The Rise of Global Infotainment* (Sage, 2008).

Turcotte, Jerome. *Rupert Murdoch: Creator of a Worldwide Media Empire* (Beard Books, 2003).

Weisberg, Jacob. *The Bush Tragedy* (Kindle, 2008).

West, Darrell. *Air Wars: Television Advertising in Elections* (Kindle, 2008).

Wicker, Tom. *George Herbert Walker Bush: A Penguin Life Series* (Penguin, 2004).

Williams, Anthony. *Wikinomics: How Mass Collaboration Changes Everything* (Portfolio Trade, 2010).

Wolfe, Michael. *The Man Who Owns the News: Inside the Secret World of Rupert Murdoch* (Kindle, 2010).

Woodward, Robert. *State of Denial: Bush at War, Part III* (Kindle, 2007).

Zakaria, Fareed. *The Post-American World* (Kindle, 2010).

www.ingramcontent.com/pod-product-compliance
Lightning Source LLC
Chambersburg PA
CBHW060231290526
45789CB00001B/3